Imposing Decency

American Encounters/Global Interactions
A series edited by Gilbert M. Joseph and Emily S. Rosenberg

This series aims to stimulate critical perspectives and fresh interpretive frameworks for scholarship on the history of the imposing global presence of the United States. Its primary concerns include the deployment and contestation of power, the construction and deconstruction of cultural and political borders, the fluid meanings of intercultural encounters, and the complex interplay between the global and the local. American Encounters seeks to strengthen dialogue and collaboration between historians of U.S. international relations and area studies specialists.

The series encourages scholarship based on multiarchival historical research. At the same time, it supports a recognition of the representational character of all stories about the past and promotes critical inquiry into issues of subjectivity and narrative. In the process, American Encounters strives to understand the context in which meanings related to nations, cultures, and political economy are continually produced, challenged, and reshaped.

Imposing Decency

The Politics of Sexuality and Race

in Puerto Rico, 1870–1920

EILEEN J. SUÁREZ FINDLAY

Duke University Press   Durham and London, 1999

© 1999 Duke University Press

All rights reserved

Printed in the United States of America on acid-free paper ∞

Designed by Rebecca Filene Broun

Typeset in Adobe Garamond by Keystone Typesetting, Inc.

Library of Congress Cataloging-in-Publication Data

appear on the last printed page of this book.

Contents

In memory of Peter Franklin Findlay (1963–1983)
Lover of history, warrior for justice, seeker of meaning

In celebration of Amaya Ruby Suárez-Findlay (b. October 6, 1998)
Light and hope of my life

Acknowledgments

Although the historical profession generally requires that intellectual production be recognized on an individual basis, all historians worth their salt are acutely aware of the crucial invisible labors of collaboration and support that sustain our work. None of us would be able to do what we do without our friends, family, and broader political and intellectual communities. Thus, this short acknowledgment is for me one of the most important—and sweetest—parts of the book.

I have shared years of graduate seminars, coffee shop discussions, and telephone conversations about theory, politics, and history with Raka Ray, Karin Rosemblatt, Roger Kittleson, Blenda Femenías, René Reeves, Seemin Qayum, Sinclair Thomson, Anne MacPherson, Nancy Applebaum, Félix Matos, and Luis Figueroa. Sarah Chambers, Jim Krippner-Martínez, Olivia Martínez-Krippner, Lillian Guerra, Ileana Rodríguez, Andy Daitsman, and Greg Crider were there for much of the process, too. Karin Wulf, Vanessa Schwartz, Deborah Cohen, Cathy Schaeff, Helen Langa, Bill Leap, and Cathy Schneider have stimulated me immensely as colleagues and friends in recent years. The History Department at American University has provided a supportive community which facilitated my rewriting of the manuscript. The insights, challenges, love, and never-ending support of Marisol de la Cadena and Ana Patricia Alvarenga can never be adequately communicated. I can only say that many of the ideas in this book would never have materialized without them; often it is unclear where my thoughts end and theirs begin.

The caring, challenging advising of Florencia Mallon, Francisco Scarano, and Steve Stern while I was in graduate school pushed me to go further intellectually than I ever thought possible. It is rare to encounter three people in one place in the academy who combine respect for passion and political commitment with such resolute insistence on academic rigor. I have been extremely lucky to have had them as my advisers and to have them now as good friends. Their emotional support and creativity as historians continue to nurture and challenge me.

Other friends in the United States may not have been as directly involved in the writing process but helped it along in innumerable ways. Deb Coltey,

Chuck Winant, Pauline Chakravarti, Ellen Baker, Danny Holt, James Couture, and Stephanie Levy have been dear friends to me; over the long years they have helped me sift through ideas and also kept me laughing, sane, and on track through different stages of this project. Daryl Gordon has been there since well before it all began—she has never let me forget that both pain and empowerment are wrapped up in sexuality. My friends and spiritual seekers at All Souls Unitarian Church have helped me along the way as well.

My students teach me in innumerable ways. They continually remind me that ideas do make a difference and that delving into the past can radically alter one's relationship to the present. Above all, they give me hope in the future and in the meaning of my life's labors. Their struggles to make this world a more just home for humanity inspires me to keep planting my own seeds in whatever way I can. Thanks to all the students who have shared their hopes and dreams with me but whom I do not have space to name here. My special gratitude goes to Andrea Morrell, Ramón Cruz, Daniel Alberdeston, Mary Finn, Erica Mott, Stephanie Schaudel, Cynthia Breunig, and Regina Langley.

Thanks also to Ramón Cruz for his last-minute census research in Ponce, providing creative insights along the way, and Janice Jayes, whose calm computer database skills came through in the end. Erick Nawrocki pulled me out of many tight spots and did a heroic job helping me piece together the index.

Many people in Puerto Rico believed in this project as well, despite its apparent oddness. The staff at the Colección Puertorriqueña and the Centro de Investigaciones Históricas of the Universidad de Puerto Rico (UPR) were extremely patient in tracing down sources for me. María Carrasco, the head of photocopying at the UPR library, transformed the meaning of xeroxing for me—she fed me a steady diet of good humor, intellectual curiosity, political solidarity, and plenty of Ponce tidbits, all while complying with my interminable requests for photocopies (even from the United States). José Flores, Milagros Pepín, Neftalí Quintana, Hilda Chicón, Edgardo, Ramonita, Sonia, Ruth, and the rest of the staff at the Archivo General de Puerto Rico (AGPR) are invaluable friends and colleagues; their tall tales, jokes, and help in locating previously unexplored sources enriched my stay in San Juan immensely. Juan José Baldrich, Pedro San Miguel, Fernando Picó, Blanca Silvestrini, and Lolita Luque were all generous with their time and energy. Mabel Rodríguez, Laura Naters, Carlos Bruno, Rafael Cabrera, Marita Barceló, José Flores, and Mayra Rosario welcomed me into their community of historians. They have given me precious friendship and intellectual insights. Carlos Rodríguez not only shared with me his work on sexuality and his ever fresh analyses of Puerto Rican society but also took personal risks to deepen our friendship. I will always treasure the long hours spent with Don Rubén del Pilar analyzing sexuality, race, class, gender, and colonialism, and introducing each other to the people and struggles we encountered in the documents at the AGPR. Special thanks to Doña Olga for her delicious food and family warmth, which sustained me through some lonely moments.

Perhaps more than anyone else in Puerto Rico, Marta Villaizán is physically responsible for this book's completion. Unaware of our eventual familial connection, she graciously hosted me in the capital's Archivo Histórico Diocesano and a year later facilitated my gaining entrance to the Ponce Municipal Archive while it was officially closed to the public for reorganization. She also housed me at her "el convento" apartment during my stay in Ponce. Her passion for history and its preservation was a constant motivation for me. Doña Gladys Tormes welcomed me into the Ponce archives at a very inauspicious time, also sharing with me invaluable recollections of her father, Leopoldo, her aunt Herminia, and her beloved city. I am forever grateful to these two committed archivists. Thanks also go to the director and staff of the National Anthropological Archives in Washington, D.C., for their help in obtaining photographs of early-twentieth-century Puerto Rico.

Lolita Vargas and Yvonne Laborde made Ponce come alive for me. The residents of Ponce's San Antón neighborhood, particularly the Cabrera family— Doña Judith, Doña Fela, Jerry, María Judith Banchs Cabrera, and Luis Alberto—opened their homes, community, and culture to me. They insisted that history and its ghosts are relevant to the present and shared their historical memories of Afro-Puerto Rican Ponceños' struggles and hopes. They, along with Humberto Figueroa and Efra Matos, nurtured the creativity that must lie at the center of all committed history.

I owe special thanks to Magaly Robles. She was always ready to listen to the stories of pain and struggle that I uncovered in the archives. She took up those voices from the past and transformed them into art. She has thus provided another means—much more effective than a book—of communicating their messages. Her fighting spirit is testimony to the power within all of us and an ever present inspiration to me.

I am grateful to the various funding sources that allowed me to complete the research and writing of these pages: the National Endowment for the

Humanities, the Jacob Javits Scholarship fund, various American University faculty grants, and the University of Wisconsin Graduate School.

I owe a great debt to those whose input boosted me through the last stages of intellectual production. Barbara Weinstein and Avi Chomsky read the manuscript several times and offered challenging, insightful comments. Valerie Milholland has been a superb editor, cajoling and encouraging me throughout. Miriam Angress patiently kept track of all the myriad details which plague authors, and Nancy Raynor carefully caught my grammatical errors.

Finally, I thank my family. My parents, Jim and Doris, are insightful students of human nature and both historians, although only my father formally exercises the profession. It is their example that set the agendas and the standards by which I labor. They have sustained me over the years in more ways than I can ever express here. Suffice it to say that I love and honor them very much. My husband, Raciel Suarez-Findlay, encountered this project rather late in the game but has consistently supported me in every way he could while I struggled with it. I owe my ability to keep it all in perspective largely to him and his unflagging love. Raciel and his family have brought the Hispanic Caribbean and its diaspora into my life in uncountable, precious new ways. Thanks from the bottom of my heart to the entire Suarez-Cardozas clan.

This book is dedicated to the memory of my brother, Peter Franklin Findlay, and to my daughter, Amaya Ruby Suarez-Findlay. I like to think that it is the kind of history Pete would have written if he had lived long enough. Amaya and this book literally went through their final birth pangs within weeks of each other. It is my hope that the questions raised in these pages can help us to build a world that accepts Amaya in all her fullness as an interracial, multicultural woman.

Introduction

Legitimacy must be clothed in magic; words must be made into things; blocks, hedges, compartments are the condition of knowledge. Thinkers must recognize the destructive lure of the natural system of symbols, equally when it devastates category boundaries as when it wrongfully closes them.

Beware, therefore, of arguments couched in the bodily medium.
—Mary Douglas, *Natural Symbols*

The mottled past still haunts Puerto Rico. Of course, you might not realize it if you visit only the center of such cities as Ponce, the second-largest metropolitan area on the island, with its carefully groomed plaza; shining marble sidewalks; genteelly pastel, reconstructed mansions of long-dead sugar barons; modern, mall-like shops; and burgeoning set of museums, which celebrate the accomplishments of the city's wealthy and powerful. But if you listen closely and visit the places in the city that have not been razed and scrubbed and remade by the recent tourist-oriented urban renewal, you can hear a cacophony of histories, carefully cleansed from the urban center.

In such working-class Ponce neighborhoods as Bélgica, La Cantera, and San Antón, the marble sidewalks abruptly halt, giving way to crumbled cement and dirt. Salsa music blares alongside occasional evening invocations of the older rhythms and lyrics of *bombas* and *plenas*. Light skin tones deepen into cinnamon and mahogany. In Don Cesar's crowded lunch joint, over a huge plate of rice and beans and octopus salad, you can hear reminiscences of loves won and lost during bomba dances, bitter memories of cane cutting and desperate, gnawing hunger, and proud invocations of the mulattos who founded local unions, the Ponce Firemen's Corp, and the city's musical bands. Elderly women on their porches offer stories of supporting children by sewing and washing for others, seeking a loving mate, and combating male infidelity. Even within the homes of the sugar elite's descendants, where wrinkled white women recall the glorious days gone by of multiple houses, servants, and demure carriage rides to church, the cleaning women slip in their own memories, which complicate the homogenizing narrative of Ponce's grandeur and lily-white moral decency. They remind the questioner that much has been omitted from such stories. Poor women did the cooking, cleaning, and caring that sustained these expansive lifestyles. The region is dotted with families of African descent who share their employers' last names, bound to them generations ago by enslavement and in many cases by blood connections, forged in semiclandestine sex.

During the years I lived in Puerto Rico, I encountered such competing historical narratives quite frequently in my personal relationships, archival burrowings, and interviews. Despite the assertions of most middle-class and wealthy Puerto Ricans I met that race was irrelevant in their society (unlike the United States, they claimed, which was plagued by racial hatred and violence), my friends and neighbors who acknowledged their African heritage insisted that race marked all Puerto Ricans profoundly, however differently it might do so on the island than *afuera* (out there, outside) in the colonial metropolis to the north.

Other official silences contradicted the quotidian sensibilities I was uncovering. Historians of Puerto Rico largely ignored or dismissed "private" issues, such as marriage, sexual practices, conflicts within the family, and conceptions of morality, respectability, and honor, deeming them irrelevant to "larger" questions such as the formation of national identity, class relations, and colonial state policies. Yet as I requested reflections from older women of all classes and races on their own and their foremothers' lives, I was struck by the frequency with which unsolicited discussions of sexuality arose. Many women cited coping with the pain of male infidelity as one of their greatest struggles. Elderly working-class women in Ponce not infrequently spoke of the prostitutes who lived in their communities, expressing either sympathy and concern or disdain for them; these errant souls had slipped from respectable status and reminded all women of what fate might await them. Women also waxed eloquent, with bright lights in their eyes, about the thrill of flirting during their weekend turns about the Ponce public square, about a first love, or about the freedom of dancing bomba until dawn.

Sexuality clearly played a central and quite complicated role in Puerto Rican women's lives. It was one of the main mediums through which they had constructed their gender, race, and class identities. Sexual norms and their enforcers regulated women's lives, demarcating the "worthy" from the "disreputable." Sexuality was also an arena for exciting exploration. Sex and power, my informants insisted, were intimately linked; sex was a cornerstone of both the reproduction of dominance and its subversions. In this book I try to give historical depth to these women's evaluations of their own lives, thus offering further legitimacy to the issues to which they repeatedly returned.

In my research, I soon found that Puerto Rican sexual practices and norms and changing racial identities had indelibly shaped each other. The intertwining of the two had also been central to politics in nineteenth- and early-twentieth-century Puerto Rico. Racially charged attempts at moral reform, conflicts over the legitimacy of various sexual norms and practices, racialized discourses about sexual respectability and honor, as well as the strategic silencing of racial differences were often key to social movements' articulation of political agendas, state interventionary strategies, and the construction of local collective identities and colonial hegemony. Consequently, I resolved to try to break down the conceptual wall between the grand, public arenas and the rather mysterious and seemingly unimportant "private" spheres of people's lives where sexuality and racial identities loomed large.

My ultimate goal in this book is to explore the possibilities and limits of sexual politics for creating an emancipatory agenda. Thus, I attempt to expose the dangers of conservative consensuses based on ideas about sexuality, racial impurity, "decency," and what is "natural." I also intend to illuminate those moments and spaces, however fleeting and small, where radical intervention is possible.[1] It soon became clear that to do so, I would have to dispense with the "heroic age" model of history. Therefore, although there are some heroes in the following pages, all of them have warts. In our quest for a more just future and for models from which to build it, we must recognize that all movements for change have had their limitations; many of these limits have been quite severe.

Yet I do *not* wish to demonstrate the futility of social and intellectual struggle. On the contrary, it is imperative to remember that alliances—whether for traditional or transformative ends—constantly shift in membership, meaning, and effectiveness. It is up to us to forge ones as inclusive and powerful as possible. Much work remains to be done. I hope that the issues raised in the following pages will spark readers to ask their own questions and refine, expand on, and challenge my conclusions.

For over a century, the relationship between nationhood and colonial rule has been one of the most enduring questions with which Puerto Rican politicians and intellectuals have wrestled. This is not surprising, given Puerto Rico's five hundred years of experience as a colonized land. Sometimes nationhood and colonialism have been seen as diametrically opposed states of being as well as political and economic systems. More often, Puerto Ricans have striven to join the two in various ways that they have hoped will provide them with a modicum of material resources and collective integrity. Whatever the relationship posited between colonialism and the nation, however, almost all Puerto Rican public intellectual and political debates are haunted by this conflictually wedded pair of concepts. Spanish and U.S. imperialism have obviously profoundly shaped Puerto Rican history, as have a variety of attempts to forge a coherent national identity. Both forces appear in this book, as people used them to coerce, regulate, inspire, and give meaning to their own and others' daily lives and political choices.

But national identity is not the only appropriate axis of analysis for the island, as scholars have begun to point out in recent years. Puerto Rico has deep internal cleavages as well. Puerto Ricans have long defined themselves along class, gender, racial, and regional lines, and they continue to do so today. I try to do justice to these concerns, showing how they often complicated the actions and alliances that many have painted as either heroic nation building or tragic colonial collaboration. Hopefully, this book will contribute to the growing impetus for moving beyond the often sterile dichotomy between nationalism and colonialism, without discarding the preoccupation with Puerto Rican material, cultural, and political integrity that underpins it.[2]

Heeding Michel Foucault, Lynn Hunt, Judith Walkowitz, and Ann Stoler, I have found that linking analyses of cultural and political discourses can yield revealing insights into the multiple, complex meanings of daily actions, state interventions, and political movements, conceptually pushing us beyond another simple binary opposition that haunts Puerto Rican historiography—that of resistance and accommodation. As dominant social orders are constructed, these pioneering postmodern historians remind us, they simultaneously incorporate and exclude different members of society in many diverse ways. Thus, they can be quite difficult—if not impossible—to transform completely or challenge frontally. Projects claiming to be radically liberatory often share key assumptions with those which they oppose, as careful analysis of Puerto Rican plebeian projects for sexual reform reveals. Made up of potentially contradictory alliances, interests, and meanings, however, dominant orders also remain unstable. Their enforcers denounce and police those whom they exclude out of fear, rather than from positions of unassailable security. Often, newly forming groups find ways to articulate their own interests and divergent meanings even while reproducing the parameters established by others. In turn-of-the-century Puerto Rico, both bourgeois feminists and plebeian women divorce petitioners did just this.[3]

Despite their brilliant insights, though, the above-mentioned authors, along with most of their fellow travelers in the field of postmodern theory and methods of historical inquiry, have focused in the last decade primarily on the bourgeoisie and the colonizers, the power brokers and "high" culture makers, whose thoughts and deeds have been relatively well preserved in the historical record.[4] Despite their protestations to the contrary, they implicitly attribute most agency to those groups which constructed the definitions and demarcations ultimately adopted as dominant in their societies. Such actors also carry a good deal of weight in this book. But equally if not more important in this volume are the laboring colonized people of coastal Puerto Rico, aspects of whose moral norms and political visions emerged through careful sifting of court testimony, oral narratives, newspapers, and political tracts of their own. They too were powerful historical agents who formed the island's history, social norms, and political discourses. Puerto Rican working women and men of all races forged complex, changing identities and sociopolitical projects. They shaped the ideas and strategies of more powerful groups in the process.

The discourses produced by Puerto Ricans and colonial agents grew out of their creators' particular lived experiences of race, class, and gender power relationships on the island and in the metropolis. In an effort to demonstrate this, I join discourse analysis with social and political history. I examine how specific historical circumstances allowed or pushed certain groups of people to link similar discursive elements, occasionally giving them surprising meanings which at times diverged from and at times converged with others. Apparently shared language and images about such questions as prostitution, slavery, marriage, and domesticity had the capacity to take on different meanings in turn-of-the-century Puerto Rico, depending on who used it and how they did so. This process of meaning making was a central aspect of various groups' struggles to form collective identities. Ideological production did not occur only after a class, national identity, or social movement had been "objectively made." Liberal Autonomists, bourgeois feminists, working-class radicals of both sexes, and Afro-Puerto Rican political activists all forged their ever changing senses of themselves—their differences from and affinities with others—*as* they created discourses and often *through* the discourses themselves.[5]

In my joining of social history with discourse analysis, I have attempted to guard against the tendency in much of the theoretical work on the history of sexuality to focus only on what has been *said* and, until recently, in much writing on race to assume a fixed, self-evident biological basis to racial identity. Consequently, in this book I consider how discourses about respectability shaped sexual practices, racial meanings, and sexual regulatory strategies. I also demonstrate how different social experiences spawned divergent discourses about the interconnections of race, class, and sexuality in Puerto Rico. Indeed, I argue throughout the book that the experiences and meanings of sexuality, race, and class are mutually constitutive: "they come into existence *in and through relation to* each other—if in contradictory and conflictual ways."[6]

Because I will use the term "discourse" frequently throughout this volume, it merits a brief discussion. Discourses are built only partly through "the words people say to each other."[7] They also emerge through the combination of images, symbols, and intellectual and cultural practices with which people produce meaning for themselves and others. Thus discourses can be created in many venues: in political and social movements; in public debates; in the pages of newspapers; in official laws and proclamations; and more informally in court testimonies; in the storytelling, jokes, and songs of neighborhoods, marketplaces, and families; and in individuals' daily actions and decisions.

The social discourses embedded in popular culture often provide a particularly powerful means for people to articulate their concerns. Such discourses "embody often unconscious values, but also express . . . social practices."[8] The discourses produced in these and many other sites are not hermetically sealed off from one another. Rather, their producers constantly draw on and respond to other discourses to which they are exposed, jockeying for collective recognition of their own meanings. Finally, the construction of discourses is a political as well as an intellectual or cultural process, in that their creators struggle over both power and meaning as they seek to weave their stories.[9]

The Workings of Race and Sexuality

The construction of postemancipation racial identities and politics in Puerto Rico has only begun to receive concerted attention from historians during the last decade. Throughout the twentieth century, the United States, in particular, has served as a powerful counterpoint in discussions of Puerto Rican race relations. The harshness of legal and economic segregation, overt racial conflicts, and organized white supremacist groups in the United States has led many Puerto Ricans to tout the comparative racial "harmony" of their society. Most students of the island's history asserted or assumed that after the abolition of slavery, racial differences and conflicts there became either irrelevant or clearly secondary to class relations. Those who argued otherwise were effectively marginalized from the centers of scholarly discourse. Fortunately, this has begun to change in the 1990s.[10] Nevertheless, the connections between racial and gender power relations in Puerto Rico still remain largely unexplored.

This book demonstrates that throughout the period in question, race was quite important to Puerto Rican familial, community, and national politics, but often in subtle, shifting ways. Discourses about race became interwoven with those of gender and class—often deflecting and refracting off them, but never completely buried. "Cultural competencies and sexual practices," as well as material resources and physical phenotype, helped create individual and collective racial identities. Consequently, they were sometimes subject to change.[11] The political meanings and uses of these identities also mutated over time, according to the perceived exigencies of the moment. Those building new political projects sometimes emphasized racial differences in order to distinguish themselves from others, and at other times deliberately downplayed them in order to cement alliances. The dominant racial hierarchy, however, valuing "lighter" over "darker," remained more or less intact, despite various twentieth-century plebeian efforts to challenge or invert it.[12]

Most discourses about honor and moral respectability, which produced powerful languages for the articulation of politics, were racially as well as class and gender based. They provided a medium for asserting whiteness or anxiety about it; for "lightening" people of African descent; and for affirming dignified blackness. Indeed, discussions of sexual morality or unruliness became a prime way for Puerto Ricans to talk about race and create racial labels, without directly naming racial distinctions. The entangling of sexual and racial meanings allowed Puerto Ricans to refer constantly to race and underscore its power in their society, but often to do so obliquely. Yet race *was* openly addressed in Puerto Rico at the turn of the century much more often than one might imagine, considering the resounding silence on the topic in most of the historical scholarship.

Sexuality remains even more marginalized than race in the historical literature on Puerto Rico. In other parts of the world, however, scholarly attention has increasingly turned to the deep concern with reshaping gender and sexual relations that permeated colonial and nationalist projects. Many have argued that such discourses about women and sexuality were largely symbolic; women's bodies and morality served as particularly powerful tropes for the formation of discourses through which were alternately expressed colonial dominance, emerging national or bourgeois class identities, and yearnings for the creation of effective nation-states. As Mrinalini Sinha puts it, "The discussion about the 'woman question' in colonial India was seldom about women; women were more often the grounds on which competing views of tradition or national identity were debated."[13] I agree that the combined symbolism of sexuality and women was especially compelling and thus could be turned to powerful use by intellectuals and politicians. Indeed, a good portion of this book is dedicated to analyzing how conceptions of "decency" and "disreputability" operated in the making and unmaking of political projects and alliances.

But sex is not only symbolic. The men and women who sought to regulate sexual practice through their individual actions, public discourse, and state interventions were not only concerned with its symbolic power. They also worried constantly about the racial, economic, cultural, and political ramifications of marriage, consensual union, prostitution, and male infidelity. As Ann Stoler and Frederick Cooper point out, "discourse about sex was not necessarily metaphoric: sex was about sex—and also about its consequences."[14] Because sexual and racial meanings were often inseparable, racialized sexual norms and practices were central to the construction of social and political orders in a number of ways in Puerto Rico.

First, they structured quotidian power relations, operating as both a diffuse glue and a site of contradiction and conflict in people's daily lives. Sexual norms provided systems of meaning through conflictually shared languages about honor and respectability. Sexual practices and their regulation also were a primary medium through which people physically experienced both power and exploitation. Sexual norms and practices, at least during the period studied here, were consistently a central component of intertwined class, race, gender, and generational relations, although they did not always operate in the same ways. Asserting moral superiority or respectability vis-à-vis others, for example, was an important way to establish one's distance from poverty and blackness, or at least from their "uncivilized" aspects.

Consequently, racially saturated sexual norms and practices were key to the ordering of society. In chapter 1 I will examine their diffuse, yet quite powerful workings in nineteenth-century Ponce.

But sexuality does not operate only in this way. It also becomes explicitly politicized at certain historical moments. This seems to be particularly true in times of change and transition. Stoler, for example, has shown that colonial authorities in Southeast Asia responded to threats from labor unrest, nationalist murmurings among the colonized, and lack of consensus among colonizers by radically shifting their strategies for sexual regulation and focusing attention on sexual transgressions by colonized men. Laura Engelstein and Isabel Hull argue that morality became particularly important in political debates as Russian and German reformers began to envision more modern societies, loosened from their feudal pasts. Sonya Rose analyzes the panic about working-class girls' alleged interracial sexual dalliances which erupted during World War II in Britain, when anxiety about British citizenship and national identity were high.[15]

In such moments of historical flux, discourses about morality, respectability, and honor are frequently used, often unconsciously, to assert distinct interests, define identities, and malign social and economic competitors. Redefinitions of racialized sexual norms and practices often clarify one's difference from an opposing group, thus confirming one's own superiority vis-à-vis others. When developing their initial social programs, for example, both elite Puerto Rican Liberals in the nineteenth century and radical labor organizers in the early twentieth century elaborated moral codes that served this purpose. Liberals hoped to create a newly virile nation, freed from what they saw as dangerously African, feminizing, and sensual popular classes. Leftist labor activists, on the other hand, sought to morally demonize capitalists, while asserting the moral and racial solidarity of working people.

Publicly invoking either new or familiar sexual agendas can also incorporate others into one's own project, effectively erasing difference and achieving internal consensus. This process of incorporation and internal homogenization is generally accomplished through the combination of two methods. The first is reform, when one group attempts to reshape others to be "properly" compliant, acceptable. In Puerto Rico, elite male Liberals attempted to moralize, de-Africanize, and thus subject to their authority women of all classes and working-class men. Bourgeois feminists, on the other hand, tried to do the same for both elite men and plebeian women. Radical working-class

men simultaneously denounced racism on the island while asserting a plebeian solidarity capable of transcending racial differences. Concomitantly,
they elaborated new conceptions of morality and gender relations that sought
to deracialize and elevate workingwomen's status while reinserting them into
an idealized, controllable domesticity. Soon after the U.S. occupation of the
island, colonial officials joined together with local elites to encourage Puerto
Ricans of the disturbingly racially fluid popular classes to marry and thus
"stabilize" their families and the social order.

The second method of homogenization is repression and exclusion. This
entails the sexual and often racial demonization of particular marginalized
groups—those who refuse to fit within the prescribed limits of morality and
"decency." In Puerto Rico from 1870 to 1920, such repressive episodes consistently centered on racially charged excoriation of unruly plebeian women,
who were labeled "prostitutes." These crackdowns were selective, however.
Their very harshness encouraged the political inclusion of those who did not
fall within the state's repressive purview. During the late nineteenth century,
the harassment of alleged, darkened prostitutes went hand in hand with elites'
concession of honorable, racially acceptable citizenship status to plebeian
men. Several decades later, respectable bourgeois "ladies" were the new actors
to enjoy inclusion in the public sphere through their participation in an
antiprostitution crusade. But neither of these campaigns simply confirmed
the status quo. Even while acquiescing to their broader terms, previously
marginalized groups used both antiprostitution drives to assert their own
interests, which often diverged in unexpected ways from those of male elites.

In Puerto Rico, where local elites were positioned on the margins of both
Spanish and U.S. empires and where during the twentieth century the United
States tried to forge a new, "modern" form of colonialism, reform and repres-
sion/exclusion were generally closely combined in some form. These attempts to consolidate a homogenous group identity or political consensus
were often simultaneously inclusive and silencing, open and closed. Such
ambiguity could shift dominators from pure contempt of subalterns to less
disparaging positions, joining denigration, ridicule, and sometimes even disgust with attempts at inclusion. Such equivocal methods of rule both encouraged collusion, normalizing social relations and reaffirming social hierarchies,
and helped produce challenges from below.[16]

In the midst of this ambiguity, though, one method of homogenization
tended to predominate over the other at specific historical conjunctures.

Concerted efforts at remaking racialized sexual norms frequently surfaced as new collective identities or political projects were being formed. Yet once these movements consolidated themselves and were able to carve out a relatively secure political space, the debates over sexual reform tended to drop away. Both bourgeois feminists and the early left followed this pattern. Likewise, the U.S. colonial enterprise and Puerto Rican elite Liberals began their projects with proposals for apparently benevolent reforms, many of which focused on sexuality, morality, and reshaping traditional familial relations. But when pressed by relatively autonomous challenges to their authority, both turned to selective repression—against discursively darkened *women* deemed sexually dangerous.

Challengers of the established order can very quickly become its defenders, particularly once they have gained some access to power; the shifting alliances that I trace here confirm this pattern. Yet neither "challengers" nor "defenders" of the status quo are purely one or the other. Those seeking to preserve the status quo must incorporate elements of the opposition's agenda to maintain their power. Concomitantly, subaltern intellectuals and leaders continually choose which elements of the old social order and discourses they will retain and which they hope to reinvent.[17] This was the case for Liberal male professionals, as it was for bourgeois feminists, working-class anarchist feminists, and Afro-Puerto Rican political activists. Ultimately, even those calling for radical change have generally sought to assert power over others; this book will demonstrate that Puerto Rico was no exception.

Why is it that sexuality and race should be so important in these struggles over collective definitions of the self and other? Perhaps the answer lies in their close connection with the human body and its alleged "naturalness."[18] Joan Scott and Elaine Combs-Schilling, among others, have noted that ideas about gender often become the "constant" of power relations because they are more easily connected to the body and what is supposedly "natural." Gender relations are therefore deemed more immutable than class relations.[19] The same can be said about race, which is often linked, at least discursively, with physical characteristics. Such assertions of unalterable authority become even more powerful when tied to questions of sexuality; they are then "undeniably natural." What better way to claim legitimacy than to ground one's project in a specific code for the interrelationship of bodies and the sexes? Even as they change, moral codes can be presented as imbued with the unassailable power of nature.

Thus, as this book will confirm, definitions of "honor," "respectability," "race," and "'proper' sexual practices" can become key to ascertaining who will be included or excluded in the nation or community being imagined.[20] This may well be the case because defining collectivities around bodily relations and what is supposedly natural provides a center and an enduring legitimacy to what is otherwise a rather arbitrary drawing of lines. The nation, as a group of scholars has noted, has an "insatiable need for representational labor to supplement its founding ambivalence, the lack of self-presence at its origin or in its essence."[21] Sex, as both symbol and practice and ever endowed with multiple, often racially charged meanings, is frequently at the center of such labor. It quickly becomes a primary battleground for collective definition at crucial moments of conflict and transition.

Intellectuals and the Making of Discourse

Building on Steven Feierman's brilliant analysis of peasant intellectuals in Tanzania, in this book I pay special attention to the popular and elite intellectuals who played pivotal roles in the creation of racially and sexually saturated political discourses. Artisans, professionals, wealthy wives and widows, labor organizers of both sexes, Afro-Puerto Rican journalists and lawyers: individuals from all sectors of urban Puerto Rican society proved themselves capable of generating politically influential discourses about racial identities and sexual norms and practices.

These individuals stood at "the nexus between domination and public discourse" and mediated the relationship between the two. They displayed "directive, organizational or educative" social capacities and were key players in the construction of shifting political alliances built around the racialized definitions of sexual norms and practices. They chose which elements to valorize or reject of the broader codes of honor and respectability; their literacy and access to print media and public-speaking forums made them more effective than others in garnering audiences for their interpretations. Analyzing their discursive practices will hopefully begin to provide an explanation for the fluctuating uses of race and sexuality—why the discourses changed when they did, and why certain elements resurfaced time and time again.[22]

But examining the role of intellectuals in the production of political discourses and projects is not sufficient. I am also concerned with the agency of the unorganized, those who were *not*, in Feierman's terms, "intellectuals defined by their social position."[23] They too created and elaborated discourses through their daily practices, conflicts, and conversations. Such discourses may not have been self-consciously political—politicization seemed to require the intervention of intellectuals, whether popular or elite—but they were powerful nonetheless. They provided the milieus, or habitus, within which intellectuals lived and from which they fashioned their politico-moral language and projects. Thus, this book explores the informal struggles over sexual and racial definitions that took place within communities and families, as well as their linkage by intellectuals to public political discourses, social movements, and state regulatory campaigns.

The Context

Most of the archival research for this project was done in the municipality of Ponce. Although I trace islandwide movements such as liberalism, feminism, and the early-twentieth-century labor movement, widening my scope in the last two chapters to include the coastal regions of the island, the book remains primarily a study of Ponce. Consequently, I can illuminate but not draw definitive conclusions about other parts of the island, particularly the mountainous central highlands. This coffee-producing region has had a quite different historical experience than the sugar plantation–dominated coasts, including the prevalence of a free, smallholding peasantry throughout the nineteenth century, the dominance of rural over urban society well into the twentieth century, and a more generalized rejection of Afro-Puerto Rican identity by the local popular classes.[24]

The period spanned by this book, 1870–1920, is crucial in Puerto Rican history. With the abolition of slavery in 1873, the island deepened its long transition to capitalism. The 1870s and 1880s also witnessed the founding of the Liberal (later the Autonomist) Party, whose leaders began to agitate for autonomy from Spain. They elaborated a distinct national identity for the island and engaged in a series of struggles over its parameters with artisans and early feminists. By early 1898, the Liberal Autonomists' drive for hegemony seemed to be complete; an autonomy charter for Puerto Rico had been won, and the Liberals were ensconced in political power throughout the island.

The U.S. invasion of 1898, however, shattered Liberal hegemony. All sectors of Puerto Rican society rushed to redefine the social and political order as proletarianization and land and capital concentration rapidly accelerated. The first two decades of U.S. colonial rule saw the emergence of both bourgeois and working-class feminisms, as well as a multiracial, islandwide labor movement and increased Afro-Puerto Rican political activism. The 1917 Jones Act institutionalized Puerto Rico's colonial status, just in time to drag the island's residents into World War I along with their colonial master. The prewar period consolidated U.S. colonialism; the political and economic terms instated in these early years would endure until the institutionalization of the Partido Popular Democrático's "Free Associated State" in 1952. The fifty years between 1870 and 1920, then, established the groundwork of Puerto Rico's modern social relations, political systems, and understandings of what it means to be "Puerto Rican." And Ponce was at the center of it all.

Ponce began the nineteenth century as a sleepy village of a few hundred souls surrounded by countryside that was sparsely populated by a racially mixed, smallholding peasantry. Puerto Rico's sugar boom—which began in 1815, was in full swing by 1830, and had peaked by 1850—changed all that. Sugar production rapidly increased from 838 tons in 1812 to 14,126 tons in 1830, exploding to 52,622 tons in 1850. As Francisco Scarano has shown, sugar radically transformed the coastal districts that it touched, quickly becoming the island's dominant industry and remaining so for much of the century. Large-scale sugar production meant the institution of plantation-based agriculture, the displacement of the local peasantry, and the importation of tens of thousands of enslaved Africans, wrenched from their native lands to produce wealth for those who claimed to own them. In Ponce alone, between four and six thousand slaves were brought from Africa between 1802 and 1846, increasing the slave population from 12 percent of inhabitants to almost 25 percent. Ponce's sudden insertion into the world economy also brought urbanization, class differentiation, and the emergence of politically powerful planter and merchant elites, most of whom were immigrants from Spain, the mainland of Latin America, and other Caribbean islands.[25] As Angel Quintero Rivera has pointed out, during the nineteenth century Ponce became Puerto Rico's "alternate capital." The municipality's booming sugar industry and port made it an economic center of the island after the 1830s, surpassing San Juan in importance until the twentieth century. During the 1870s, Ponce gave birth to the pro-autonomy Liberal Party and to Puerto Rico's earliest formal formulations of national identity.[26]

Ponce is also a fascinating place on the island to trace race relations. In 1860, for example, free and enslaved people of African descent made up 57 percent of the municipality's population.[27] Afro-Puerto Ricans heavily influenced Ponce's culture and politics. Their impact was felt in areas as diverse as the heightened racial self-consciousness of its white elite, the music played in the streets of urban working-class neighborhoods, and the strength of the Republicano Party in the early twentieth century. In addition, the early Puerto Rican labor movement maintained a significant presence in the city between 1900 and 1920. Finally, the city was an organizational center for the bourgeois feminist movement from the 1890s on. Through the late nineteenth and early twentieth centuries, then, Ponce was a city where national identity and race, class, and gender interests were openly and intensely debated—an ideal venue for this volume.

The book begins with an analysis of the various honor codes that structured daily life in nineteenth-century Ponce. Chapter 2 moves to a discussion of the national project elaborated by elite male Liberals during the 1870s and 1880s. They saw "proper" mothers and a whiter pleb as the keys to creating both the competent rulers and docile workers who would comprise the "great Puerto Rican family." The new, de-Africanized, appropriately virile nation would be built through morally reforming women. In response to liberalism, Puerto Rican bourgeois feminists began to articulate their own moral vision of egalitarian elite marriages, superior feminine morality, and the white, wealthy women's right to intellectual and sexual fulfillment. Yet these early feminists' desires to maintain their class privileges and distinguish themselves from the "disreputable" darker women of the working classes ultimately prevented them from posing a radical challenge to the Liberal project.

Chapter 3 delineates how talk by the Liberals of moral reform ultimately translated into repression in practice. An 1890s campaign to regulate prostitution and thus cleanse Ponce's urban space of "sexually wayward" plebeian women was instrumental in forging a cross-class and cross-gender consensus in favor of creating a "decent" city, just at the time when the Liberals were launching their final successful drive to political power. Potential political challenges from artisans and bourgeois feminists were neutralized by the prostitution panic, previous Liberal emphases on racial distinctions between elite and urban plebeian men were silenced, and working-class moral norms rigidified as the targeted women were deemed repositories of blackness and sexual danger. Thus, Liberal hegemony in its stronghold of Ponce rested partially on the denigration of sexually threatening, discursively darkened workingwomen.

The Liberal-led consensus began to break apart, however, with the invasion by the United States and its institution of an allegedly benevolent colonialism. Access to divorce seems to have been an important ingredient of pro-U.S. sympathies among many women. As I outline in Chapter 4, U.S. officials soon set about implementing their own sexual reforms, focused on marriage and divorce, which they expected would tame and modernize their newly acquired tropical colonies. The liberalization of access to divorce sparked an explosion of women's protests against domestic violence, male infidelity, and economic abandonment. The women who flooded into court to demand divorces implicitly denounced as a farce the Liberals' dream of a harmonious "great national family" and applauded what they interpreted as U.S.-sponsored "democratization of the family."

The emergence of a vibrant labor movement in the early twentieth century definitively splintered Liberal hegemony, as delineated in Chapter 5. Leading labor activists denounced racism among both the upper and working classes, while asserting that working-class unity in the struggle against "wage slavery" could overcome intraplebeian racial tensions. Female and male labor organizers began to formulate a newly self-conscious sexual politics based on popular sexual norms and practices. In the process, they rejected the fusion of immorality, blackness, and femaleness that for so long had permeated dominant social assumptions in Puerto Rico. In Chapter 5 I analyze the ideologies of free love, fiesty working-class womanhood, and solidarity with prostitutes with which working-class radicals challenged Liberal notions of respectability, cross-class male alliances, and citizenship. Male labor leaders dreamed of their own version of male dominance, however. They sought to enclose working-class women in an idealized, safely circumscribed domesticity that closely mirrored that of the local bourgeoisie. Those plebeian women who challenged this vision were effectively marginalized.

In Chapter 6 I demonstrate how during World War I, when labor, feminist, and Afro-Puerto Rican political demands were escalating, the excoriation of prostitutes once again became a prime tool in the hands of those seeking to maintain stability and create political consensus. This time, however, it was U.S. colonial officials, followed by many local elites, who insisted that jailing sexually suspect women was the only hope for the survival of democracy. In a chillingly familiar pattern, ruling "benevolence" turned to repression when faced with pressure for change from working people and women. The medium was once again racially charged sexual demonization, and its prime target, plebeian women.

The social movements and political constituencies that had consolidated since the U.S. invasion all crystallized around the wartime antiprostitution campaign. In an attempt to advance their own political interests, bourgeois feminists enthusiastically cooperated with the state. They lent legitimacy to its repressive activities by attempting to "morally rehabilitate" the jailed women while articulating a more woman-centered discourse about prostitution than was that of colonial officials. Female and male workers, however, as well as Afro-Puerto Rican professionals and other dissident members of the two principal political parties, produced a chorus of protest against the mass arrests. Countering the state campaign with their own analyses of racially neutral citizenship and sexuality, they drew on earlier radical sexual discourses to posit that the targeted women were the quintessential representatives of a working class fighting for dignity and democratic rights.

In the end, the repressive campaign against "sexually suspect" women was implemented, but colonial officials and their local allies were unable to forge a supporting political consensus similar to that of the 1890s. The very promises of social equality and justice that had cemented U.S. colonial hegemony could be transformed into critiques of abuses by U.S. officials. Sexual controversy was a linchpin of these battles, fracturing prior political alliances and creating new ones. Its roots lay in the conflictual, racialized sexual norms and practices constructed by Puerto Ricans during the nineteenth-century slavery and sugar boom, to whose workings I now turn.

Chapter 1

Respectable Ponce: Deciphering the Codes of Power, 1855–1898

My sister is a poor orphan, with no patrimony but her honor.
—Presbítero Velez, "Contra Andrés Nieves Servano," 1901, AGPR

The declarant says that she has had romantic relations for about a year with Antonio Laubriel, who visited her house with her parents' consent. But people began to murmur that she was pregnant, which was untrue. Since she had already been slandered by the public, she decided to go and live with my lover. . . . The declarant states that Laubriel neither persuaded her nor forced her to go with him. That night she lost her virginal state, which she had carefully conserved until then.
—"Sobre rapto de Francisca Vega," 1887, AGPR

On Christmas Eve 1894, sixteen-year-old Teresa Astacio ran off in the middle of the night with Santos Vargas, a *pardo* laborer who had been hired to pick coffee on the farm of Teresa's father. The next morning, the news spread like wildfire in Montes Llanos, the rural sector of Ponce where the Astacios lived. After unsuccessfully searching for the two, Don Dionicio Astacio, a widowed smallholding landowner, stormed into the home of the *alcalde de barrio* and denounced Vargas for kidnapping his daughter and "robbing her of her purity."[1]

When the couple was finally located and brought into court several months later, they told rather different stories. Facing the possibility of a lengthy prison sentence for having dishonored a virgin, Santos insisted that after they had established a courtship, Teresa admitted to him that she was not a virgin and asked him to take her away with him. The two left Teresa's home, had intercourse, and began living together. Despite her alleged lack of virginity, Santos claimed, he had intended to marry Teresa and thus redeem her stained honor. But when he left her alone one night about a week later, Teresa left Santos to take up with his good friend Balbino Zayas, who was also a landless day laborer. Balbino and Teresa had been living together at the home of Balbino's father ever since. Consequently, Santos was no longer interested in marrying his former sweetheart; he prevailed on the court to recognize his claim that he had not deflowered her and consequently to refrain from punishing him.

Teresa, on the other hand, insisted that although she had left her father's house with Vargas, intending to make love and live with the impoverished laborer after only a two-week courtship, she had indeed lost her virginity that fateful Christmas Eve and therefore was honorable. Teresa confirmed that she had left Santos to live with his pardo friend Balbino, but not, as Santos had implied, owing to her immorality. Rather, she left "because it was not convenient to continue living with Vargas. He set me up in a house that didn't even belong to him, and he made me serve him like a servant; I'm not accustomed to that."

When interrogated about his role in the drama, Balbino said that he had never asked Teresa whether she had been a virgin when she left her father's home; it had "never occurred to him to do so." A number of wealthy, white, landowning neighbors, however, did not show the same disinterest in Teresa's virginity. Their testimony centered on her "unstained" sexual reputation. Teresa had never been known to have had a romantic relationship with anyone before. Before her sexual escapades of the last few months, she had always been "properly contained" within her father's house and therefore had been considered by everyone who knew her to be a virgin and a respectable young woman.

Before the court could render a decision in the matter of marriage and the reparation of Teresa's honor, however, Don Dionicio and Teresa appeared before the judge and pardoned Santos Vargas. Teresa was no longer interested in marrying him (if she ever had been), and Don Dionicio perhaps feared that the court would either formally find that his daughter had indeed not been "pure" when she left with Santos or that it would order a socially unacceptable marriage.

Officially recorded cases of cross-class romances between poor, Afro-Puerto Rican men and daughters of allegedly white landholders, even illiterate landowners such as Don Dionicio, were rare in the nineteenth century. Nevertheless, Teresa and Santos's story—and the story that each told about it—offers some fascinating glimpses into a number of issues to be explored in this chapter.

The script of female honor, based on the maintenance of a woman's virginity and sexual fidelity, which, once lost, was only reparable by marriage to the conquering male, was clearly well known by all parties involved. Teresa, Santos, Don Dionicio, and the Astacios' neighbors all employed elements of this discourse in their presentations to the magistrate. Yet each hoped to achieve different ends by appropriating the common language of honor and respectability. Indeed, honor, as we can see from this case, could be profoundly contradictory. Restoring Teresa's honor by ordering her marriage to an impoverished pardo man would have subverted the class and race hierarchies that cemented Don Dionicio's superiority over landless Afro-Puerto Rican laborers, rather than confirming them, as the defense of female honor was intended to do. In addition, the very definition of respectability could vary widely from class to class. Balbino's acceptance of Teresa's shifting sexual alliances contrasted markedly with her white, wealthy male neighbors' preoccupation with her chastity.

Furthermore, the divergent social expectations of women across Ponce's class spectrum helped produce very different experiences of womanhood, as Teresa so pointedly stated. She had never experienced the brutal poverty of the landless laboring classes, nor had she performed the kinds of domestic labor expected of her by her plebeian lover. In fact, she may well have been accustomed to enjoying the fruits of servants' domestic labor herself. Being served, rather than having to serve others, was important to her understanding of what it meant to be a respectable woman.

Finally, Teresa's case shows that women did not passively reproduce patriarchal social codes. Rather, they struggled with the men in their lives over the precise definitions of acceptable gendered labor and sexual conduct. Even while accepting the dominant tenets of honor and gender obligations, women often attempted to manipulate them to their own advantage. And like Teresa, who took up with a man of African heritage and then challenged the accepted wisdom that he "owned" her by establishing a more satisfactory sexual alliance with another, sometimes women even dared to openly defy them.

Honor, Power, and Social Conflict

In nineteenth-century Puerto Rico, as in much of Latin America, concepts of honor were based on gendered and racialized beliefs about social ordering, appropriate behavior, and personal worth. Discourses about honor expressed, justified, and enforced the gender, race, and class hierarchies on which society was built.[2] Honor, in other words, was an assertion of power over or in relation to others.

Honor was often invoked by nineteenth-century Ponceños, especially those who enjoyed its benefits, as "natural" and therefore unquestionably legitimate, impervious to change. When linked to the physicality of people's bodies through supposed biological givens such as race and sex, this assertion of naturalness gained added power. In the name of the "natural" privileges implicit in their honor, women and men accepted as white asserted their superiority over Puerto Ricans of African descent; parents claimed authority over their children's lives; and men of all classes insisted on their right to control women. However, neither honor nor the social codes that bestowed or denied its benefits were natural phenomena. They were the products of social contention.

As such, honor did not simply constitute a set of abstract beliefs. Rather, it was embodied in the concrete practices of people in their everyday lives—in sexual relationships, local labor and other economic relations, social interactions, and the courts. These practices had crucial material effects on people's lives, impacting on their possibilities for marriage or sexual partnership, community standing, and economic well-being. As Steve Stern has pointed out in his study of colonial Mexico, honor was only one of several axes around which gender, racial, and class power could be organized.[3] It did, however, provide a powerful medium through which nineteenth-century Puerto Ricans understood and gave meaning to their world and its social order.

In addition, honor discourses did not constitute a singular, unitary code of social respectability that all people interpreted in the same way.[4] Rather, as we saw in Teresa Astacio's story, a variety of discourses about honor, discernible in different groups' language and practices, existed in Puerto Rico by the mid–nineteenth century. At different points, these discourses converged, diverged, and even came into open conflict with each other. The moral norms they delineated marked the outside limits of acceptable behavior and power relations for whichever group was formulating them.

Because they sought to win, consolidate, or contest power relations, all discourses about honor and respectability were internally contradictory. These discourses helped order society, but they did so in defense against disorder. Moral norms had to be continually reiterated and actively enforced precisely because they were constantly contested; less powerful individuals and groups often tried to turn the precepts of respectability to their own advantage or invented their own definitions and values. The result was ongoing, multileveled struggles over the terms of "decency." These struggles in turn encoded the great societal conflicts of race, class, and gender. Puerto Ricans' practices and beliefs about respectability provided part of the tension-ridden ground out of which grew the state interventions, collective practices, and social movements that I analyze in this book.

The honor codes that I consider in this chapter were not transhistorical phenomena. They were probably consolidated in Puerto Rico during the sugar boom of 1800–1845. As Francisco Scarano has noted, the rapid expansion of plantations in Puerto Rico's coastal areas, accompanied by massive influxes of both enslaved Africans and wealthy, "white" immigrants, dramatically polarized and rigidified Ponce's racial and class hierarchies. The more fluid social relations that Scarano and others assert marked eighteenth-century Ponce may well have produced sexual norms substantially different from those examined here.[5] In addition, enslaved peoples from various parts of Africa and the Americas, as well as free immigrants, brought their own sexual practices and conceptions of honor with them to Puerto Rico. During the early nineteenth century (1800–1830), when large numbers of people from around the globe were flooding into the island, the collision of cultures may have created a society in which it was more difficult to identify regional definitions of honor. A rigorous investigation of these hypotheses, however, lies beyond my scope here; the sources available to me were produced after the height of the sugar boom in 1845. Rather, I will decipher those honor codes produced once the plantation regime and its cultures were consolidated in Ponce. My analysis will span the pre- and postabolition periods, since the diffuse honor codes created in Ponce's families and communities displayed a marked consistency both before and after 1873.

The Workings of Honor

Honor in Public

Honor had meaning only in relation to other people. One's ranking on the honor scale depended partly on how one compared with those in the surrounding community in matters of lineage, wealth, and perceived racial categorization. According to dominant definitions, the whiter and wealthier, the more honorable an individual. In addition, the accomplishment of gender-appropriate behavior determined men's and women's honorability vis-à-vis their social equals. But honor depended heavily on social recognition and public opinion. Only if acknowledged as honorable and paid the proper public deference by one's community could an individual enjoy honor's benefits, no matter how much money or noble a lineage he or she might possess.

Therefore, public standing—the image of a person accepted by the community—ultimately established that person's honor or lack thereof. Indeed, reputation could be more important than one's own actions. In battles over honor, the public construction of reputation became reality. If a young woman was considered a virgin, she was one.[6] Regardless of whether she had actually had intercourse with a man, if a woman was rumored to be "lost," her social standing and chances for marriage could be ruined. Cecilia Miranda was forced to confront this ugly reality when she insisted on attending a "society" dance to which she had pointedly not been invited. Upon her arrival, Gumersindo Beltrán informed her that many people were "disgusted" by her presence there and insisted that she leave; she "was said to be a lost woman and was not worthy of frequenting respectable society gatherings."[7]

Even racial categorization, which supposedly was determined "naturally," could be established through the way a person or group was perceived by others. Phenotype certainly had a good deal of bearing on one's racial identity. Yet money, "good manners," a "respectable" lifestyle, and stylish dress could "whiten" a person. Juan Serrallés, for example, was the son of Juana Colón, an Afro-Puerto Rican woman who was the lover for some years of the wealthy sugar baron Don Sebastian Serrallés. At his birth, Juan was listed in the baptismal record for black and mixed-race people; this indelibly marked him as a "pardo." When he was sixteen, however, Juan was legally recognized as a "natural" (that is, illegitimate) son by his father, thus raising his social status—and probably signaling his father's willingness to provide him with at least some educational or financial support. Years later, when Juan was thirty-three, he petitioned the Crown and the Catholic Church for a certificate of legitimation. It was eventually granted, and Juan was accorded the right to use the honorific title of "Don," thus publicly claiming the status of a white person. In the 1871 census, Don Juan Serrallés appeared as the owner of substantial amounts of land, as well as a number of slaves. He had completed the journey from black to white.[8]

Concomitantly, in sugar areas such as Ponce, outward signs of poverty—

ragged dress or plebeian forms of speech—could mark a person as "blacker" than others with similar physical characteristics. "African" behaviors also "darkened." They encompassed all sorts of Afro-Puerto Rican–based cultural activities, such as dancing the bomba and practicing witchcraft, in which many phenotypically "white" plebeian people participated.[9] Teresa Astacio, whose sexual saga opened this chapter, may well have threatened her racial status by taking up with poor, pardo men. Racial identities, then, and their accompanying social standing (or lack thereof), were socially constructed. Puerto Ricans' whiteness, in particular, needed to be perennially reasserted. Popular culture was especially important in this process, simultaneously marking Ponceños racially and providing a space where biological differences could be confounded.

The Dominant Honor Code

The honor system of Puerto Rico's nineteenth-century elites was premised on the sexual control of women and the exclusion of people who were poorer, of African heritage, or enslaved from the community of respectability. Men fought out battles over honor and social power among themselves on the racialized field of women's bodies. Women of means also sought to assert themselves as respectable members of "decent" society. Moneyed people of both sexes defined their social standing and whiteness in opposition to the people of African descent who surrounded them on the streets, in their shops, laboring in their fields, and serving them in their homes.

CONTROLLING AND DIVIDING WOMEN

Control over women's sexuality was a cornerstone of the dominant honor code. Respectable women were required to be virginal before marriage and unswervingly faithful to their husbands once married, which demanded that women be carefully guarded against outside male incursions and placed under constant surveillance. Once destroyed by sexual activity, rape, or rumors of such encounters, a woman's reputation could be fully restored only by marriage, usually to the man who had "conquered" her.[10]

One important exception to this general rule existed. It was not unheard of even for young white women of the "respectable" classes to have premarital intercourse with their boyfriends, once marriage had been promised. The extensive nature of "betrothal sex" provided the foundation for the frequent presumption that women were no longer virgins once they had established a public relationship with a man. Courting, then, for "respectable" white women was a serious business; it usually meant closing off the possibility of marrying anyone else.[11]

A man's word in this matter could be enforced in the courts. As long as a woman "belonged" sexually to only one man who had publicly intended to marry her and was her social equal, he had the legal responsibility to follow through on his promise and restore her honor.[12] Thus, women deemed properly virginal and worthy of the man in question could count on some protection from public opinion and the colonial courts. "Betrothal sex" and its enforcement, however, did not challenge the dominant honor code's underlying premises about the sanctity of female virginity, the costs of losing it, and male sexual ownership of women. Neither did it question the legitimacy of class and racial hierarchies. Equality of social standing between the two partners was usually necessary to invoke court enforcement of the marriage promise.

A family's honor hinged on its women's sexual reputations. This obsession with the sexual control of women was rooted in desires to preserve racial precedence and material patrimony as well as interests in consolidating male power over women. Enforcing female virginity and marital fidelity ensured that children of an undesirable race would not be introduced into the family's legitimate "bloodline." Honorable daughters had potentially high value as readily tradable items on the marriage market; stained reputations ruined opportunities for the economic and political alliance building that accompanied marriage. Patriarchs also depended to a great extent on the sexual restriction of "their" women in the creation of a home and family over which they exercised control. Thus, sexual regulation of "respectable" women was crucial in defining racial identity, maintaining familial and economic social positions, and confirming male dominance.[13]

But feminine respectability did not depend only on sexually controlling "decent" women. Wealthy white women's honor was also premised on the disreputability of poor and Afro-Puerto Rican women. Elite women were assumed by their peers to be respectable unless "proven" to be otherwise. Adherents of the dominant honor code considered white women of the laboring classes, on the other hand, to be sexually suspect. Women of African descent, particularly those unwilling or unable to "whiten" themselves through dress and behavior, were believed to be inherently disreputable. Plebeian women's social inferiority and alleged sexual licentiousness provided the necessary counterpoint to elite women's status. Only in relation to poorer, darker, disreputable "others" could "respectable" women assert their honor. In addition, plebeian women provided a socially acceptable outlet for the sexual energies that a properly virile man was expected to indulge. Their conquest by socially powerful men theoretically ensured that "honorable" women would not suffer sexual or other types of affronts from men of their own class. Thus, women of the moneyed classes had powerful motives for accepting the dominant honor code's terms, despite the fact that it was premised on their sexual and social control: it both granted them social preeminence vis-à-vis plebeian women and justified elite women's material privilege as "naturally" emanating from their chastity and supposed racial purity.

At first glance, the honor system's strict insistence on female virginity and its rigid class- and race-based demarcation of "pure" from "disreputable" women seems oppressively seamless, buttressed as it was by material resources, legal definitions, and respectable society's opinion. But even among the classes and racial groups in which acceptance of this honor code reigned supreme, there were some who by their actions quietly put the lie to its totalizing legitimacy.

Long-term concubinage of white couples was not unheard of among the leisured classes. Once her abusive husband disappeared to the United States, Doña Nieves Gaston, the educated daughter of a respectable wealthy widow, set up house with Don Pablo Niuri, a neighboring plantation owner. Doña Nieves and Niuri lived together not only in the relative privacy of his country home, but also publicly frequented his city properties, to the great distress of Doña Nieves' mother and, presumably, their neighbors. Doña Nieves and Don Pablo seem to have successfully borne the brunt of their peers' disapproval, at least enough to continue living together for an extended period of time. Perhaps the combination of their material wealth and political connections with the fact that Doña Nieves' husband had abandoned her allowed them to survive their community's censure.[14]

But those married women who entered into extramarital affairs while still living with their husbands risked much more than social ostracism, no matter how well off they might be. Their transgressions posed an especially grave threat to the social order. By rejecting the edicts of unquestioning female fidelity and sexual submission to their husbands, these women challenged the principle of exclusive male control over women's bodies. Consequently, state agents dealt with them harshly. Magistrates routinely imposed jail sentences of six years or more on "adulterous" wives, permanently separated them from their children, and stripped them of their property. A single extramarital foray, no matter how discreet, was enough to convict a woman, "because such cases are presumed to embody a great perversion; they are inherently a scandal from the moment they are discovered." Men, on the other hand, could be convicted of adultery only if they kept a mistress in the same house as their wife *and* "committed continual public scandals."[15] In my research I found no convictions of adulterous husbands, unless they were carrying on an affair with a married woman of their own class. In such cases, it was their violation of the other man's exclusive sexual rights to his wife, not male infidelity per se, that concerned the courts.

The fact that some married women did take lovers and brave the possibility of discovery despite the severity of the punishments they faced speaks to the depth of their passion and their yearning for a more fulfilling emotional life than that afforded by the often suffocating social restrictions that surrounded them. Unknown is how frequently elite women made such dangerous choices; only those situations which became so conflictual that they burst into the judicial realm and were transcribed in court documents surface in the historical record. The preserved cases probably represent a small fraction of the actual numbers, but these tantalizing historical remains remind us that even in the heart of the *gente decente,* women tested the razor-sharp edges of respectability's limits.

MALE HONOR

Whereas adherents of the dominant honor code distinguished sharply between "pure" and "disreputable" women, men were afforded a bit more flexibility. The poorer a man and the more "African" he looked or behaved, of course, the less honor he might profess under the dominant principles of respectability. Simply being male, however, as long as one was free, gave plebeian men a potential claim to a modicum of honor, as long as they accepted their inferior social position vis-à-vis more powerful men.

The lowest levels of the Ponce municipal court, for example, sometimes found in favor of pardo plebeian men in disputes with their social superiors over honor.[16] This stood in marked contrast to Afro-Puerto Rican women's supposed inherent degeneracy. In extraordinary cases, even a male slave could be endowed with hints of honor, if he was a highly skilled worker and properly subservient. José Dionicio, an enslaved artisan who rented himself out to his owners' acquaintances, defended himself successfully against charges of robbery by calling one of these employers as a witness. The white man insisted that he had "always esteemed José Dionicio as a man of good will and deed, loyal, and trustworthy." The slave Fernando was also given good conduct marks by the municipal court based on his "consistent hard work and submission to white people."[17]

Proper subservience was key, though. Those plebeian men, especially of African descent, who dared to challenge openly the will of their wealthy white "superiors" were swiftly and brutally disciplined. Escolástico Negrón, a black peasant who owned land adjacent to Don Ventura Toces, was whipped, brought in chains to the municipal jail, and punished with a lengthy sentence and heavy fine for refusing to acquiesce to Toces's encroachment on his property. Toces's witnesses, all members of the Ponce city council, applauded the punishment, citing Escolástico's reputation among whites as "an uppity, troublemaking black."[18]

Unlike wealthy white women, whose respectability hinged primarily on their sexual reputation, men's honor depended on a number of elements. The most important corresponded to men's principal function in the familial structure—the provision of income: men of all classes needed to have a reputation as trustworthy in economic and social transactions.[19] *Pícaro* (thief), *pillo* (thief), or *embustero* (liar) were the insults most likely to prompt court cases demanding reparation of a man's honor. Men were also expected to provide financially for their families. Within the dominant honor code, propertied and independently wealthy men were the most honorable of all. Plebeian men, however, considered hard work essential to establishing one's honor.[20]

Plebeian conceptions of virility also included physical reprisals against those who insulted one's honor. Teodoro Ruiz insisted in court that beating José Colón with a broomstick was only the "natural" result of their having exchanged heated insults. Ruiz testified that "he could not contain himself; he was in one of those moments when a man loses his reason."[21] Wealthier, whiter men who could more consistently depend on the state to protect their interests tended to take such cases to court, but they too could not let a cutting insult stand unanswered.[22]

An integral part of proving one's manhood for men of all classes was the capacity to protect the women of the family from the sexual incursions of other males. Fathers, brothers, lovers, and husbands had to be constantly on guard to "defend the honor of their women," especially against those men who were darker or poorer than themselves. As pointed out earlier, male protection of women was often difficult to distinguish from sexual surveillance. Wealthy patriarchs attempted to keep their daughters and wives "safely" isolated from the world outside of their luxurious homes and narrow social circles. But men of more modest means could not even contemplate such domestic seclusion of "their" women. Plebeian women worked extremely long hours in Ponce's shops, marketplaces, and fields and thus had contact with a wide cross section of society. Divisions between the public and the private were not marked, for the poor's homes were extremely small, often no more than one dirt-floored room covered with palm thatch. "Domestic" labor and interactions frequently spilled into "public" spaces. Partly because of this contradiction between practice and ideal and because they could not count on the courts to decide in their favor, nonelite men seem to have resorted more often to overt violence against other men while policing/protecting "their" women; they were involved in the overwhelming majority of assault cases focused on conflicts of this kind. Juan González Delgado, for example, tracked down a *jornalero* (day laborer) who had insulted his sweetheart and hacked the man with a machete.[23]

The corollary to controlling and protecting one's "own" women from male marauders was the necessity of sexually conquering others. Men of all classes and races unequivocably asserted the right to have multiple sexual partners while insisting that "their" women remain chaste.[24] Nonmonogamous men were usually not subject to open community criticism for their sexual forays. Gaspar Salichs, the Spanish overseer of one of Ponce's largest sugar plantations, informed his young, blond wife-to-be and her father of his relationship of many years with a black laundress; the marriage went ahead as planned.[25] Family accounts of Eduardo Salich, a respected Ponce architect, were replete with casual comments about the numerous children he sired with women "of the servant class."[26] Alfonso Cabilla y Escalera, a store clerk who lived in the workers neighborhood of La Cantera, spent the night with his lover once or twice a week. The rest of the time he spent with a few other "lady friends." He expressed surprise at the suggestion that his lover might have been jealous; the woman's female friends and neighbors also described the couple's relationship as a "very tranquil marital life."[27]

Thus, a sexual double standard permeated the dominant honor code. The right to sexual conquest was a silent cornerstone of male honor. It applied to all free men, regardless of their class or race, yet this male bonding over women's bodies was not egalitarian. Wealthy men often resolved the contradiction between the need to conquer and protect/control women by sexual adventures among women of the popular classes. They asserted the right to rape, seduce, and establish longer-term informal sexual relationships with plebeian women, while marrying women of their own class.[28] Economic power meant sexual access to women, including those who "should" have been the exclusive property of poor men.

When they could, plebeian men fought back against these incursions from powerful men. The owner of a small rural store arrived home to find the local tax collctor raping his lover; he threw himself on the man and beat him out of the house.[29] Ramón Amorós, an artisan living in the Playa sector of Ponce, used more subtle tactics. When a young merchant developed a romantic relationship with his daughter, Amorós acknowledged social hierarchy while issuing a barely veiled warning to the man. He "reminded [the merchant] of the difference in class between the two, and let him know that if he had no intentions of marrying the girl, it would be best to terminate the relationship in order to avoid problems." The young man broke off the romance.[30] More often than not, though, wealthy white men probably prevailed in their forays into plebeian sexual fields. Neither the courts nor the police consistently challenged their actions.

Plebeian men, for their part, were not allowed such open sexual access to women. "Respectable" women of the leisured classes were decidedly off-limits to men of the laboring classes. On the rare occasions that men of humble origins did dare to establish relationships with women of a higher social status than themselves (and manage to have their attentions returned in kind by the women), they were halted as quickly as possible by the women's family and the courts. Or, as in the case of Teresa Astacio, who did consummate relationships with "socially undesirable" men, the woman lost the social status she had previously enjoyed as an honorable member of "respectable" society, becoming, in effect, racially "darker" than she had been before.[31]

PLEBEIAN WOMEN IN THE DOMINANT HONOR CODE

Both enslaved and free workingwomen frequently negotiated cross-class, interracial sexual encounters or relationships. At times, this sex could be overtly coercive. Documentation of openly violent cross-class sexual advances is not overwhelming, for very few plebeian women and girls dared to denounce wealthy rapists in a judicial system that was heavily weighted in favor of their assailants. But several cases have survived which confirm that rape was an undeniable subcurrent in class and race relations. Hortencia Rivera was not alone in her experiences. Soon after her fourteenth birthday, a wealthy neighbor spoke to Hortencia's mother, saying "that he wanted me to be in his house, to serve his wife; that he would treat me as a daughter; that he would dress me, and give me shoes, and take care of me very well. Seeing that he was offering so much, my mother agreed that I could stay in his house." But several days after beginning her work as a servant, the "lady" of the house went to visit some friends, and Hortencia was left alone with her employer, Clotilde: "He called to me and proposed that I do certain things with him, and I told him that I couldn't bear to do that. Then he said to me, 'If you won't do it, you'll see how fast I'll bring another one here who will; you'll be out on the street, and all the things I promised to you, I'll give to her.' You see, before, he had offered to give me all kinds of new dresses, and even a pair of new shoes. But I told him that it would be better for me to go back home. And then he answered that that was not necessary, but that if he couldn't get it one way, he'd get it another." Several nights later, Hortencia was awakened by "two terribly strong arms which pinned me down on the bed; I tried to free myself, and in the struggle with him, I fell to the floor, and I tried to run from the room, but he dragged me back, and threw me on the bed. I called out for the lady of the house, but she didn't answer. And there he finally did what he had wanted to do."[32] Hortencia's testimony provides a rare window onto the complicated power dynamics that permeated cross-class sexual encounters. Hoping at first to advance her station in life, Hortencia soon found herself bargaining over her sexual integrity. Setting limits on a male employer's assertion of power over her body, she found, could have terribly violent consequences.

But Hortencia's story also hints at the difficult ground between coercion and consent that many plebeian women negotiated. Certainly, not all sexual relations between workingwomen and employers or other relatively powerful men began as rapes, although the threat of violence may have loomed frequently in the background. Like Clotilde Rivera, most men were probably aware that they had to offer something if they wanted to gain ongoing sexual access to the women they desired. For women of the laboring classes, whose lives were often consumed by the daily grind of poverty, the prospect of material advantages, no matter how small, must have been a powerful incentive to participate in sexual relationships such as the one Rivera proposed. Rivera was perfectly aware of this; he warned Hortencia that he could easily replace her with someone who would accede to his demands.

Thus, although cross-class relationships were built on profound power differentials, plebeian women did often manage to wring some economic benefits from them. Isidora Font, a freedwoman who worked as a laundress for the prosperous Restaurada plantation, bore a daughter to the overseer. When he married a young, "honorable" white woman some years later, the man arranged for Isidora and their daughter to be given a room to themselves in the home of a mulatto farmer who rented land from the plantation's owner. Although Isidora could not afford to give up her work washing field hands' clothes, the father of her child did give her some money toward her expenses. Her relationship with the overseer may also have allowed her to avoid the brutal fieldwork to which her sister and cousins were assigned. Undoubtedly, many relationships of this kind established powerful emotional and familial bonds. Isidora Font's daughter continued to visit her paternal grandmother regularly after her father married. Both grandmother and father persisted in maintaining their close connection to the child (and very possibly Isidora herself) despite the new wife's outraged protests.[33] Some plebeian white women also acquired a rather comfortable economic status through long-term concubinage arrangements with wealthy men. White women such as these were probably more accepted by "respectable" society than were Afro-Puerto Rican mistresses.[34]

But the economic benefits and social standing negotiated in any informal cross-class or cross-race relationship remained very fragile for poor women. As "nothing more than wanton mistresses," they were extremely vulnerable. Despite the emotional and social ties forged over the years, their male lovers frequently abandoned them to marry more respectable white women. They were then left "desperate and without a penny for their children," as one woman cried out to a judge.[35]

Plebeian white women could try to block their man's wedding by insisting that they had been offered marriage before starting the sexual relationship. Although they generally failed to prevent the marriage if they were of a lower social class than their lover, many of these women often did manage to negotiate some sort of regular financial support. Afro-Puerto Rican women, however, were fully aware that no magistrate would believe such a claim about a wealthy white man from them. On the rare occasions when they appeared in court to protest abandonments, therefore, they asked only for small lump-sum amounts of money for child support and were generally awarded much less than their requests, if they were lucky enough to get anything at all.[36]

Thus women were frequently caught in intense competition with each other for men's income, attentions, and social status. If men were wealthy enough, their "legitimate" wives did not suffer financially from their affairs, although many agonized over their husbands' infidelities.[37] For plebeian women in these cross-class relationships, the competition with legal, "respectable" wives was much more serious, given that wives had a legal basis on which to demand maintenance in the courts.[38] But as disreputable, lower-class mistresses in the eyes of the powerful men who peopled the judicial system and other state bureaucracies, plebeian women had little to no honor capital on which to trade and thus no legal recourse.[39] For them, losing a man's attentions was literally a life-and-death matter; financial support from a moneyed lover could well mean the difference between survival and near starvation for themselves and their children.

Within the dominant honor code, then, plebeian women might negotiate some space for themselves, but they rarely won. The entire system of beliefs and practices that buttressed an exploitative society was predicated on their inferiority. Their labor provided the lifeblood of wealthy women's and men's luxurious lifestyles. Their supposed moral degeneracy supplied the necessary counterpoint to "decent" women's respectability. And their sexual availability to elite men—sometimes coerced—allegedly ensured that white, wealthy women's honor could be properly guarded.

But women of the popular classes did not passively submit to the terms that honorable Ponceños attempted to impose on them, for they often managed to wrest some material concessions from their moneyed lovers. And their daily struggles helped form popular moralities that, while still weighted in favor of whiteness and men, granted more flexibility to women in their sexual choices than did the dominant honor code.

Plebeian Respectability

The "popular classes" in nineteenth-century Ponce were very diverse. Often working alongside and living near enslaved people, their multiracial members included smallholding peasants, sharecroppers, landless laborers, and

Respectable young women of the moneyed classes (from José de Olivares, *Our Islands and Their People as Seen with Camera and Pencil* [St. Louis: N. D. Thompson, 1899])

plantation-employed artisans in the rural areas, and artisans, small shop-keepers, domestic laborers, street vendors, militiamen, and wage laborers in the city.

Thus, it is potentially problematic to speak of general patterns of popular morality, as I do here. Studies of Puerto Rico have documented that even in

A Proper Courtship (from the Helen Gardner Collection, National Anthropological Archives, Smithsonian Institution)

the twentieth century, significant differences in attitudes toward marriage and female virginity existed between peasant communities of the coffee high-lands and the multiracial coastal sugar proletariat.[40] In the nineteenth cen-tury, the municipality of Ponce encompassed both huge sugar plantations and small landholdings, although by the early twentieth century, it was dominated by great corporate-owned sugar tracts. Thus there was no single, uniform "popular honor code" in Ponce during this period.

Census data offers some clues to the sexual practices, such as marriage versus concubinage, that prevailed among various groups. Yet censuses tell us little about what these practices *meant* to the people involved. Was a woman living in concubinage considered shameful or respectable by her community?

Cleaning Rice (from the Helen Gardner Collection, National Anthropological Archives, Smithsonian Institution)

Did a low incidence of marriage reflect disdain for the institution itself or simple inability to pay for the religious ceremony? Luckily, in judicial documents illiterate men and women were recorded speaking about their conceptualizations of morality and respectability. Although filtered through the pens and frequent paraphrasings of the court scribes, the moral values and daily struggles of plebeian people emerge from the pages of Ponce's criminal cases.

Unfortunately, the originating barrios of these cases were often not recorded, so tracing attitudinal patterns to regions is generally impossible. In addition, defendants were the only parties for whom racial and occupational information was consistently provided; other witnesses often cannot be placed on the race/class spectrum. Consequently, a detailed picture of the diverse popular moralities that undoubtedly jostled for acceptance in nineteenth-century Ponce is unfeasible. I cannot, for example, definitively state how urban artisans' respectability codes may have differed from those of smallholding peasants or landless jornaleros, nor how fluid racial identities may have produced differing moral codes within the same class. Yet I can begin to draw some general conclusions about key elements in the value systems of the popular classes during the nineteenth century.

RACE AND POPULAR RESPECTABILITY

In some ways, the obsession with racial purity and segregation that so marked Ponce's professional and upper classes in the nineteenth century was a world apart from the multiracial reality of the popular classes. Black, white, and mixed-race men worked, gambled, made music, and bet on cockfights together. Women of all physical types mingled in the city's marketplaces, shared washing spaces at the rivers, and gossiped as they worked in the streets and fields. Enslaved and free people of African descent engaged in small-scale trade with one another and with plebeian whites.[41]

In both rural and urban areas of Ponce, poor people established interracial sexual partnerships and lived in close quarters with people of races different from their own. In 1860, for example, in the rural sugar barrio of Sabanetas, two-thirds of the married white day laborers had Afro-Puerto Rican spouses. The urban barrio of La Cantera was quite racially mixed; Afro-Puerto Rican and "white" families lived next door to one another and sometimes even shared housing. Ten percent of the ninety-one allegedly white seamstresses in La Cantera lived with or were married to men of African descent. Two of the four Afro-Puerto Rican cigar makers had white partners. Between 6 and 16 percent of the neighborhood's other male artisans—masons, carpenters, blacksmiths, painters, and shoemakers—were in identifiable interracial consensual or conjugal relationships. Probably many more than this had such relations on a more informal basis; nothing definitive can be deciphered about the sexual arrangements of half of the neighborhood's free adults ($N=$ 489) who were listed as "single" with no apparent partner.[42]

The lower middle classes—shopkeepers, clerks, accountants, and the like— counted many people claiming to be white in their ranks. These men and women, whom I have dubbed "marginal Dons," lived and worked in close quarters with Afro-Puerto Ricans and impoverished whites, sharing neighborhoods and similar living conditions. They often lived in concubinage rather than marrying, and not infrequently, men of this social strata established permanent primary relationships with women of African descent. The daughters of this social group attended social gatherings where they danced with Afro-Puerto Rican men—something unheard of among women of the moneyed classes.[43]

Yet race was important in poor people's conceptions of identity and social status. Until the 1870s, African slavery was a bedrock of Ponce's economy and social relations. For generations after abolition in 1873, Ponceños lived with the memory of slavery and the continuation of the brutally unequal power relations it spawned. Thus, however powerfully Africanness permeated the cultural and physical makeup of Ponce's people, for many it remained a stain to be denied. The very "whites" who lived, worked, and established recognized families with "blacks" were quick to assert their racial superiority when pressed.

The marginal Dons, especially, were engaged in a constant scramble to assert their worth. Their intimate proximity to the poorest and darkest sectors of Ponce society made their social position quite fragile. They often clung to their supposed racial superiority in order to distinguish themselves from their neighbors. Many such families, even when poor and probably barely able to feed all the mouths in the house, owned an enslaved woman and her children: owning other human beings provided them not only labor and additional income but essential social status as well.[44] It is precisely this class of people that turns up most frequently in nineteenth-century slander cases, in which they often defend their honor against insults from Afro-Puerto Ricans.[45]

Plebeians' claim to whiteness could be challenged, however. Because of the racial mixing so common among the popular classes, anyone was open to charges of having an African blemish in their history. For example, Julia and María González, two "white" sisters who lived with their widowed mother in a single room connected to an artisan's workshop, shouted at their "white" neighbors, "You're nothing but mulattos, and we have the money to buy you," and "You're a mulatto, descendant of pirates."[46]

Those claiming whiteness were not the only ones concerned with distancing themselves from the taint of slavery. People of African descent also drew racial lines among themselves. Mulatto artisans striving for "decent" status scorned the bomba drumming in the plantation barracks and black sections of the town, fearing that such "African" culture could destroy their carefully constructed refinement.[47] José Dergniz, a black man from the town of Guayama, encountered the racism of such self-styled, civilized Ponce Afro-Puerto Ricans. Dergniz danced a few numbers at an artisans dance filled with people of African descent, but was soon pulled aside: His dark color and unknown origins repulsed people there, he was told. For all the pardo Ponceño artisans knew, he could be an escaped slave, therefore he should leave the dance or wear a mask if he insisted on staying.[48] Alleging intimate connections to slavery was a powerful insult. Cancia Moreno, a mulatta washerwoman, knew this full well when she called her parda neighbor a "slut . . . who gave birth to a slave's child under a ceiba tree."[49]

Many Afro-Puerto Ricans, however, insisted on their right to social recognition and human dignity without denying their blackness. The mulattos Gregoria Soler and her artisan husband turned the dominant meanings of the honor discourse on its head; they proudly stated in court before a white magistrate that they were "honorable people."[50] Don Pedro González, the white manager of a small shop, tried to slap María Nicolasa Moreno and called her a "dirty black" when she brought back some defective products he had sold her grandson. But María Nicolasa fought back, shouting that he was "nothing but a stingy *jíbaro*" and that she was "just as good as he was." Her daughter-in-law chimed in, retorting that she and María Nicolasa were "better than González's whole family."[51] And when the white *comisario de barrio* slapped Juan Laboy and called him a thief, the mulatto laborer hit him back and shouted, "Oh, if only we were equals; I'd break your very soul in two!"[52]

Thus, Ponce's popular classes lived a very different racial reality than the doctors, lawyers, merchants, and plantation owners of "decent society." For the humble classes, rigid distinctions between white and black were impossible. People of all races lived, worked, and loved together. Moreover, everyone knew that very few, if any, white people were truly "racially pure." Still, struggles over racial definitions and hierarchies permeated social relations among working people. So-called whites and even many people of African descent, who would have been scorned in Ponce's wealthy, respectable society, maintained that in the final analysis, "whiter was better." These persistent racist strands in popular culture were implicitly questioned in turn by those Afro-Ponceños who insisted, sometimes in the very terms of honor denied them by others, that they be treated with respect and recognized as dignified human beings.

POPULAR MORAL CODES AND FEMININE RESPECTABILITY

One of the richest sources for deciphering plebeian moral codes in Puerto Rico are *rapto,* or seduction, cases. They provide one of the few historical records of the meaning that poor people attributed to their sexual practices, illuminating generational as well as gender conflict. And perhaps most important, in many rapto cases young plebeian women's voices are not silenced by the clamor of elders, men, and the privileged who surrounded them in court.

Thus, raptos and other judicial records allow us to reconstruct the multiple levels of struggle that produced distinctly plebeian moral codes in Puerto Rico, as well as to understand those codes on their own terms—not simply as deviations from or variations on the dominant honor code. Working people constructed definitions of feminine respectability that did not hinge solely on virginity and lifelong "ownership" by a single man. Rather, plebeians considered serial female monogamy a perfectly honorable lifestyle—many young women clearly preferred it to the restrictions of marriage. Flexibility in partner choice and economic stability, not women's virginity or marriage, seem to have been of paramount concern to laboring Ponceños, who struggled together for survival. Plebeian women and men had differing expectations of consensual *vida marital,* however: Women sought steady financial support as well as freedom from familial surveillance and physical and sexual aggression. Men, in contrast, often tried to contain women's attempts freely to choose acceptable partners, attempting to keep women under close control.

Raptos were a well established social practice among Puerto Rican working people by the nineteenth century. The classic form was deceptively simple: After having established a romantic relationship with a youth, a young woman would leave her parents' home and go with her boyfriend to the house of a friend or relative of his. If the young man had saved money and had planned the move for some time, he might have his own house or a rented room. Once away from parental surveillance, the couple would have sex, the man in the process "taking possession of" the woman's virginity. They would then set up "marital life together," either remaining in the household to which they had originally gone or moving off on their own.[53]

Because he had stolen the young woman's honor, according to the dominant script, the raptor was required by law either to marry his sweetheart or to suffer the punishment of one-and-a-half year's imprisonment, plus the payment of one thousand pesos to the woman as reparation for lost honor, as well as formal recognition and provision of financial support for any child who might have been conceived during the liaison.[54] As in cases of "betrothal sex," female virginity and a prior, explicit male offer to marry were the essential prerequisites for the courts' protection of women's assumed interests.

In nineteenth-century Ponce, rapto cases were generally filed by the parents or other close relatives of the young woman involved in the elopement. Their responses to the couple's move usually took one of three forms. First, parents might accept the young people's move and not bother with attempts at marriage enforcement. Because this type of parental response never appeared in court and thus created no historical record, its frequency is unknown. The second response, by far the most common in court documents, was immediately to report the girl's disappearance to the local comisario de barrio and start judicial proceedings to enforce the couple's marriage. Third, parents might extract a promise from the girl's lover to marry her within a set period of time; these agreements were reached either through informal negotiation or the comisario de barrio's mediation. If the wedding was not carried out as agreed, the girl's family, sometimes joined by the girl herself, appealed to the court to enforce it.[55]

All working people knew the terms of the dominant honor code and were fully aware that the law of the rich was based on them. Therefore, when plebeians went to court, they used arguments they knew would be familiar and hoped would be convincing to the presiding magistrates. Both parental and legal discourses were premised on assumptions of women's passivity and men's voracious, conquering sexual instincts. Men were supposed to be the actors in the rapto drama, suggesting the establishment of a nonmarital household, carrying their sweetheart away from the benevolent paternal home, and initiating illicit sex. To be "vindicated" by the courts, the young woman had to be successfully presented as an innocent victim, done in by her boyfriend's insistent pressures. Inés Serna's mother echoed scores of other parents when she insisted that she "had no idea why the girl might have left so suddenly—Juan must have pressured her to do so."[56]

The existing studies of raptos in colonial Latin America do not substantially challenge this view of the women involved in the practice. Verena Stolcke acknowledges that some young people in nineteenth-century Cuba tried to choose racially or economically questionable marriage partners, but she insists that elopement was ultimately a timid, individual challenge to the dominant social system. Ramón Gutiérrez argues that raptos functioned primarily as a ritual reproduction of male power. In colonial New Mexico, he notes, men frequently accused the women whom they seduced of non-virginity. Through raptos, Gutiérrez asserts, men tested each other to see whose women could be conquered and, in the process, almost uniformly sexually dominated women.[57] Studies such as these focus on seduction cases among the more privileged members of society or between socially unequal partners. In such contexts, young people seemed to have used raptos mainly as a way to force their parents' hand when the older generation was opposed to the couple's desire to marry.

In Ponce, however, all parties involved in the vast majority of nineteenth-century rapto cases were of humble economic origins. Probably because there generally was no substantial difference of social status between the partners, the young men did not challenge the young women's claims regarding their virginal status before the elopement.[58] And for largely the same reasons, the parents who initiated the majority of the rapto petitions in Ponce were trying to ensure a rapid marriage, often over the girl's objections, rather than reluctantly agreeing to an undesirable match.

Perhaps as a result of these differences in the gendered and generational conflicts that surfaced in nineteenth-century Ponce rapto cases, I take issue with Gutiérrez's contention that "women were pawns" in the practices of seduction.[59] Among plebeian Ponceños, raptos were not a preordained step in a seamless dance of male domination. Rather, in defiance of both magistrates' expectations and parental exhortations, women of the Puerto Rican laboring classes emerge from these judicial documents as sexual and social agents, struggling with their partners, parents, and wealthy judges over the terms of bodily and economic integrity as well as the meaning of marriage and respectability.

Parents and family members sought to ensure that "escaped" young women would receive ongoing financial support and respect from their lovers. Thus they employed the classic language of violation of women's honor/virginity to mobilize the state's disciplinary power in their favor. In the process, they implicitly challenged an underlying premise of the dominant honor code—that they and their families were incapable of claiming respectability and, therefore, social worth. Desiderio Rodríguez echoed scores of other parents when he asked the court to punish the young man who had seduced his daughter and now refused to marry her. The youth was "mocking both justice and the honor of my daugher," Desiderio testified.[60] Ercilia Reyes's artisan father said that she was "lost" after sleeping with her boyfriend.[61] And Presbítero, a thirteen-year-old orphaned day laborer, cried out that his sister was "a poverty-stricken orphan with no patrimony but her honor."[62]

It is impossible to ascertain definitively how much of this testimony was devised simply for the courts. It appeared consistently enough, however, that it is difficult to dismiss it as solely opportunistic manipulation. Marriage and female virginity may have been more important for those sectors of the laboring classes who owned property or aspired to "full" respectability, such as middling peasants, shopowners, and the upper artisan echelons. In 1860 in the urban neighborhood of La Cantera, for example, 50 percent of the Afro-Puerto Rican masons and the sole white mason, half of the Afro-Puerto Rican and one-third of the white shoemakers, and one-third of all carpenters, regardless of race, were married. This was a significantly higher marriage rate than that of the neighborhood's laundresses (less than one-fifth) or day laborers (one-quarter).[63]

But even many humbler Ponceños seemed to agree that virginity was preferred, if not essential, in a young woman. Francisca Vega, a seventeen-year-old illiterate parda seamstress provides a good case in point. Francisca preserved her virginity for an entire year while Antonio Laubriel, a young carpenter, visited her family's house to court her. But then, Francisca bitterly recounted, "the public began to murmur that she was no longer a virgin, and pregnant, which was not true." Francisca's father, an illiterate shoemaker (who, interestingly enough, was not married to her mother), began to scold and beat her when he heard the rumors. Because she was already "slandered" by public opinion and her father would not listen to her assertions of purity, Francisca "proposed to [Antonio] that he take her from the house. If he didn't, she would leave on her own." The two left together one night and set up a household. When Francisca's father took Antonio to court, demanding that he marry the girl, Francisca refused to press charges against her sweetheart, insisting that marriage did not matter to her. Francisca's mother, an illiterate laundress, pardoned Antonio, and the case was closed.[64]

Francisca Vega's story shows clearly that marriage and women's premarital virginity *were* valued to some extent among Ponce's laboring population. Francisca wanted to maintain her own reputation as sexually "pure" and hoped to marry as such; she was incensed when gossip destroyed that goal. Her father, unmarried himself, violently punished Francisca when he thought that she might have circumvented his surveillance efforts. But in the popular classes, lack of virginity did not irrevocably mark a woman as undesirable, nor was marriage necessarily always the only acceptable goal. Once brought low by her neighbors' wagging tongues, Francisca Vega initiated a live-in sexual relationship with her boyfriend and rejected marriage—the antithesis of the passive victim that her father tried to make her out to be. Her mother too chose to back Francisca's decision, even though she would have easily won a rapto petition asking that Antonio marry her daughter.

It is no accident that Francisca's parents had such different responses to her supposed fall from virginal grace. Men, as we have seen, had a much greater stake in maintaining sexual control over the women of their family. Plebeian women, on the other hand, often considered marriage solely as an insurance against financial disaster and abandonment; Francisca's mother apparently trusted Antonio's commitment to her daughter's financial well-being. Consequently, virginity and even marriage itself was unnecessary.

Similarly, 35 percent of the 211 young women whose parents protested their elopements in nineteenth-century rapto petitions openly stated that they had not been virgins before beginning their current relationships. All parties knew that such admissions immediately destroyed any possibility of state intervention to ensure their marriage; parents tried desperately to deny their daughter's testimony. Not being virgins did not, however, appear to provoke shame in the young women. Neither did it deter the young men involved from publicly recognizing the relationship and intending ultimately to marry their sweetheart in the few such cases where the women wished to marry.

It is possible that this allegation of prerapto sexual activity with other men was a ruse employed by some young women to save their lovers from jail and themselves from losing income. They may have seen renouncing their public reputation as prerapto virgins as the lesser of many evils, having arrived at this conclusion after a great deal of pressure from their lovers. Despite intense pressure from parents to retract their assertions of nonvirginity, though, I encountered only one girl's admission of sexual misrepresentation in the rapto cases I reviewed. Whatever the motivations behind such a high percentage of young plebeian women who refused to present themselves as virgins, it is clear that they were willing to embrace a public reputation as nonvirginal and settle for consensual union rather than marriage. Such moves would have been unthinkable for most women of the upper classes, for whom marriage or public virginity were the only legitimate alternatives.

Clearly, these were not the only acceptable sexual options within the popular classes. The majority of Ponce's laboring people lived in consensual union.

Between 1841 and 1847, only 15 percent of free Afro-Puerto Rican men and women, 20 percent of all former male slaves, and 31 percent of all white women (which included upper- and middle-class women) were married or widowed.[65] In 1860, Ponce's plebeian urban barrio of La Cantera also displayed low marriage rates; about one-quarter of both free Afro-Puerto Ricans and whites were married.[66] Thirty years later, the profile of plebeian sexual practices had changed very little. In 1892, in the city's Callejón de Comercio, for example, a mulatta washerwoman owned a small two-room shack. She and her mechanic lover lived in one room; she rented the other room to a literate black seamstress and her lover, who worked as a barrel maker. Their neighbors were carpenters, tailors, chocolatiers, shoemakers, *industriales,* and many seamstresses and laundrywomen. All except the neighborhood shopkeeper were living in consensual union.[67]

"Concubinage," as Puerto Rican elites dubbed the widespread plebeian practice of nonmarital cohabitation, was based on a patriarchal quid pro quo. Workingmen's incomes were miserably low, but women's were even lower. Consequently, surviving alone was economically unthinkable for most women of the popular classes. Living with other women was also relatively unfeasible, because most adult women had themselves and several children to support. Thus, almost all women made the choice to exchange sex and, if living regularly with a man, domestic labor for a portion of male earnings.

Very few plebeian women could afford not to earn their own income as well, even if married or in a stable relationship. Interspersed with their never-ending domestic tasks, they worked long, sweaty hours waiting on customers in stores and cafés, cutting cane, picking coffee, vending small items on the street, and sewing, washing, and ironing others' clothes. The working classes, both urban and rural, clearly could not have survived without women's labor and income. This economic vulnerability and interdependence helped forge a strong solidarity between laboring men and women, particularly when faced with threats from outside the family or community, such as wealthier people's encroachment on a small plot of land, refusal to pay wages, or attempted sexual incursions against plebeian women.

As a result, many working people recognized ways other than sexual "purity" for women to establish their respectability. Faithful mothering and hard domestic and income-generating work were essential female virtues.[68] Women's sexual reputations were not unimportant, however. Rather, as discussed above, among many sectors of the Ponce working classes, as long as a woman was sexually faithful to one man for a period of time, she was considered respectable by her neighbors.[69]

Some working people established lifelong consensual unions; this may have been the popular ideal. But many plebeians seem to have practiced serial rather than permanent relationships. Juana Garay, the daughter of a rural day laborer, had already lived with three men by the age of eighteen.[70] The sexual history of Teresa Astacio, whose story opened this chapter, was apparently of little or no import to her second jornalero lover. Women often had children with a number of different men. Many relationships ended when men violated the patriarchal pact too severely. If living in concubinage, women could leave men who failed to provide financial support or whose efforts at surveillance slipped too frequently into physical abuse.[71]

Consensual union's greater flexibility may have been the reason that such a significant number of young women establishing a household for the first time seemed utterly uninterested in marriage. Only 25 percent of the young women in nineteenth-century rapto cases stated that they wanted to marry their raptors. Forty-five percent did not express any desire to marry, although their parents were generally eager for them to do so. A further 30 percent explicitly rejected marriage in their testimony. For 75 percent of the 211 women involved in contested raptos, then, marriage appears not to have been the ultimate economic aspiration or proof of social worth. Rather, like thirteen-year-old Alejandrina Matos, whose mother had always counseled her not to fall in love, they may have seen that in a society which did not recognize the right to divorce, marriage could become a chain irrevocably binding them to soured relationships.[72]

But women still depended on men's income for survival. Leaving one man was not much of an option unless another one was readily available or unless a woman's family was able to take her back in. Both alternatives were much less feasible if a woman already had several children. Thus, young childless women just setting out on their first live-in relationship may have been much less interested in the permanence implied by marriage than they would be later in life, when their survival options became more limited.

The rapto cases provide a window into the expectations and practices of young, mainly adolescent plebeians. *Juicios verbales* offer a different slice of the Ponceño life cycle. Many of the couples who appeared in these types of cases had been living together for some time (a few for over ten years) and had one or more children. Marriage had not been broached since they originally moved in together, if ever. But now the man had either left his lover for another woman or had stopped providing her regular financial support for one reason or another. Those juicios verbales which involved younger, childless couples originated when the youth had broken off a formal engagement and left his fiancée pregnant.

Juicios verbales, then, were generated mainly by men betraying their responsibility for economic contribution to women and children. These plaintiffs faced a situation very different from that of the majority of the rapto women who were in the early stages of consensual unions and whose young men were prepared to live with and support them for the time being. In marked contrast to the rapto women, 82 percent of the "white" and 85 percent of the plaintiffs of acknowledged African heritage in juicios verbales requested marriage—the only social status recognized by the state through which women could make financial claims on their sexual partners.[73]

In addition, 65 percent of the very parents who insisted so vehemently on their daughter's marriage in rapto petitions were not married; they had probably set up their first household in the same way their daughter had. Thus, even the parental concern for marriage expressed in the rapto cases may have been based largely on the "older and wiser" knowledge that women needed some insurance against future economic troubles. Those parents who trusted that their daughter's lover would be a financially dependable partner may not have thought to enter the courts and raise the issue of marriage.

Examining rapto and juicio verbal cases together suggests that many women of the popular classes became interested in marriage only when they could no longer trust that male income would be regularly available. Marriage also became a more attractive option once children appeared on the scene; motherhood meant increased monetary needs, less time to earn one's own income, and potentially more difficulty in finding a steady lover who would be willing to support several people. Financial stability, then, not rich people's respectability, was plebeian women's bottom line.[74]

Thus, workingwomen helped forge a wider range of socially acceptable sexual options for themselves than those available for wealthy women. Their undeniably important labor forced a broader definition of female respectability that included productive and reproductive work, motherhood, and consensual union. They defied both parental and elite definitions of them as passive and helpless. A significant number also implicitly questioned the legitimacy of marriage; by leaving undesirable partners and publicly choosing new ones, women of the popular classes helped create a distinctly plebeian moral norm of serial monogamy.

Nevertheless, women of the laboring classes did not lead a free and easy sexual life. The fear of unwanted pregnancy was never far away. And although they played an important role in supporting themselves and their families, women were dependent on male income for survival. Although plebeian men may not have expected virginity from their partners, they did assert the informal "right" to exclusive control over women's sexuality as long as they supported them financially. Ultimately, the tenets of the sexual double standard and male ownership of women's bodies remained intact in popular normative standards, despite their relative flexibility. But these norms required continual reinforcement. Women had their own interpretations of how they should function.

Surveillance: Policing the Boundaries of Respectability

The outer limits of what constituted acceptable behavior among the popular classes were hotly contested. Consequently, working Ponceños invested a great deal of energy in patrolling one another. Their strategies ranged from gossip to physical violence to calling for police and judicial intervention. Surveillance operated in the neighborhood, at the workplace, within the family, and in the courts. Its practitioners sought both to contain subversion of male and parental power and to curb extreme abuses of them.

Adult women zealously regulated one another's behavior. Through gossip and slander, women were important agents in the creation and maintenance of gender roles and sexual norms. The informal news networks that women wove throughout rural and urban communities wielded great disciplinary power. Gossip served a number of functions. It defined the parameters of acceptable male behavior, often clarifying the line between appropriate discipline and abuse. It consolidated the social status of "respectable" women and could wreck the pretensions of those, like Francisca Vega, who aimed too high.[75]

Perhaps most important, gossipers endeavored to prevent other women from sleeping with their male partners. Plebeian men often insisted on their masculine right to have multiple sexual partners. This meant the diversion of precious economic resources, for no woman with an eye to survival would sleep with a man, whether as mistress or principal partner, without exacting some material support in return. Plebeian men earned painfully low incomes. Dividing them between several households reduced the funds available to each woman even further. Thus, the conflicts between women over male attentions were quite intense; not infrequently they escalated into physical fights. Such friction between women did not necessarily mean that they absolved men of responsibility. Rather, it was generally easier for women to try to discipline each other than to confront directly the men who controlled a good portion of the purse strings and enjoyed community sanction of the sexual double standard.[76]

Surveillance functioned especially intensely within the family. From an early age, boys were expected to earn income for the household. Girls helped their mothers with child care, cooking, tending animals, and other domestic tasks, as well as earning money through embroidery, street vending, and so on. Children's labor had to be supervised and disciplined for the family to survive economically. This task usually fell to adult women or older female siblings. Mothers were held responsible for girls' sexual regulation until their "proper" establishment in either marriage or consensual union. Parents also enlisted the help of their friends and neighbors in keeping track of their teenage daughters.[77]

If children persisted in challenging their parents' surveillance boundaries, both mothers and fathers could resort to violence—the stakes were too high to brook frontal opposition. Young people's response to parental beatings was strikingly gendered. Boys ran away to work on plantations or to apprentice themselves to artisans, whereas girls could not hope to survive on their own economically. Instead, they relied on sexual alliances to escape their parents' beatings, running off with boyfriends. The young women in a full 35 percent of the 211 rapto cases cited parental violence as a principal reason for their having set up a household with their sweetheart.[78]

But the freedom from surveillance that these young women sought by running off with their boyfriend could be short lived. Boyfriends, lovers, and husbands often subjected their women partners to intense sexual surveillance as well. José Jaime Napoleoni rejected his pregnant girlfriend because she attended a dance without his permission.[79] Manuela Guiet's husband enlisted the aid of neighbors, a local schoolteacher, and the police in his efforts to spy on her as she worked as a seamstress and shoe repairer; he was convinced that Manuela's long hours away from home meant that she had taken a lover.[80]

Men could sometimes be brutal in the enforcement of their right to control their woman lover's perceived sexual behavior. José Nicolás Baldiris, a mason, proclaimed to the court that because Juana Rita Montalvo was his concubine and he gave her money daily, she did not have the right to speak to other men. When he "caught" her conversing with a male neighbor, he beat her and later raped her as she was washing clothes by the river running by the city.[81] Miguel Montes, a day laborer, did not live with his girlfriend, but this did not prevent him from biting her in the face and beating her with a stick when he found her talking in the house of her male neighbor.[82]

It would be a mistake to read the scores of similar cases that surface in nineteenth-century judicial records as proof of women's unmitigated subjugation to men or of a "natural" male propensity toward misogynist violence. Rather, domestic violence was a product of what Stern has called a "contested patriarchal pact"—the struggles between men and women over gender rights and obligations bound up in labor, financial resources, sexual fidelity, and physical mobility.[83] Women generally did not dispute men's right to demand monogamy and domestic labor from them, as long as they received consistent financial support for themselves and their children. But women persistently attempted to link the provision of these services and their partner's right to monitor their whereabouts to men's economic responsibility. If men did not provide for their families, women insisted that they do so, often quite vociferously. At times, they also attempted to withhold domestic labor or sex until their partner complied with his part of the pact. If a man did not provide a modicum of financial security, a woman might also seek out a new partner. Men, for their part, resisted this linkage of their responsibilities and rights. They often claimed unlimited authority within the family, as well as a "natural" right to multiple sexual partners.

The conflicts between these gendered interpretations of the general patriarchal pact often exploded in violence. Felipa Luid, for example, fought frequently with her lover Julio "for not bringing home anything with which to feed the family." One night when their argument got especially heated, Julio stabbed her several times, fatally wounding her.[84] By their own admission, men often initiated the violence to quell women's challenges and insubordinations, but it was not unusual for a plebeian women to hit her partner back.[85]

Women embroiled in such cycles of conflict sometimes took a partner to court, but most magistrates simply admonished the husband to treat his wife better. The stiffest penalty I encountered against a violent husband was ten days in jail. Many women called on informal community and family resources rather than turn to the courts. As mentioned above, female gossip could curb some male abuses. The homes of women friends and family members often served as refuges. These allies probably agreed with Doña Rosa Estoruell, who cried out "as a mother, I couldn't be indifferent to my daughter's plight."[86] Finally, women facing violence from their partner cashed in their chips with male family members; men had a particularly gendered responsibility to protect their wronged relatives. Often, those men who intervened on the behalf of a woman ended up physically confronting the partner who had stepped beyond the limits of his legitimate authority.[87]

Surveillance, then, was multileveled and multidirectional, and it occurred in the midst of complicated alliances. Parents tried to regulate children's labor and daughters' sexuality. Men kept vigilant watch over women. Women disciplined one another through gossip and physical confrontation while attempting to keep men in line economically and sexually. The alliances and conflicts in these complex webs of cross-cutting interests were rarely clear-cut or stable. Women might call on the very family members whose violence they had fled to curb their partner's excesses. The youths who promised a life free of parental restrictions to young women often spun out their own surveillance mechanisms with which they hoped to control their lover. Sexual competitors could also be close friends or cooperative neighbors. For most laboring Puerto Ricans, family and community were profoundly ambivalent arenas of security and violence, surveillance and support.

Likewise, sexuality and its struggles encompassed a wide variety of experiences. We should guard against reducing them to repression, surveillance, and grudging quid pro quo exchanges. Sex was also *para gozar* (for pleasure). Nineteenth-century Puerto Rican women as well as men found great pleasure and excitement in flirtation and sex. This is a silent but eloquent message of the women adulterers who risked prison and the loss of their children, property, and reputations for passion. Workingwomen's desires too were occasionally preserved in the historical record. Margarita Marcucci stated that she had "gone to the sexual act with pleasure."[88] Daniela Colón told the court that "her passion for her lover was overwhelming; it simply was too big to contain." She insisted that he take her with him to a private place where they could make love.[89] Indeed, considering the precarious material conditions of the Puerto Rican poor, the intrigue of flirtation and sexual liaisons was a precious ray of light in plebeian life—an affirmation of hope, joy, solidarity, and strength in the midst of the daily grind.

The seemingly monolithic honor system of nineteenth-century Ponce was actually quite diverse—filled with fissures of conflict and, therefore, as we shall see, susceptible to historical change. Indeed, it is misleading to speak of one honor code, no matter how conflict ridden. It is much more accurate to describe the value systems of Ponceño society as a series of interlocking codes riven with internal tensions, all of which shared aspects of some values and challenged others.

Throughout this chapter, I have sought to examine honor and respectability through women's eyes and words, illuminating their agency in the struggles over morality and sexual practice. Women both challenged and reproduced hegemonic codes of respectability. The married wealthy white woman engaged in an extramarital affair might insist that her daughter follow the precepts of virginity and assert her superiority to all people of African descent. A mulatta seamstress might reject marriage in favor of concubinage while policing the sexual activities of her women neighbors. Women, then, were active participants in the formation of the conceptualizations of honor and respectability that shaped nineteenth-century Ponceño society.

Indeed, the historical record hints at the existence of a feminine moral code, one that yearned for male fidelity, economic stability, the fulfillment of female desire, and freedom from physical and sexual violence. By and large, nineteenth-century Puerto Rican women did not seek to eliminate male dominance or gender difference but instead sought more reciprocal patriarchal pacts and, sometimes, more flexible definitions of respectability and honor. During most of the nineteenth century, these desires remained diffuse, present only in women's daily, individualized struggles in fields, streets, and homes. It was not until the 1890s that bourgeois women would articulate elements of these yearnings into a self-conscious Puerto Rican feminist discourse on morality. It would be at least another decade before workingwomen spoke out forcefully to define their own more inclusive and radical feminist sexual politics. The roots of both feminist visions, however, lay in the lives and aspirations of the thousands of Puerto Rican women who preceded them.

Chapter 2

Motherhood, Marriage, and Morality: Male Liberals and Bourgeois Feminists, 1873–1898

Differentiation . . . is dependent upon disgust. . . . But disgust always bears the imprint of desire.
—Peter Stallybrass and Allon White, *Politics and Poetics of Transgression*

By the 1870s it had become clear that great changes were afoot in Puerto Rico. The second half of the nineteenth century witnessed the abolition of slavery (1873) and the failure of the *libreta* system, a state campaign to force free landless men into labor on large estates. As these systems of overt domination crumbled under pressures from the island's enslaved people and landless laborers, as well as shifts in Puerto Rico's position in the world economy, the elite's economic and political consensus began to fracture.[1] The more progressive male members of the island's landowning and professional classes began to cast about for new ways to organize their society. They soon focused on moral reform, drawing on aspects of the coastal regions' dominant conceptions of honor and respectability.

Like many of their counterparts in other parts of Latin America, the Puerto Rican Liberals who agitated during the nineteenth century for the abolition of slavery and, later, autonomy from Spain were preoccupied with the education of women.[2] They insisted that the creation of responsible, intelligent mothers was necessary to purify the island's unhealthy racial heterogeneity and to move beyond the economic and political stagnation in which they believed Puerto Rico was trapped. But Puerto Rican Liberals were not concerned only with white middle- and upper-class women's intellectual fate. They also focused on the need for female education among the popular classes; Liberals were convinced that properly educated plebeian women would be critical weapons in their struggle to form a disciplined, whitened wage labor force. "Proper" education for women of any class, however, could not focus simply on feminine intellectual development. Puerto Rican male

Liberals insisted that above all, women had to be morally transformed; the island's racial, political and economic health depended on it.[3] Throughout the 1870s and 1880s, then, moral reform would be a central concern of these men.

By the mid-1890s, the first bourgeois feminist murmurings had begun to emerge in response to Liberalism. Early Puerto Rican feminists politicized aspects of women's long-standing grievances. They protested male sexual privileges, posited a new female moral superiority, and stretched the boundaries of the Liberal gender discussion, especially in the area of sexuality.

The discourses of both Liberals and feminists marked an important political move away from the overt repression that had underlain Ponce's slavery-based regime and toward more benevolent social reform. Moral transformation, both groups proclaimed, would create a new, reinvigorated society. Yet the proposed reforms were premised on elements of the dominant honor code; thus their proponents assumed the right to assert racial superiority and consolidation of power over the groups whose lives they hoped to better. Despite their breaks with Puerto Rico's coercive past, neither Liberal male nor bourgeois feminist ideas constituted a call to social equality. Rather, both groups envisioned newly harmonious hierarchies that would ultimately maintain the social, political, and economic power of the professional and landed classes. Competing definitions of morality provided an important medium through which they asserted the legitimacy of their aspirations.

Liberalism and "La Gran Familia"

Liberalism first emerged as an organized movement in Puerto Rico with the founding of the Partido Liberal Reformista in 1870, encouraged by Spain's Liberal Revolution of 1868. During the early 1870s, the Puerto Rican Liberal Party agitated for the abolition of slavery and the extension of Spain's newly liberalized constitution (except its provisions for universal male suffrage) to Puerto Rico. Some early Liberals promoted political and economic autonomy from Spain, but these positions did not gather strength within the party until the 1880s. In 1887, autonomy advocates founded the Partido Autonomista in Ponce; from then until the U.S. occupation in 1898, autonomy remained the dominant political and economic goal of Puerto Rican Liberals, most of whom were white professionals or middling landowners.[4]

As an economic and cultural center of the island, Ponce was a critical hub of Liberal organizing and intellectual production during the 1880s and

1890s.[5] By 1887, Ponce's mayor, appointed by the Spanish governor, reported that Liberal Autonomism had gained the sympathies of 90 percent of the municipality's voting population. Liberals held twenty-seven out of thirty seats on the city council and had the last word in most of Ponce's political affairs.[6]

Facing severe repression from the colonial state later in that "terrible year," the Autonomists lost much of their formal political power. Nevertheless, they continued to be a crucial social force in Ponce and other coastal sugar regions throughout the following decade.[7] The Liberals founded Ponce's main daily newspaper, *La Democracia,* in 1890 and steadily gained support among both the middling and laboring classes. In 1897 they finally acquired an autonomy agreement from Spain. The following year, a few months before the United States invaded Puerto Rico, they won a smashing islandwide electoral victory against both the pro-Spain Incondicionales and the splinter Orthodox Autonomist Party.

During the late nineteenth century, the Liberals began to consolidate an ideology that articulated a new vision of Puerto Rican society, one they hoped would be more adequate to the social relations that began to emerge after the abolition of slavery in 1873. To replace the brutality of slavery and the libreta labor regime, they posited a benevolent but hierarchical paternalism as the glue which would hold society together under Liberal leadership and which would more effectively mold a pliable workforce.

Liberal professionals and landowners wove their paternalist vision from powerful discourses linking racial identity, sexuality, and labor discipline. Through them they simultaneously attempted to define the nation, position themselves as its leaders, and clarify their own collective identity vis-à-vis both the racially mixed masses and the conservative hacendados who they accused of exploitative labor practices and backward social vision.

Puerto Rico's national character, the Liberals reassured colonial officials, metropolitan rulers, and local readers, was essentially peaceful. Social conflict had always remained at a minimum, particularly when compared with Haiti and its slave-led revolution, or Cuba, where the struggle to end slavery and gain independence from Spain had exploded in a bloody, decade-long war.[8] The centuries of racial and cultural mixture in the "intimate relations of domestic life" that had preceded and continued during the plantation slavery boom had made Puerto Rico a "country untouched by discord."[9] Puerto Rico would advance through legislative change, not rebellion, they insisted.

But however much they may have touted their island's alleged interracial tranquillity, the Liberal Autonomists frantically worried that it lacked a spirit of progress. Slavery, along with the Africans whom the slave trade had dragged to Puerto Rico, had destroyed the moral fiber of the country, debasing both masters and slaves, who "satisfied their voluptuous appetites" together.[10] It had created disdain for hard work. The enslaved Africans' moral degradation had also infected white peasants, who had been forced by the *libreta* regime to work alongside them.

According to the Liberals, the resultant rampant interracial promiscuity corroded the productive capacities of the rural poor. Writer after writer worriedly echoed Governor Caspe's comment that "the family in the Puerto Rican countryside is not morally constituted." Concubinage, especially, was denounced as a great evil, "extending itself everywhere, destroying all bonds, . . . gradually devouring the entire rural population." Liberals believed that, "isolated in the midst of nature's exuberance" and contaminated by Africanness, peasants were literally drowning in the uncontrolled satisfaction of their desires. Sustained productive labor was impossible to maintain in such a context.[11]

In their elaboration of these discourses, the Liberals implicitly defined themselves in opposition to those whom they discussed so fervently. The rural masses thus provided the perfect "racially erotic counterpoint" to Puerto Rico's emerging bourgeoisie.[12] Their alleged racially stained immorality, deemed abhorrently different from that of the respectable "sons of Spain," simultaneously confirmed the Liberals' self-discipline, racial purity, and right to lead the country.

But it was not only the rural poor who had succumbed to the allure of interracial sexual degeneration. Liberal Autonomists could not bring themselves to acknowledge openly the sexual relations with poor and Afro-Puerto Rican women that were so integral a part of moneyed men's lives. They did, however, protest the threat posed to "respectable society" by popular music and dance—represented as dangerously feminine and African. The *danza,* created and played by mulatto musicians, had infiltrated the casinos and drawing rooms of the elite.[13] Liberals lamented that as a result, respectable young men now displayed no interest in "the great manly moments of [political and intellectual] struggle" that should preoccupy "virile citizens." Rather, elite youth had collectively succumbed to the "seductive murmur" of the danza and "beauty's magic attraction." Unlike the "pure, virile, patriotic" notes of the "Marseillais," which so inspired enlightened Europeans, the danza represented all that destroyed elite Puerto Rican men's love of nation as it drove them to "intoxication with soft luxuriousness . . . and moral decay."[14]

The most honest of the Liberals admitted that even they shared in Puerto Rico's racial and cultural heterogeneity. Desire permeated their denunciations: "Do not think that I am cursing the danza. Her melodies rocked me to sleep in the cradle and excited me in my adolescence; they evoke all my lovely memories of youth. I have still not learned to curse that which I love."[15] Such passages, rare though they were, hinted at an awareness hovering at the edges of elite society that Africanness was a part of all Puerto Ricans, disseminated through the many intimacies shared with women of the popular classes. Yet the sensual power that allegedly exuded from Afro-Puerto Ricans and all that they touched ultimately had to be expunged. It feminized and weakened the rational, orderly, European potential of Puerto Rico's male elite, which was the island's hope for progress.[16]

Clearly, Puerto Rico needed national invigoration. The Liberals sought to free their island, their class, and implicitly themselves from the emasculating, all too African sensuality that they feared haunted them. Creating a civilized society and bourgeoisie required a disciplined march toward rational, de-Africanized virility. But this would not be an easy task. Puerto Rico's popular classes and social relations had to be reshaped and a new, visionary class of leaders formed who could effectively emancipate the island from its history of open exploitation and promiscuous racial mixing.

Birthing the Great Puerto Rican Family

Familial imagery was an integral part of the language Liberal Autonomists used to describe ideal social relations in the proto-nation they hoped to build. As Angel Quintero Rivera has pointed out, Liberals asserted that Puerto Rico would now be "la gran familia" (the great family). Carefully subordinated incorporation of social inferiors rather than their blatant subjugation would be the order of the day.[17]

Luís Muñoz Rivera, one of the great "fathers" of Autonomist Liberalism in Puerto Rico, filled his writings with familial references. One of his favorite images linked whiteness, the formation of the new national family of Puerto Rico, and autonomy. His focus was often the Liberals, the "sons of Spain" who were striving to break the slavish bonds of colonialism with their repressive father and gain paternal status themselves. " 'You were born in the

colony,' they murmur, 'and you carry the seal of dishonor upon your fore-
head. It matters not that you are sons of our sons, that the same blood
nourishes you, nor that you speak the same language.' . . . The natives of
Africa no longer have masters. But the natives of Castile still do."[18]

For Muñoz Rivera, Puerto Rico's political and economic autonomy would
ensure full sovereign white manhood for professional and elite Liberals. Once
able to govern themselves, they could claim the fatherly right to consolidate
their rule over others—especially the freed Afro-Puerto Ricans. "Oh, to be a
journalist; *direct the masses; / produce popular struggles; /* fight for shining ideas;
and for great causes," he trumpeted.[19] Many of Muñoz Rivera's Liberal comrades maintained that enlightened hacendados and professionals should serve
as the protective fathers of the "sons of labor." "[The hacendado] visited the
plantations which produced his wealth with the pure affection of a father who
caresses the little blond heads of his children."[20] The popular classes, in turn,
inspired by their Liberal leaders' social reforms and personal examples, would
gell into a productive workforce.

Liberals insisted that once properly obedient rural laborers had been
formed, jornaleros and professionals would be joined in a great community
of male workers. In effect, the Liberals were incorporating the plebeian
codes of male respectability, examined in Chapter 1, which linked virility to
labor. Liberal intellectuals enthusiastically described the future Puerto Rican
brotherhood of hardworking men; the most progressive among them excoriated slothful, exploitative hacendados. This harmonious fraternity, however,
would be led safely by the professionals. As the medical doctor in Salvador
Brau's novel *¿Pecadora?* passionately proclaimed to a poverty-stricken rural
peón, "Appearances . . . ? Don't let them fool you. I'm nothing but a worker
like you; we simply . . . cultivate different fields and *in mine there are fruits
that you lack.*"[21]

In Liberal tracts of the 1870s and 1880s, exemplary workers were always
white.[22] Producing these model laborers and a cohesive national Puerto Rican family from the distasteful, dissolute interracial mass would require de-
Africanizing the rural poor. To accomplish their goal, some Liberal Autonomists advocated a combination of sexual regulation and carefully contained
miscegenation. White peasant women should be prevented from coupling
with black men, so that they could produce more white babies to populate
the laboring classes. Mulattas, although overly sensual, could be counted on
to follow the "instinctive pull toward self-perfection" and seek lighter (and

even white) male partners.[23] By and large, however, Puerto Rican Liberals did not place great emphasis on biological methods for cleansing "the African stain" or on European immigration as did their counterparts in Brazil, Venezuela, and Cuba.[24] Rather, Puerto Rican Autonomists hoped to subject plebeian men to moral reformation, which would "whiten" their behavior, if not their skin.

Thus, while reconceptualizing their workforce and body politic in familial terms, wealthy male Liberals called continually for the reform of the family itself, especially that of the rural popular classes. The family was the great school of society; if it did not function "properly," many Liberals believed, any other reforms would be fruitless.[25] The key to this internal collective transformation was the reshaping of Puerto Rican women. The de-Africanized male fraternity of la gran familia was to be built through the reconstituted moral energies of loving, faithful white wives and mothers.

The Liberals Speak: Motherhood and Morality

Public discussions about women's moral and intellectual condition exploded during the late nineteenth century. They focused on two main themes: female sexual morality and motherhood. Liberals worried endlessly about what they deemed poor rural women's immorality. They also passionately denounced bourgeois women's alleged superficiality and mindless flirtation. Puerto Rican women of whatever class, it seemed, were unfit mothers, a major cornerstone of Puerto Rico's weakness.

Expanded female education—with carefully class-differentiated content, of course—would solve both problems for those women deemed racially redeemable. Proper education would lift both groups of salvageable women · into class-appropriate white respectability, wifely partnership, and responsible motherhood. Well-educated mothers would then raise the de-Africanized, disciplined laborers, on the one hand, and assertive, virile white citizens, on the other, who were necessary to form a newly prosperous Puerto Rico.

Rural Reform

Indeed, some Liberals insisted, the lighter-skinned women of the countryside had higher moral potential than their men. Although poor white rural women were enslaved by their sensuality, exhibiting a "certain infantilism," they were not actively immoral. Rather, they had submitted to "the role which nature has assigned them in the perpetuation of the species." If given a proper education, "based, above all, on moral transformation and rigor," these women could rise above their "natural instincts" and "stupifying isolation" to faithful, practical motherhood.[26] Previously enslaved and other black women, however, could never be so effectively reformed. Slavery had left them, at best, stupid and brutish, "reduced to a purely vegetative state," and, at worst, monstrous mothers who murdered their children.[27]

Those few poor, white rural women who did marry showed potential, Liberals claimed. They were monogamous, wore themselves to the bone doing domestic work, and submitted to the will of their husbands, as was proper. They would never be true ladies, with well-developed intellects, but they could train future generations of hardworking laborers. As Salvador Brau so pointedly stated, "Let us not make these women *wise,* but neither let us leave them abandoned as utterly irrational."[28]

The only hope for rural workingmen was this feminine reform from within. Many Liberals were convinced that male jornaleros and peasants were nothing but "discolored" sexual beasts, preying on young women's unawakened desires and forcing them into a life of "rank sensuality." Unlike their women, rural men sexually roamed beyond marital boundaries.[29] Only the creation of upstanding, popular, white rural womanhood could contain the unbounded lusts and consequent lack of discipline that permeated the rural male population. If poor women could be elevated to marital *compañera* (companion or partner) rather than sexually degraded *hembra* (woman) of their man, they would achieve through moral suasion and example what the state in all its repressive power had failed to accomplish—the formation of a de-Africanized, controllable rural labor force.

Thus, the Liberals began to tinker with some aspects of the dominant honor code's definition of popular gender hierarchies, reevaluating whiter poor women's moral status vis-à-vis men of the rural popular classes. Poor rural men, not all poor women, were morally debased, although they might be reformed. For the most part, however, the Liberals' gendered racial conceptualizations remained intact; "unwhitened" plebeian women remained inherently and permanently degenerate. Implicitly, then, it was from them that Puerto Rico needed to be liberated. Desires for women of African descent and all that they symbolized had to be suppressed—at least in public.

Also, the Liberals' tacit insistence on male monogamy did not apply to themselves or other men of their class. Liberals refused to criticize the multiple extramarital sexual encounters with poor women that most wealthy white men enjoyed. Thus, for all their concern with elevating some poor rural women to a new level of "moral womanhood," Liberals failed to acknowledge elite men's role in their sexual subordination.[30]

The Moral Transformation of "Respectable" Women

During the 1880s, Liberals more seriously contemplated the expansion of Puerto Rico's body politic and began to invoke the concept of political legitimacy based in "the people." But "the people"—who at that point consisted of propertied men—had to be formed. Puerto Rican male professionals and landowners did not yet display the "virile" interest in political matters that marked enlightened Europeans. Remaking elite mothers and through them, the family, would usher in a new era of Europeanized bourgeois modernity.[31] Male Liberals began to call for reform of the "respectable" marital relationship and for the women of their classes to be transformed through education from useless ornaments to intelligent mothers and wives.[32]

The discussion linking bourgeois motherhood, marriage, and female education began as early as the 1850s in the pages of the newspaper for women, *Guirnalda de Puerto Rico,* and continued throughout the long decades of Liberal self-definition.[33] The largely male authors of the Liberal publications for women during the 1870s and 1880s all insisted that women of their social class were potentially the intellectual equals of men. These women, the authors asserted, should develop their minds for more effective mothering, not simply define themselves by their beauty or pass their time flirting.[34]

A rigorous female intellectual education would give women interests in life beyond their beaus, Liberals asserted. It would also improve bourgeois marriages by maintaining men's interest in their wives long after the physical attractions of courtship had faded. Educated wives would now be the helpmate and comfort of their husband; they could "understand, aid, and even replace him occasionally, in times of great necessity."[35] Most important, these well-educated women would provide Puerto Rico with an army of capable mothers to produce future generations of active, manly citizens.[36]

Although white bourgeois women held the key to Puerto Rico's future, the Liberals believed, their sexual potential made them highly suspect. They were not depraved like many women of the popular classes, but the majority of them seemed to be devoid of a moral core. As one author wrote, even while maintaining her virginity, a flirting woman "lets herself be stung / by all sorts of bees."[37] Such women were capable of adulterous affairs if not satisfied in their marriages.[38] Consistently, then, the resounding call for "the rational emancipation of women: new word, fertile dogma" that echoed through Liberal writings of the late nineteenth century was profoundly hostile to female sensuality.[39] Warnings like the following were not uncommon: "Sensuality, embodied as it is in the customs of our century, has given forms to our dance which can only be called grotesque and completely incompatible with decency. It is imperative that any self-respecting woman not allow herself to imitate them."[40] Elite women established the line between unassailable whiteness and African-tinged immorality, but they could also blur it with frightening ease. Hence the Liberals' reminders that "a woman's honor is extremely delicate" and that it was a *woman's* responsibility to maintain her sexual reputation intact.[41]

Liberals throughout the late nineteenth century agreed that female education was intended to liberate bourgeois women from the dangers of passion and flirtation. These "dangers" threatened many components of elite identity: familial honor; the alleged link between class privilege, racial purity, and female sexual control; and male claims to exclusive ownership of women's sexuality and sentiments. In exchange, Liberals offered bourgeois women new vocations as maternal nation-builders and intellectual companions of their husbands. Although still defined by their relationship to the family, women should be valued for their minds rather than their physical appearance alone.

But this new Liberal exaltation of the intellectual bourgeois wife and mother did not mean that elite women could define themselves. Enlightened *men* were to deliver women from their centuries of ignorance and frivolous flirtation; women were not to agitate on their own behalf. Indeed, Ferrer closed his influential 1881 essay on women's right to education with a firm admonition that a woman should be totally identified with her husband, demonstrating "complete unity of will, thoughts, and aspirations." His words left no doubt as to who Liberals expected would control this new, safely white, bourgeois familial unit. "Submissive and obedient to the will of her husband, she cannot fail to comply with his every mandate, since we all know that the argumentative [*altanera*] woman, moving beyond her sphere of rights, utterly fails to dominate with her demands. Rather, she exasperates and irritates the natural pride of her man."[42]

Yet Ferrer's final admonition hints that the Liberal dreams of harmonious

Peasants Threatening the Health of the Nation (from José de Olivares, *Our Islands and Their People as Seen with Camera and Pencil* [St. Louis: N. D. Thompson, 1899])

hierarchy with themselves at the helm were as yet unrealized.[43] Ferrer inadvertently acknowledged that educated, "respectable" white women could push beyond the male Liberals' careful definition of the expanded but still subordinate female "sphere of rights." In fact, the very feminine education that Liberals advocated could create its own contradictions. As the poet Lola Rodríguez pointed out in 1875, "Women's education could be an obstacle to the ill-conceived ends of frivolous men, because a lettered woman will not always have the flexibility that the male ego requires."[44]

In the 1890s, educated bourgeois women did indeed begin collectively to stretch the boundaries of the heretofore male-defined discussion of women's morality and right to education. But these early feminists remained confined by their fears of another group of "argumentative" women—those of the dark popular classes. Ultimately, the feminists chose alliances, however conflictual,

Rural Domesticity (from José de Olivares, *Our Islands and Their People as Seen with Camera and Pencil* [St. Louis: N. D. Thompson, 1899])

with men of their own race and class rather than with racially and sexually suspect workingwomen.

The Bourgeois Feminists Speak

Many of the early feminists were an integral part of the Liberal political and cultural milieu. Like their counterparts throughout Latin America, they were Liberal Party activists, Liberal intellectual and artistic collaborators, and wives and relatives of prominent Liberals.[45] Those who were not directly involved with one or another aspect of Liberal politics were profoundly influenced by the Liberal ideas and debates with the Incondicionales that filled Puerto Rico's newspapers, drawing rooms, and social casinos. Thus, Liberalism provided the political ground out of which the vast majority of nineteenth-century Puerto Rican feminists grew. And as we shall see, these women would accept the broad limits of Liberal discourse, no matter how far and in what radical directions they may have attempted to stretch them.

The Luxury of a Decent Home of Means (from the Helen Gardner Collection, National Anthropological Archives, Smithsonian Institution)

In the 1890s, bourgeois feminists began to form a fragile network across the island. By 1894, its members had become sufficiently well organized to publish their own newspaper, *La Mujer*. Founded in Humacao by Ana Roqué, the wife of a hacendado, the paper served for several years as a forum for bourgeois women throughout the island to exchange ideas and information about their lives.[46] The majority of its articles focused on the need for and implications of female education. Unlike the previous Liberal publications aimed at female audiences, however, *La Mujer* was edited and written by women. A few of the women who published articles in *La Mujer* also wrote short stories and novels in which they exposed issues usually left untouched in the pages of the newspaper. In the feminist fiction of the 1890s, husbands beat wives,

Puerto Rican Lady (from José de Olivares, *Our Islands and Their People as Seen with Camera and Pencil* [St. Louis: N. D. Thompson, 1899])

women experienced extramarital sexual yearnings, and rich white men raped innocent *parda* girls.[47]

The early feminists did not represent a monolithic ideological block. Some writers enthusiastically endorsed the economic independence of all women and the partial dissolution of the elite gendered public/private dichotomy. Others asserted the eternal nature of women's domesticity and femininity, denouncing any hints of the possibility of mixing women's moral sphere with the male world of politics.[48]

Nevertheless, certain common themes are discernible in these women's intellectual production. The intersection of sexuality, morality, and female education was key in their theorizing of women's subordination and the prospects for their emancipation. While agreeing with Liberal men that educated mothers were essential in the creation of a responsible citizenry, nineteenth-century feminists insisted that education had other, equally important purposes for women. Women thirsted for knowledge, the feminists proclaimed, and this yen for intellectual expansion was legitimate in its own right. In addition, they recognized that women's economic vulnerability forced them to rely on their sexuality for financial survival. Education would free all women from the prisons of their bodies; through it, they could gain both intellectual and economic autonomy. The feminists also posited a superior bourgeois female morality that would be legitimated in the eyes of society once women were properly educated. Both bourgeois men and bourgeois marriage itself could then be effectively transformed, replacing the Liberals' benevolent patriarchy with an egalitarian partnership built on intellectual and spiritual love.

Throughout their discussions of feminine education and its connections to the economics of sexuality and gendered morality, the early feminists called attention to the complicity of men of their own class in the subordination of women, something most Liberals refused to do. In their fiction, they went even further, denouncing the infidelity and sexual abuse practiced by men of all classes against women. Ana Roqué de Duprey also elaborated a relatively daring theory of female sexuality that outlined the possibility of feminine desire and pleasure within the parameters of the dominant honor code.[49]

For the first time, bourgeois women *as a group* had begun to speak for themselves rather than being spoken about. In the 1890s, bourgeois feminism had not yet become a movement dedicated to agitating for specific social and political goals as it would in the twentieth century. However, it is clear that women from Puerto Rico's upper and professional classes were beginning to reflect on their own position in society and question the immutability of power relations, especially within the family. These early feminists were forming a consciousness of themselves as a group with particular interests. *La Mujer* and the feminist fiction published during the 1890s played an important role in this growing collective self-definition.[50]

But these feminists not only tried to reenvision the bourgeois family and their place within it. They also defined themselves in opposition to plebeian women. Women of the laboring classes were generally too African, too public, and believed to be too frankly sexual to be included, even rhetorically, in the early feminists' community of women. Not unlike their male Liberal relatives and contemporaries, bourgeois feminists could conceive of women of the popular classes only as "little sisters" to be remade in their own image or as dangerously sexual beings, who threatened the very essence of female respectability. They denied any connection between their own experiences and the lives of the plebeian women who sought justice in the courts. Thus despite their efforts to address the concerns of laboring women, speaking *for* themselves ultimately meant that early feminists scornfully spoke *about* the unreformed workingwomen whom they defined as so different from themselves. In the process, they asserted their own racial and moral superiority.

The nineteenth-century female feminists were the first group in Puerto Rico consistently to advocate women's economic self-sufficiency.[51] Although they did not question the primacy of motherhood or critique class relations of power as socialist feminists would do two decades later, bourgeois feminists were acutely aware of women's economic vulnerability. Plebeian women's misery was plain to see in Puerto Rico's fields and streets. And in the protracted economic crisis that beset the island's sugar regions after abolition, anyone could fall on hard times. Once married, middle- and upper-class women should devote themselves to motherhood, the feminists wrote, but even they should be able to earn an income in hard times. Unmarried daughters might need to keep their parents and siblings afloat, and poverty-stricken widowhood was a constant threat.[52]

Many feminists themselves faced this reality. Olivia Paoli, one of Ponce's most vibrant and radical bourgeois feminists, is a case in point. Olivia's father, a local landowner, lost his fortune in the economic crisis of the postabolition period. Olivia married a Liberal journalist who died at a young age, leaving her to raise seven children. She supported them by teaching out of her home, freelance writing for newspapers, and, during U.S. colonial rule, through employment as a social worker. Likewise, Ana Roqué, who married a wealthy hacendado, had to work as a teacher to survive after all her money was depleted in 1884. The feminist poets Fidela Matheu and Trinidad Padilla met similar fates.[53] The fragility of these women's class status may well have fed their critiques of elite gender and familial relations. It probably also influenced their reaction to women of African descent; in a society where slavery had only recently ended and where financial stability was unreliable, moral and racial identities took on heightened importance.

The early feminists also saw clearly that women's economic survival was integrally linked to their sexuality. Poor women, especially, needed "to insure [their] subsistence in order to permanently separate from vice." Trading sex for money through the "immorality" of concubinage was hard to avoid for those plebeian women who could not support themselves.[54]

Middle- and upper-class white women did not face the same sexual dangers as did women of the laboring classes. They were, by definition, "honorable." In fact, keeping their virginity intact, at least in public opinion, was crucial for bourgeois women's livelihood; without it, marriage was practically impossible. Yet they still depended on their beauty and manipulative flirtation to snare a husband who could support them. In a significant divergence from Liberal writers' exhortations to bourgeois women to reject frivolity, the feminists pointed out that women of the moneyed classes had been forced to depend on their sexual wiles. Their superficiality and flirtation did not stem from willful vanity; rather, they were survival strategies developed to cope with the economic and social realities faced by "respectable" women. Thus the construction of feminine gender roles, the feminists argued, was intimately linked with both women's economic dependence and sexuality.[55]

Female education, the feminists insisted, would solve these problems. It would allow women of all classes to separate sexuality and economic survival and to be economically autonomous if necessary. But the bourgeois feminists' theorizing was quite carefully class-differentiated. In the initial issue of *La Mujer*, Roqué laid out the editors' program: Ultimately, "respectable" women would devote themselves to motherhood, whereas plebeian women would work their entire lives for wages. The education received by the two groups would be radically different as well. Bourgeois women should be exposed to a broad range of academic subjects; workingwomen were to be given only "practical" vocational training.[56]

The feminists also insisted that although the domestic sexual division of labor should remain intact, the gender power relations of marriage had to be transformed. When women married to cement familial financial and political alliances or for other purely economic reasons, husbands owned their wife's body and mind; women "were only a *thing,* belonging to their lord."[57] The distrust and lack of love in such matches led to husbands' physical and emotional abuse of their wife.[58] In the new feminist order, however, an egalitarian marital relationship would prevail. Wives and husbands would be joined in an intellectual and spiritual union, freely chosen by both partners. "The woman would thus truly be the companion of the man, because marriage is above all the union of two souls. . . . And how happy the home is when it houses two spouses who love each other, who respect each other above all, and when he seeks in her all the consolation for his trials, and the approval that in the great conflicts of life, one conscience gives to another!"[59] The sentimental tone of the feminist writings on bourgeois marital reform was often quite similar to that of Liberal tracts, but one crucial element was changed: not one feminist mentioned wives' submission to their husband in the great "union" of marriage.

On the contrary, bourgeois women would domesticate and moralize their men. Women of the "respectable" classes, the feminists asserted, were not in need of moral training, as the male Liberals claimed; they were morally superior to men and always had been. Once educated, bourgeois women would be able to lift the men in their lives to their own elevated moral level.[60] The early feminists were turning the Liberal men's moral reform proposals against them; now it would be *bourgeois* men who would be domesticated and tamed of their vices by women.

Chief among these elite male failings was sexual infidelity, a crucial subtext of the feminist discourse on female education and the transformation of marriage. Male extramarital affairs were a constant source of pain and financial worry for women of all classes. This was such common knowledge that when a woman committed suicide, criminal investigators assumed that the cause was jealousy of her partner's mistress.[61] In my interviews, I also found that the historical memory of the women of Ponce's leisured classes is still full of this anguish; they frequently made comments about their grandparents' generation such as, "He cost his wife terribly; she suffered her whole life with the weight of those horns he placed on her head."[62]

Ana Roqué exposed this suffering in her fiction, openly denouncing the male extramarital sexual desires left unnamed by the Liberals.[63] The pages of *La Mujer* were also filled with veiled references to the philanderings of bourgeois men. Superficial charms, the authors warned, would not keep a husband's heart; only intellectual companionship could guarantee men's lifelong love. Thus, education would not only release women from trading on their own sexuality for financial support but also meant freedom from other women's sexual threats and husbands' straying.

Not surprisingly, feminists called for an end to the sexual double standard, insisting that monogamy should be required of men as well as women.[64] Male sexuality unchecked by love, the feminists implied, was bestial, predatory, and abusive, regardless of the man's social standing. In Roqué's story "Sara la obrera," for example, a wealthy merchant who felt no affection for his wife abused her and raped her best friend. Men might use more subtle tactics in their sexual advances, but the result would always be the same: no matter how sweet their words, men were capable of taking sexual advantage of women.[65]

Lower-class women of African descent posed the most powerful sexual threat to "respectable" women and familial sanctity, however. The elite feminists' sympathy for the economic plight of workingwomen vanished when they appeared as sexual competitors. Feminists never acknowledged that the material "favors" received from well-to-do male lovers were an important motivation for many laboring women's willingness to continue "illicit" sexual relationships. Instead, the early feminists were convinced that such relationships were a result of plebeian women's uncontrollable sexual desires and seductive powers. Feminists appear to have shared the pervasive conviction among elites that black women embodied animalistic sexuality. They thus assumed that women of African descent shamelessly provoked male lust and tempted married men to betray virtuous wives. "That Cuban woman had in her the magnetic power of a boa constrictor, and in her lips the voluptuousness of Oriental odaliscs, whose only purpose is pleasure. . . . [She] sought to entangle him in her net of seductions; and he felt in his heart and nerves an electric quivering when he realized such an exciting woman was looking at him in that provocative way."[66] Such unbridled plebeian sensuality threatened to destroy the bourgeois family with its exotic powers. Once again, it was women deemed dangerously African who posed the greatest threat to elite Puerto Rican vitality.

Such fears of sexual competition and betrayal were part and parcel of the feminists' profound distrust of heterosexual sexual activity in general. This apprehension is not surprising, considering the often life-threatening physical dangers of pregnancy, childbirth, abortions, and venereal diseases that accompanied sexual intercourse for women.[67] During the nineteenth century, it was also probably quite difficult, if not impossible, for "decent" bourgeois women to express their own sexual needs, given the dominant prescriptions against women's sensuality. Consequently, bourgeois marital sexual practice may well have been dictated by male desire and not very satisfying to the women involved. Incorporating pleasure into their conceptualizations of sexuality was likely particularly unthinkable for the early feminists because female sexual desire was so closely associated among Puerto Rican elites with the allegedly bestial sensuality of poor black women. The vast majority of white, bourgeois feminists could not admit to such tainted feelings. Thus, feminists called on both men and women to rise above the claims of the body and instead build heterosexual partnerships based on intellectual compatibility. Respectable women, especially, were exhorted to tame their man's sexual drives through "the lovely, pure essence of their divine love."[68]

At first glance, as in their calls for female education, the feminists' antisensuality often appeared similar to that of the Liberals, but the motivations behind the positions of the two groups were quite different. The Liberals' exhortations were meant to produce a disciplined rural, male labor force and to keep women from challenging male claims to exclusive possession of female sexuality. The feminists, on the other hand, strove to discipline men sexually *of their own class,* free women of all classes from unwanted male sexual advances, and eliminate the sexual competition from plebeian women.

One nineteenth-century feminist, though, did not simply advocate women's escape from their bodies. Ana Roqué de Duprey, widely known as one of the founders of the twentieth-century bourgeois women's suffrage movement, also developed a theory of female pleasure and sexual fulfillment. In her fiction, Roqué insisted that women experienced sexual desire as powerfully as men: "A woman is not an angel; she is being full of passions, just like a man."[69] Both sexual satisfaction and financial support were essential to a woman's happiness. This reality could be denied only at great cost to marital tranquillity; a husband's failure to satisfy his wife's sexual needs could drive even an honorable spouse to extramarital fantasies. "The wife passionately embraced herself while her husband slept like a saint. And as always happens when the laws of Nature are violated, while seeking their natural equilibrium, these laws break through all social norms, and follow their powerful path. . . ; despite her honorable intentions, Julia's passion grew greater, crazier, and dominated her more every day."[70]

For Roqué, freely chosen marriage for love was the resolution of the potential contradiction between the "laws of Nature," which gave women undeniable sexual desires, and the "laws of society," which dictated female chastity. Such a relationship would be mutually monogamous and built on the basis of intellectual and spiritual compatibility. If a woman's intellect was satisfied, Roqué implied, her sexual desires would be channeled in appropriate directions.[71]

Roqué's insistence on middle-class women's right to sexual satisfaction, as well as the wider feminist demands for male monogamy, female intellectual fulfillment, and the delinking of women's sexuality from their economic livelihood, could have posed profound challenges to bourgeois gender power relations. Yet despite the radical potential of Roqué's ideas about sexuality, she and other nineteenth-century feminists were incapable of reconceptualizing the dominant definitions of respectable feminine behavior. Roqué may have condemned male sexual abuse as the root of much of women's supposed moral weaknesses. But although men's sexual predations were despicable, ultimately they "required that women know how to guard their honor."[72] Roqué failed to acknowledge that the honor system itself reinforced women's subordination, perhaps because no matter how restrictive its tenets, the dominant honor code accorded women of her race and class social superiority and power over other women. In Roqué's worldview, then, women's premarital virginity and fidelity during marriage remained paramount; if they were lost, so was their female bearer, regardless of the reasons. Women could exercise sexual agency, Roqué asserted, but only within the limits of a lifelong monogamous marriage.[73]

Likewise, Roqué never suggested that women openly challenge their husband's sexual indiscretions. She implied that bourgeois wives' successful domestication of men would be accomplished through silent moral example rather than through the much too plebeian strategy of direct confrontation. The quiet, chaste perseverance of respectable wives would eventually awaken male morality and rekindle husbands' potential for true monogamous love.[74]

Nowhere does adherence by the feminist elite to dominant definitions of feminine respectability and its importance to their own class and racial identity emerge more clearly, though, than in their discussions of plebeian women. Bourgeois Puerto Rican feminists did address issues of great import to workingwomen that Liberal males completely ignored: the right to economic self-sufficiency, the connections between sexuality and women's economic dependency on men, and sexual abuse of poor women by wealthy men. But nineteenth-century feminists never claimed commonality with their darker, poorer "*hermanitas*" (little sisters). Rather, they posited themselves as these women's morally superior leaders: "Are we to say to the people that all classes exhibit the same vices and behave the same way? Impossible! If this were true, how could we aspire to educate them?"[75]

To early feminists, female members of Puerto Rico's laboring classes were not "women" but *campesinas* (peasants) or *obreras* (workers)—the term "woman" was reserved for ladies of the leisured classes. The female intellectual capability and special moral sensibility so touted by feminists remained, in their minds, white as well as middle- and upper-class qualities. The vast majority of Puerto Rican women, an article in *La Mujer* asserted, "barely have moral or religious ideas, nor notions of human dignity."[76] Likewise, although the early feminists recognized that all women traded on their sexuality for male financial support, the fact that one group did it "honorably" and the other through "vice" kept them from explicitly drawing the connection between the two. Racialized respectability remained a crucial dividing line between women, especially because plebeian women were potential competitors for the economic, social, and sexual attentions of elite men.

Women and men of the popular classes could gain acceptance into the feminists' "gran familia" only through combining hard work, education, and unquestioning adherence to bourgeois norms of sexual propriety.[77] And as in Liberal writings, feminist images of "decent" plebeian women were emptied of all hints of Africanness. A case in point is Roqué's tragic heroine Sara, the hardworking, educated seamstress who, although of mixed Spanish and African heritage, "seemed more indian than parda."[78]

Popular women's morality, which embraced premarital sex, serial monogamy, and concubinage as eminently respectable social practices, remained beyond the feminist pale. The same feminists who called for female education to ensure plebeian women's economic livelihood invoked the supposed rampant immorality of poor women to prove their own respectability and worthiness to elite men.[79] The feminists' reaction to a novel by the Liberal writer M. González García illuminates how they defined themselves in opposition to plebeian women. They were horrified by González García's attribution of the "immoral" behavior of the laboring classes to supposedly "decent" and "distinguished" women.

[The book] is quite offensive to Puerto Rican families of the distinguished classes, to whom it imputes a complete lack of education and a detestable culture, neither of which is true.

What will foreigners who read this book think of Puerto Rican ladies? Will they believe that we all pass our time going at each other with fisticuffs . . . that here, all sleep together in the same bed? . . . [González García] paints our society as one where ladies act like market women. . . .

It is certainly true that the scenes with which this writer presents us do take place, *but not in the distinguished class.* We have seen such scenes many times among the scum, the dregs of society, among those women without any education or culture whatsoever."[80]

Indeed, in many respects, the feminists of the 1890s seemed to be striving to replace male Liberals as the defining agents of the new social hierarchy.[81] Many of the early Puerto Rican feminists were, on the whole, quite conservative in class and racial terms. The newly educated bourgeois woman would not overturn the social order, they assured their readers, but would be the savior of the planter class, now facing hard times in the sugar industry's crisis. Her industriousness and superior morality would maintain both her family's honor and some semblance of its previous social standing.[82] Some of the 1890s feminists also contended that they and other women of their troubled class would be crucial players in the battle against the rising radical political tides around the world. "Consider how necessary it is to contain that great force that nihilism and socialism can currently muster, while they count women like Sofia Perosky, Vera Zassulitchy, and Luisa Michel among their adherents. In order to save our society which is so gravely threatened, we must educate the women who alone as mothers and as Christian wives can stem the tide which advances upon the saintly boundaries of the home."[83] If the bourgeois gender order were modified somewhat to allow educated women a place at the helm, class and race relations could remain undisturbed.

Thus, while the early feminists clearly challenged several basic Liberal assumptions about power relations between the sexes, acknowledging some of the urgent problems facing plebeian women, they were ultimately unable— or unwilling—to breach the class and racial barriers between themselves and laboring women. In the nineteenth century, desires to maintain their social and material privileges and distinguish themselves from the "disreputable" women of the working classes bound feminists tightly into the male Liberals' racialized class enterprise. Puerto Rican feminists of the 1890s built their project on the redefinition and defense of bourgeois white womanhood. Consequently, they were just as concerned with excluding most women from the feminine version of the "gran familia" as with asserting all women's right to economic and sexual autonomy. This suspicion of plebeian women ensured the feminists' silence as the Liberals' rhetoric of rural moral reform translated in practice into a repressive state campaign against sexually threatening urban women during the last decade of the century.

Chapter 3

Decent Men and Unruly Women: Prostitution in Ponce, 1890–1900

The poor count among themselves many highly honorable families, but despite this, the Mayor and the Municipal Council have ordered prostitution among them. The poor have been obliged to accept prostitution as a neighbor. Prostitution now resides within honor.

Tired of invoking the law, which has refused to come to their aid, honor and decency will fall vanquished at the feet of prostitution, who struts about crowing of her impending triumph. Decency and honor, humiliated and ashamed, flee to hide in the fortress of justice, but in vain.
—Ramón Mayoral Barnés [Canta Claro], "La honradez vencida por la prostitucion," *La Democracia,* December 29, 1898

In 1891, the portrait of Rafael Cordero, a black cigar maker and teacher, was hung in Puerto Rico's principal elite cultural center, el Ateneo Puertorriqueño. A previous attempt to include the deceased Cordero in the pantheon of illustrious Puerto Rican men of letters had been roundly rejected by the Ateneo's membership twenty-five years before. Now, however, social and political conditions had shifted radically on the island, or so the eminent intellectual and Liberal party activist Salvador Brau exclaimed in his ode to Cordero, penned especially for the occasion. Brau's eulogy celebrated Cordero's interracial, cross-class school and stern, patriarchal pedagogy. Rafael Cordero had created a disciplined, racially harmonious community of elite and plebeian children in his classroom, and thus deserved the title of "intellectual father" of modern Puerto Rico.[1]

On New Year's Eve 1896, Isabel Salguero was denounced by the Ponce police for "trafficking in sex" without registering on the city's prostitution rolls. Several young men had complained to the police that Isabel was infected with a venereal disease. Regardless of whether she had actually exchanged sex for money, Salguero's alleged infection marked her indelibly as a prostitute. The judge gave Isabel ten days to enroll as a prostitute. The next day, after a forced vaginal examination at the Hygiene Hospital, the city's hygiene physician pronounced Isabel free of venereal infection. Despite her clean bill of health, however, the judge and policemen assigned to the case continued to search for Salguero, who had fled Ponce after the coerced "hygiene" examination. They tracked her to Yauco, a town thirty-two kilometers away. The case was dropped only once Salguero's neighbors in Yauco insisted that she had left Puerto Rico in a boat headed to the Dominican Republic.[2]

At first glance, these two events seem quite unrelated. One heralded the dawn of a modified Liberal political project advocating universal male suffrage and an ambivalent identification with respectable, urban workingmen, many of whom were of African descent. The other constituted a small skirmish in the decade-long campaign to regulate prostitution in Ponce—a drive that had rapidly become a systematic state crackdown against plebeian women suspected of "immorality." Contrary to initial appearances, however, the simultaneous emergence of a political opening for workingmen and state repression against sexually suspect urban workingwomen were intimately linked.[3]

In this chapter I examine how the drive to regulate prostitution in the city of Ponce emerged out of the unnerving social, economic, and political changes sweeping Puerto Rico's sugar regions. I analyze the struggles of the targeted women and the campaign's impact on their lives and communities. Finally, I explore how the campaign helped shape the new political discourses of the 1890s fashioned by both elite and popular male intellectuals and activists. The antiprostitution campaign provided an opportunity for plebeian men to intervene in the political debates of the moment. It played a central role in creating a cross-class, cross-gender consensus about the terms of Ponce community membership, based in the increasingly powerful concept of decency. Its implicit blackening of the targeted women and concomitant de-Africanization of all those deemed "decent" also facilitated the racial neutralization of political exchanges between working-class and elite men in the city. Ultimately, the symbol of the prostitute and the highly charged political currents that swirled around it helped consolidate elite male Liberal power in Ponce, amid a variety of political challenges.[4]

The moral panic about sexually wayward women was not a conscious creation of male elites, however well it eventually may have served their political interests. The campaign to cleanse "decent" neighborhoods of unruly, implicitly Afro-Puerto Rican women had no single, identifiable cause. It also had a number of unforeseeable political, material, and cultural effects. The narratives of sexual danger swirling through the streets and salons of 1890s Ponce both disciplined workingwomen's lives in new ways and incited new political imaginings—most of them profoundly misogynistic.[5]

Indeed, the prostitution regulation campaign was supported wholeheartedly by many of the same men who in the 1870s and 1880s had rejected coercion in favor of reform. In Ponce's urban environment, where plebeian women very publicly rejected the boundaries of bourgeois propriety, the Liberal rhetoric of gentle, paternal moral transformation of poor women quickly showed its repressive potential. Once in the city, the potential good mothers of the countryside were summarily redefined as disreputable, darkened whores. For many women of the urban popular classes, then, the actual practice of Liberal moral reform meant increased repression.[6]

Roots of the Regulatory Campaign

The 1890s were a time of unsettling social and economic changes in Ponce. Despite efforts to modernize the sugar industry, the region's economy contracted throughout the 1870s and 1880s. By the 1890s, coffee from the highlands made up the bulk of Puerto Rico's exports, and Ponce's sugar economy was in the depths of a profound crisis. Only twenty-two of the eighty-six sugar estates thriving in the region fifty years before had survived. The masses of laborers, especially urban working people, suffered the brunt of the economic crunch. Artisans and wage laborers faced unemployment, low wages, and increasing costs of basic imports.[7] The rate of urbanization after abolition in 1873 also increased dramatically, swelled by *libertos* (former slaves) and migrants from smaller towns seeking work and the relative freedom they hoped the city could offer them. Ponce's urban population nearly tripled in twenty-five years, growing from only 9,166 residents in 1871 to 24,654 in 1897. Many of the new Ponceños were libertos who moved to Ponce's urban center to seek shorter work contracts and greater freedom of movement and residence.[8]

The Unruly Poor

For the wealthy white people who held economic and political power in Ponce, the dramatic increase of poor, largely Afro-Puerto Rican people in "their" city was quite frightening. Complaints abounded of homeless people sleeping on the porches of "decent" families and of disrespectful poor people stoning police officers. Worried comments about "vagabond," unemployed men appeared regularly in *La Democracia,* Ponce's main daily newspaper. Elite anxiety was fueled further by the apparent Africanness of the burgeoning urban popular classes. Liberals and Incondicionales alike represented such poor neighborhoods as La Cantera, Bélgica, and San Antón as dark, dangerous places, where ignorant, unruly people danced the bomba to African rhythms and believed in witchcraft. Working-class funerals "closely resembled African or Haitian voodoo customs, with cries and vulgar songs."[9]

Institutions to keep troublesome people off the streets and out of the sight of "respectable" people mushroomed. The Asilo de Pobres for the enclosure of beggars and vagrants was constructed in the 1890s, as was a new jail and a special section of the Tricoche Hospital dedicated to confining indigent children who roamed the streets too frequently. They joined the recently built asylum for the mentally ill and various hospitals that were dedicated to isolating those with leprosy and women infected with venereal diseases. The city council also passed resolutions prohibiting begging. Thus, the efforts to regulate prostitution were part of a broader attempt by local elites to cleanse Ponce's urban landscape of social undesirables.[10]

Perhaps most disturbing of all, however, were the growing numbers of working-class women, many of them Afro-Puerto Rican, who crowded Ponce's streets in the decades following emancipation. Their labor, mainly as laundresses, market women, and seamstresses, swelled the burgeoning informal economy. Gaining access to a wage of their own gave women in the city more sexual and economic autonomy than their rural sisters, especially when they pooled their earnings with other women. Slightly more than a quarter (26 percent) of Ponce's urban families were headed by women. Households of unrelated women also were not uncommon in the city by 1897, accounting for 9 percent of all household groupings. It may well have been easier for urban women of the 1890s to leave abusive or ungratifying sexual relationships than it had been earlier in the century or in rural areas, although survival without male financial support must have been extremely difficult. In 1899, women servants typically received three dollars per month; seamstresses earned only fifteen cents for thirteen-hour workdays.[11]

In a society where economic survival for the poor hung by a thread in the best of times and the sex for money quid pro quo was a fact of life for all women, the move into selling sex as one of a variety of income-earning strategies was probably not so unthinkable for laboring women. During the acute economic crisis that wracked Ponce in the early 1890s, workingwomen may well have turned more frequently to occasional prostitution. Work was hard to come by for all urban laborers, and more rural migrants arrived in the city every day, adding pressure to an already overloaded labor market. Women's bodies, though, were always available to them as a way to earn a few pesos.

Whether they sold sex or not, plebeian women generally did not conform to dominant standards of female respectability. Working-class women often settled their conflicts with fisticuffs and shouting matches in their yards. In urban neighborhoods, 65 percent or more of adult plebeian women lived in consensual union rather than marrying. And in the urban space of Ponce, poor women's "disreputable" behavior was present for everyone to see. Workingwomen, the majority of them of African descent, not only filled Ponce's great marketplace and walked the streets hawking foodstuffs, sweets, and other goods during the day but also socialized at night without chaperones, often renting coaches with groups of girlfriends, flirting and sometimes drinking at neighborhood taverns. On weekends they attended bomba dances, where the drums beat until dawn.[12] Thus, regardless of their biological phenotypes, many urban women of the laboring classes "acted black" in the eyes of the elite.

In 1891, complaints about these "rowdy, unruly, immoral women," who wealthy white residents of Ponce insisted must be prostitutes, began to appear in the local newspapers. "Decent" residents called on the city government to cleanse their neighborhoods of these women. The municipal government quickly complied, passing a number of regulations requiring "scandalous women" to be removed from the sight of "respectable" folk.[13]

Although elite men penned most of the initial complaints, they were not the only ones unnerved by these unequivocally public, unattached women. White women of Puerto Rico's middle and upper classes, including the early feminists, defined their own respectability in opposition to workingwomen's supposed inherent degeneracy. And many workingmen also must have been disturbed by their increasing inability to control plebeian women's sexual and economic activity. A Ponce artisan newspaper of the period denounced the "scandals" caused by disrespectful women.[14]

"Unruly" Market Women Selling Their Wares (from José de Olivares, *Our Islands and Their People as Seen with Camera and Pencil* [St. Louis: N. D. Thompson, 1899])

Political Changes: Feminists and Artisans

By 1894, women of the Puerto Rican middle and leisured classes had begun publicly to demand changes in power relations between the sexes. Although Puerto Rico's nineteenth-century female feminist circle was small, it caught the attention of elite Autonomist men. Authors in *La Democracia* periodically referred to articles in the feminist newspaper *La Mujer,* and full-fledged debates between feminists and leading Autonomists sometimes broke out.[15] In addition, the 1890s witnessed a growing awareness in Ponce of the shifts in gender relations occurring in Europe and the United States. *La Democracia* frequently reported on the increasing number of women in other countries who worked outside of the home as professionals and wage laborers. Its writers also discussed European and North American women's political mobilization.[16]

The Ponce Marketplace (from José de Olivares, *Our Islands and Their People as Seen with Camera and Pencil* [St. Louis: N. D. Thompson, 1899])

Faced with a growing autochthonous Puerto Rican feminism and fearing an explosion of female mobilization such as that taking place in Europe and the United States, the Autonomist Liberals' earlier public sympathies for women's emancipation began to break down. The chorus of Liberal voices that had hailed male-led female education as the key to good mothering and moral womanhood during the 1870s and 1880s ceased entirely. Instead, authors published in *La Democracia* in the late 1890s consistently expressed fears that feminism or even expanded education for women would destroy the institution of motherhood, bring about female sexual license, and encourage women's autonomous political activism.[17]

The generalized panic over sexually promiscuous plebeian women occurred at precisely the same moment as elite men's worries over bourgeois feminism began to heat up. Ponce's Reglamento de Higiene, which sought to systematize prostitution regulation, was promulgated in 1894, several months after *La Mujer* began its publication. By 1898, when the prostitution scare had

The Private in the Public (from the Helen Gardner Collection, National Anthropological Archives, Smithsonian Institution)

reached a fever pitch in Ponce, diatribes against feminism were published regularly in *La Democracia*.

Elite men feared feminine disorder, and these worries were especially acute in sexual and moral matters. The rowdy women of the streets symbolized the rebellious potential of bourgeois women. Such a threat had to be contained, as this racially charged quote from the prominent Autonomist Luis Muñoz Rivera demonstrates: "We pity the fallen woman, but we must avoid at all costs her contact with the honorable woman. Let us offer shelter and bread to the Magdalene who repents. But total rejection is the only possible response to the Magdalene who persists in dirtying herself. In this way, her contaminating spray will not reach our faces, nor tarnish the purity of our society."[18] As bourgeois women challenged the legitimacy of Liberal men's authority, drawing clear, racially coded lines between "respectable" and "disreputable" women seemed of paramount importance. One way to do so was physically to eject troublesome workingwomen from "decent" people's milieu. Over the course of the decade, the attempts to demonize and segregate allegedly sexually wayward women from "decent" society—especially "decent" bourgeois women—would quite effectively reinforce the limits of respectable white womanhood for the middling and upper classes.

But the growing numbers of uncontrollable laboring women and the potential revolt of women of their own classes were not the only challenges facing elite Ponceños. Male artisans were also organizing. In the late nineteenth century, they founded newspapers, social clubs, mutual aid societies, cooperatives, and worker education centers in Ponce. By the mid-1890s, as Angel Quintero Rivera has noted, Ponce's largely Afro-Puerto Rican artisans were asserting their right to be considered fully cultured citizens.[19] They created the music that filled the local elite's ballrooms and helped found such important social institutions as the firemen's corp. Sources from the period hint that the mulatto artisans' insistence on dignity in the eyes of the wealthy may also have entailed attempting to separate themselves from the taint of slavery. An artisan newspaper article from the 1880s drew a sharp dichotomy between the "poor, defenseless slave who obeyed his master" and the proud artisan who "has dignity in his labor and decorum in his personality and noble resolutions."[20]

The male artisans' growing organization could not be ignored. Liberals feared the specter of socialism and regularly exhorted artisans to reject its tenets.[21] Also, in 1887, the Liberal Autonomists had been brutally driven out of political power in Ponce's municipal council by Spanish officials and the pro-Spanish Incondicional Party. Many Liberals lost property and employment and were even jailed. After that year, it became clear to Liberal leaders that they could no longer expect political inclusion on equal terms with the Incondicionales. To regain the political clout they had previously exercised, they would have to broaden the electorate and win the support of the increasingly organized working classes.

Thus during the early 1890s, as they struggled anew with political marginalization, Liberal Autonomists began to develop a discourse of ambivalent identification with the plebeian men, particularly urban artisans, whom they now hoped to incorporate into an active political constituency. The new ideal laboring man would be a citizen as well as a hard worker. He would no longer be moralized by feminine influence. Instead, Liberals acknowledged artisans' "muscular," "virile" hard work, collective organization, and struggles for intellectual advancement. Such leading Liberals as Salvador Brau and Luis Muñoz Rivera even declared that the dedication and discipline of "sober workers" could serve as a model for elite society, as long as they accepted Autonomist political leadership and did not aggressively assert distinctive Afro-Puerto Rican identities or interests.[22]

This ambiguous inclusion conceded respectability to male artisans and deracialized elite political discourse about them. The overt references to slavery and racial differences that underlay Liberal writings of the 1880s disappeared almost completely in the 1890s. In their place a racially neutral language of cross-class fraternal manhood emerged, quite possibly responding to the artisans' desire to escape slavery's weight. Racism and, with it, attention to race, the Liberal Autonomists asserted, were dead. All respectable men could now be joined in a great color-blind family of citizens. "Among us concerns about color or race do not exist. For the exercise of our rights and the defense of our ideals, the most knowledgeable physician is the same as the humblest typographer," they insisted.[23] Elite Liberals also advocated jury trials, freedom of the press, and universal male suffrage. When they finally won a charter for the implementation of autonomy from Spain for Puerto Rico in 1897, universal male suffrage was one of its key tenets. A few months later, male workers rewarded the Liberals for their efforts by overwhelmingly voting them into office.[24]

The Liberals sought to confirm distance between themselves and the popular classes, though, even as they invoked the intimacy of a cross-class, racially neutral political brotherhood. Their newspapers' frequent denunciations of the unruly poor—particularly women—intensified throughout the 1890s. This language resonated racially, despite its general avoidance of overt racial labeling. Images of disorder, degeneration, and particularly sexual disreputability all powerfully evoked blackness and racial "impurity." As the prostitution regulation campaign progressed, "uncontrollable" plebeian women of all phenotypes were morally denigrated, targeted for state harassment, and implicitly racially marked—a compelling political counterpoint to the newly respectable, de-Africanized male artisans now confirmed as members of the body politic.[25]

Labeling women as prostitutes drew sharp, racially coded gendered lines that distinguished the "respectable," urban poor from the "dishonorable" pleb. Autonomists could not advocate consistent repression against the very men with whom they were forging a new political pact, "free of racial hatreds." Instead, those who were most politically and economically vulnerable—poor urban women—now became the targets of sexual control campaigns and the objects of the fears and dangers associated with blackness.

Liberal Autonomists and pro-Spanish Incondicionales, the men who made up the opposing ends of the elite political spectrum, may have differed on questions such as the scope of male suffrage, but they consistently displayed a wholehearted consensus on the necessity of isolating boisterous plebeian women. The Liberal Autonomists enthusiastically supported the regulation of prostitution beginning in 1891 under Incondicional rule and intensified the campaign once they gained control of Ponce's municipal government in 1898. This crackdown, they hoped, would entirely separate what they defined as disreputable urban workingwomen from the new, racially neutralized national community they were attempting to form. In a society where women's character and worth were defined largely by their sexual reputation and sexual reputations were intimately linked to racial identities, it is not surprising that the exclusion of unruly plebeian women from the community of *gente decente* would be carried out in a campaign to regulate sexuality that had powerful racial overtones.

Lynn Hunt has noted that during times of great social change, groups remake their collective identities by targeting victims in moments of unconscious "sacrificial crisis." Often these explosions of exclusionary panic express a great fear of sexual boundary loss. Ann Stoler also has pointed out that racial, class, and sexual discourses can combine to produce particularly powerful methods of identifying and rejecting marginal members of the body politic, thus "mapping the moral parameters of . . . nations."[26] This was certainly the case in 1890s Ponce. The fervor to regulate prostitution originally sprang from increasing elite anxiety about economic crisis, urban growth, and potentially radical social movements that characterized Puerto Rico's late-nineteenth-century sugar regions. Plebeian women's unregulated labor, increasingly autonomous sexual practices, and loud public presence posed a disturbing challenge to male elites, also unnerving wealthy women and many workingmen. The unruly urban women became the target of deflected anxieties and negative racial stereotypes. The exclusion of "disreputable," discursively darkened public women from the rest of urban Ponce society both expressed elite male fears of the subversive potential of feminism and the popular classes and safely demarcated loyal wives and male workers as "respectable," racially neutral members of la gran familia. The Puerto Rican proto-nation, as it came to be defined in the 1890s, had no place for uncontrollable women of the dark popular classes.

Regulating Prostitution

By 1894, the initial attempts to eject plebeian women suspected of being prostitutes from "decent" neighborhoods converged with a growing public hygiene movement within the Puerto Rican medical profession. Among their adherents, hygenists counted Liberal medical doctors such as Manuel Zeno Gandía and Francisco del Valle Atiles, who figured prominently in the moral reform debates of the 1880s. Del Valle also was an avid eugenicist, in the 1880s advocating the whitening of the Puerto Rican peasantry through miscegenation and arguing after 1910 that prostitutes were biologically inferior to the rest of the populace.[27]

The hygenists were primarily concerned with public health issues. They devoted much attention to altering the personal and sexual habits of the poor as well as to curtailing their racial heterogeneity. Unlike the more radical proposals of Argentine socialist physicians, Puerto Rican hygenists, by and large, hoped to alter the poor's conduct, not transform the economic and social conditions that caused poverty. Social problems were medicalized; they stemmed from the "want of living a sanitary life, which produces an anaemic race, and it is an accepted principle that a sickly race is a vice-ridden race."[28] Good hygiene and a strong society required clear definitions and strict social demarcation of healthy and sick, moral and immoral, rich and poor, white and black. Convictions of this sort, which in the hygenists' discourse rested on the unassailable authority of science, eventually lent a special force to state attempts to control alleged prostitutes. Their simultaneous advocacy of sexual surveillance and insistence on racial purity further normalized the equation of "disreputability" with blackness.[29]

Hygiene doctors' interest in prostitution sprang from concerns about controlling venereal disease. Syphilis and gonorrhea were quite common, and their long-term effects on the body were frightening—oozing sores, swelling and often loss of limbs, blindness, sterility, and insanity.[30] Prostitutes, however, not the men who bought their services, were believed to be the root of the incurable venereal disease "plague" that afflicted Puerto Rico. Thus, women, not men, would be the object of the regulatory campaign.

The influence of the hygiene movement systematized and gave scientific, medical legitimacy to state attempts to regulate prostitution. From 1894, when the Ponce municipal council passed the first "prostitution hygiene" legislation, until the campaign ended in 1900, police and medical surveillance of workingwomen's sexuality would take precedence over the informal family and community methods of surveillance that until then had kept women more or less in check. The authors of the Reglamento sought to formalize and define the structure of women's labor as well as to regulate their sexuality. Women's bodies and labor practices became subjected to medicalized state surveillance, to be invaded and "evaluated" at will.

After 1894, women suspected of being prostitutes were required to register on an official list, pay a "hygiene tax," and submit to biweekly pelvic exams by designated hygiene doctors. All registered women had to carry a special passbook, in which their residence and clean bill of health was confirmed. They were expected to work out of a licensed brothel. If found to be infected with a venereal disease, women were involuntarily isolated in a special "hygiene hospital." The exams themselves were painful, humiliating events, often carried out in police stations, in full view of policemen and bystanders. The examiners routinely used speculums that were shunned by doctors in gynecological treatment of "respectable" women. The usually unsterilized metal instruments were jammed unceremoniously into women's vaginas.[31] As the campaign, as well as resistance to it from alleged prostitutes, intensified through the second half of the decade, vaginal exams were officially sanctioned as "appropriate punishment" for "disrespectful" behavior on the part of targeted women.[32]

In addition, the Reglamento, as the regulatory legislation was called, created a special hygiene police task force for identifying and tracking suspected prostitutes. Several plebeian neighborhoods were designated as special prostitution zones, into which all "public women" were to be forcibly relocated. It was now illegal for anyone alleged to be a prostitute to live or move about in "decent" sections of the city.[33] Thus, surveillance mechanisms expanded rapidly once elite medical and moral concerns converged to focus on purifying "respectable" Ponce from prostitutes' dangers. But these institutions and practices were not all-powerful. The very women they were meant to contain shaped and limited them.

Pre-Reglamento Prostitution

The few surviving records of prostitution in Ponce before 1894 hint that before the implementation of the Hygiene Reglamento, prostitution in Ponce

was a diffuse, rather fluid occupation. María Rodríguez, for example, identified herself in 1890—and was considered by her neighbors—as a washerwoman, not a prostitute, although she had occasional sexual encounters with
different men for which she accepted money.[34] Those women who may have
sold sex more consistently to earn their living appear to have moved in and
out of the trade. Seventy-five percent of the 103 women listed as prostitutes in
the first citywide police surveillance list of 1893, for example, did not appear
in any subsequent list or criminal record.[35]

Not surprisingly, considering the political trend in the 1890s toward silencing overt discussions of race, the surviving documents from the regulatory
campaign make no direct reference to the targeted women's race. The last
names of some women provide clues to their racial identity; names of prominent Ponce hacendado families such as Font, Oppenheimer, Rosaly, or Serrallés are relatively clear evidence that the women who bore them were of
African ancestry—probably the descendants of slaves. But most of the women
whose names appeared on the "hygiene" lists, in court cases, and in newspaper reports had last names (such as Martínez) that were common among
people of all races. Consequently, the phenotypical markers or self-accepted
racial identities of most of the targeted women cannot be ascertained. In the
course of the campaign, however, all "scandalous" or "disreputable" women
became discursively darkened, regardless of their ancestry.

Although the race of alleged Ponce prostitutes was not named, the sources
do provide some information on their social origins. The majority of the
women in police prostitution lists whose birthplace was identified had migrated to Ponce from smaller towns. In 1892, eight of the nine women living
in the Vista Alegre section of town and suspected by the police of selling sex
were migrants. Sixty percent of those on the 1893 citywide list of prostitutes
had journeyed to Ponce, 93 percent of them from coastal towns.

Interestingly, women migrants from the same town and identified by the
police as prostitutes do not seem to have lived together or recruited one
another into the trade.[36] This may suggest that young women migrating to
Ponce who lacked networks from their town of origin were more likely to
make their living from prostitution; they may not have had access to the
social connections necessary for finding affordable housing or earning sufficient income in other ways. Once established in a community, they may have
moved on to other means of supporting themselves. Of course, because such
migrant women did not live with extended family members or other "protec-

tive" elders, they may also have been more likely to be identified by police or their neighbors as sexually deviant, whether or not they directly sold sexual favors.

If the identity of the prostitute was not rigid or permanent in these early years, neither did the structure of the trade fit the 1894 Reglamento's ideal. Sizable brothels run by an appointed manager and serving substantial numbers of clients, such as emerged in Europe or even Buenos Aires and Guatemala City, did not exist in Ponce. Instead, when prostitutes lived together, they did so in small groups of two to three women, each one contributing a few pesos a month for rent.[37] The majority of women who sold sex for a living did so as individual freelancers, with no permanent base of operations. Forty-eight of the fifty-four women on the 1894 list of registered prostitutes—89 percent—were individual *meretrices* (prostitutes) who had no consistent supervision.[38] The clearly defined prescriptions of the Reglamento, then, did not fit the much more ambiguous reality of the sexual economy of Ponce's popular classes. Rather, plebeian women appear to have sold sex intermittently and independently. Indeed, prostitution may have served as a female alternative to proletarianization. It was up to the police to create a more readily identifiable and centralized prostitute population that could be medically and socially controlled. They did their best to comply with "respectable" public opinion.

Expansion of Surveillance

After the promulgation of the Reglamento in 1894, state intervention in the lives of poor women exploded. In 1884, scandalous women constituted a scant 2.5 percent of Ponce's recorded crimes. By 1896, however, fully one-third of all charges pursued—at least one each day—were prostitution related. Denunciations of prostitutes continued to climb through the end of the decade. No proof of prostitution had to be provided for a woman to be harassed by the police; "suspicion of immorality" was sufficient grounds for arrest. Police began arresting and fining working-class women by the hundreds, hauling them into court and accusing them of being unregistered prostitutes.[39] By 1898, the penalties for such suspicion had escalated: 52 percent of the alleged prostitutes were jailed in addition to being charged the customary fines.

In 1898, the blueprint for a proposed new jail included for the first time an entire section set aside for women, complete with a venereal disease examination and isolation room. Clearly, women were swelling the prison population as a result of police crackdowns against prostitution. Serving a jail sentence was no small matter in those days. Rape by prison guards was not uncommon, and the conditions were horrid—the food was often putrid, pools of fecal matter lay about on the floors, and there was little, if any, ventilation.[40]

Certainly, many women did register and ostensibly submit to routine medical examinations as a result of the Reglamento's enforcement. Fifty-four initially signed up on the prostitution rolls in 1894, and in the ensuing years, hundreds more appear as registered in police delinquency lists and court cases, though often only after being harassed, fined, and even jailed. It seems that the sharpening of police repression in the later years pushed a good number of women onto the official register. Of the eighty women who appeared in the surviving police records and court cases more than once during or after 1896, 82.5 percent eventually registered.

Some evidence exists that once the register was established in 1894, women's stints as identifiable prostitutes began to lengthen. Seventy-five of the 103 women on the 1893 (pre-Reglamento) police list of prostitutes residing in the city never appeared again, whether in surveillance records or denunciations. In stark contrast, only 35 percent of the women named in Ponce's only surviving list of registered prostitutes, drawn up several months after the promulgation of the Reglamento, did not reappear. Sixty-five percent of the women recognized as prostitutes in the early post-Reglamento months, as opposed to 25 percent a year earlier, were still surfacing within the net of police harassment and registry enforcement in subsequent years.[41]

Unfortunately, it is impossible to tell with any certainty how many women eventually enrolled as officially recognized prostitutes. The police records themselves are incomplete, and except for the initial 1894 registry list, no prostitution rolls or medical reports were preserved. Also, the women appearing in police records were only the most unruly, requiring overt disciplinary attempts; many more may have registered and lived relatively peacefully within the Reglamento's parameters.

It is clear, however, that the targeted women frustrated some of the state's attempts to regulate their sexual and economic practices. Many of those arrested by the police refused to register on the official lists. They often failed to appear in court or pay the fines routinely levied on them by magistrates; over 60 percent of the fines were never paid. Some of those who did register as prostitutes manufactured counterfeit passbooks and handed them off to one another to avoid the hated exams. The scores of denunciations lodged against registered women are ample testimony to the fact that they continued to live, move about, and practice their trade outside the designated zones. Hygiene doctors complained that the registered women "refused to accept their authority" and often refused to "submit" to the exams.[42]

Hospitalizations of poor, "sexually suspicious" women also increased. As noted earlier, those found to be infected with venereal disease were summarily locked away in a special hospital set aside for that purpose. It is worth emphasizing here that no cure for venereal diseases existed in the nineteenth century. Available "therapies" were limited to injections of massive doses of mercury, arsenic, and other toxic chemicals. The treatments themselves were often lethal, and when patients survived them, they produced painful side effects such as tongue fissures, massive hemorrhaging of the bowels, and loss of teeth. Thus, internment in the hygiene hospital did not cure infected women. Its sole purpose was to isolate them from society. This was made quite clear by the "indeterminate sentences," high spiked fences, barred windows, and perpetually locked doors that kept the hospital and the women within it "secure" and prevented family and friends of the "patients" from visiting.[43]

But just as they resisted police attempts at surveillance, the women accused of prostitution did not submit passively to the conditions imposed on them by an ever more invasive medical profession. It was precisely their ongoing subversion of the hospital's control mechanisms that generated such a constant concern for security among medical authorities. The women shouted to people passing by in the street and loudly cursed the hospital staff, causing "unbearable scandals." The head of the Hygiene Hospital complained of frequent escapes made by sick women. Police records mention women "fleeing" the hospital without authorization. Two made an especially spectacular break by climbing out an unguarded window and down a rope made of sheets knotted together.[44]

Plainly, the Reglamento and the state campaign it authorized created new arms of state bureaucracy and interventionary bodies, as well as a rapid expansion of state intrusion into the lives of working-class women, all focused primarily on the regulation of sexuality. Despite the rapid proliferation of its surveillance apparatuses, however, the state was unable to control effectively many of the women it targeted. Indeed, the women's widespread refusal to comply with official mandates helped fuel the growth of state intervention in their lives.

The hygiene police never denounced any man for purchasing sex, nor were any men sent to the hygiene hospital for being infected with venereal disease, although they too obviously passed the diseases on to their sexual partners. Indeed, it is nearly impossible to piece together any conclusions about the male patrons; they are conspicuously absent from the historical record. Police, politicians, and concerned private citizens alike studiously ignored the role of men in prostitution. Men visiting prostitutes presumably could still enjoy respectable status. It is even possible that they included some of the "gentlemen" who so vociferously denounced the sale of sex, although we cannot know. This was a highly gendered campaign—only women bore its weight.

Morality and the Prostitution Panic

There is little reliable evidence that the number of women actually selling sex increased through the course of the campaign. No records of prostitution in Ponce were kept before the 1890s. But although we cannot tell with any certainty whether the actual number of women selling sex increased, we *can* identify an explosion in moral panic about prostitution in Ponce during the 1890s.

The press began to publish reports of all police arrests of women, identifying the women by name and applauding the intensifying crackdowns. After 1895, when the regulation campaign really picked up steam, newspaper editors consistently equated women who "caused a ruckus" with prostitutes. No actual sale of sex had to be established, even by police accusation, for a woman to be publicly labeled as beyond the moral pale. This public shaming by the local press served as an extrastate method of control. It was a formalized mode of the gossip that had long been the principal method of policing neighborhood boundaries of respectability. The exclusionary power of the printed word was staggering in a society where most people were unable to wield it. And newspapers spread one's reputation—or damage to it—across the entire city. The press's authority, unlike informal gossip, was not limited to specific neighborhoods. Journalists thus escalated the perceived threat of prostitution and encouraged the adoption of repressive measures to deal with it. They helped both to create the moral crisis and to construct the misogynistic discourses and practices that "resolved" it.[45]

The prostitution panic evoked powerful racial echoes as well, at least for elites. Behavior considered scandalous by wealthy Ponceños—loud music, rowdy verbal exchanges, or physical fighting—had long been associated with both poverty and blackness. Likewise, Afro-Puerto Ricans, especially women, were rumored to embody dangerous sensual powers. In urban Ponce during the 1890s, scandal, poor women, and "immorality" all fused in a particularly compelling discourse with darkened undertones. No overt racial labeling of the targeted women was necessary. They acted black. They inhabited dark, menacing neighborhoods. Their alleged sexual waywardness was black. They threatened to stain Ponce's decency with their impure disreputability. In short, they embodied—symbolically and sometimes physically—the shameful blackness from which many "respectable" Ponce residents sought to liberate themselves.

With the press's racially resonant reports whipping up fears about the darkened "plague" of prostitution that had supposedly descended on Ponce's "decent" sectors, individual neighbors seem to have also become much more disposed toward accusing unattached women of being prostitutes. They could now spread rumors about women's sexual reputations without having to take personal responsibility for their insinuations. Residents denounced "suspicious"-looking or too loud women to the police and the mayor's office daily, where before almost no such complaints had been made. By 1898, the identification and purging of prostitutes had become a veritable obsession in Ponce.[46]

Even though most poor Ponceños were illiterate, they clearly were aware of the contents of local newspapers. Once female "scandal"—or disturbing the peace—became synonymous with "prostitute," women began to appear at the offices of local papers to publicly defend their sexual reputations and insist that they were not, in fact, whores. Delfina Vásquez, like many other workingwomen, was denounced by the police as a prostitute for letting men into her house and "causing a scandal." When the incident was reported by *La Democracia,* Delfina protested in person to the newspaper's editors, who printed her declaration: "As her neighbors and all those who know her can testify, she has never caused disturbances of any kind. This error, [she insists] without a doubt, is due to the bad faith of those responsible for the enforcement of the Hygiene Reglamento, who often overstep their bounds in their zeal to comply with their duty. The meeting that took place last night in her house, Miss Vásquez adds, was not at all scandalous. Rather, it was nothing more than she and her sister, accompanied by two male friends, singing and playing the guitar, without disturbing any of the neighbors."⁴⁷

Delfina spoke for many working-class women in her protest that the Re- glamento's enforcers had gone too far. Almost any behavior that drew atten- tion to oneself or evoked Afro-Puerto Rican culture could now mean police harassment and public stigmatization as a prostitute. Within a year after the Reglamento's implementation, talking back to store owners, allowing men in one's home, dancing in an "unseemly" way, or being on the streets too late at night could mean denunciation and even arrest as a prostitute, as well as prompt reporting of police citations and judgments in the press. In 1895, police repression against Afro-Puerto Rican working people's bomba dances, now labeled *bailes de prostitutas,* became commonplace.⁴⁸

Association with women identified as prostitutes was also dangerous. The police assumed that Luisa Arias was a prostitute and denounced her when they discovered her dancing with some registered women. Felícita Martínez, along with her two registered relatives, was denounced for *paseando por las calles* (walking the streets), although she had not been seen soliciting and was not on the prostitution rolls.⁴⁹ The gravity of being marked in such a way was graphically illustrated in 1898, when a young, working-class woman, driving in a carriage one evening with another woman and two *jóvenes alegres* (lively young men), was arrested by the hygiene police. Desperate to escape the public censure and shame sure to follow such an experience, the woman tried to poison herself.

After this incident, some local newspapers criticized the hygiene police for arresting innocent women. *La Democracia* insisted, however, that after fur- ther investigation, it was clear that the police had not been in error. The young women had engineered "nocturnal escapes" from their parents' houses before; therefore, they could not possibly be honorable. In the eyes of the wealthy Liberal editors of the paper, being out at night branded women as prostitutes. Firm lines must be drawn, the editors continued, between women who carefully preserved their "reputations, worthy of consideration and respect," and those who, like the suicide victim, were "victims of their own imprudences."⁵⁰ Women who did not remain within the bounds of respectable femininity had no one to blame but themselves. And the costs of pushing the limits had become very high.

The Reglamento created other ways to damage women's sexual reputa- tions. After its implementation in 1894, plebeian men began to denounce women to the police as infected with venereal diseases. The receipt of such an accusation, founded or not, was sufficient to "prove" a woman's status as a prostitute and immediately subjected her to police harassment, involuntary vaginal examinations, and court orders to register.[51] A woman's sexual reputation now could be linked to her supposed state of health, and the word of men, whether embittered former lovers, actual sex purchasers, or hygiene physicians, had the weight of law. For poor women, being sick had become criminalized, and the inference of disease had become another weapon in men's arsenal of sexual control.

The campaign to "contain" prostitution seems to have reinforced the boundaries of male control over women in other ways as well. After 1898, it became impossible for a registered woman to remove herself from the official prostitution list without proving that she was in a long-term monogamous relationship with a man who would take "responsibility for her behavior and public conduct." The state would relinquish its sexual surveillance "rights" only if control were effectively exercised by individual men.[52]

Already-registered prostitutes were not the only ones to be pushed more firmly into patriarchal sexual and economic arrangements. As we have seen, working-class women, especially those who "acted black," were increasingly being accused of prostitution, whether or not they actually sold sex. To refute these charges, it was often necessary to prove that one was "owned" and "supervised" by a man. Josefa Torres, for example, was able to escape arrest only by proving that she lived in consensual union. She brought her lover in to testify that she was indeed monogamous. María Vega caught the attention of the hygiene police when she caused a ruckus in a small restaurant. She was eventually arrested for "exercising the hygiene traffic" after not heeding the initial denunciation. But María insisted to the judge that she had never been a prostitute and that her lover, Juan Méndez, supported her financially. María won her release from jail only after having Juan come into court as well and obtaining a note from their *comisario de barrio* (the neighborhood representative of the municipal government) confirming that she was "living honorably with Méndez."[53]

If starting a relationship could save one from charges of prostitution, leaving the partnership might turn out to be another matter. In the 1890s, when proof of having a steady man in one's life could be the only protection against police harassment, plebeian women may have been less willing to contemplate leaving unsatisfactory or even abusive relationships. Clearly, the campaign to cleanse "decent" Ponce neighborhoods of threatening, "immoral" women had a disturbing impact on the lives of many urban workingwomen. But its effects did not stop there. The campaign also affected working-class moral norms.

Working people held a wide variety of opinions about prostitution and about who *was* a prostitute. The rural men drinking at small roadside stands where María Martínez and her male companion stopped to eat and drink one evening almost all assumed that she was *de mal vivir.* But a shoemaker and a cigar roller in the city did not see anything out of the ordinary in having seen her in the streets with this unfamiliar man much later that night. Some of the wealthier artisans who aspired to respectability openly abhorred prostitutes. But the case of Ezequiela Saldaño, who left the prostitution rolls by establishing her monogamous status, proves that at least some plebeian men were willing to establish and recognize publicly relationships with confirmed prostitutes. This suggestion is supported by a few more slivers of surviving evidence from other urban areas. In the neighboring town of Coamo, a forty-year-old mechanic freely admitted living in concubinage for two years with a known prostitute. Oral history from the tobacco town of Cayey has preserved numerous accounts of prostitutes being "rehabilitated" into honorable respectability by upstanding male workers who fell in love and married them.[54] For some workingmen, apparently, the label of "meretriz" was not anathema.

Even those among the popular classes who strove to distinguish themselves clearly from prostitutes often recognized the economic pressures that forced women to sell sexual favors. María Vega, for example, acknowledged in her defense against prostitution charges that supporting oneself in such a way could happen to any poor woman. She was simply fortunate not to have been "obligated" to do so. In 1899 the Ponce Republicano Party paper *La Patria,* pitched to a popular audience, expressed a much more sympathetic view of prostitution than *La Democracia.* Prostitutes were not "the other"—disgusting, purposeful sinners—as the Liberal press painted them. Rather, to many working people they were unlucky women, friends, and neighbors who had fallen on hard times, "poor girls who had to serve" the whims of men.[55]

Yet popular codes of respectability were still premised on male sexual control of women, although plebeian men were not able to exercise this control nearly as tightly as were men of the upper and middle classes. Although community norms allowed them to leave abusive or unsatisfying relationships, women were still required to be monogamous while in one;

men were not. "Slut" or "whore" were the worst insults that could be slung at a woman of the working classes.[56] Thus, the moral panic created during the 1890s in Ponce, with its intense stigmatization of alleged prostitutes, found echoes among the laboring classes.

The continual repressive police intervention against women suspected of selling sex probably placed a strain on plebeian moral norms. Alleged prostitutes were harassed by the police, and registered women were visited by hygiene physicians and kept under surveillance by hygiene inspectors. These actions set them apart in the communities in which they lived. Discreetly allowing different male visitors into one's home was one thing. But once this sort of behavior began to attract police attention, it may well have become an intolerable presence. In addition, the fear of being dragged into the municipal jail, denounced in court, or written up in the press for visiting or recreating with friends or neighbors who were "confirmed" sellers of sex must have made it more difficult to maintain close relationships with women who earned income from sexual encounters.

Finally, the creation of special zones for prostitutes placed an additional stress on low-income communities. After the Reglamento's promulgation and the subsequent crackdown to push alleged prostitutes out of the central, wealthier areas of town, increasing numbers of prostitutes and unruly women moved to the poor neighborhoods designated as prostitution zones. After 1894, residents of plebeian sections of the city, especially those included in the zones, first began to complain to the police and local newspapers about disturbances by prostitutes.[57]

Laboring people did not complain about prostitutes only to the press. The rocketing rate of police intervention against "suspicious" women also must have been based, at least in part, on information provided by the women's low-income neighbors. Despite working people's general distrust of the Guardia, they seem to have called on the police with escalating frequency once the presence of "troublesome" women increased in poor sectors of the city. The unequivocal labeling of unattached, rowdy women as prostitutes by the press and the police may well have fueled resentment against these women, especially among plebeian women in established relationships who had no desire to lose precious portions of their lover's or husband's wages to alleged "traffickers in sex." Thus, self-defined "respectable" workingwomen may have played a key role in the intensifying cycle of repression against disruptive or nonmonogamous women.

It is unlikely that the label of "prostitute" had the same racial meanings for plebeians as for elites. But the Reglamento's zealous enforcement generated a hardening of plebeian *gendered* moral norms. Although the campaign began as a response to elite calls for cleansing their urban space, it also resonated with some aspects of popular respectability codes. For the first time, working-class people themselves began to participate in large-scale denunciations of alleged prostitutes, making the campaign, at least in part, their own.[58]

Citizenship for Prostitutes?

But the Reglamento's enforcement did not only produce hardening attitudes toward prostitution by Ponce elites and plebs. The identity created by the Reglamento also seems to have engendered a sense of rights among some registered women. Cecilia Cadiz and Emilia Brito, two well-known prostitutes, were hauled into court, accused of violating the Reglamento by trafficking in the central streets of the city. Instead of accepting the judge's scolding, however, the two women turned the case on its head and raised demands that they be justly paid for their labor.

Cecilia and Emilia had gone for a drive in the countryside in a rented carriage at 1:00 A.M. with two well-heeled youths who lived at the Colegio del Divino Maestro. Cecilia recounted that "after having used the witness and her friend, the men refused to pay them, *and when she defended her rights,* one of them, the bigger one, threatened to beat her." Emilia backed up Cecilia's story, insisting that "they used them, and did not remunerate them for their work, and still have not done so." Lorenza Colón, the woman who headed the casa de citas where Cecilia and Emilia lived, also used the language of rights to insist that the two should be respected by the courts and paid for their night's work. She said that "the two women were *only exercising their rights with these two men—you see, they are registered prostitutes."* The judge dropped the case against Cecilia and Emilia, but after their two customers claimed to have paid the carriage driver the next day for the women's sexual services, no attempt to redress the prostitutes' demands for pay was made. This understanding of the Reglamento was echoed some time later by a Ponce policeman. When denouncing a woman whom he suspected of prostitution, Ignacio Chandón noted that he had "ordered her to register on the prostitution roll, *so that she could freely exercise the hygiene traffic;* without doing this, she could not practice said traffic."[59]

Thus during the latter half of the 1890s, the Reglamento's surveillance mechanisms appear to have generated some unexpected results. Registered women may have begun to develop a fledgling concept of prostitutes' rights—the counterpart to their many onerous duties. Cecilia, Emilia, and Lorenza were not afraid to assert in court that selling sex was *work,* not simple promiscuity, and that they had the right to be fairly paid for their labor, like any other working person. They also claimed the right to practice their trade in peace, based on their having registered and paid their "hygiene taxes." They had complied with their part of the pact with the state; now they demanded protection by its courts from abusive customers.

Yet the fragility of disreputable women's rights was exposed whenever they clashed with the interests of male customers, police, newspaper reporters, neighbors, or doctors. Emilia and Cecilia never received their pay. Customers' and neighbors' accusations of infection or physical movement beyond prescribed parameters were grounds for immediate arrest or fines. Any registered woman was subject to involuntary hospitalization if found infected by a venereal disease carried by male customers. Ultimately, prostitutes' desire for fair treatment before the law have been lost to the silencing weight of history. Not so for Ramón Mayoral Barnés, alias Canta Claro, a young workingman who appropriated the power of the pen to add a different note to the shrill chorus railing against the plague of prostitution in Ponce.

Popular Decency and Democracy: Canto Claro Speaks

Perhaps the sharpest expression of the plebeian reaction to the regulatory campaign came from Mayoral Barnés, a clerk "of humble means" who lived with his lover and children in Vista Alegre, one of the neighborhoods designated by the Reglamento as a prostitution zone. Throughout 1898 and 1899, under the pen name Canta Claro, Mayoral mounted a vitriolic campaign against both unruly women and elite Liberals. The women, he claimed, were destroying the fabric of plebeian communities. Yet the Liberals had supported and intensified the regulation campaign, which, as Canta Claro saw it, had created the prostitution problem in the first place. Through this popular intellectual's intervention, prostitution became a central arena for discursive battles over class privilege and definitions of respectability and democracy.

Mayoral Barnés occupied an ambiguous class position. Like many of the "marginal Dons" I discussed in Chapter 1, he teetered on the brink of moral and material vulnerability. On one hand, he lived in open concubinage with an Afro-Puerto Rican woman. He did not own his own tools, workshop, or home. He worked in a small neighborhood store, for a wage so low that he paid no taxes. He could not afford to live anywhere other than in the impoverished sector of Vista Alegre. As such, he was a dependent man, as his occupational category of *dependiente* implied. On the other hand, Mayoral Barnés enjoyed unquestioned white racial status, wrote voluminously and quite eloquently—this in a city with, at best, a 30 percent literacy rate—and had at least sporadic access to a printing press, with which he briefly produced his own newspaper. Certainly Mayoral possessed some privileges unavailable to the majority of his neighbors. He positioned himself accordingly. Studiously silent on questions of racial difference, which would have set him apart from many Ponce working people, Mayoral Barnés identified very clearly as a member of the laboring classes. His lot, he repeatedly proclaimed, lay with them—not with the elites. Just as vociferously, however, he tried to establish himself as the political and oral spokesperson and guide of Ponce workingmen.

Canta Claro's appearance in Ponce's political arena was part of the unnerving realignments unleashed by the U.S. invasion of Puerto Rico in the summer of 1898. After Spain's defeat, the rural poor sacked hacienda stores where debt records were kept and destroyed coffee and sugar crops. Poor people throughout the island, emboldened by the United States's image as the world's first republican democracy and its 1860s "war against slavery," began to push against the political limits imposed by Spain and Creole elites. In the heady first months of U.S. rule, full democratic rights and equality before the law, previously impossible under Spain's restrictive colonial policies, seemed within the grasp of unpropertied men. The Republicano Party, born out of an Autonomist splinter group called the Ortodoxos and led by the Afro-Puerto Rican medical doctor José Celso Barbosa, quickly began to gain ground among the popular classes against the Liberals. The Republicanos advocated immediate annexation to the United States and excoriated the Liberals as the elitist descendants of Spaniards who hoped to maintain their power over an oppressive social order. Republicano newspapers often linked the Liberals to slavery and Spanish rule.[60] The U.S. occupation, then, ripped open some of the contradictions and resentments that lurked just beneath the surface of the fragile Liberal project. In Ponce, the initial plebeian political challenge to

Liberal authority would be expressed in Canta Claro's discourse about disreputable women.

The campaign by Mayoral Barnés against prostitution in his community began in mid-1898, when he wrote a series of letters to the Ponce Ayuntamiento, then dominated by elite Liberals. He complained that prostitutes had flooded the humble Vista Alegre neighborhood as a result of its designation in 1894 as an acceptable red-light district, and he demanded that the Municipal Council control or relocate the women and their clients. After several months of governmental inaction, he began to pen satiric columns in *La Democracia* using the pseudonym of Canta Claro. In early 1899, when the editors denied him further editorial space, he turned to publishing his own newspaper, dedicated in large part to railing against prostitution.

Mayoral's acerbic wit and unrelenting stinging critiques of the Liberal political establishment caused an uproar in Ponce. The issue of prostitution exploded into public political controversy all over the city. *La Nueva Era* and other Ponce newspapers engaged Canta Claro in debate.[61] Mayoral organized his neighbors to carry various petitions to the mayor, who denounced him publicly a number of times. Several of Mayoral's most blistering columns were printed up as leaflets and distributed in the main plaza and throughout poor neighborhoods. Flyers attempting to discredit him were in turn plastered to the walls of several public buildings.

Mayoral's campaign created ripples throughout the municipal government. On December 6, 1898, *La Democracia* listed control of prostitution as one of the top three priorities established by the new Liberal administration in Ponce. Police intensified their arrests and harassment of women during November and December 1898 as the Alcaldía received daily complaints about the unsavory presence of prostitutes in the city. General popular concern with prostitution seems to have escalated sharply with this pitched public discussion. Puerto Rico's U.S.-appointed secretary of state eventually intervened from San Juan in an attempt to resolve the controversy.[62]

Three basic points are key to understanding the political explosion fueled by Canta Claro in Ponce. First, the protests were some of the first clear, urban, plebeian criticisms of Liberal rule in Ponce and therefore marked a political watershed. In Ponce, prostitution was the trope through which the most publicly articulate strand of sharpening male, working-class consciousness was expressed.[63] The discourse produced by Mayoral and his supporters suggests that the early development of a distinct worker culture and identity in Ponce was grounded at least partially in the exclusion of those women who refused to comply with dominant popular-class norms of "proper" feminine behavior. For many, the newly emerging turn-of-the-century sense of male, urban, plebeian solidarity had clear limits—and they were distinctly antiwoman.[64]

Second, Canta Claro developed a passionate public discourse about the meaning of democracy and its connection to prostitution. This discourse centered on vindicating *male* working-class respectability as the true repository of democratic values. The counterpoints to this popular male respectability were both the rich, who falsely claimed to be "decent," and the prostitutes themselves, who were a "scourge" in working-class communities.

The law, Canta Claro insisted at every turn, was not the universal protector of all citizens, as the wealthy Liberals claimed. Rather, it was a weapon of the ruling classes to be used against the poor, and the Hygiene Reglamento was the prime example of this hypocrisy. In the name of the "decency of the people and highly cultured nature of the great city of Ponce," the ruling Liberals had cleansed their neighborhoods of boisterous women, only to foist them off in unbearable numbers on the poor. The rich's definition of "the people," Canta Claro trumpeted, excluded the vast majority of Ponce inhabitants.[65] "By proceeding in this way, the aristocratic elements of the city have sought to benefit solely themselves, while prejudicing the principles of democracy; and since democracy almost never has a mouth with which to complain, nor a hand with which to write, the aristocrats don't think twice before approving regulations which exalt wealth at the expense of poverty."[66]

Mayoral's identification of democracy with the "little man" was integrally linked to U.S. authority on the island. Like thousands of his contemporaries, Canta Claro looked to the United States as Puerto Rico's liberator from Spanish despotism and as the power that could force Creole elites to comply with the full political promise of democracy.[67] "Since the implementation of [the Hygiene] Regulation, we have been protesting against it, but because during the period of Spanish domination the poor almost never obtained justice, it is not surprising that this Regulation still stands; although Spain's Law still rules us today and it tolerates prostitution living on the same street as morality, American Law will force justice on Spanish rule and force it to proceed correctly. American Law will not tolerate such a situation, not under any circumstances."[68]

In actions such as the promulgation of the Hygiene Reglamentos, the

Liberal Ponce elites had betrayed their promise to serve the people. In the process, they had proved themselves unfit to govern anyone. Turning dominant moral presumptions on their head, Canta Claro insisted that those who claimed respectability and thus social legitimacy based on their economic and political dominance were immoral.

Thus, Mayoral attempted to wrench the definition of both decency and democracy from the hands of Ponce's dominant classes. He loudly proclaimed that the rich did not have a monopoly on either respectability or political rights. "Don't as many decent families live outside the 'zone of stone' as within it? Don't these families pay taxes, the same as those who live within the zone of stone?" Poor, forthright folk were the true standard-bearers of respectability, fighting against the moral corruption fomented by the rich. This superior popular decency, Canta Claro warned, might soon "fall at the feet of prostitution, ashamed and vanquished."[69]

Indeed, it was the poor's respectability that legitimized their claims on the state and demands for political rights. Mayoral's writings were saturated with references to "poor and decent" people and with calls to defend "the Law, Morality, and Order." He referred to himself frequently as "a peaceful and honorable citizen," seeking justice "in the name of the poor and honorable class."[70] In Mayoral's rhetoric of rights and justice, "civilized" governments owed equal treatment to all honorable citizens, whether rich or poor. Citizenship should no longer be based on wealth but on decency, which, as defined by Mayoral, was potentially available to all men.

This popular respectability did not conform to elite norms; it included public concubinage, interracial partnerships, or serial monogamy. By emphatically proclaiming himself and his neighbors, most of whom were also probably living in non-state-sanctioned sexual arrangements, as honorable, Mayoral openly challenged the dominant honor system and the negative meanings it ascribed to subaltern sexual practices. For Mayoral, for example, poor women of African descent living in concubinage could be respectable. In this sense, then, Canta Claro heralded a new era in popular sexual politics. His was the first public plebeian voice in Ponce's history to draw connections between sexuality and political power. He was also the first plebeian to develop a coherent public discourse that defended specific popular sexual practices and norms. Indeed, Mayoral ultimately based his claim to citizenship on the positive value of the very sexual practices that for so long had been excoriated by both male and female Puerto Rican elites.

But Canta Claro acted as a moral regulator as well as a champion of popular morality. Implicit in his discourse on respectability was the assumption that only the *moral* poor, *as defined by men like him,* should be allowed to participate in the body politic. To be sure, Mayoral defined respectability differently from those controlling state power, but he also drew rigid lines between "moral" and "immoral."

Men in particular should regulate the "proper" behavior of women. In this, the third key tenet of Mayoral's protests, he shared a central assumption with the men who drafted the Hygiene Regulations. For Canta Claro, as for the police and elite commentators of the period, any woman who stepped outside the bounds of acceptable feminine behavior was a prostitute. And once "identified," prostitutes should be shown no mercy. These women were immoral stains on the community, making a previously respectable collectivity a "fount of infection." The women themselves were to blame, not the circumstances that might have caused their behavior. They should be hounded from the city entirely and held in camps in the countryside.[71]

Thus, for all his criticisms of the Liberals and their prostitution policies, Canta Claro heartily concurred with them and all other parties that had produced the regulatory campaign—prostitutes were "disgusting scum" who should be separated from respectable folk. To this self-proclaimed standard-bearer of working-class male political expression, the greatest danger to the health of the new democratic body politic was troublesome *women,* and they could be dealt with effectively only by repression. Ultimately, Canta Claro agreed, however conflictually, with Liberal strategies toward threatening women, although he may not have shared elite racial characterizations.

Mayoral Barnés did not stand alone in his position on unruly women, especially after the implementation of the Reglamento. A Ponce artisan newspaper from 1889 complained about "scandalous" women who were not disciplined sufficiently by police. Similar protests accelerated in the artisan-edited *La Bomba,* "the organ of the people," in 1895 and 1896. Eighty percent of the neighbors who signed Mayoral's petitions and accompanied him in his frequent visits to City Hall were men. Along with seven young artisans, he founded his own newspaper, *Canta Claro,* to protest "the scourge of prostitution." And Mayoral held frequent discussions with his artisan neighbors in a corner barbershop, where he no doubt held forth about the evils of prostitution.[72] Thus, it seems safe to say that Canta Claro's writings crystallized attitudes about sexuality and gender circulating among a good number of

Ponce's laboring men, although Mayoral likely did not speak for all working people, given that interpretations of prostitution varied widely in the city's plebeian neighborhoods.

Whether or not Canta Claro can be proved to be truly representative of "respectable" plebeian male opinion of this period, he certainly emerged as the city's dominant popular political voice of the time. In the end, he was marginalized; his meager financial and political resources were ultimately no match for the Liberal elites of Ponce. Unlike the women targeted as prostitutes, however, Canta Claro was able to appropriate the power of the written word for a short time and force consideration of his opinions in the local halls of power. The antiprostitution campaign provided him a platform from which to intervene in public political discussions.

Despite Mayoral Barnés's more inclusive definitions of democracy and decency, the vociferousness of his writings combined with post-Reglamento resentment in poor neighborhoods temporarily to drown out less restrictive attitudes about female morality and prostitution. By proclaiming himself the sole voice of the disenfranchised, Canta Claro drove alternative plebeian discourses underground, at least in the public debates of the late 1890s. Thus popular intellectuals such as Mayoral are not sui generis liberatory voices. Discourses advocating greater democracy can also enforce hierarchies of privilege and power—in this case one that sought to consolidate male control over female sexual practice, public behavior, and economic activity.[73]

The Ponce campaign to regulate prostitution emerged at a crucial time—a period when the economy was in crisis, society was in great flux, a public hygiene movement lent scientific legitimacy to state intervention into the sexual practices of the poor, and new political actors were appearing on the scene. The Liberal opposition was pushing for expanded democratic rights and constructing a new, racially neutral political discourse, while trying to build a broader political constituency. The regulatory campaign was not a conscious strategy of male elites to contain the challenges to their authority— instead, it emerged out of a rather messy convergence of all these elements. Yet it played a pivotal role in the political alliances and conflicts of the period.

The racialized moral panic that built up around the presence of unruly, supposedly immoral plebeian women in the heart of "decent" Ponce had a complicated ripple effect. In addition to its very negative impact on the lives of the women targeted by police and their neighbors, it produced a closer convergence of elite and popular moral norms than had occurred before. By the late 1890s, almost everyone in Ponce, from "respectable" working-class men and women to bourgeois feminists and elite men from all positions on the political spectrum, could unite in their scorn of "the prostitute." All these groups were "decent" in relation to the (for some, racially) degenerate, "scandalous women," who were now unequivocally considered outside the community of moral citizens.

In addition to uniting many diverse groups, however conflictually, in a common discourse about "decency," the regulatory campaign also hardened and reinforced the boundaries of feminine respectability. No "honorable" woman would dare step outside their limits for fear of being labeled a prostitute. This also held true for the early Puerto Rican feminists, who constructed their sense of respectability and racial superiority in opposition to the darker women of the popular classes. Although they occasionally called for education to save workingwomen from "vice," during the 1890s bourgeois feminists refused to step forward in defense of plebeian women's rights to freedom from police repression and medical surveillance.

The panic over prostitution not only sharpened divisions between elite and plebeian women but also blunted the potential radical edge of the early feminists' sexual theory. The power of feminist attempts to reconceptualize the meaning, role, and practice of sexuality for women was neutralized by a social context that vehemently reinforced the necessity of female monogamy and sexual possession by men. It is surely no coincidence that Ana Roqué de Duprey's novel *Luz y sombra,* in which she laid out her theory of women's right to sexual pleasure, was originally written in 1894 but not actually published for another decade. During the height of antiprostitution fervor, women who wished to remain "honorable" could not safely express such ideas.

Many workingmen, although they may have disagreed with aspects of the regulatory campaign such as its racial resonances, concurred with the basic gendered reasoning behind it. Even within Mayoral and his supporters' sharpening class consciousness, concern for the maintenance of male privilege and control over women could provide a powerful glue binding them to elite men. Ultimately, both feminists and some urban male workers—the potential organized threats to the Liberal project of "the great Puerto Rican family"—made common, although conflictual, cause with those elites who strove to exclude unruly poor women from the Puerto Rico being fashioned during the 1890s. Both groups defined themselves as much by their rejection of "dangerous" (and, for the feminists and perhaps some artisans, darkened) women of the popular classes as by their oppression at the hands of wealthy men.

Consequently, the campaign to regulate prostitution and the resultant moral panic enabled the Liberals to "manage" this very tricky moment of political and cultural flux. They did not plan it this way, but eventually, the campaign worked to their advantage. New groups were allowed into the nascent proto-national community to varying degrees, at the same time as many of their challenges were neutralized. The deepened, unbreachable divisions among women confirmed the apparent permanence of Puerto Rico's social hierarchies and may have made it safer for the Liberals to construct a more inclusive, masculine political project. Concomitantly, as the diseased prostitute became the symbolic receptacle for all that was nasty, immoral, and black, the regulation campaign likely facilitated the erasure of race from the Liberals' political discourse about workingmen.

Thus, the expansion of democracy was built partially in Ponce on the racialized sexual stigmatization of "wayward" working-class women. The marginalization of an already vulnerable group gave the political and cultural order a crucial element of stability, preventing previously excluded groups from posing too radical a threat to Liberal power. It was not until a working-class feminism emerged that a different popular discourse about prostitution and morality would develop—one that resurrected the more flexible, inclusive currents in plebeian communities. Until then, the overwhelming consensus would prevail that unruly women were the scourge of Puerto Rican society and that decent men had the right to discipline them in any way they saw fit.

Chapter 4

Marriage and Divorce in the Formation of the

New Colonial Order, 1898–1910

[The United States] has lifted the anchors which hitherto held it to the American continent, and has drifted far over the seas into that arena of colonial international relations from which it has heretofore striven to keep clear. What the result will be no man can predict. We have primitive civilizations to civilize, indolent populations to stimulate, hostile populations to pacify, ignorant populations to educate, oppressed populations to lift into manhood and teach the principles of liberty and the art of self-government.
—Charles Morris, *Our Island Empire* 1899

The right to divorce heralds the advent of a new civil, republican, and genuinely democratic regime.
—Rafael Toro Vendrell, "Demanda de divorcio—Doña Elisa Guménez y Ramírez contra D. José Colón y Carrasquillo, 1901, AGPR

I don't believe there is a court on this earth that would require me to live with such a low-life man as you. . . . If they have to kill me, you will not get me to return.
—Rafaela Nuñez, "Don Luis Besante y Lespier contra Doña Rafaela Nuñez y Fernández," 1903, AGPR

The U.S. invasion of Puerto Rico in 1898 abruptly interrupted the local Liberal elites' long campaign for social reform, political hegemony, and increased political and economic autonomy for the island. The previous thirty years of debates over national identity were redirected by powerful, new colonial interests. For a time after the invasion, Creole elites readily embraced their new subordinate role in hopes of higher profits, expanded local political influence, and the maintenance of social hierarchies. As I will show, Puerto Rico was also shoved along new routes by increasing pressures from working people. The protests by Canta Claro of Liberal policies in Ponce were not the only popular explosion unleashed in the aftermath of the U.S. occupation.

In the early years (1898–1910) of the United States's "encounter" with Puerto Rico, a new colonial construction of the island's state and society began. Once again, family and sexual relations became a focus of efforts to reshape Puerto Rico. But the new colonial administration was not overly interested in the "plague of prostitution" that had so galvanized the "decent" population of Ponce during the 1890s. Rather, like the early Liberal Autonomists, U.S. colonial officials hoped to incorporate the Puerto Rican masses into their new project through moral reformation, among other strategies. Colonial officials and informal agents alike believed that "Americanizing" the family would legitimate the emerging colonial order. They endeavored to homogenize their new colonial subjects sexually, to reduce diverse popular sexual practices and morals to a unified standard of heterosexual marriage and two-parent families, thus instilling their Anglo-Saxon, bourgeois social and cultural ideals in the island's populace. Therefore, remaking familial sexual arrangements held the attention of authorities during the first years of the U.S. occupation. The legalization of divorce, along with the facilitation of civil marriage, quickly became important elements of early U.S. efforts to bring racially fluid Puerto Rican moral "backwardness" up to the "modern" standards of the self-styled "civilizer of primitive nations." Purging prostitution from urban spaces temporarily dropped from the political agenda.

In Puerto Rico, feminist agitation did not legalize divorce, as in Europe, the United States, and much of the rest of Latin America. Puerto Rican feminists did not broach the issue of divorce in the nineteenth century. Instead, in an ironic twist of history, male U.S. colonial officials, with the eventual collaboration of local male elites, institutionalized the right to full divorce much earlier in Puerto Rico (1902) than occurred elsewhere in Latin America.[1]

Colonial officials hoped that shifting the legal structures of marriage and the family in Puerto Rico would overcome the deep-seated reluctance to marry among the island's popular classes. By reforming the sexual practices and definitions of the Puerto Rican poor, colonial agents and local elites sought to produce a recognizable, acceptable order in the island's domestic and public life. The benevolent paternalism of successful U.S. colonialism would ideally be mirrored in and consolidated by the new definitions of marriage and divorce. Early U.S. strategies in Puerto Rico confirm that definitions of morality and sexuality lie at the heart of colonial power relations. In Puerto Rico, the dream of sexually disciplining the popular classes went hand in hand with the creation of new forms of male dominance over women. Both, it seemed to officials, were key to colonial success.

But definition of sexual arrangements in Puerto Rico did not lie only in the hands of imperial authorities and local elites. Broadening the scope of legally sanctioned marriage elicited little interest among Puerto Ricans. Access to divorce, on the other hand, unleashed a quiet flood of popular response. Married women flocked to the courts to demand divorces in the early twentieth century. Although previously ignored by Puerto Rican historians, their actions constituted one of the many popular eruptions of discontent after Spain's rule collapsed—perhaps less dramatic but more widespread and certainly more enduring than the famous partidas sediciosas who sacked Spanish properties in the wake of the U.S. occupation.[2] The surge of early-twentieth-century divorce petitions expressed a resurfacing of the long-standing yearnings of Puerto Rican women for more egalitarian gender relations that bourgeois feminists had partially articulated during the 1890s: reliable economic support, an end to the sexual double standard, and safety from male violence. In their appeals to the courts for divorce, Puerto Rican women voiced their keen awareness that marriage was not necessarily a homogenizing, stabilizing institution, as colonial officials and elite Puerto Rican men insisted. Rather, bitter struggles over gendered interests and power imbalances often lay at its heart. Now even plebeian women had a formal forum in which to voice their demands, however diffusely, and to receive some type of legal redress—however feeble and inadequate.

Indeed, divorce is an illuminating example of the complexity of U.S. colonialism in Puerto Rico. The right to divorce, like the eight-hour workday, trial by jury, and the right of habeas corpus, was imposed by the United States on a sometimes reluctant Puerto Rican elite. These progressive reforms were not a product of U.S. benevolence. Rather, they were state concessions which had been politicized through decades of struggle by marginalized groups within the United States and which were then exported as part of an allegedly "gentle, civilizing" colonial project.[3] Puerto Rican popular backing for such reforms was immediate and enthusiastic. Their institutionalization planted the roots of a deep support for U.S. rule. The legalization of divorce under the rubric of equalizing legal rights confirms Alice Conklin's contention that in addition to extracting profits and creating hierarchical differences, modern colonialism has "had a universalizing and democratic component" that has given it powerful legitimizing force.[4] But implementation of divorce and its sister reforms was not sufficient to ensure justice on the island. The Puerto Rican women who sought marital equity in the new judicial system discovered, as did workers, Afro-Puerto Ricans, and other marginalized groups, that there were quite severe limits to the new colonial order, however benevolent it may have seemed at its inception.

Divorce in the Nineteenth Century

Throughout the nineteenth century, divorce was virtually impossible to obtain in Puerto Rico. The Spanish Civil Code of 1889 did finally grant the possibility of civil matrimony and divorce from nonreligious marriages. But the state did not hear religious divorce petitions. Practically all marriages continued to be performed by the Catholic Church; ecclesiastical courts were the only body that could dissolve these bonds of marriage.

Divorce was staunchly resisted by church officials. After receiving a petition, years generally passed with no decision by the ecclesiastical officials. All but three of the admitted divorce petitions for the entire colony of Puerto Rico between 1840 and 1898 had no final verdict. Of the three that did receive a decision, only one, involving quite wealthy families, was granted an annulment. It is quite conceivable that the petitioning wife bought this release from her husband's physical abuse. The other two were conceded only temporary separations, despite the husbands' proof of their wife's lengthy extramarital affairs.[5]

Perhaps this is why, from 1840 to 1898, only twenty-six cases from the entire island were filed and pursued to this advanced stage. Puerto Ricans knew that seeking a divorce, no matter how grave the conflict between spouses, was a losing proposition. The vast majority of those who did persist in requesting divorce from the ecclesiastical courts were women, who filed twenty-two of the twenty-six cases.

Male adultery clearly caused great pain to many women. Doña Salustiana Capó, for example, bitterly testified that her husband was always gallivanting about with *queridas* (sweethearts). His most troublesome mistress was a woman who had borne him a child before his marriage with Doña Salustiana and whom he continued to visit regularly. The "illicit" relationship had now produced another child; her husband had legally recognized both children. It may well have been this "indiscreet and insistent" public acknowledgment of his extramarital relationship rather than its existence per se that drove Doña Salustiana to denounce her husband's adultery so vehemently.[6] However, husbands' infidelity was not the petitioners' principal complaint; it was raised in only one-fourth of the cases filed.

Abandonment or lack of male financial support, which would become the central issue in twentieth-century divorce cases, was mentioned in only five of the cases (23 percent) as well. The low incidence of abandonment charges was probably due to popular awareness that the church refused to grant divorces; it was useless to waste precious time and money requesting a formal dissolution of marriage. Moreover, among the popular classes, it may have been relatively common for a woman who had been abandoned by her husband simply to look for another man who would establish an informal relationship and provide some modicum of financial support to her and her children. Given the widespread practice of serial consensual union among Puerto Rican working people, it was probably not too difficult to find a new partner, regardless of one's marital status. Some women of the more moneyed classes, such as Nieves Gastón, whose case I discussed in Chapter 1, also entered into nonmarital sexual relationships once they had been abandoned by their husbands. However, most probably did not dare to flaunt social convention so openly; they often returned to live with their families.[7] One thing remains clear: financial abandonment was not legitimate grounds for divorce in the church's eyes under any circumstance, and Puerto Rican women knew it.

The driving force behind women's divorce petitions in the nineteenth century was domestic violence. Every one of the women plaintiffs unequivocally stated that she could no longer bear her husband's physical abuse.[8] Women of all social strata—from wealthy white owners of numerous properties to Afro-Puerto Rican laundresses—spilled out stories to church authorities of brutal beatings, lashings with horsewhips, and knife wounds. These women must have known that they had no chance of actually being formally released from their abusive marriages. Once a divorce petition had been accepted, however, the church was obliged to place the woman in *depósito,* in the home and under the care of a "respectable family." Meanwhile, the husband was to pay for his wife's room and board and in theory was denied access to her personal property. The husband was also prohibited from harassing or visiting his wife during the course of the divorce proceedings. Thus, most of the nineteenth-century women petitioners demanded to be placed in depósito. It served as both protection from male abuse and a way to get access to some financial support.

This protection came at a high cost, though. The depósito was designed to contain physically women who sought to escape their husband's control. Close surveillance was a requirement of any depósito placement, to "protect the husband's honor" until his wife could be returned to him. Women in depósito were not allowed to venture out of their designated living space unaccompanied, have social interactions, or engage in any outside economic transactions. Women unable to propose an acceptable depósito placement were placed in the Casa de Beneficencia, the San Juan asylum for the mentally ill and prison for sexually wayward women.

Plebeian women divorce petitioners faced an especially onerous existence, for they were expected to work for the families with whom they were placed (and to whom they were paying monthly "support" fees). Depósito essentially locked them into enforced domestic servitude. Afro-Puerto Rican Juana Soler, for example, married a mulatto artisan after obtaining her freedom from slavery. After suffering months of beatings from her husband, Juana filed a divorce petition with the church. She was placed in judicial depósito in the house of her former owners. Juana was left there, laboring in exchange for their "protection" indefinitely. No verdict was ever decreed in her case.[9]

The depósito became a battleground where estranged wives, husbands, placement heads of households, and church officials struggled over whose interests the institution would serve. Some women managed to have their own families designated as the depósito placement; they certainly enjoyed more autonomy than did such women as Juana Soler.[10] But most women petitioners of modest means were not so fortunate. Some plebeian women refused to perform the labor expected of them in placement households, or they simply escaped and looked for work elsewhere. Micaela Díaz provides a good example. She insisted that her abusive husband was too poor to pay her depósito costs: "Since I must attend to my own subsistence, I must be at liberty to look for a house of good antecedents and morals where I can rent myself out, and where they will pay me a monthly wage in addition to my food so that I can buy clothing and shoes."[11]

Husbands had the right, however, to contest placements if they thought their wives were being treated too leniently. The church tended to uphold their patriarchal right to control their wife's physical movement and social and economic interactions. Juan Portalín, Micaela Díaz's day-laborer husband, complained that Micaela "intends to wander about freely from house to house. . . . The depósito of a married woman is not undefined; it is not intended to serve her pleasure. . . . I cannot, I should not be required to consent to this diversity of depósito to which my wife aspires. It insults my authority, it slanders me, it torments me. She has made a vile toy of my honor." The ecclesiastical tribunal agreed with Juan. Within a few weeks, church officials not only denied Micaela's petition for a more flexible depósito but also canceled her divorce petition, effectively denying her any protection from her husband's beatings she might have won.[12]

Thus under Spanish rule the prospects for Puerto Rican women seeking redress for domestic violence or other marital conflicts were bleak. The small number of divorce petitions filed during the nineteenth century reflected this harsh reality. The U.S. occupation and the resultant reforms in family law would elicit a very different reaction.

The New Colonial Order

The invasion by the United States was met with open arms by most Puerto Ricans. Local elites dreamed of vast markets for their coffee and sugar once free trade with the great northern power was established. U.S. capital, they were sure, would also establish banks for desperately needed agricultural credit. The leadership of the Liberal Autonomist Party (soon to become the Federales) never considered that their hard-won local political autonomy might not be respected by the world standard-bearer of democracy. Initially, both they and the opposition Republicanos were enthusiastically proannexationist.[13] Statehood would mean economic prosperity with continued, perhaps even expanded political power for local elites and a careful maintenance of social hierarchies.

Working people also celebrated the U.S. occupation, but for very different reasons. Overall, they saw the United States as a liberator from Spanish (in which they included local elites) oppression. Most plebeian Puerto Ricans expected that the United States, with its growing labor movement and its reputation as a great democratic nation, would usher in a golden era for workers. Influxes of capital would expand employment opportunities. New, abundant imports would provide cheaper food and basic goods for the working classes. A benevolent state would now intervene on behalf of workers. And perhaps most important, especially for Puerto Ricans of African descent, the principles of the United States Constitution seemed to hold out a radical promise of social and legal equality for all people. Certainly the Puerto Rican elites who had owned their parents as slaves and currently exploited their labor were not to be trusted to implement important social reforms. Antonio "el negro" Guilbe, for example, shocked the Ponce elite and delighted local plebeians by parading through the streets gun in hand, with a U.S. flag wrapped around his shoulders, his crowd of companions loudly cursing members of the city elite. The Republicanos, in particular, used such sentiments to win Afro-Puerto Rican support for their party and for annexation to the United States. Thus, hoping for economic well-being and the overthrow of social hierarchies, the working classes of Puerto Rico also initially welcomed U.S. rule as a great step toward a more just future.[14]

Some of the early moves by the new rulers of Puerto Rico seemed to confirm popular expectations. Colonial officials implemented many Progressive Era reform experiments from the United States on the island. Sanitation brigades were set up quickly in larger cities such as Ponce, where open sewage was a serious health hazard.[15] Colonial officials and U.S. observers noted the popular "thirst" for instruction. Before too long, the skeleton of a free public education system for both boys and girls was established. A national normal school, the University of Puerto Rico, opened in 1903.[16] Trial by jury and the right of habeas corpus were instituted for the first time in 1899. And in April and May of that year, Major General Henry, the commanding officer of the U.S. occupying forces, decreed the eight-hour workday and exempted all working women and men from income taxes.[17]

But the new, allegedly compassionate colonial order had its ominous side as well. The same decree which established that "eight hours in twenty four shall be considered a day's work in the Island" also declared that only property owners could be members of municipal councils. Just a few months later, the new presiding U.S. military officer ordered that only literate or tax-paying adult men could vote. This marked a substantial restriction of voting rights from the universal male suffrage won from Spain in the Autonomy Charter of 1898. In addition, those eligible to run for office were further restricted to the wealthiest two-thirds of each municipality's taxpayer rolls.[18]

The warning signs were not restricted only to electoral matters. Colonial charity boards set up to dispense public relief after a devastating hurricane in 1899 soon developed a variety of methods to coerce impoverished rural Puerto Ricans into plantation labor. Racist attacks by white U.S. soldiers on

Afro-Puerto Ricans were not uncommon. The U.S. generals Guy Henry and George Davis severely checked the freedom of the island's press, allowing no criticism of the military government in Puerto Rico or U.S. neocolonial policy in Cuba. The United States's highly touted "gifts" of social equality and freedom of speech stopped at imperialism's door.[19]

The colonial handwriting was indelibly inscribed on the wall with the passage of the Foraker Act by the U.S. Congress in 1900. This legislation finally instituted civil government in Puerto Rico and established the anxiously awaited free trade between the United States and the island. But the structure of governance imposed on Puerto Rico was much more restrictive than that won by the Autonomists from Spain in 1898. The governor and a majority of the legislature's "high" chamber, which doubled as a Cabinet, were to be North Americans appointed by the U.S. president. The remaining members of both legislative chambers could be Puerto Ricans elected by popular (although restricted) male vote. All laws passed by the Legislative Assembly, however, were subject to approval by the U.S. Congress. The presiding judge of Puerto Rico, along with all members of the island's Supreme Court, was also to be appointed by the U.S. president. New civil and penal legal codes were to be drawn up; the priority was not to make the legal system more just but to make it "compatible" with United States law. It was in the context of this general legal overhaul that the debates over marriage and divorce took place in Puerto Rico.[20] This "modern" colonialism both excluded and included its new subjects from its democratic promise.

The United States government was willing to use force if necessary to maintain its tight control over Puerto Rico's politics and economy. A military government had been maintained for over two years after the initial invasion, despite there being no evidence of meaningful anti-U.S. sentiment. But most colonial officials were well aware that there were limits to how much could be openly imposed upon the island's populace. The success of a peaceful, "benevolent" colonial enterprise in Puerto Rico was crucial if imperialist advocates within the U.S. were to defuse domestic critics and counter the anxieties fueled by nationalist insurgencies in Cuba and the Philippines.[21]

Also, social relations among the Puerto Rican popular classes seemed bafflingly fluid. To white North American eyes, the island's coastal plebeian communities were indiscriminately interracial. Generations of open sexual and social racial mingling had produced a confusing "racial mass," within which blacks and whites could not be easily distinguished. Such flexible racial relations and identities were unintelligible—and consequently inferior—to white North Americans steeped in the United States's rigidly bipolar racial system. The Puerto Rican laboring classes were believed to be just as unrestrained in their sexual behavior as they were in drawing racial boundaries. They seemed to have sex often and with many people, creating large families and living in consensual union rather than marrying.[22]

This alleged dissoluteness marked plebeian Puerto Ricans as childish or even prehuman. "They sin, but they sin only as animals, without shame, because there is no sense of doing wrong. . . . They are innocently happy in the unconsciousness of the obligations of morality. They eat, drink, sleep, and smoke, and do the least in the way of work they can. They have no ideas of duty, and therefore are not made uneasy by neglecting it."[23] For the most part, then, the Puerto Rican poor were represented by the new colonial officials as innocently inert, slumbering in a premoral natural state, ready to be shaped into civilized adults by the guiding hand of the United States. Puerto Rico, like Europe's colonies, could become a "laboratory of modernity," as well as a site of efficient exploitation.[24]

Ultimately, the efficacy of U.S. reforms and rule over the island would have to be based on a thorough "Americanization" of Puerto Rican society. Puerto Rico might even serve as a showcase for how to deal with the thousands of immigrants from southern and eastern Europe who were flooding into United States cities. Much of the preoccupation of mainland Progressive Era reformers with assimilation of foreigners was echoed in the reports of colonial observers.[25] As an early military governor of Puerto Rico stated, "Allowances must be made for the difference in customs, in language and the associations of years, all of which are hard to eliminate in a short time, *but which must be changed before any advance can be made.*"[26]

Local culture and the social relations of everyday life would have to be altered to consolidate colonial rule. Whether or not the total assimilation of Puerto Ricans to the bourgeois, white, Anglo-Saxon, Protestant model of American culture were possible, at the very least colonial officials sought to eliminate any resistant edges from Puerto Ricans' attitudes toward "things American." Progressive reforms would cement the popular classes' allegiance to the United States. A rudimentary education in the trappings of American patriotism was to be substituted for Puerto Ricans' sense of their own history. English would be taught systematically in the new public school system; by 1907 it had become the primary language of instruction. Protestant missionaries from the United States were encouraged to evangelize the population. And finally, a more modern familial policy was necessary if the "backward" Puerto Rican social system was to be replaced with a "rational" North American one.

Benevolent Discipline: Marriage and Divorce Reform

The family forms, sexual practices, and morality of island residents—particularly those of the laboring classes—were an ever present subtext in the U.S.-authored hearings, reports, and commentaries about Puerto Rico that proliferated in the first years of North American rule. For colonial agents, moral standing was a potent marker of identity, of one's very relationship to civilization. U.S. observers and local elites alike were concerned about the high incidence of consensual unions, serial sexual relationships, and female-headed households among the popular classes on the island. All agreed that the island's 50 percent out-of-wedlock birthrate was unacceptable. A productive, properly disciplined workforce and stable political order could be built only on a base of marriage and "legitimate" families. As A. C. Sharpe, the colonial attorney general for Puerto Rico, said in 1899: "Family life is the recognized basis of true civilization. American law and institutions regard the relation of the husband and wife as one of the most sacred guaranties for the perpetuity of the state. Marriage is recognized as the only lawful relation by which Providence has permitted the continuance of the human race, and the history of mankind has proved it to be one of the chief foundations of social order."[27] Thus, in an eerie echo of local Liberals' early rhetoric, U.S. colonial officials insisted that the push to bring the island out of an inert, disordered state of nature and into civilized ways of life had to begin within the home. The relatively fluid popular Puerto Rican definitions of the family had to be regulated and homogenized into a unified standard. Marriage was key; it would help establish an acceptable social order under the eye of the state.

Consequently, the inculcation of marriage on a mass scale was a serious matter. A series of legal reforms were quickly instituted in hopes of encouraging the Puerto Rican popular classes to marry. In March 1899, the legalization of civil marriages was confirmed by decree and municipal judges prohibited from charging fees for performing the ceremony. Two years later, this stipulation was codified and broadened in the civil marriage reform law. The legislation was enthusiastically endorsed by the governor, who wrote that it "is intended to and should accomplish a great moral reform on the island."[28] Hopes were still high when the following year a law was passed that granted the right to celebrate marriages to all ministers, rabbis, and judges on the island. Governor Hunt gushed that "scarcely any act of the legislative assembly was more important."[29]

Yet there is no evidence that all these attempts to make marriage more accessible to the poor of Puerto Rico had any significant effect. The census data from the first decade of the twentieth century shows a relatively stable rate of marriage, hovering around 50 percent. The roots of plebeian alternative conceptions of respectability and conjugal life were much deeper than U.S. officials had ever dreamed. Many laboring Puerto Ricans were actively *un*interested in marrying—not simply prevented from doing so. It was the right to divorce, not access to marriage, that eventually provoked a popular explosion of interest.

This was the second thrust of colonial officials' attempts to lure Puerto Ricans to marriage. Accessibility was not the only key. Marriage also had to be made more attractive. As they pushed for the legalization of divorce on the island, North American officials asserted that people might be more likely to marry if they could leave a marital situation gone awry. Women in particular, they feared, resisted marrying because it allowed them no escape from bad relationships.[30] The right to divorce would hopefully popularize marriage. Indeed, picking up on mainland feminist arguments, officials implied that the right to divorce would actually transform marriage. Being able to leave unworkable relationships would help ensure that the marriage contract would be based on freely chosen love. Those whose relationships endured would enjoy happy matches; those who severed the marital tie would have the chance to choose a more satisfactory partner in the future. The result would be more democratic, less "despotic" marriages—a neat analogy to the change from Spanish to North American colonial regime.[31]

The interest in full divorce did not spring only from colonial officials, however. Petitions for relief from husbands' violence, lack of financial support, and release from unwanted relationships began to arrive at the governor's palace as soon as word spread that the new colonial administration was sympathetic to divorce.[32] Popular pressures for the full legalization of divorce were joined by that from many prominent members of both Puerto Rican elite-led political parties, who had long been staunch anticlericalists and advocates of marital reform.[33] Liberal political activists such as Rafael Toro

Vendrell welcomed this shift as a crucial step toward democracy and freedom. Rather than a threat to stability, divorce represented liberation from the unjust exercise of power, "a step forward in defense of family happiness."[34] Toro Vendrell proclaimed that "the singular importance of the transition from the rigid military system to the governance of the people by the people is that it affects the ties of matrimony and family, which until now condemned husbands and wives to suffer perpetually the unhappiness and misfortune of a misguided choice or of an unforeseen disgrace."[35]

United States colonial officials did not have a completely free hand in reforming divorce law on the island, though. Initially, some conservative elites emphatically opposed the moves.[36] However, the 1902 Civil and Penal Codes drafted by Puerto Rico's Legislative Assembly in a general overhaul of the island's legal system included greatly expanded divorce provisions. The legalization of full divorce does not seem to have generated significant debate in the assembly. Concomitantly, very little discussion of divorce appeared in the Puerto Rican press after 1901. Thus, it appears that despite the opposition of some powerful Puerto Ricans in 1899, by 1902 a consensus had been reached that a broadened application of divorce was either acceptable or unavoidable.[37]

Despite the legalization of full divorce, the new Civil Code retained a number of key patriarchal rights; they probably helped gain the support of the more conservative Puerto Rican politicians. Although wives were now allowed to represent themselves and their property in court as well as to exercise professions, husbands were still the only legal representatives of the "conjugal unit" and retained sole rights to administer marital property. Wives could not use conjugal property for anything other than the "purchase of articles for the use of the family." Every wife was also still explicitly required to "obey her husband and follow him where he elects to reside."[38] *Patria potestad* (parental authority over children) was supposedly transformed from an exclusive male right to one shared by both husband and wife. But the 1902 code stated that "if there should be any disagreement between the husband and the wife, the decision of the husband shall prevail in all cases relating to family affairs."[39] As in the broader colonial project, democratization and benevolent rule had their limits; the heralded legal transformation of marriage still codified male power over women.

It was probably in the area of divorce that the new Civil Code most directly affected the lives of ordinary Puerto Ricans. For most people of the laboring classes, stipulations regarding property and its control were largely irrelevant, for they owned very little. The right to end relationships, however, potentially affected all married couples, regardless of class. The 1902 code made all marriages civil contracts, regardless of the religion of the participants or the celebrant. Consequently, even Catholic marriages could now be legally dissolved. The grounds for divorce were also greatly expanded, now including adultery by either spouse without gender distinctions, "cruel treatment" by either party, habitual drunkenness or narcotics use, and the abandonment of either party for more than a year. The sexual double standard faced a potential legal challenge. Violent, unworkable, or unreliable marital relationships could now be terminated. It would not take long for the popular response to materialize.

The Demand for Divorce

Word spread quickly among those excluded from the circles of formal colonial power that the previously lifelong bonds of marriage could be broken. Soon, women and men began to stream into the courts to demand divorces. Their petitions gave voice to popular definitions of marriage that often diverged sharply from those of colonial officials. Women's anguished testimony in particular put the lie to colonial assertions that marriage was the basis of peaceful social order. Rather, their petitions illuminated the struggles over gender power relations that permeated familial life.

The new judicial forum shifted the terms of these struggles. Although women still could not effectively discipline men into compliance with their side of the marital contract, they could at least obtain officially sanctioned release from unbearable relationships. For many Puerto Ricans, especially women, divorce would become one of the institutional changes that distinguished the *época de los americanos* (time of the Americans) from *los tiempos aquellos, cuando los españoles* (that time long ago, when the Spaniards ruled) and cemented already strong support for U.S. rule among the popular classes. Although this support remained intact, broadly speaking, through the first decades of the twentieth century, it did not reliably produce the kinds of social behaviors that colonial officials desired. Puerto Ricans enthusiastically took advantage of institutional openings established by the new, "benevolent" colonial regime. They did not, however, docilely embrace the homogenizing colonial vision of family and society. Neither the civilizing effects of marriage nor a man's right to uncontested power over his wife was accepted by the Puerto Rican women who filled civil courts with their divorce petitions.

The marital reforms codified under the new colonial regime produced a set of options quite different from those available in the nineteenth century. Although judicial records did not mention the race of petitioners or defendants, we can tell that divorce was utilized by women and men of all social classes in the twentieth century. Despite the island's high rate of consensual unions, plebeian Puerto Ricans did marry—enough, in any case, to now request divorce in significant numbers.[40] As in the nineteenth century, women were the majority of the plaintiffs; they constituted two-thirds of all divorce petitioners. The results they achieved were much more reliable, though, than under the previous regime: by 1909, obtaining a divorce generally took only a few months, and rarely was a petition denied. Indeed, by the end of the first decade of U.S. rule, divorce had become legal routine, a prosaic institutionalized practice.[41] This was a far cry from the long years that nineteenth-century women petitioners spent languishing in depósito, waiting for a response from church officials, usually to have their petitions rejected.

The response to divorce legalization was striking. Divorce petitions steadily rose from a minuscule share (1.5 percent) of all civil cases filed in the jurisdiction of Ponce during 1900 and 1901 (*N* = 651 for the two years combined) to a fifth of all Ponce civil cases filed during 1911 (*N* = 253).[42] It seems safe to assume that at least in the other island coastal districts that encompassed the majority of the population, the response was similarly enthusiastic. When compared with the numbers of divorce cases filed during the nineteenth century, these figures are even more remarkable. More than six times as many divorce cases were filed in a twelve-year period—and in a single judicial district—than were filed for the entire island in the preceding sixty years. Puerto Ricans' use of divorce also appears to have continued throughout the early twentieth century. Although systematic archival research was not done for the years following 1911, Ponce newspapers reported several divorces a day in the municipality throughout 1917 and 1918.

What prompted Puerto Ricans to request divorce in ever increasing numbers? What were they hoping to obtain by doing so? To understand its popular meanings in the early twentieth century and divorce's possible ramifications for colonial hegemony requires examination of Puerto Ricans' expectations of marriage. The meaning of marriage for Puerto Ricans was not based on a single marital code, such as U.S. colonial officials sought to establish. Rather, marriage was a contested patriarchal pact that linked sexual, reproductive, and economic rights and obligations. Men and women generally knew what they were expected to deliver in a marriage. But a great deal of contention simmered under the surface of this broad consensus; men and women had different definitions of what constituted acceptable behavior and power relations within the broad parameters of gendered marital roles.

The ability to provide financially for one's family, a prime element in male honor, emerged in divorce petitions as the most important expectation of men's marital performance. Husbands were expected to *ponerle casa* (provide a home) for their wives; this ideally meant setting up a household separately from both partners' families, even if only in a rented room. If a married couple could not afford to live on their own, a good husband at least lived with his wife and contributed to the larger family income on a regular basis.[43]

Ramón Alvarado, an impoverished day laborer, tried to excuse himself from these requirements by arguing to the court that work close to home was hard to find. But several male neighbors, rural wage laborers themselves, rejected his statement. They condemned the fact that Ramón did "not support his wife, nor attend to her needs." He even refused to live with her. Now she was reduced to scraping by on her own, picking coffeee and washing other people's clothes.[44]

As intimated by this testimony, married women of all classes hoped that their husband's earnings would be sufficient to release them from the necessity of working outside the home. This remained an unobtainable dream for most women of the popular classes; their income was generally an indispensable part of the family budget. At the very least, however, wives insisted that they should not have to be the sole support of the household.[45]

Regardless of the percentage of the familial income they earned, wives were responsible for all the domestic labor of the household. Middle- and upper-class women simply supervised the labor of their servant women, but plebeian women worked long, hard hours in their own homes as well as in those of other women. Cooking, cleaning, washing clothes, caring for children, and finding firewood, water, and foodstuffs and bringing them to the home were all women's jobs. This was unpaid labor automatically owed to any man who provided a woman with financial support. Women seemed to agree that they were responsible for all domestic work, for conflicts over this issue seldom arose in divorce petitions.

Husbands expected their wife to be monogamous, also asserting their right to sexual access on demand, regardless of their wife's desires. Women seemed hard-pressed to control when they had sex with their partner as long as they continued to receive money from him. María Rita Ortiz, for example, left her husband and moved in with her parents to escape his beatings. But because he did not stop sending her portions of his weekly wages, she felt that she could not deny him his *vida marital.* For three months, until she filed for divorce, he visited her secretly at night to demand sex from her at her parents' home. She reluctantly complied, as a good wife was required to do.[46] Not all women were so compliant, however. José Martínez moaned that his wife "has always maliciously denied [me] my conjugal rights. She has thus caused me all sort of moral suffering, even to the point of disturbing my health, making me lose a huge amount of weight, and causing me great mental anguish."[47]

Evidently, although conventional wisdom assigned wives and husbands clearly demarcated roles in marriage—sex and domestic labor from women in exchange for financial support from men—the terms of the marital contract were contested. Women struggled against the onerous definitions of marital authority that men attempted to impose on them. Men generally agreed that their primary responsibility was to support their family financially. But they often asserted that if they did so, they should have free rein in the treatment of their wife. Don José Colón y Carrasquillo, for example, readily admitted that he exhibited a "bad character," regularly insulted and publicly humiliated his wife, and even committed "physical excesses." But to do so was his right, he insisted, because he had never failed to provide for her financially.[48]

Many men feared women's challenge to their authority. This, they insisted, was the root of the violence that often exploded within families. Female insubordination was unacceptable. Juan José Príncipe defended his unremitting beatings of his wife in these terms in a letter to his mother-in-law: "She . . . wanted to give orders more than her owner," thus she deserved every slap she had received. "Sooner or later, she will have to obey. I know the duties of matrimony, but you have not taught them to her. . . . You are foolish if you believe that I am going to let a woman do what she likes with me like all those other 'good' husbands."[49] A reporter for *La Democracia* concurred with this vision of absolute male authority, writing that a wife "should never allow [her husband] to treat her other than as a child . . . she should never openly challenge her husband's ideas. Above all, she should prevent herself from causing the marital 'scenes' that are always avoidable."[50]

Thus, for many men, women's conjugal duties were not restricted to provision of sex and domestic labor. A wife should also submit unconditionally to her husband. And if she did not, a man had the right to "discipline" her in any way he saw fit.

Women, however, disagreed. Wives did generally accept that they owed domestic labor and sexual fidelity to their husband if they received regular financial support. They were also keenly aware that without at least a portion of a male income, most of them were only one step away from starvation. But male violence and the sexual double standard rankled them. Women knew that the quid pro quo of marriage and heterosexual partnership in general was an unequal exchange.

We saw earlier that plebeian women consistently subverted their partner's attempts at surveillance and control. The married women who appeared in twentieth-century divorce courts were no different. They protested their husband's extramarital affairs, which drained precious financial resources and sometimes publicly humiliated them. They resisted domestic violence through familial and informal community intervention, often calling on neighborhood networks of women.[51] They argued back and sometimes even hit back when their husband's assertions of authority became too severe.

If these strategies failed to make their marriages livable, no small number of wives left their husbands, usually to start up a relationship with another man who they hoped would treat them better or provide more adequately for them and their children. For some, then, plebeian women's assertion of their right to serial monogamy did not stop at the gates of marriage. Adultery and, as the decade progressed, abandonment were the primary causes for men's divorce petitions. Three-fifths of all cases filed by men ($N = 47$) alleged abandonment of the conjugal household. All but three linked their wife's refusal to return to the woman's establishment of a live-in relationship with another man. An additional quarter of male petitions alleged wifely adultery. Nine-tenths of men's divorce complaints, then, hinged on women's sexual relationships with other men. Clearly, all wives did not passively accept their husband's claim to total dominance. In effect, these women's actions constituted a popular, informal divorce practice. Its roots lay in plebeian moral norms forged in an era when legal divorce had been unavailable.

Most women so accused went to great pains to explain that they had not stepped outside the normative limits of wifely behavior by choice but had been driven there. Juana Evangelista Rodríguez, the wife of a shopkeeper, testified that "if her husband had not abandoned her with a child, denying the necessities of life to both of them, she would not have thrown herself into the arms of another man. Although she recognizes that her husband has a legitimate basis on which to divorce her, she wishes to clarify the desperate situation in which she found herself forced to live with another. This would have never happened otherwise, for while she lived with her husband, she was always faithful to him—she never wavered in her conjugal loyalty, not even in her thoughts."[52] These women agreed with the requirement of female monogamy. But financial necessity took precedence over absolute moral principles. And ultimately, in their responses to their husband's accusation, "adulterous" wives asserted, however humbly, that the roots of female infidelity lay in male irresponsibility.

As discussed in previous chapters, a man's "right" to exclusive sexual ownership of his wife was a linchpin of male power. The violation of this "right" was the basis of most husbands' divorce petitions. For men, female abandonment was a code word for adultery. Women also denounced men's abandonment of them in divorce court, but their grievances differed from those of male petitioners. The meaning of abandonment, like that of so many other popular concepts, was gendered; women did not define men's abandonment primarily as sexual but focused on men's chief marital function—money.

In the nineteenth century, most wives who requested divorce were seeking protection from domestic violence. After implementation of the 1902 Civil Code, however, a different profile appeared: male abuse or adultery still figured prominently in a significant number of women's petitions, but the vast majority (85 percent) cited financial and physical abandonment as the principal cause of their requests.

Because many plebeian women became interested in marriage only when they could no longer trust that male income would be regularly available, the steady availability of financial support was key in the decision to enter or reject marriage. Likewise, once divorce became widely available, women of all classes appear to have chosen this option only after all informal methods of familial and community intervention failed to force the husband to meet his financial responsibilities. Thus the defining issue for women in heterosexual relationships continued to be reliable access to male income. Generally only when husbands definitively violated this aspect of the conjugal quid pro quo would wives petition for divorce.

Certainly, domestic violence remained a presence in many women's lives. Thirty percent of women's twentieth-century divorce petitions described extensive beatings and cited them as important bases for the divorce request. But violent partners were not much more likely to be disciplined by the courts under U.S. rule than they had been during the Spanish colonial era. No legal or institutional protection was available to battered women short of divorce, and most women, especially mothers, were too dependent on their partner's income to risk that option. (Only 15 percent of all petitions were based solely on male violence.) Thus, until male financial input became totally unreliable, women generally seem to have found ways to live with their husband's violence, keeping it in check as best they could. Numerous wives spoke of their "constant efforts to appease [their] husbands and to maintain domestic peace."[53] Like the women discussed in Chapter 1, battered wives called on family members to intervene on their behalf, fled to their neighbors and friends, and, in the last resort, called in the police.[54]

Similarly, men's insistence on having multiple sexual partners continued to inflict great pain and stress on women in the twentieth century. Like the bourgeois feminists of the 1890s, female divorce petitioners of all classes spoke bitterly of their husband's infidelities. The wealthy Ezequiela Rosa del Busto complained that her husband had carried on an affair for many years. Her description of her "respectably" silent suffering would have made her a perfect heroine in one of the nineteenth-century feminist novels. "Extraordinarily prudent, for many long years I put up with this insult to my dignity; in silence I wept the tears that the screws of jealousy squeezed from my love, and forgave—even if I could never forget—the continual disturbances that my unfaithful husband incited in the intimacy of our home."[55]

Plebeian women also resented husbands' extramarital wanderings. Mercedes Velez, the wife of a mechanic, testified angrily that "letting himself be dragged along by his lowest passions, [her husband] frequently fled the loving attentions of his wife in order to run about tasting the repulsive caresses of despicable prostitutes."[56] As noted in previous chapters, women of the laboring classes not only suffered the emotional stress and social shame they shared with wealthier wives but also were locked in intense economic competition with their husband's mistress. Cornelia Segarra traded blows and insults with Segunda Ortiz, a laundress she suspected of being her husband's lover. Cornelia also recounted bitterly that her husband had struck her when she protested the money he spent on Segunda: "He shouted at me that only Segunda had the right to live in his room with him, and that the funds that he could have given to [me] he now would give only to her."[57]

The new divorce terms codified in 1902 presented a potential watershed in women's struggle against the sexual double standard. The equalization of adultery standards for both sexes marked the first time that a legal challenge had been made to men's age-old patriarchal right of multiple sexual partners. Again, however, while economically dependent on their husbands, most women must have found their newly gained legal right to divorce on the basis of infidelity difficult to exercise.

Other obstacles lay in their way as well. Although a potential challenge to male privilege was now codified, it remained extraordinarily difficult for a woman to prove her husband's adultery in a court of law. In several cases, even numerous eyewitnesses' testimony of a man's extramarital affairs was not sufficient to convict the husband and obtain a divorce. In contrast, several men were granted divorces solely on the basis of testimony from neighbors who had "heard [only] through public rumor" that their wife had had an affair.[58] Consequently, unless men's adultery was paired with cessation of all financial support, popular patriarchal custom prevailed over formal legal restrictions of male sexual practice. This cornerstone of male honor and privilege remained largely intact.

Thus, access to male income continued to be the bottom line for most women. As long as steady male contributions to the household economy continued, unhappy wives were apparently reluctant to sever the marital bonds permanently, despite sometimes facing severe physical abuse and persistent infidelity. This reluctance was probably exacerbated by the courts' general unwillingness to pursue charges of adultery against men. Married women did, however, struggle to carve out a more humane space for themselves within these limits. And if they encountered potential partners who appeared to offer better terms, some women were perfectly willing to leave their marriage and set up household with another man.

When husbands' financial support ceased altogether, however, women now could move to break their marital ties. And this they did, in large numbers. Eighty-five percent of all female divorce complaints listed abandonment as the primary charge. In petition after petition, women testified to the bone-grinding hardships of life without a reliable male income. Carmen Lucca had lived for several years with her mother, sister, and daughter, all of whom worked twelve to fourteen hours a day to feed, clothe, and house the family. Her husband had not contributed anything to the family's income for "as long as I can remember," even when he was gainfully employed in a bakery.[59]

Carmen's husband and several other plebeian male defendants denied that they had violated the marital contract. While each admitted that he had given his wife nothing in the way of financial support for some time, all insisted that this was due to their poverty. Material barriers, then, prevented them from fulfilling their individual responsibilities as husbands. Wives and their supporting witnesses, however, scoffed at these arguments, pointing to the money their husbands spent on drink and women, as well as to how hard they themselves worked to earn a few pennies a day, which they then devoted entirely to the maintenance of their family. These women insisted that familial senses of responsibility were gendered. Their husband may have been poor, but that did not give him the right to desert his family.[60]

Carmen Lucca told the court that she wanted her "wayward" husband to live with and support her and her daughter. But because the judge did not enforce Carmen's economic claims against her husband, she demanded a divorce. Most women filing divorce petitions had similar stories. They would probably have preferred enforcement of the male end of the conjugal exchange but accepted the best they could get: permanent release from the violated contract.

Municipal judges seemed reluctant to grant women divorces for petitions alleging solely infidelity; this perhaps meant striking too close to home in censuring male privilege. But women were extremely successful in obtaining divorces based on financial abandonment; not one of these petitions in the period reviewed was denied. Thus, financial responsibility, not sexual privilege, was the point of possible judicial discipline of men.[61]

But judges generally ordered no economic relief for workingwomen divorce petitioners, despite their legal ability and women's desperate pleas to do so. (The 1902 Civil Code provided for successful women petitioners to be granted alimony, not to exceed one-third of their former husband's income.) Only propertied women stood to substantially gain economically from a divorce; they immediately recovered administrative rights over their own property and received half the marital property as well.[62] Divorce was hardly a panacea for women's worries, then, especially for members of the working classes. Wronged wives might come to the courts seeking marital justice from the new colonial state, but they rarely found full relief.

In many ways, the early U.S. colonial attempt to reform the sexual mores and family definitions of the Puerto Rican popular classes illustrates well Foucault's theory of modern disciplinary power.[63] Such power, according to Foucault, abandons outright coercion in favor of a process of subjection that brings increasing numbers of individuals under its scrutiny. By combining a widening surveillance net with proliferating discourses about specific practices or groups of people, disciplinary power channels and controls meanings and practices, even as it produces new identities. Thus, disciplinary power is both restrictive and productive. It does not depend on public displays of force; rather, it penetrates into the most intimate recesses of people's lives. Ultimately, it disciplines them into *self*-discipline. It is "elegant" and ultimately very effective, creating a totalizing web of power that incites participation from all within its reach. Sexuality is often one of its "dense transfer points."[64]

Focusing on the strategies of colonial agents who worried about popular resistance to marriage in Puerto Rico might lead us simply to confirm Foucault's brilliant conceptualization of the workings of power. Certainly, there are many parallels. Marital reform under early U.S. rule sought to tame what colonial agents and local elites saw as the sexual cacophony of the working classes and to reduce it to one unison note—the respectable, "civilized" state of marriage. This in turn would help establish an acceptable social order more readily available to state surveillance. The two-pronged strategy of increasing access to marriage and legalizing divorce developed by colonial agents had many sources; popular pressures as well as colonizers' interests helped produce the U.S. strategy for marital reform. In the process, the official meaning of marriage itself was transformed; new meanings of old institutions were codified by the state.

But close attention to other aspects of the move toward marital reform in Puerto Rico invites us to expand on Foucault's insights. Many of the intended subjects of the new disciplinary strategy refused to participate in it fully. Puerto Ricans appropriated those elements of colonial marital reform which served their interests and rejected those which did not. They enthusiastically took advantage of the opportunities to end unworkable relationships, rushing to the courts to petition for divorce. But they did not go on to marry in significantly larger numbers, as colonial strategists had hoped. Puerto Ricans' responses to the colonial reforms confirm that they had their own definitions of marriage and its responsibilities. They were also quite cognizant of their own gendered interests and did their best to advance them through whatever fissures they could find or force open in the colonial edifice. Thus, attention to diffuse popular actions can show us that disciplinary power is not always as effective as Foucault's theory implies. Its ripple effects do reach into the intimate spaces of people's lives. But people have the power to make divergent decisions and act on them, thus challenging the totalizing patterns in Foucault's conceptualization.[65]

The reform of divorce and marriage in Puerto Rico also illuminates the contradictory effects of early U.S. colonialism on women's lives in particular. In a striking parallel to the patterns that Leila Ahmed traces for European colonialism in the Middle East, colonial officials' appropriation of feminist projects from their home country helped shift the parameters of institutions that had historically restricted women's options. However much the new colonial agents may have learned (or co-opted) from feminists at home, they never intended to challenge male power over women. The new definitions of marriage and divorce that were codified in Puerto Rico in 1902 and subsequently worked out in the courts were meant to reconstruct a patriarchal family, where husbands could still exercise power over women, although less overtly.[66]

Clearly, the right to terminate abusive, shameful, or unreliable marriages was important to Puerto Rican women, who constituted the majority of divorce petitioners. Indeed, the right to divorce—heretofore ignored by historians of the construction of U.S. colonial hegemony in Puerto Rico—may well have been one of the social reforms that won the U.S. colonial regime support among marginalized Puerto Ricans. Certainly, the explosion of divorce petitions—the vast majority of which were granted—in the decade following implementation of the new Civil Code implies that this may have been so. Popular commentary in Ponce today also hints that some Puerto Rican women still associate U.S. rule with an increase in options for their sex. Several Ponce working-class women mentioned to me that their grandmothers were able to rid themselves of "useless" husbands only "after the Americans came."[67] Ironically, the dissolution of formal marital relations may have been more important in cementing popular support for U.S. rule than was the colonizers' attempt to stabilize society through encouraging marriage.

As I have discussed, Puerto Rican women had yearned for more reciprocal gender relations throughout the nineteenth century. Although women seem to have accepted the patriarchal balance of the marital pact, they continually struggled against men's assertion of absolute physical and sexual power over them. After the implementation of the 1902 Civil Code, however, women had a new weapon in their battles. For the first time, women were able to obtain some legal redress for complaints against husbands. An unworkable marital contract could finally be terminated. Indeed, Lillian Guerra has found that men frequently complained about such increased options for women in popular twentieth-century folktales and jokes.[68]

But there were limits to the efficacy of this new arena of struggle, just as there were serious, gendered limits to the "benevolent" nature of U.S. colonialism in general. After 1902, men could rid themselves of a wife who refused to submit to their claims of sexual ownership. Divorce served their interests relatively well. Divorce did *not* protect women from male abuse, however. The courts were not quick to punish husbands' infidelity. Nor did they enforce men's compliance with their financial responsibilities. Release from a bad marriage was better than the extremely limited options that existed in the nineteenth century, but it certainly did not provide the full relief sought by most women. The potential (although partial) challenge to male privilege posed by the 1902 code remained largely unrealized. The colonial state was not a dependable ally for women in their struggles for justice within the family.[69]

In 1898, Puerto Rican women had not yet managed to create effective strategies for enforcing their alternative moral codes through the state. Nor had most plebeian women articulated their desires for male fidelity, economic stability, and freedom from physical and sexual violence into self-consciously political demands. Yet women in Puerto Rico did aggressively turn a new institutional opening to their own advantage as much as possible. Women's response to the increased accessibility of divorce ripped open the dream of "civilized marital unions" on which both Puerto Rican Liberals and the new colonial rulers sought to build their power. Women's diffuse but insistent voices cried out to the U.S. colonial regime that facilitating marriage was not sufficient to stabilize the family. In the family, as in the larger society, stability without justice was an empty ideal.

Chapter 5

Slavery, Sexuality, and the Early Labor Movement,

1900–1917

If we are slaves of an immoral state, let us break the chains that bind us, and
preaching the Union of all the sons and daughters of labor, let us establish on
the face of the earth a more moral world.
—Alberto García, "Moralidad," *Porto Rico Workingman's Journal*, 1905

I understand that all women and all men have the right to direct their own [sex-
ual] lives and accept each other mutually, without limits or privileges of any kind.
But these freedoms must be won; they are not yet established. Let us fight for
them—this is the struggle for liberty and justice!
—Luisa Capetillo, *Mi opinión sobre las libertades, derechos, y deberes de la mujer,* 1911

Not all popular dissent from the Liberal project was articulated as diffusely as
the thousands of divorce petitions filed after 1902. In the early years of U.S.
rule, a dynamic labor movement also began to brew in Puerto Rico. The first
decades of the twentieth century witnessed an outpouring of working-class
organization, agitation, and intellectual production on the island. Fueled by
accelerated proletarianization, hopes for democratic reforms under the new
"progressive colonialism" of the United States, and the international circula-
tion of socialist and anarchist ideas, Puerto Rican working women and men
began to fashion a political alternative to the hegemonic Liberal consensus of
the 1890s. No longer would laboring people allow the parameters of the
island's political, economic, or cultural agendas to be set solely by elites.

These diverse, newly self-conscious, working-class politics and culture
often included striking reconceptualizations of gender and sexuality. Early
working-class Puerto Rican feminism, whether male or female, was much
broader than the struggles for women's suffrage and equal wages for which it
has primarily been heralded; sexuality was also important in the articulation
of these new politics. Working-class radicals' revisioning of moral norms and

sexual practices became a key method of asserting their superiority over their opponents.

Labor activists also helped initiate a new public discussion of race in Puerto Rico, an aspect of the movement often ignored by its historians. Challenging both the hostility toward sexually suspect urban workingwomen and the public silence on race that reigned in the 1890s, they simultaneously affirmed racial differences and deflected attention away from plebeian racial divisions onto discussions of women's subordination and the need to unite all working women and men in a common struggle against capitalism. Thus, labor organizers simultaneously spoke about race, attempted to sever it from its previous association with sexual morality, and subsumed it within their morally charged definitions of class.

There were limits to the early labor movement's gender and racial inclusivity. For all its innovations, the early Puerto Rican male left was not uncompromisingly feminist, as many historians have claimed. For as Joan Scott has noted, while social change often entails the questioning of gendered norms, it can also produce attempts to preserve some semblance of stability in the face of disorder. Often this search for equilibrium is expressed in efforts to ensure the survival of a more or less familiar gender hierarchy.[1] In Puerto Rico, many radical twentieth-century workingmen attempted to preserve some form of male-defined social order in Puerto Rico, even as they defended women's rights to equal pay, suffrage, and freedom from sexual harassment. In their advocacy of women's containment in an idealized domesticity, as in their call for moral reform of the popular classes and their assertion of the primacy of collective (in this case, class) solidarity over both racial and gender interests, anarchist labor activists echoed some elite Liberal yearnings. Thus, they formed an alternative, not purely oppositional political culture that shared—however conflictually—some key elements with that of their most bitter enemies.

Only a handful of radical workingwomen dared to differ from this analysis. Although they avoided racial issues altogether, they consistently challenged both the ravages of capitalism and the gendered hierarchies *within* the working classes. These courageous women, epitomized by Luisa Capetillo, a working-class intellectual and organizer, asserted that incidences of plebeian men's sexual infidelity, economic abandonment, and physical violence were indeed pressing political issues, as was women's economic exploitation under capitalism. In this chapter I demonstrate that in the twentieth century's first decades, as today, such far-reaching critiques of power remained, for the most part, marginalized women's work.[2]

Finally, I trace the shifting politicization of sexuality within Puerto Rico's early labor movement and its decoupling from racial identities. During the first decade of the twentieth century, a radical sexual ethics began to take hold among the movement's leaders and organizers. These plebeian intellectuals penned passionate defenses of prostitutes, whom they presented as the quintessential example of capitalist exploitation; developed critiques of marriage and women's sexual exploitation; and advocated the practice of free love. Throughout, radical leftists refused to identify either sexual virtue or its lack with any particular racial characteristics, instead focusing on the "immoralities" of wealthy men. By the time the United States (and, consequently, Puerto Rico) entered the First World War in 1917, however, most of these radical discourses on sexuality had disappeared from the left's lexicon. Only the issue of prostitution remained, a faint echo of the broader agenda for sexual reform that had briefly appeared in the creative birth pangs of Puerto Rico's radical working-class movement.

Emergence of the Puerto Rican Labor Movement

As I have discussed, the U.S. invasion of Puerto Rico in 1898 unleashed debate within the laboring classes over the meaning of democracy, as well as ardent pressure for expanded civil rights. The occupation also swept great economic changes across the island. With the influx of U.S. capital into sugar production, the transition to capitalism that had begun during the 1870s accelerated dramatically. Sugar rebounded from its moribund state of the 1890s to regain its previous position as the bedrock of the island's economy. By the 1920s, it made up 65 percent of Puerto Rico's exports.[3] The great sugar *centrales* established by U.S. corporations devoured increasing amounts of land in their push for radically expanded production and profits; between 1900 and 1910, the land planted in sugar rose from 72,000 to 118,000 acres, while production levels soared from 61,000 to 285,000 tons. Thousands of men labored in the cane fields for miserably low wages during planting and harvest seasons. Descendants of enslaved Africans who had cut cane for generations were joined by peasants pushed from their plots by the ever expanding sugar plantations and by thousands of migrants from the now stagnant coffee farms of the highlands.[4]

U.S. capital also transformed the cigar industry. Although tobacco farming remained in the hands of smallholders, U.S. companies focused their energies on taking over the processing and manufacturing stages of cigar production. Centered in Cayey, San Juan, Caguas, and Bayamón, with additional workshops and factories in Ponce and Arecibo, cigar production rapidly expanded in the early twentieth century and was soon reorganized on an industrial scale. Large factories, mainly owned by U.S. corporations and employing hundreds of male cigar rollers and female stem-strippers, replaced the small artisanal shops of three or four male *tabaqueros* that had previously produced the bulk of Puerto Rico's cigars.[5]

Thousands of women entered the waged labor force during the great wave of proletarianization that swept the island in the first decades of U.S. rule. Between 1904 and 1920, the tobacco industry was the largest single employer of women, displacing domestic service, which had been women's primary source of employment in the late nineteenth century. Tobacco-strippers' wages were even lower than those earned by their male counterparts; most women worked from ten to fourteen hours a day in the tobacco shops, earning forty cents or less for a full day's labor. Many women also canned fruits in factories, shelled coffee in warehouses, or made hats in their homes, where they could mesh income earning with domestic labor.[6]

Out of this political ferment and accelerated economic change emerged working people's first attempts at islandwide organization. Puerto Rican workers formed their first general labor federation in October 1898, shortly after the U.S. occupation of Puerto Rico. For the next few years, acute internal conflicts rent the fledgling labor movement. By 1905, however, the Federación Libre de Trabajadores (FLT) had established itself as the preeminent labor organization on the island.[7]

In 1915, after more than a decade of organizing unions and strikes around the island, the FLT founded the Socialist Party. For the next nine years, the Socialists enjoyed great electoral successes in Puerto Rico's coastal sugar regions, tobacco-producing centers, and urban areas. By 1920, the Socialist Party had built a substantial following in the majority of the island's municipalities; in that year, the party won over 50 percent of the vote in ten municipalities and between 20 percent and 47 percent of the vote in thirty-one more.[8]

In these early years and especially before 1911, the labor movement that coalesced around the federation was quite diverse. Debates on political and organizing strategies raged between the two main tendencies within the movement: the young organizers and worker intellectuals who embraced many tenets of anarchism, and those who controlled the FLT's administration and advocated working for gradual reform in salaries, working conditions, and civil rights.[9] There was wide disagreement about the ultimate goals of the movement even within each of these two factions.

Puerto Rican working women and men began to articulate their own self-consciously political discourses, which they developed and disseminated in public speeches and mass demonstrations. The early labor movement also produced an intellectual and artistic explosion. Workers organized their own musical bands, literary competitions, publishing presses, libraries, and local study circles. The Centros de Estudios, which provided small libraries and regular discussions on theoretical and practical issues facing workers, had a surprisingly broad reach. These centers were coeducational and frequented by workers loyal to the elite-led Unionista Party, as well as by socialists and anarchists.[10] Working men and women wrote essays, novels, poetry, and plays, which they read out loud and performed to large, enthusiastic audiences across the island in theaters, union halls, worker demonstrations, and town squares. Worker newspapers mushroomed throughout the island in addition to the FLT's official newspaper, *Unión Obrera.*

The epicenters of anarchist organizing and intellectual production were in the tobacco-processing cities of San Juan, Santurce, Caguas, and Bayamón. It was in the tobacco-rolling shops that Puerto Rico's radical worker culture was born and most quickly flourished. The new, militant proletarian politics grew out of a long tradition of autodidacticism in the tobacco industry, built around the institution of worker readers. The readers were hired by the tobacco workers themselves, to whom they read out loud newspapers, fiction, poetry, and essays by the great Latin American and European radical thinkers of the day. Passionate discussions of the merits of various organizing tactics or theoretical positions frequently broke out among the tobacco workers, lending a highly interactive nature to the already collectivized practice of workshop reading.[11] Workers initiated into this autonomous popular education in the tobacco shops were the first to found Puerto Rico's worker libraries, theater troupes, and Centros de Estudios of 1900–1910.

Although not as central to the new movement as San Juan and the tobacco-based towns, Ponce was an important focal point for the FLT's activities.[12] Throughout 1906 and 1907, Ponce was a center of FLT organizing; although consistent involvement was difficult to maintain at times, FLT rallies there attracted as many as two thousand people at a time. The great cane strikes of this period always encompassed Ponce, and smaller protests by tobacco workers burst out in the city as well. Some of the FLT's first womens unions were formed there by prominent free-lover female organizer Carmen Rosario, as were early longshoremens, blacksmiths, and bakers locals. The Ponce FLT rank-and-file frequently hosted workers' theater productions and produced packed May Day celebrations each year.[13] Thus, the new ideas developing within the radical labor movement also circulated in plebeian Ponce.

Libertarian socialism, or anarchism, was the principal ideological current in the first decade of the Puerto Rican labor movement. Although only a portion of the FLT's leadership fully embraced libertarian socialism, Rubén Dávila points out that these dynamic anarchist organizer-intellectuals disseminated their ideas widely through the newspapers, theaters, reading rooms, pamphlets, songs, and novels which they produced and which were quite popular among the working classes. This social and cultural movement never developed a coherent, unified theory but was made up of a wide variety of rather diffuse discourses.[14]

A number of basic themes did arise consistently in the writings of the early male worker intellectuals. Denunciations of state and church control over social institutions and popular worldviews abounded. The radical plebeian authors scoffed at attempts by proautonomy and nationalist planters to whip up patriotic sentiment against U.S. colonial rule; the problems of Puerto Rico, labor leaders insisted, would not be solved by creating a nation with the rich at the helm and social hierarchies undisturbed. Their allegiance was solely to all working people, regardless of national borders. Likewise, anarchists asserted, "bourgeois democracy" and the "freedoms" so touted by all political parties on the island were useless without a true redistribution of economic and political power.[15] Ownership of property should be collectivized and laborers should manage their places of work. Workers should organize and educate themselves in order to shed the individualistic, subservient practices and beliefs of the past.

These early radical labor organizers were struggling to make an islandwide working class out of a quite diverse population. Working people in Puerto Rico before World War I labored under widely variant circumstances: performing domestic services for individual families, doing piecework at home, picking coffee as tenants on others' land, producing goods and services as artisans in small shops, and working together in large numbers on plantations or in factories as wage laborers. They also were fragmented by gender, racial, regional, and previous class identities. Islandwide unity was anything but a given. Thus the early FLT labor organizers sought to forge an imagined community politically, built on rhetoric and practices they hoped could convince people of their common interests and of their capacity to organize collectively. Their most powerful political rhetoric drew on popular culture and symbols that resonated with coastal working people's historical memories, daily lives, and dreams of a transcendent future: slavery, female sexual exploitation, proud virility, outspoken working-class women, and tranquil domesticity.[16]

Slavery and Race in the Labor Movement's Discourse

Federation organizers and journalists persistently invoked slavery and the struggle for emancipation in their speeches and writings. Often, they linked the history of enslavement and the supposed cultural degradation of working people. Like the Liberals, many FLT activists saw themselves as a moralizing vanguard that would lift the laboring classes into an enlightened, united modernity. Progress, education, and the eradication of "backward ignorance" among the poor were the catchwords of the day.[17] But even as the federation's moralizing, modernizing hopes resonated with aspects of the Liberals' own early writings, they defined the legacy of slavery and racial humiliation quite differently.

Instead of distancing themselves from blackness and racial diversity, numerous federation organizers claimed them as an integral part of Puerto Ricanness. Many FLT members and leaders were clearly of African descent themselves. They also affirmed this heritage for the entire working class. "The white man was our father. The black woman was our mother," wrote one "white" FLT leader.[18] The dangerous "others" who weakened the social fabric of society were not blacks but the racist, allegedly white elites, "aristocratic . . . ferocious enemy of the colored race," whose ancestors had owned slaves and who now accused proudly black activists of *odios africanos* (African resentments). No one in Puerto Rico, not even the wealthy, could legitimately claim pure whiteness, FLT activists warned. "Here, we are all of color, including you . . . all recent descendants of blacks. Especially those men of *La Democracia*" (once the Liberals, now the Unionistas).[19]

Federation organizers also acknowledged the specificity of Afro-Puerto

Ricans' experiences. They denounced the past abuses of slaveowners and the struggles of enslaved people to wrest a modicum of dignity from life. Historically, racism had infected working people as well; nineteenth-century artisans had drawn careful color and racial distinctions among themselves, often striving to "better" themselves by distancing from their neighbors or family members who were more African in appearance. Blacks in contemporary society also suffered more than others, for they continued to face racist attitudes among both rich and poor whites.[20] Thus, racial prejudice within the working classes had to be denounced.

Working-class whites were exhorted to discard their false sense of superiority and accept their commonality with workers of African descent. Blacks and whites now worked side by side for their wages. All laboring people faced a common enemy—the economic slavery of twentieth-century poverty. Union organizing, education, and political unity across color lines were the roads to emancipation. This time, the exploited would free themselves, regaining an "honorable virility." The main obstacles to this interracial class unity lay in employers' attempts to divide workers along color lines.[21]

Not infrequently, FLT members explicitly linked racialized chattel slavery and the new "wage slavery" both in print and in public speeches. More often, though, they did not directly draw the connection, producing a seemingly colorless class rhetoric of denouncing "modern slavery: the exploitation of men by men." In the coastal and urban regions of early-twentieth-century Puerto Rico, however, where chattel slavery had marked much of the population, such language undeniably carried deep racial connotations. These reverberations implicitly racialized the FLT's broader class discourse, particularly when the speeches were delivered by black and mulatto men, likely giving it special appeal to workers of African descent.[22]

Indeed, between the U.S. invasion and World War I, race seems to have reemerged into the arena of masculine political discourse, after having been silenced by the Liberals 1890s political pact with urban artisans. The FLT was not the only group to attempt to mobilize Afro-Puerto Rican men by addressing them directly. Rank-and-file Republicanos, led by the black physician José Celso Barbosa, seem to have done so even more. They consistently presented themselves as the "party of the men of color" and "the party of Lincoln." Even more frequently than the FLT, they accused the Unionistas, a party formed by the Liberals and dissident elite Republicanos, of race hatred. Black Republicanos persistently called on Unionistas of African descent to free themselves from their *amos* (masters) and the "servile status" they claimed the Unión leadership forced on its black followers. Slavery and freedom had become popular metaphors in the hotly contested politics of the era, and they resonated powerfully with the racial identities and historical memories of many Puerto Ricans.[23]

Those federation activists who addressed racial questions directly struggled mightily to balance their defense of Afro-Puerto Rican dignity with their theoretical and political commitments to interracial class unity, which threatened to elide attention to blackness. Such FLT leaders as Ramón Romero Rosas, Eugenio Sánchez, and Eduardo Conde generally did not deny racial differences, as the Liberals had done, for they recognized that to do so was neither possible nor desirable. Rather, they stressed the need to undo racial hierarchies and unite working people amid their cultural and ethnic diversity. Even these men, however, insisted that "when organizing under the flag of labor . . . the existing barriers between whites and blacks are erased completely in the heart of the [union]."[24] Twentieth-century intraplebeian racial tensions could be eliminated through common labor organizing struggles and a simple shift in white workers' attitudes. Thus FLT leaders simultaneously spoke about racial differences within the working classes and minimized their importance. Black Republicano activists shared this discursive strategy. They insisted that party unity must supersede racial differences, even as they passionately denounced fellow Puerto Ricans' racism.[25] For both groups, because chattel, race-based slavery had ended, twentieth-century racial conflicts were attitudinal, not structural.

Not so for gender oppression, however. Almost every major FLT writer in the early years of the labor movement—even those who remained studiously silent on racial issues—directly addressed questions of gender as important loci of the class struggle. In the years before World War I, leftist labor leaders recognized that women's oppression was rooted in both waged labor exploitation and the dominant moral norms and sexual practices of the day. The institutions of marriage and the family, as well as the economic structures of capitalism, had to be transformed before women could be emancipated fully. Yet with the exception of Ramón Romero Rosas, radical activists never acknowledged that women's racial identities might shape their experiences. Thus, they implicitly recognized gender as a separate and more enduring social difference than race, demanding more extended analysis and practical reforms. Once again, as in Ponce during the 1890s, concerns about racial divisions within the newly forming community were deflected in part by focusing on gender and sexuality. The new leftists, however, sought a more inclusive vision—whatever its limits—on both counts than had their Ponce predecessors.

Gender and the New Working-Class Politics

It was probably no accident that the worker politics emerging out of Puerto Rico's tobacco factories demanded an end to women's oppression as well as an end to racial and class hierarchies, private property, religion, and nationalism. Tobacco was one of the first industries to incorporate women as wageworkers on a large scale; unlike mass embroidery and clothing production, which were mainly done by women in their homes until well into the 1930s, women's labor in tobacco was organized in collective workplaces. Although they tended to be concentrated in the lower-paid tasks, such as stem stripping, and were often kept in separate rooms, women tobacco laborers did work in the same factories as men. In 1910, women represented 27.8 percent of the tobacco industry's workforce, up from only 1.6 percent in 1899. By 1920, the percentage had increased to 52.9 percent.[26]

By 1907, the FLT had established unions of women tobacco strippers, coffee processors, domestic servants, and laundresses throughout the island. Women organizers and union members not infrequently addressed federation rallies of thousands of people. In Ponce, Santurce, Mayagüez, and Arecibo, girls and women often made up the majority of the performers in radical musical and dramatic presentations. They also attended the new workers' theater productions in large numbers, where they interacted enthusiastically with the plays, poems, and didactic "dialogues," hissing at the evil bourgeois characters and applauding the workers.[27]

Despite their clear presence in the labor movement and the strong impetus they must have provided it, workingwomen's voices are not well represented in the movement's historical record. The vast majority of the authors published in the early workers' newspapers were men, and virtually all the surviving novels and plays of the period were penned by men. Consequently, we can only hope to reconstruct a bare skeletal sketch of how radical women attempted to shape the new working-class politics in Puerto Rico. In the final section of this chapter I will focus on female anarchist analyses of sexual politics, but now I turn to what radical men had to say about sexuality and definitions of womanhood.

Historians of the early Puerto Rican labor movement have long acknowledged that its leaders developed a new understanding of gender relations,
especially in the tobacco sector. Influenced by the radical currents of Spanish,
Cuban, and Argentinian anarchism, the story goes, the male left leadership
welcomed women workers into their movement. With their entrance into
the world of collectivized waged labor, women were recognized officially as
comrades in the struggle. From its inception, most historians of the labor
movement insist, the FLT committed itself to organizing the women swelling
the tobacco labor force, advocating women's suffrage as well as equal pay for
equal work. Women's emancipation was an integral part of the "tradition of
dissent" forged in the early labor movement; this new gender vision "represented a negation of the *machista* ideology of the plantation culture's hierarchical paternalism."[28]

María Barceló Miller and María Baerga Santini diverge starkly from this
dominant interpretation of the early Puerto Rican male left. They contend
that radical men's organizing of women and rhetoric of sexual protection were
completely self-serving, alleviating a threat to their own wages and reasserting
their status as power-wielding patriarchs.[29] Certainly, patriarchal self-interest
may well have played an important role in the positions developed by the FLT.
But comparing the federation with its predecessors on the island and to
analogous movements elsewhere demonstrates that the early Puerto Rican
left's gendered discourses were more complicated than either the heroic historical narratives produced during the 1970s and 1980s or the newer frontally
critical analyses suggest. Deborah Levenson-Estrada's and Anna Clark's studies of Guatemalan and British male labor activists, respectively, point toward
a subtler interpretation, one which examines the historical specificity of male
dominance and which acknowledges the potential coexistence of men's desires for control over women and genuine advocacy on their behalf. Workplace and community class solidarity can create powerful sympathy for
women coworkers, even amid patriarchal behaviors and attitudes.[30] Thus, I
argue that, pushed by women, Puerto Rican male leftists helped build a more
ambiguous gendered movement than has been previously acknowledged by
most historians. Before World War I, radical men sought both to include and
to contain women, to transform gender relations, and to maintain working-
class male power.[31]

The FLT did spawn important new gendered discourses. The labor movement's newspapers and literature rejected the ideal image of the genteel, well-

educated "angel of the home" that elite Liberal men had tried to popularize throughout the late nineteenth century. Instead, radical working-class male intellectuals celebrated plebeian women's historic feistiness. The working-class woman warrior became one of the early labor movement's feminine icons. Puerto Rican anarchists applauded revolutionary Barcelona women who "fought at the barricades, by the side of their husbands, brothers, and sons against the king's soldiers, sacrificing their beautiful blood and lives in the holocaust of a high, humanitarian ideal."[32] Equally praiseworthy were the "valiant, manly" Italian women who fought off strikebreakers in a Tampa tobacco factory—"now those are *real* women!" crowed the anarchist press.[33] Under the proper conditions, workingwomen's aggressiveness could serve the movement well.

The FLT also maintained an official position in favor of organizing women workers rather than attempting to exclude them from the labor force. Eugenio Sánchez, a long-term organizer and union officer, insisted that women should be trained as cigar makers; as long as they were organized and demanded equal pay for their labor, they were no danger to male workers.[34] The federation backed up its conviction by hiring women organizers. This practice contrasted with the strategies of early labor movements in the United States, in Britain, and in Chile's copper mines, where male workers actively resisted women's presence in the workforce and in labor organizations.[35]

Stirring odes to the emancipation of women appeared in male workers' writings. Manifestos such as this one were not uncommon: "Today we proclaim that Woman is not ours; revolutionary men believe that she belongs to herself. As the old ideas crumble, we new men hope that those women who own themselves, and are our true and free comrades, will rip off their bonds, raise their heads to gaze at us fearlessly and love us as women, not as slaves."[36] Many labor leaders insisted that workingwomen were comrades, companions, and sisters in the struggle—not simply sexual objects.[37]

For a few early male leftists, revolutionary women were the hope for resolving society's contradictions and ushering in an era of freedom and justice.[38] But another discourse was much more prevalent, and deracialized sexuality was key to it. Throughout the radical press and cultural production of the period, victimized, downtrodden, workingwomen came to symbolize the exploitation of the entire working class. The power of this imagery sprang in part from its joining of many aspects of the sexual and economic oppression that had in fact long haunted plebeian women.

Sorting Coffee (from José de Olivares, *Our Islands and Their People as Seen with Camera and Pencil* [St. Louis: N. D. Thompson, 1899])

A long line of impoverished widows, unfortunate single mothers, and desperate young female factory workers trudged through the pages of left publications and across the stages of anarchist dramatic productions. These representations of women deprived of male financial support by the premature deaths and political persecution of their husbands, bludgeoned by inhumanly low wages, and almost always raped or seduced and then abandoned to raise children alone by wealthy, immoral men, became the quintessential symbols of the ravages of capitalism. Unlike the early Liberal writings, the images remained decidedly raceless.[39]

Rape or sexual abuse at the hands of rich men was a constant theme, and it

Making Chewing Tobacco (from José de Olivares, *Our Islands and Their People as Seen with Camera and Pencil* [St. Louis: N. D. Thompson, 1899])

must have resonated strongly with many women's experiences. But male leftists were not denouncing solely actual abuses that occurred against plebeian women. Rubén Dávila Santiago points out that FLT organizers used this characterization of rape as a particularly powerful trope to "awaken a virile response from the [male] worker against the 'possession' of the most intimate capital."[40]

Thus, in the worker literature of the early twentieth century, and quite possibly in workers' daily lives as well, class struggle between men was played out on the field of competing male "rights" to sexual possession of women. To radical Puerto Rican male workers of this period, female waged labor in factories meant both potential female political mobilization and women's increased economic and sexual vulnerability. It also translated into plebeian men's waning ability to control sexually and economically as well as to protect

A Working-class Neighborhood in Cayey, an FLT Stronghold (from José de Olivares, *Our Islands and Their People as Seen with Camera and Pencil* [St. Louis: N. D. Thompson, 1899])

"their" women. The new working-class movement sought to strengthen laboring men's social position vis-à-vis both elite men and plebeian women. Radical men's construction of rape as always a cross-class act of domination, from which the noble workingman would liberate "his" woman, neatly expressed these desires.

Unlike many late-nineteenth-century Ponce male artisans, however, who had also feared their waning power over women, most of the new radical men did not openly call for the excoriation of women who stepped outside the "proper" bounds of the family. Instead, they condemned the capitalist system and the rich who directed it for destroying the fabric of working-class families. Thus, the early labor movement's gender politics diverged significantly from the misogynistic conservatism that dominated the political exchanges of 1890s Ponce.

Nowhere is this clearer than in discussions of prostitution. The radical

Cigarette Factory Workers in Ponce (from José de Olivares, *Our Islands and Their People as Seen with Camera and Pencil* [St. Louis: N. D. Thompson, 1899])

workers' discourse of the early twentieth century stands in stark contrast to the revulsion of "respectable" Ponce male artisans and elites toward prostitutes and "rowdy women" during the late nineteenth century. In the new popular analysis of sexual politics, prostitution was not women's fault, as it had previously been constructed, nor was prostitution racialized. Rather, its roots lay in a color-neutral capitalism, which relegated plebeian women to such brutal poverty that they were forced to sell their bodies to survive. "Only misery creates whores," proclaimed an anarchist newspaper. Daughters and sisters of workers, prostitutes were an integral part of the laboring classes—not a "different type" of woman, to be isolated from respectable working folk. "The miserable prostitute is the proletarian's sister; her history, like his, is written with tears of blood. . . . Labor's flesh, prostitution's flesh—the same misfortune."[41]

Thus, the early Puerto Rican leftists resurrected and consciously politicized a more inclusive current in popular sexual norms that had been driven underground although not completely destroyed in Ponce by the moral panic of the 1890s. They recognized plebeian women's economic precariousness and publicly acknowledged the impact this vulnerability could have on women's sexual practices. They consciously rejected rigid, often racialized

Workers in a Ponce Cigar Factory (from José de Olivares, *Our Islands and Their People as Seen with Camera and Pencil,* [St. Louis: N. D. Thompson, 1899])

divisions between respectable and disreputable womanhood. Ultimately, they converted the prostitute, along with the woman warrior, into one of the prime symbols of the Puerto Rican working classes.[42]

This more accepting discourse on prostitution permeated the labor movement's press and literature. But it was not the left's only innovation in sexual matters. A small group of anarchist leaders and organizers also began to articulate a politics of free love. Two Ponce organizers, Carmen Rosario and Francisco Santiago, publicly celebrated a "free and loving contract" in Ponce in 1907, presided over by Eugenio Sánchez, a national FLT officer. *Unión Obrera* announced it as "the first free-love ceremony celebrated in Puerto Rico. It heralds a new, enlightened era." Signs emblazoned with free-love slogans hung on the walls of the Caguas anarchist study center directed by Juan Vilar. Artisans in the sugar town of Guayama insisted on their right to live in "free union" with their partners, even when ordered to marry by local magistrates. The mulatto tobacco roller Emiliano Ramos from Cayey, who later edited an anarchist newspaper in Bayamón, was a widely recognized adherent of free love. Julio Aybar, a leading FLT official, also publicly affirmed his commitment to the ideology.[43]

Among early-twentieth-century anarchists, "free love" had a very particular meaning. Like their counterparts in Spain, Argentina, and Brazil, Puerto Rican free-love advocates rejected the dominant honor code and its sanctification of marriage. Marriage, they proclaimed, was built on social convenience or economic dependency, not on love and mutual compatibility. It also facilitated church and state control over the family and created false distinctions between "honorable" and "dissolute" women. "It is well known that 'honor' is an empty word, invented to protect your privilege," accuses the wife of a wealthy man in an anarchist short story. Indeed, anarchists insisted that marriage was the ultimate form of prostitution, legitimized by the church and the state. Ideal relationships, anarchists wrote, should not be built on economic considerations. Rather, men and women should unite "guided solely by love." Couples should form "naturally," with no intervention from either church or state. Unworkable relationships should be left at will by either partner.[44]

The advocates of free love drew on anarchist ideas from Europe and Argentina to develop their critique of marriage and the honor system. But these Puerto Rican sexual radicals were also building on the moral norms of the popular classes within which they came of age. Female virginity was not so important as a woman's fidelity once in a relationship. Serial monogamy, rather than marriage, was the ideal form of heterosexual partnership. And the honor system, with its dichotomy between respectability and disreputability, existed only to support social hierarchies; women, especially, were damaged by such distinctions.[45]

Thus, during the first decades of the twentieth century, working people's protests against the abuses of the rich spawned a conscious politicization of the sexual norms of the popular classes, as well as public affirmation of these norms' superiority over those of the more privileged classes. An inclusive discourse on sexuality was briefly consolidated in the Puerto Rican labor movement before World War I, one which embraced prostitutes as comrades in suffering and which, at least in theory, rejected marriage and the distinctions it legitimized between "respectable" and "disreputable" women. These stances, along with FLT authors' determined refusal to racialize their representations of women, began to undo the seemingly natural link between racial characteristics and feminine virtue. Instead, the authors asserted that gendered class identities were the primary determining factors of moral status. They also insistently reversed the class assumptions of the dominant honor code. Wealthy men, not workingwomen, were immoral.

The emergence of a more radical and inclusive public discourse on sexuality and female respectability did not signal the death of the conservative popular morality articulated by Canta Claro and his followers, however. San Juan leaders of the pro-Republicano labor organization Federación Regional were outraged that the FLT allowed "disreputable" women to participate in its demonstrations. "Alongside the sons of labor and the respectable ladies who took part, also marched women who were not worthy of being hidden in the darkest corners of the city—they even waved signs and carried banners!" The Federación Regional also lambasted FLT workers for living in "the most public and familiar concubinage." This practice infected even members of the FLT's top directorate. The Federación Regional contended that such behavior undermined the moral example that labor leaders should set for the rest of the working class and destroyed the budding labor movement's attempt to prove to the rich that workers were, indeed, honorable.[46]

Federation members lashed back with stinging critiques of both the Federación Regional's belief that the interests of labor and capital could be reconciled and its statements that "our women are prostitutes because they are not married and live honorably with their compañeros." FLT speakers scoffed at the Federación Regional's sexual conservatism, linking it to what they considered a more general betrayal of the working class.[47]

Gender, Sexuality, and the Limits of the Male Left

The early left's organizing strategies and discourses about women and sexuality did indeed mark an impressive shift when compared with the public prostitution bashing and rigid, often racialized definitions of female respectability of the 1890s. But close scrutiny of the sources indicates that there were important limits to the FLT's gender radicalism, as there were to its discourse on race. Total consensus on the validity of the new sexual politics was never reached. In addition, male leaders of the labor movement rarely, if ever, acknowledged working-class men's role in the subordination of women. Finally, many of the men who publicly advocated free love and "women's emancipation" in general hoped to construct a new domesticity within which to confine "their" women.

The cursory written record of the debate over death benefits at the FLT's 1910 congress provides a glimpse at the conflicts over sexual norms that existed within the federation itself. At issue at this islandwide gathering of delegates was which types of relationship the FLT would recognize as legitimate, thus entitling surviving female partners to male workers' death benefits. A group of union members proposed that consensual unions be included along with married couples for full death benefit compensation. Santiago Iglesias, Manuel F. Rojas, and Juan Gómez García (three men often credited with the shaping of the "mature" Socialist Party), along with several others, vehemently opposed the initial language of the proposal, which simply required that a couple had "lived together consensually." After a heated debate, a compromise was reached that recognized couples who had lived in "free and loving union" for at least five years, who had children together, and in which the man had officially declared the woman as his partner.[48]

The basic principle of "free and loving union" had been officially recognized by the FLT, but not without long debate—and in a much more limited form than originally proposed. The approved version codified a more conservative definition of popular sexual norms. Bearing a child to a man was made paramount, rather than partnership in and of itself. And without a man's official, public declaration of his commitment, women could be left with nothing in the way of financial compensation for the permanent loss of male income. Ultimately, the power of relationship definition—which could have serious material consequences for women—was left in the hands of men.

Likewise, in the very early years of the labor movement, there was clearly no consensus on the issue of women in the workplace. A San Juan workers newspaper which proudly called itself socialist and which published articles by a Spanish anarchist feminist insisted that women should not work in factories. Puerto Rico's economy was not strong enough to sustain both sexes as organized wage laborers; there was not even sufficient work for all men. Women, these writers warned, would replace male workers; the loss of male jobs and the public presence of women in factories would produce social disintegration and widespread immorality.[49]

Tobacco rollers, supposedly the most "enlightened" of all male workers, were not impervious to such ideas about women entering their industry and job categories either. Juan José Baldrich has characterized their position as "an uneasy combination of enthusiasm and hesitancy." In 1914, men in the tobacco unions complained of the threat posed by "invading women."[50] To its credit, the FLT, led by Eugenio Sánchez, eventually reaffirmed its official policy to organize rather than exclude women. But a year later, female workers still encountered frequent foot-dragging and hostility from their male "comrades."[51] Clearly, then, neither gender-inclusive organizing nor sexual radicalism were uncontested positions among FLT male militants. The celebrated feminism of the early Puerto Rican male left was far from unanimous, despite the movement's relative inclusiveness.

In addition, even the most progressive male anarchists rarely acknowledged the role of workingmen in women's subordination. Instead, early-twentieth-century workingmen's literature created stock villains of lecherous wealthy men, "señoritos" who sexually preyed on plebeian women's economic vulnerability. A colorless working-class unity was to be built around this sexually saturated excoriation of elite men.[52] Male anarchists generally remained silent about the sexual double standard *within* the working-class, plebeian men's infidelities and the instances of their own abandonment of partners and children. Likewise, women's need for sexual and economic autonomy from men of their own class was rarely, if ever, mentioned. Instead, FLT male militants attempted to legitimize their project by invoking a demonized, masculine other that allegedly threatened their own benevolent protection of "helpless" workingwomen. In the end, radical male workers were no better than male elites in admitting their own sexual privileges.[53]

J. Limón de Arce, the only male anarchist author to acknowledge (and briefly at that) workingmen's violence against women, insisted that it was solely a product of the men's degradation under capitalism. In Limón de Arce's vision of the new socialist man, restored to true manhood by collective struggle and class consciousness, domestic violence would wither away. Plebeian men's abuse of workingwomen was not an expression of male dominance independent of class exploitation.[54]

Thus, to male anarchists, capitalism was the sole cause of women's suffering. "It is [capitalism] that robs the virtue of future generations and the vitality of women . . . it is the horrible house of immorality and the school of dishonor."[55] Capitalism bound women into a brutal double day of labor, in both the home and the shop. It destroyed families, forcing women to leave their children and sick, elderly parents alone.[56] And perhaps most threatening of all, women's double exploitation eroded relations between the sexes.

Many anarchist men insisted that women's wage labor was destroying the sanctity of the domestic sphere.[57] Under capitalism and its allegedly newly imposed burden of wage labor, women were indomitable shrews; conflict within the home came from their constant complaints. Women "are no longer tender companions, idolized friends, but slaves, irreconcilable enemies of the worker."[58] It was the rich who "have taught men and women to hate each other, to decalre a war to the death against each other, to stupify each other with unjust accusations; they have only divided homes more and more with their vile messages."[59] Federation organizers thus deflected attention away from those roots of gender conflict which lay within the working classes, even as they acknowledged the presence of such conflicts.

Revolution, however, would free women from wage labor to focus all their energies on the home and thus would sweeten and tame them.[60] The utopian future, male anarchists trumpeted, held not only a society without racial hierarchies, classes, or states but also a reconstituted, conflict-free, working-class domesticity. "The wife happily awaits the arrival of her husband or beloved companion at the door of a comfortable home, not a miserable hovel, in order to shower him with tenderness and caresses after his long day's work, *not to make him suffer and embitter his existence.*[61] Thus, the same anarchists who advocated free love, female suffrage, and the organization of women workers also dreamed of a gender order not unlike the Liberal bourgeois ideal—a clear separation of domestic and "public," "productive" spheres, with women safely circumscribed within the former and men proudly owning the latter.

The novelist and organizer Santiago Valle y Velez painted a bucolic picture of such an ideal relationship: After moving in with her lover, Valle's heroine Magdalena stops selling vegetables in the marketplace and herding sheep. She tends the family garden and peacefully dedicates herself to the "labors of her sex," while her lover, Pascual, earns all their income.[62] The anarchist free-lover Angel Dieppa concurred with this vision, insisting that "women are made naturally for childrearing and the home, better than for the rough labor to which the present system has condemned them."[63] Other anarchists asserted that women should be "converted into mothers" in order to make the home a "temple of instruction" for their children.[64] No male leftist journalist suggested that women should not be economically dependent on men, that domestic labor be collectivized, or that men might do such work.

Thus the early radical men largely avoided direct challenges to plebeian male privilege in Puerto Rico. Conflicts between working women and men always came from outside the working class—whether in the form of rapacious "señoritos" or from the economic structures of capitalism and the social institution of marriage. While all these factors were indeed key elements in the reproduction of women's subordination, radical men consistently ignored or downplayed plebeian male desires for control over women. For many male anarchists, the answer to the "woman question" lay in establishing a classless world of reconstituted, separate gender spheres, where workingmen could be benevolent patriarchs, providing for, protecting, and guiding "their" women. This restoration of the "natural" order that had been destroyed by class exploitation would reinstate gender differences while eliminating class and racial divisions.

Certainly, this vision must have reverberated powerfully with plebeian women, as well as with men. Few workingwoman would not have welcomed release from the fear of hunger and the long, grueling hours of waged labor they performed in addition to their unending domestic work. The dream of domesticity implicitly assured women that their men would provide dependable protection and financial support. Thus, in FLT rhetoric, domesticity became a privilege for all to enjoy. This compelling metaphor for the future defended working-class social and familial integrity and appealed to plebeian women without threatening laboring men's privilege too severely.

For the FLT's domestic "natural order" also legitimized male leadership of women. Women had to be educated out of their religious superstitions and ushered into class consciousness by radical men. The downtrodden female victims of capitalism would be transformed into women warriors through class struggle *led by men*. A poem published in *Unión Obrera* perhaps said it best: "Rise up, woman! . . . Be valiant! . . . *You learn from me*. . . . You are the muse who inspires me, the rebellious walkiria who encourages me in the struggle. . . . This, woman, is how I dreamed of you. . . . *This, woman, is how I conceived of you in my mind.*"[65] Valiant, rebel workingwomen were to challenge only the wealthy, never men of their own class. The radical man, in turn, would shape the militant woman, even intellectually and politically "conceive" her, as she in turn inspired him in his regenerative labors.

Indeed, in the narratives spun out about the early labor movement, working-class feminism has itself become the creation of radical men. Ramón Romero Rosa, one of the early Puerto Rican male leftists most concerned with the recognition of women as productive intellectual beings, was careful to point out that *men* would liberate women. Workingmen "should explain to her how much she is worth as a woman and an intelligent being."[66] Early-twentieth-century women's radicalism, we also are told by many labor historians, sprang from male tobacco workers and their farsighted organizing.[67]

Women workers probably did learn a great deal from their male counterparts. But the limited historical record provides hints that laboring women were not only politicized by the radical workshop culture but also instrumental in forging the relative egalitarianism of the early labor movement's gender discourses. Women tobacco stemmers' complaint to Ramón Romero Rosa that the union was ignoring women workers prompted the FLT to begin to organize women in 1905. Likewise, the FLT's 1908 call for women's suffrage was initiated and pushed at its islandwide congress by *women* members, among them Luisa Capetillo. And in 1915, a group of women workers published a protest in *Unión Obrera* against the behavior of some of their male comrades. Workingmen were not true socialists, the women insisted, if they tried to prevent women from joining labor and political struggles, denied women their right to intellectual development, or kept women from earning their own living. These female militants stated in no uncertain terms that laboring men sometimes chose to be obstructionist, instead of allies. They used socialism's language of universal equality to challenge male dominance within the working classes.[68]

It is clear, then, that at the very least, workingwomen formed some of the initial incentives to broaden the labor movement's attention to women's needs. In addition, they underscored issues that even the most radical men of their day avoided, such as women's need for economic autonomy from men of their own class and workingmen's attempts to maintain power over women. It is also possible that women's labor movement activism, together with their acute understanding that very little separated them from women who sold sex for a living, contributed to the FLT's progressive discourse on prostitution. Workingwomen apparently had their own definitions of what revolutionary social change should mean. Some of their concerns were eventually incorporated into the left's agenda and ultimately presented as men's innovations. Many more were probably silenced by the chorus of male voices and power struggles that dominated the labor movement.

Very few sources remain that could provide us insight into the female world of the early left. As I noted, women's voices were rare in the FLT and anarchist newspapers. The labor movement's talk of women's rights was usually carried on—at least in print—by men. Not one issue of Luisa Capetillo's newspaper for workingwomen, which circulated for about a year in San Juan, has been preserved. Records of the accomplishments and ideas of such women organizers as Carmen Rosario, Martina González, and Paca Escabí have barely survived through scanty comments in FLT newspapers; none of these women wrote memoirs or series of essays as did male workers such as Ramón Romero Rosa, Bernardo Vega, or Jesús Colón. Consequently, the richness of debate, ideas, and experience that surely existed among left women and between them and the men around them has largely been lost to history. Fortunately for feminist historians, however, one workingwoman of this period did manage to leave a substantial historical record. Luisa Capetillo—anarchist, feminist, and labor activist—published four books in which she presented her own analysis of power relations and dreams of justice.

Feminism "Desde la mujer": Luisa Capetillo's Sexual Politics

Luisa Capetillo's politics were forged in the anarchist fervor of early-twentieth-century Puerto Rico. She was a reader in the Arecibo tobacco workshops as a young woman and received her first taste of collective political action in the great 1905 cane strike. She continued to lead labor-organizing drives and strikes throughout the island and in Florida until her death from tuberculosis in 1922.

But the labor movement was not Capetillo's only formative experience: her mother was an important source of inspiration as well. A one-time governess, reduced in her youth to washing and ironing others' clothes, Capetillo's mother not only taught her daughter to read and write through studying such European thinkers as John Stuart Mill, Hugo, Tolstoy, and Madeleine Vernet but also lived with Luisa's father without marrying and insisted on regularly attending and participating in workingmen's discussions of literature and politics—the only woman to do so in nineteenth-century Arecibo. Capetillo dedicated her first feminist publication to her mother, who, she said, "never forced me to agree with tradition."[69]

Capetillo's analysis of power relations also came from her own experiences with male domination. At eighteen, she began a relationship with Manuel Ledesma, the son of a wealthy landowner whose clothes her mother washed, bearing two children over the years she spent with him. During this time he kept her under strict surveillance at her mother's house, while he had affairs with other women. Eventually he left her and her children with no financial support. Capetillo and her mother struggled to keep their family afloat,

Luisa's father having left as well. Once Capetillo began her public career as a labor activist and journalist, Ledesma took her children away; never again was she able to maintain direct, consistent contact with them. Capetillo also faced sexual propositions from comrades within the movement, and she later had a third child whose father never recognized him.[70]

Thus, Capetillo's feminism did not spring solely from either European theorists or her political formation within the male-dominated Puerto Rican labor movement. "The majority of my studies I have carried out in relation to myself," she proudly stated. She also drew directly on the practice by the Puerto Rican popular classes of *rapto* and serial monogamy to formulate her critiques of marriage and advocacy of free love.

Capetillo never directly acknowledged racial differences in her writings, although she frequently spoke of women as slaves to both men and capitalism. Apparently she considered gender and class to be the main axes of exploitation. For Capetillo, sexual autonomy was as key to women's emancipation as economic self-sufficiency, education, and class struggle. By 1910, when she founded a newspaper in San Juan for workingwomen, she had decided that her feminist campaign had to promote "women's freedom in *all* aspects of our lives."[71] This included opening discussion on "the sexual question" (although not explicitly on race) and placing it at the center of politics. "In the modern age, women have been conceded rights and privileges, but they are still slaves. Enslaved, not in intelligence, or in their labor, but by sex. In intelligence, women rival men; in their work, they are equal in activity, initiative, and perseverance. They have freedom and rights in everything, except in love, in the right to freely and frankly choose. This, male egotism still denies them."[72]

Luisa Capetillo's formulation of sexual politics marked a historical watershed. Although the early left had already opened a space for such a discussion and some anarchists had begun to articulate a radical sexual ethics, sexuality was not considered a political *priority* by the labor movement or left parties. As we have seen, prostitution and cross-class sexual abuse were symbolically important in the movement's self-definition. Likewise, early radicals discussed the need to shift the terms of the sexual contract between men and women. But these and related issues were not considered "truly political"; they were not formally recognized as organizing tenets of the workers movement. Not one of the numerous official published platforms of the FLT or the Socialist Party, for example, ever mentioned divorce reform, the rights of "illegitimate" children, or the recognition of "free unions," despite the fact that these issues were of clear concern to working people and were debated within the labor movement itself, especially during its first decade. They remained secondary questions, on the periphery of formal politics. Wages, working conditions, the right to organize workplace unions, worker education, debunking ruling-class nationalism, and, later, electoral campaigns, on the other hand, were all given center stage by the male-led worker organizations and publications. In short, production, patriotism, and parties were "really" political and therefore had priority over sexual issues, an assumption with which Capetillo may have agreed during her early years in the left. Her first collection of essays focused almost exclusively on restructuring the relations of production, although women workers figured significantly in her analysis.[73]

But by 1910, Capetillo was loudly asserting in no uncertain terms that sexuality *was* political, indeed central to a revolutionary agenda. Her play *Influencias de las ideas modernas* ends with a woman worker exhorting women to reject the institution of marriage, as a crowd of workers shouts: "Long live free, loving unions! An end to exploitation! An end to the reign of the wage!"[74] Thus, Capetillo tried to break the primacy of production; for her, bodily autonomy was essential to a broader liberatory project.

In addition, Capetillo was acutely aware that individual men, as well as social institutions and economic structures, oppressed women. Certainly lack of democratic rights, horrifically low wages, and terrible working conditions trapped workingwomen in a cycle of poverty and powerlessness. Yet men also helped create and fought to maintain the laws, customs, and economic relations that perpetuated women's subordination. Men "are guilty of our ignorance, our slavery, of which they take advantage."[75] And not only wealthy men were to blame for plebeian women's misery.

Workingmen were known to abandon their partners and children economically, but perhaps even more painful was their sexual betrayal of women. Capetillo opened her first feminist tract with a passionate denunciation of male infidelities and returned to the theme frequently in subsequent essays and plays. Capetillo expressed the deep rage women of all classes felt at men's "right" to multiple sexual partners.[76]

Capetillo also sharply criticized men's frequent preoccupation with the sexual control of women. Neither financial support nor marriage contracts gave men the right to own women and their bodies. Rather, men should control their own sexual drives; they should remain virgins—"not belong to a woman"—until fully mature and ready to settle down and create a family. Those men who assumed sexual ownership of women, were unfaithful, or did not fully love their partners should be left, with no second thoughts.[77]

Thus Luisa Capetillo not only rejected the dominant honor code's obsession with female virginity and fidelity but also actually applauded those women who stepped outside the bounds of propriety. Indeed, women had a responsibility to leave unsatisfactory or abusive relationships. Those who did not were "stupid" or "idiots." Capetillo was especially contemptuous of women who hung on to the social and economic privilege gained by their attachment to a man. Such women, she scoffed, were weaklings who were willing to lose their dignity to avoid conflict and controversy.[78] This right to leave unworkable relationships was the essence of Capetillo's definition of free love.

Capetillo's vision of free love coincided in many ways with that advanced by her fellow male anarchists. Unlike her male comrades, however, Capetillo was careful to point out that conflict within couples arose not only because of the permanence and coldly contractual nature of marriage but also because of men's failure to treat women properly on a consistent basis. And while Capetillo firmly advocated both men's and women's right to leave unworkable relationships, she also recognized women's particular economic vulnerabilities. Consequently, Capetillo insisted on men's economic responsibility for all their children, regardless of their relationship with the mother. In addition, she repeatedly stressed the importance of women's economic self-sufficiency. Again, Capetillo's contempt for the economic dependence of middle- and upper-class "ladies" was clear: "The woman who accepts slavery because she does not know how to work is an idiot."[79]

But economic issues were not the only area where Capetillo broke new ground. While advocating the control of male sexuality, she also spoke boldly of women's capacity for sexual pleasure and their right to experience it. Women, she insisted, "have strong sexual appetites, which, like in a man, are a great virtue." Denying women the satisfaction of their desires, she argued, could even harm their health.[80]

Thus, Luisa Capetillo broke the silences that had preserved many aspects of male dominance within anarchist men's versions of free love. In her reconceptualization of heterosexual relationships, she attempted simultaneously to address multiple aspects of women's concerns—economic vulnerability and the ability to escape male abuse, control of male sexual drives and women's right to experience their own. In Capetillo's feminism, women's autonomy was inseparable from male economic and sexual responsibility.[81]

Capetillo did not analyze only sexual relationships and waged labor exploitation. In her program for feminist change she also sought to build solidarity among women. Such alliances were critical for any true social change, but before they could be formed, women had to reach beyond their sexual and economic competition and reject the false distinctions between the labels "respectable" and "disreputable" that divided them.

Capetillo exhorted women to refrain from fighting among themselves over men's sexual attentions and accompanying economic favors. Recognizing that women of all classes suffered from male infidelities, she firmly rejected the bourgeois feminists' demonization of their plebeian sexual competitors. Men and their philandering were the real source of the problem, she maintained. Rather than attacking or distrusting each other, women should unite in confronting unfaithful men, forcing them to choose a single partner and enforcing their economic and emotional commitment to that woman.[82]

Divisions between "respectable" and "disreputable" women were false social constructions, Capetillo insisted, here again rejecting bourgeois feminist definitions of womanhood.[83] Nonvirginal or nonmonogamous women were not "fallen"; they were exercising their right to sexual autonomy. And those called "prostitutes" by society were forced into the sale of sex by poverty, not a dissolute character. In fact, Capetillo wrote, these women were no different from the wealthiest, most "honorable" lady, for all married women exchanged sex for male income. Despite their class differences, women occupied analogous structural positions, dependent on and exploited by men. In their recognition of these commonalities lay the seeds of true social transformation.[84]

Perhaps the best example of Capetillo's call for women's cross-class alliances is her play *Influencias de las ideas modernas.* Angelina, the daughter of a factory owner, is radicalized through her exposure to spiritualism and anarchist and socialist writers and prevails on her father to give up their family's wealth. The instruction of Doña Marina, the widow of a worker and mother of a valiant proletarian son, eventually converts Angelina from a well-meaning lady dispensing charity to a committed radical. Doña Marina's son leads the factory laborers in a strike that, combined with Angelina's pressure on her father, compels the capitalist to turn over the factory to the striking workers and finally to join their utopian community, along with his daughter.

In a final ode to free love and classless collectivity, the play closes with Angelina and the labor leader, other worker couples, and even Doña Marina and Angelina's father joining in free union.[85]

Here, in contrast to male anarchist works, women are not simply the inspiration and support for male-led class struggle. They are the creators and shapers of radical consciousness and cross-class projects. Bourgeois feminist and male Liberal utopias are also challenged; in Capetillo's dreams of social justice, the enlightened rich do not lead the masses. Instead, the revolutionary moment begun by cross-class female encounters and forced open by collective, working-class action produces ripple effects that ricochet between the wealthy and the workers. Capetillo's reconstruction of the societal family, in which wealthy (white) women freely chose to live in consensual union with radical workingmen and proletarian widows provided the vision for social reform, was a far cry indeed from the gran familia of Puerto Rico's male Liberals.

But how well received was Capetillo's feminist project? Bourgeois feminists knew of her activities but largely declined to answer her (in hindsight, rather naïve) call to renounce their material privileges and stand in open solidarity with the working classes. Plebeian women's response to Capetillo's project is especially difficult to judge because such sources as her workingwomen's newspaper have been lost. But despite her impassioned calls to solidarity among women, Luisa Capetillo's writings display little trace of the strong feminine network that sustained feminists in Europe, the United States, and among the upper classes in her own country. Rather, her words betray a strong undercurrent of frustration at society's lack of response to her ideas.[86]

It is entirely possible that Capetillo's assertion of both sexes' right to separation at any time was too frightening to working-class mothers. Plebeian women, especially those with children, faced deepening social and economic vulnerability with the increased mobility, fragmented communities, and shifting social relations of the early twentieth century. With no ability to count on state enforcement of child support outside of marital relationships, Capetillo's call for male economic responsibility was probably not nearly sufficient to counterbalance the fear of male desertion.

Capetillo's refusal to acknowledge the contradictions in women's lives may have limited her popular appeal as well. Her unrelenting scorn for all women, plebeian or wealthy, who depended on male income or feared to leave unsatisfactory relationships excluded great numbers of potential female allies.

Despite her call for women's alliances, judgment seems to have come more easily to Luisa Capetillo than did empathy. She had braved single mother-hood, poverty, and social condemnation with her head held high; those women who hesitated to follow her lead were not worthy of consideration.

Capetillo's stinging critiques of male dominance and the priority she gave to her sexual politics probably also contributed to her marginalization within the left. Not surprisingly, resistance to Capetillo's feminist message was keen among working-class men. She bitterly complained that numerous working-women stopped subscribing to her newspaper because self-described "en-lightened" union men labeled it immoral.[87]

Luisa Capetillo fought an extremely steep uphill battle in her campaign to "liberate women in all aspects of [their] lives." Although she gave public voice for the first time to many aspirations of plebeian women and exposed some of the silences that lurked in the counterhegemonic sexual discourses of male anarchists, Capetillo's lonely feminist struggle was not enough to overturn the deeply entrenched structures and practices that supported male-dominant sexual norms—of either the elites or the popular classes.

Her position must have been weakened even further by the decline of anarchism within the Puerto Rican labor movement. U.S. colonial officials carried out a sweeping repression against anarchists during 1911 and 1912, forcibly closing study centers and jailing key activists.[88] Many anarchist orga-nizers fled Puerto Rico; Capetillo herself lived in exile in New York, Florida, and Cuba for several years following the crackdown. Concerted state repres-sion opened a space for the movement's dominance by "reformers." Men such as Santiago Iglesias and Eduardo Conde successfully consolidated their position as the principal leaders of the FLT during these years; Rubén Dávila charges that they failed to protest vigorously the state's actions against FLT anarchist members because it eliminated their competition.[89]

The new leadership bequeathed an uneven legacy to the Puerto Rican left. They founded the Socialist Party and built it into a significant mass move-ment; the period between 1915 and 1930 is usually celebrated as the heyday of the left in Puerto Rico. But the new leadership also tied the FLT firmly to the increasingly conservative American Federation of Labor in the United States. And perhaps most important for my purposes here, they closed the small but significant space that had opened for questioning gendered power relations within the left.

Along with the anarchists was also suppressed their broader critique of the family and sexual relations. With the exception of the Bayamón newspaper *El Comunista,* which circulated for a few short months during 1920, and Luisa Capetillo's last book, published in 1916, discussions within the labor movement of free love, the institution of marriage, and the sexual double standard all ceased during the second decade of the twentieth century. Even Juan Vilar, who allegedly supported free love and women's equality in his early days as an organizer, study center director, and children's theater producer in Caguas, made no mention of sexual issues in his book *Páginas libres,* which was published in 1914, after his release from a long stint in prison.

The broad analyses of the "woman question" that Luisa Capetillo and some of her male anarchist comrades had developed were effectively silenced. The focus on production that had always marked the Puerto Rican left's understanding of "the political" became even more pronounced and eventually fused with its post-1915 prioritization of electoral politics.[90] Radical sexual reform was definitively eliminated from the labor movement's agenda—indeed, the suppression of such discussions may well have boosted the left's popularity among the male electorate. Thus, with the institutionalization of the labor movement and the growth of its influence on the island's formal state structures was lost the fleeting historical moment when, in however conflictual and flawed a way, Puerto Rican working people's struggle for justice linked critiques of capitalism and sexual power relations.

Prostitution, however, remained prominent in the iconography of the labor movement. The early left's understanding of plebeian women's sexual and economic oppression under capitalism produced a powerful symbol which would long outlive the early-twentieth-century discussions of free love and the honor system and which became effectively decoupled—at least in the left's public discourses—from racial connotations. The analysis of prostitution that was eventually incorporated into the fabric of radical politics safely skirted questions of plebeian men's dominance of women while including "fallen" women as members of the racially diverse working classes. But when the U.S. colonial state embarked on a campaign of sexual repression reminiscent of the nineteenth-century hygiene campaigns, the new analysis of prostitution did provide the basis for a very different response from members of the working classes and Afro–Puerto Rican professionals. This time, instead of facing a cross-class misogynist consensus, the targeted women would encounter a broad coalition of allies.

Chapter 6

Saving Democracy: Debating Prostitution During World War I

There are only two sides to this question. Just as a person is today either pro-German or anti-German, so a person in Porto Rico is either pro-prostitution or anti-prostitution; and I believe that the man who is pro-prostitution is as dangerous to the community as a person who is pro-German.
—Howard Kern, *Special Report of the Attorney General of Porto Rico*

I sincerely hope that the people of Ponce do not support this policy [of arresting prostitutes]. For if they did, I would have to say that my people servilely kissed the very chains which oppressed and dishonored them."
—Rafael Martínez Nadal, quoted in "El mitín de anoche," *El Águila de Puerto Rico,* August 2, 1918

Look, esteemed gentlemen, for the origin of prostitution, and you will incontrovertibly find that . . . *you* are the guilty ones.
—Anonymous woman author, "Vale mas precaver que tener que remediar," *El Águila de Puerto Rico,* October 9, 1918

By the end of the second decade of U.S. rule in Puerto Rico, the social ferment that followed the 1898 invasion had deepened considerably. Afro-Puerto Ricans, particularly within the Republicano Party, continued to denounce racism on the island. Labor strikes broke out relentlessly. Women of various social classes had begun to agitate for the right to vote. Amid this unrest, the United States conveniently "granted" Puerto Ricans citizenship and conscripted them into the colonial military, just in time for the United States to join World War I in 1917. Soon after announcing its entrance into the war, the United States began drafting troops for training. Puerto Rico was expected to offer its share of the men to be sent to the European theater of conflict.

During World War I, the colonial state tried its best to contain the proliferation of grassroots movements and discourses in Puerto Rico. Official
attempts to enforce a pro-U.S., procapitalist consensus intensified between
1917 and 1920. Shrill appeals to order, patriotism (to the United States), and
moral rectitude appeared everywhere. As in the 1890s, a state campaign to
control prostitution emerged at the center of this attempt to consolidate a
clear hegemonic consensus over "national" values. At a moment when previously marginalized Puerto Ricans were increasingly contesting their for-
merly prescribed social limits, the question of prostitution made the local
headlines and quickly became a major focus of debates over the nature of
democracy in Puerto Rico. But the public frenzy over prostitution did not
follow the same trajectory that it had in Ponce during the 1890s.

Now, prostitution was named as a threat from the highest reaches of the
colonial government. Efforts to "cleanse" society of promiscuous women
were implemented through an islandwide coordinated campaign, not in
piecemeal municipal efforts. Prostitution should be eradicated completely,
state officials trumpeted, not simply confined to the "darker," poorer corners
of society as it had been by nineteenth-century regulation. The state's capacity to enforce its will had greatly increased as well. The repression of World
War I took only a few weeks to reach full force in Puerto Rico, rather than
building over the course of a decade, as it had twenty years earlier.

During this period, at least in the northern United States, the vast numbers of unassimilated immigrants created as great a threat to the homogeneity
of national identity as had former slaves. For privileged Puerto Ricans, however, the "danger within" was not European immigration but blackness and
the growing challenges from organized laboring people as a whole. Thus, the
charges of disease and immorality hurled against targeted women probably
carried racialized class connotations, as they had during the 1890s, despite
their apparently racially neutral tone. But Afro-Puerto Ricans, as well as
socialists, attempted to challenge the implicit linkage between blackness,
poverty, and female disreputability.

During World War I, the drive was to save men of all classes—specifically
soldiers—from venereal disease–infected women. The nation's virility—and
through it the future of the "honorable family"—was at stake in the battle
against prostitution. But not only the state used prostitution-focused discourses and reform activities to advance its agenda. Bourgeois women, by
now a social force to be reckoned with, actively collaborated with the state

campaign, hoping to increase their own political, professional, and moral legitimacy. No longer were they isolated from alleged prostitutes. Rather, male elites and colonial officials enthusiastically welcomed the entrance of "the ladies" into the realm of public moral reform. Their sustained contact with imprisoned, infected women would purify the strayed sheep, not mar their own "decency," as had been feared two decades earlier.

As doctors, police, state functionaries, and many "respectable" citizens proclaimed "promiscuous" women a particularly potent threat to the nation's well-being, popular protest of the repression against working-class women erupted. Unlike the 1890s in Ponce, the targeted women did not stand alone. The more inclusive discourses on sexuality articulated by the women and men of the labor movement had planted firm roots in popular sexual practices and norms over the past twenty years. However flawed these discourses may have been, they, along with the widespread proletarianization of the previous decades, the emergence of self-consciously Afro-Puerto Rican public intellectuals, and the growing militancy of workingwomen as a whole, provided a ground for alternative analyses of the meaning and roots of prostitution. It was no longer so easy to divide workingmen from supposedly disreputable women of their own class, even in the public hysteria over sexually dangerous women that erupted during World War I. Groups opposing the state campaign insisted that the targeted women embodied legal rights central to a healthy democracy—now imperiled by the wartime repression of dissent and difference.

In the end, public consensus over the terms of decency and democracy proved impossible. Even the two dominant political parties—the Republicanos and the Unionistas—split over the question of prostitution; significant members of both parties opposed the state's eradication campaign. Although the state did carry out its repressive program against sexually suspect workingwomen, it had to ram its agenda down the reluctant throats of much of the Puerto Rican populace. The ongoing resistance of targeted women and their allies established important limits to the state's long-term objectives of sexual containment.

The Context

Severe economic crisis had begun to grip Puerto Rico by the second decade of U.S. rule. Excluded from the trade and investment preferences given to local sugar production, the coffee-producing highlands stagnated after the U.S. invasion. Thousands of laborers and their families left the island's mountainous interior and migrated to coastal areas in search of work. The tobacco industry provided little relief; between 1910 and 1920, employment in this sector dropped 25 percent, while production rose only 12 percent. In the coastal sugar regions, production tripled, as U.S. corporations devoured land and introduced increasingly sophisticated technology. Employment levels, however, remained almost unaltered. Income from the cane fields, for those lucky enough to find work there, was very low and sporadic at best. During the long months of "dead time," between harvest and planting periods, cane workers were laid off with no salary. By 1917, Puerto Ricans desperate for employment were streaming to New York and other U.S. industrial centers. Ponce seamstresses wrote letters to local papers, calling on the city's population to aid them in the struggle to survive. Women who worked in sweatshops, they reported, earned only one dollar per day; those who sewed in their homes earned only a few cents per day. The seamstresses were not alone in their misery. Petitions from people begging for work or the funds to emigrate flooded the governor's office. Many laboring Puerto Ricans faced starvation, especially in the countryside. Suicides of working people were reported daily in Ponce newspapers. By 1926, the island's official unemployment rate—which did not include the seasonal cane workers—had reached 30 percent. Simultaneously, Puerto Rico's local food production had dropped by two-thirds.[1]

The years surrounding World War I were also marked by intense social mobilization in Puerto Rico. Almost all groups involved in the movements of these years weighed in on the prostitution question, viewing the antiprostitution campaign as a powerful symbol and a political opportunity to assert their own interests and hone their identities in relation to both the alleged prostitutes and those whom they opposed.

The Socialist Party, as I have discussed, was founded in 1915 as the political wing of the FLT; it steadily increased its share of the vote and by 1920 had the support of a third or more of the electorate in a majority of the island's municipalities. Urban squatters faced with government-sponsored eviction from their shantytowns called on the Socialists to help them in the struggle to defend their homes. Labor organizing continued apace. Cane workers, typographers, cigar rollers, and dockworkers, among others, held significant walkouts during this period and were often met by police repression. In

August 1918, Socialist public speakers demanded the recall of Governor Yager, citing his abuses against working people.[2]

By 1918, women were in the forefront of the labor militancy. They jammed Socialist study circles and meetings in Ponce by the hundreds, far outnumbering the men.[3] Workingwomen demanded higher wages, better working conditions, and a minimum wage for women workers and protested managerial physical and sexual abuse. More than one thousand women seamstresses and embroiderers signed a petition to the Puerto Rican legislature in 1918 urging the approval of "a law that would liberate them from the inhumane exploitation which they have suffered from time immemorial."[4] A year later, delegates representing ten thousand Puerto Rican laborers held the First Congress of Women Workers, where in addition to the aforementioned demands, they invoked the right of every woman and her family to have a "comfortable and healthy home," insisted on the implementation of universal women's suffrage, and called for a special session of the legislature to address women's concerns. Women hatmakers, tobacco strippers, pasta makers, coffee shellers, seamstresses, and laundresses went on strike throughout the island during these years. In Ponce and San Juan, women tobacco strippers walked out numerous times in solidarity with striking women in neighboring factories. Their pickets were often marked by violent confrontation with the police. When a woman striker was wounded by policemen at the La Marina tobacco factory, for example, her female comrades rained bricks, metal piping, rocks, and worktables onto the heads of armed men in the street below.[5]

Middle- and upper-class women were also on the move. Between 1915 and July 1917, they worked in coalition with Protestant clergy and the Socialist Party to prohibit the sale and manufacture of alcohol in Puerto Rico. The successful Prohibition campaign was a watershed in bourgeois women's social activism. It legitimized "proper women's" presence in public political organizing and debates. It also gave further impetus to the movement for women's right to vote.[6]

Ponce was an important center of bourgeois feminist activism. It was the birthplace of the first such organization, the Liga Femínea, and was home to many prominent feminists. After winning the Prohibition battle in July 1917, Ponce "ladies" did not limit themselves to suffrage agitation. They took on other moral reform projects that often developed rather draconian overtones. Anxious to "combat the damage" done to working-class children whose mothers had to leave them at home while working, women from a number of

Ponce's leading families began to set up an interventionist network. They identified "children at risk," took them from their mothers, and placed them with families of "clean customs" where the children were supposedly given clothing, sent to public school, and taught a trade. The bourgeois female reformers were so successful at their work, a local newspaper proclaimed, that the Juvenile District Court named them special prosecutors and pledged to aid them in their efforts to purchase a farm that might someday house a technical school for the "rescued children."[7] In addition to asserting a public social role for themselves, insisting on the right to define the parameters of "proper" motherhood and familial relations for all Puerto Ricans, bourgeois women activists were rapidly laying the groundwork for expanded state intervention into the private affairs of working-class Puerto Ricans.

Finally, particularly within the Republicano Party, Afro-Puerto Ricans continued to denounce the racism that permeated the island's society.[8] *El Águila,* the Ponce Republicano newspaper of the period, was edited by Alonso Gual, an Afro-Puerto Rican man. Like its Republicano predecessors in the city, the paper periodically featured articles delineating the history of Spanish repression against blacks in Puerto Rico, accusing the opposition Unionista leadership of wishing to return to the nineteenth century and its unbridled racial exploitation. Racism ran deep in Puerto Rico, *El Águila's* writers declared. Negative stereotypes of blacks were everywhere—in jokes, movies, and popular literature. The exhortations of wealthy white Puerto Ricans to nationalist patriotism were useless in the face of such ongoing discrimination; there could be no viable nation without respect and dignity for all citizens, regardless of their skin color. The United States, at least, had enshrined the ideal of racial equality in its constitution—its rule was preferable to that of racist Puerto Rican elites. Gual stated in no uncertain terms that he and his black compatriots were quite proud of "our dark pigment"; it was this racial self-assurance, he insisted, that made the Unión Party leadership so uncomfortable. Numerous articles in *El Águila* also celebrated Afro-Puerto Rican musical talent, professionalism, and collective solidarity in the local regiment "de color" of the U.S. Army.[9]

Afro-Puerto Ricans' persistent public voice combined with the proliferation of other popular discourses and organizing, as well as the generalized economic distress, to create an acute awareness on the island of the need for social and economic reform. Both Ponce Republicanos in *El Águila* and reformist Unionistas in the pages of the San Juan–based daily *La Correspon-*

dencia insisted that the wealthy had a responsibility to ease the plight of the poor. Working parents were forced by an unjust social system to leave their children unattended; they were not to blame for their children's unruliness. Gual went so far as to hint that if the rich were unwilling to redistribute some of their resources, working people might wrench away all their wealth—and be justified in doing so. During the early 1920s, even the popular womens magazine *Mujer* made references to the need to go beyond moralizing the poor—the elimination of poverty was necessary. *Puerto Rico Ilustrado,* perhaps the most popular magazine of the period, also occasionally ran pieces describing the horrible working conditions of the poor.[10] Thus, the working class's politicization of poverty had had an effect on public discourse about the poor by 1918. Public awareness of the material roots of social dislocation and crime had increased greatly since the nineteenth century. Even some privileged Puerto Ricans recognized poverty to be socially produced, rather than biologically inherent.

By World War I, popular conceptions of sexuality were also shaping public discussions of plebeian women and moral decency. Socialists and anarchists were not the only groups publicly to defend plebeian women's respectability and sexual dignity. Afro-Puerto Rican Republicanos in Ponce also insisted on workingwomen's right to honorable status. Several months before the national crackdown against prostitution began, a police officer attempted to arrest a young Ponce waitress walking home from work, charging her with prostitution. Both *El Águila* and the woman's employer called for an end to such abuses, which they said "were all too common in this city." *El Águila* also published a long editorial on a similar case in San Juan; Alonso Gual called for the resignation of the arresting policemen and the judge who had ignored the accused women's pleas of innocence. In addition, Gual penned a passionate piece arguing that every woman, regardless of social status, deserved respect. All women in public places should be assumed to be "innocent until proven guilty" in matters of morality. Rich or poor, black or white, rowdy or demure, they should all be treated as ladies. Gual even expressed sympathy for prostitutes themselves, ruined, as he said, by society's injustices, not their own ill will.[11] Thus, *El Águila* urged a race- and class-blind presumption of feminine respectability.

By the second decade of U.S. rule, both Socialists and some Afro-Puerto Rican Republicanos were translating inclusive, informal popular sexual norms into new public moral standards that disavowed the supposedly natural equation of blackness and poverty with disreputability. In the process, they challenged the honor hierarchy that reinforced race and class power differentials among women, and they set the stage for a response to the state's antiprostitution campaign radically different from that articulated by Ponceños in the 1890s.

The solidarity with targeted women that they and hundreds of others expressed in the months to come was probably facilitated by the massive process of proletarianization experienced by most Puerto Ricans during the early twentieth century. By this time, U.S. capital's voracious push of both urban and rural residents into waged labor and abject poverty had diminished some of the economic and social status diversity that had marked plebeian Puerto Ricans during the nineteenth century. No longer was it so simple for a working person to draw lines of respectability distinguishing oneself or one's family from public, allegedly disreputable women.

The first twenty years of U.S. colonial rule in Puerto Rico also coincided on the mainland with the Progressive Era, a time of great reforming fervor. Temperance, women's suffrage, and the consolidation of institutions for social reform were at the forefront of United States politics. These movements and state policies profoundly influenced developments in Puerto Rico, including the antiprostitution campaign.

Prostitution was a key issue for many North American Progressive reformers long before the United States entered World War I. Throughout the United States, coalitions of feminists, social hygienists, and social purity advocates formed on the local level. These coalitions were committed to the eradication of prostitution (hence their "abolitionist" title). They insisted that state regulation encouraged vice and unfairly targeted the women who sold sex. Progressives turned to scientific studies and state intervention as the means for abolishing prostitution. Women reformers, in particular, represented a broad political spectrum, from radical feminists to conservative members of mothers clubs. Most of them, however, based their critique of prostitution on a denunciation of women's sexual and economic exploitation and the sexual double standard. Prostitution became an important trope through which white, middle-class U.S. women expressed their rage at male domination.[12]

But despite U.S. female reformers' insistence that men were at the root of the prostitution economy, for the most part municipal governments intervened against women who sold sex, not the men who bought it. Police pursued and arrested prostitutes. The women were locked away in reformatories to be made the object of innumerable eugenic studies. Male pimps gained greater power over the trade and the women on its front lines. This pattern was repeated in hundreds of communities across the country, adding up to a diffuse but very powerful movement whose main result was repression against working-class women and girls.[13]

The wartime antiprostitution campaign that emerged in the United States built on the reforming zeal that had swept the nation during the Progressive Era. In a great hue and cry to "protect our boys from venereal disease," the federal government molded its first nationally coordinated crusade against prostitution. By the end of the war, eighteen thousand women had been detained in the United States. Only one-third of them had been charged with prostitution; the rest were listed simply as "promiscuous." Abolitionist activists were recruited into the U.S. campaign. Most enthusiastically cooperated with state surveillance, arrest sweeps, and efforts at "rehabilitation." The feminist protests over draconian legislative moves which had proliferated during the years 1910–19 were silenced or futile during the war. Despite the efforts of some feminists to protect working-class women from the worst effects of the arrests, by early 1919 in the United States, "the prostitute had become the war's venereal scapegoat, vilified, shunned, and eventually locked up."[14]

Much of the public discourse during the Progressive Era about prostitution's "white slavery" fused protest of the sexual victimization of (native-born) women with acute anti-immigrant sentiment.[15] Once the United States entered World War I, these types of warnings against "the enemy within" broadened and intensified. In Puerto Rico as well as in the United States, surveillance and repression against individuals or groups deemed dangerous to the national interest escalated dramatically. All mail to the island was censored in the drive to ferret out "German sympathizers." The state avidly prosecuted Puerto Rican journalists criticizing U.S. colonialism, and police placed Socialist labor organizers under heavy surveillance. Children on the island were ordered to come to public schools in military dress. Refusing to sing the U.S. national anthem marked one as a traitor.[16] This sweeping repression of dissent and marked disregard for individual civil rights directly fed into state crackdowns against sexually suspect workingwomen. Alleged prostitutes were a diseased danger, the state proclaimed, the enemy on the home front.

The Puerto Rican Anti-Prostitution Campaign

The colonial state's antiprostitution campaign in Puerto Rico was a direct offshoot of the U.S. government's mainland efforts. As soon as troops began to mobilize domestically, the U.S. surgeon general, the secretary of the navy, and other federal officials began to send letters to Governor Yager and the Puerto Rican attorney general Howard Kern urging the implementation of an "active anti-venereal campaign" on the island. As in the United States, the ultimate goal was to "exterminate" prostitution in order to protect the health of the soldiers.[17]

During the first seven months of 1918, the area around the Las Casas training base near San Juan was the focus of police activity. More than two hundred women suspected of prostitution were arrested, most of whom were convicted for violating the "Five Mile Law" and sentenced to fifteen days in prison. But Kern, the island police chief, and medical officials were not satisfied. Almost half the men arriving in Las Casas were already infected with venereal diseases. Establishing a five-mile "moral zone" around the camp was not a sufficient preventative measure.

In early August, Kern sent a circular to all municipal judges, prosecutors, and police forces announcing the opening of an islandwide campaign to "cleanse prostitutes from every town and barrio." To Kern and his Puerto Rican supporters, prostitution was a "plague" to be "exterminated"—"the rotting part of the social organism." The health and, ultimately, the virility of Puerto Rican soldiers was paramount; the only way to ensure these elements was to eliminate promiscuous women from society entirely. Once again, as in the 1890s, medical concerns lent a presumably neutral veneer of scientific legitimation to state repression.[18]

Kern insisted on coordination of efforts between all branches of the judicial system, the police, and "helpful citizens." He then called a press conference for sympathetic journalists, at which he made clear that "suspect" women could be arrested without cause and submitted to involuntary vaginal exams by the police. Infection with a venereal disease was de facto proof of prostitution.[19] Kern also pronounced that questioning the new policy within official ranks would not be tolerated. "If there is any weak link in this chain, report it in order that it may be corrected. If any official fails to do his duty, report him and he will be replaced and a more efficient and patriotic man will be appointed in his place. . . . *It is not our task to ask or reason why, but to do.*"[20] George

Shanton, Puerto Rico's colonial chief of police, demanded the removal of the overseer of military sanitation who balked at the idea of mass arrests. Kern also sharply rebuffed a municipal judge who expressed concern about the new policy's potential for conflicts with "personal rights and liberties."[21]

Within a few weeks, all towns in Puerto Rico had been "inspected." Those pronounced "infected by prostitution" were placed off-limits to soldiers, and troops from those towns were not allowed to return home for leave. Manatí, Puerta de Tierra, and San Juan received particularly heavy surveillance. Throughout, however, no systematic investigations, surveillance, or arrests of venereal disease–infected *men* were ever made. Working-class women bore the weight of this new wave of repression, just as they had in the 1890s.[22]

In Ponce, the equation of "scandalous woman" with "prostitute" that had emerged during the prostitution panic of the 1890s seems to have dissipated somewhat by 1917. Before the 1918 antiprostitution campaign, the police logbooks clearly distinguished between those women who were simply rowdy and those considered to be prostitutes.[23] From 1905 until the state's wartime crackdown, prostitutes appear to have been left alone by the police as long as they were discreet about their activities. Police intervention occurred only when alleged prostitutes crossed recognized social boundaries by inviting children into their homes, drinking with adolescent boys, stealing from their neighbors, or fighting openly in the street. Often, the women were simply warned to stop their untoward behavior. Arrests were relatively rare; prosecution and convictions even more so.[24] Neighbors' complaints did periodically prompt police roundups of alleged prostitutes, but no prosecutions or imprisonment ever resulted. The women were merely given a scolding and advised to move.

The past was not completely undone, though. Prostitutes were still subject to a good deal of surveillance. Police continued to keep lists of alleged prostitutes, carrying out "investigations" of suspicious women when city residents took their complaints of misbehavior to the press.[25] Clearly, at least some "respectable" citizens were not satisfied with the moral state of their city. Kern's wartime campaign against prostitution had firm ground on which to build.

And build it did—extraordinarily quickly. Within two weeks of the publication of Kern's circular, hundreds of women were arrested and sentenced to prison in Ponce alone. Not a day passed without the arraignment of several women accused of prostitution before the city's municipal judge. Arrested women began to arrive under police guard at the Ponce district jail from

Mayagüez, Isabela, San Sebastián, and Aguadilla. By August 19, 273 women had been imprisoned at the Ponce jail. Less than a month later, their numbers had swelled to 348; soon they numbered 450. Most were convicted and given sentences ranging from six months to a year—far exceeding the imprisonment rate and term length of the 1890s. State repression had returned with a vengeance.[26]

The picture in the rest of the island was quite similar. Two hundred and fifty women were imprisoned in the Arecibo district jail within a week of the national campaign's initiation. On September 1, with both the Arecibo and Ponce jails filled to overflowing, the Mayagüez district jail was designated as a third prostitution imprisonment center, quickly accepting 180 women. Early October saw 95 more women jailed in San Juan. On February 1, 1919, Howard Kern triumphantly reported that in less than four months, 1,197 women had been arrested across Puerto Rico. And, he gloated, "those not sentenced were practically interned with their families in towns [outside of San Juan]."[27]

The mass arrests caused quite a splash among the Puerto Rican populace. The campaign immediately made front-page headlines in newspapers across the island. The flatbed truck convoys and trains carrying arrested women from smaller towns to the main holding jails in Arecibo, Ponce, and Mayagüez were met along the way by crowds of people. Five hundred turned out near San Juan in a single day to gawk at the women. These trips must have been excruciating for the arrested women—not only did they face up to a year in jail, but now they also had become a national spectacle, publicly branded as prostitutes, and exposed to the alternately curious, pitying, and hostile eyes of the entire island.[28]

In a highly accelerated version of the 1890s, new surveillance forces and practices quickly spun out of the antiprostitution campaign. Ponce's police chief, Miguel Hurtado, established a special "morality" police force, intended to keep working-class neighborhoods along the edge of town and the riverbanks under close surveillance, because they were the areas of highest "promiscuous activity." Police began to close public dances. They burst into the homes of "suspicious" single women and interrogated them, their families, and neighbors about their friends, visitors, lifestyles, and livelihood. Only those lucky enough to be residing "under the power" of a live-in boyfriend or parent were let go without detention. Some couples living in consensual union were forced to marry to avoid the woman's imprisonment. At least one woman was arrested and charged with prostitution because she refused to "make commitments to prolonged relationships with any man."[29]

Soon the Ponce police were arresting anyone they could find having non-marital sex. Lovers trysting in the back rooms of stores, at the riverbank, or even in their own private rooms were hauled into the police station and subjected to questioning. The men were invariably let go, whereas the women were forcibly "inspected" for venereal disease and often charged with prostitution or immorality. Across the island in San Juan, working-class couples leaving the cinema or taking evening walks were arrested.[30]

Across the island, women reformers leaped to help in surveillance activities as their counterparts had done in the United States. The Puerto Rico chapter of the Women's Christian Temperance Union (WCTU), jointly led by Rosa Chevremont and Edith Hildreth, a North American woman, quickly established groups of "feminine police" in San Juan, Arecibo, and Mayagüez. Hildreth asked the "ladies" of the island to help this "force for moral reform" expand women's role in preparing Puerto Rican society to defend democracy in the European war.[31]

Tomás Bryan, a municipal judge in Mayagüez and a particularly zealous pursuer of alleged prostitutes, applauded the WCTU's efforts. He urged Mayagüez's "chaste, timid ladies of honor" to join the feminine police and "persecute clandestine prostitution," obtaining evidence to use in convictions and keeping lists of suspicious neighbors. Women's long-standing practices of gossip and informal neighborhood surveillance would make them invaluable allies in the thrust to eradicate female promiscuity. "Mothers, wives, and sisters," he trumpeted, "this campaign presents you with the first great opportunity to destroy the most powerful enemy of your homes and, therefore, of your happiness."[32]

Indeed, evidence suggests that the crackdown may have found a good deal of support among "legitimate" wives, partners, and mothers. In Naguabo, where a widow took in a number of women fleeing police persecution, a group of women neighbors demanded that she expel them. A Ponce "mother of a family" also wholeheartedly endorsed the attorney general's new policy: Her son had been "captured" by one of "those women." For some time he had refused to listen to her motherly advice, abandoning her to spend all his time and money with his lover.[33] The charge to "protect our men" had popular reverberations that stretched far beyond the colonial state's immediate wartime concerns. For many women, the call to arms was a much more personal one, for it also meant defending their own economic and emotional interests. At last, "decent" married women could strike out at their sexual competitors and count on the state's repressive force to back them.

A mere ten days after the campaign's initiation, a "detective" of the feminine police crowed that respectable women had made great strides in their drive to protect the virtue of the home. Island newspapers were avidly covering the campaign. Hundreds of infected women had been arrested and locked away securely, with the support of the attorney general's "firm position." "Public opinion has been raised, and the public conscience has awoken. We women have won a glorious victory!"[34]

The Unión and Republicano Party leaderships, Puerto Rico's chapters of the Rotary Club and the Young Men's Christian Association (YMCA), mayors, municipal judges, and Protestant and Catholic clergy throughout the island all joined in the acclaim of Kern's efforts.[35] This consensus is particularly striking when viewed in the political context of the times. Republicano and Unión Party leaders were locked in bitter conflicts over interpretations of the Jones Act, proposals for fiscal reform, "Americanization" of Puerto Rico's populace, and the proper method of "self-government" for the island. Apparently, only state repression against allegedly morally ambiguous workingwomen could unite them. But state officials and their supporters were to find that "the public conscience" was not monolithic and that all women did not agree that this campaign was a victory for their sex.

The Opposition

Even before the state's islandwide campaign began, individual women protested the attack on prostitution. In May 1918, a young domestic worker named Leonor Crespo was arrested by the police in San Juan and accused of being a prostitute. Leonor insisted that she was honorable and prevailed on her employers to testify on her behalf. After subjecting her to an involuntary internal examination, even the court-appointed doctors pronounced Leonor a virgin; she was finally acquitted of all charges in Puerto Rico's District Court. In Mayagüez, numerous women charged with prostitution maintained their innocence. They were not as lucky as Leonor: all were convicted in the early days of the state's campaign. A Ponce waitress, similarly harassed by the police, obtained the public support of her employer and local Afro-Puerto Rican journalists. On August 19, 1918, Susana Torres won an acquittal from accusations by a neighbor that she had infected him with venereal disease; after demanding an examination, she was found to be a virgin. In Ponce, *El Águila* gave these stories front-page headlines, warning against indiscriminate sweeps by the police. Suspicion of being "horizontalists," Alonso Gual wrote, was not sufficient cause for arrest. "This is like holding a whip of fire to the backs of unfortunate women who happen to be out of favor with police officers."[36] The righteous protests by individual working-women, along with the Afro-Puerto Rican Republicano press's encouragement of their position, sparked a storm of opposition in Ponce which reverberated across the island.

On August 20, 1918, three weeks into the islandwide campaign and one week after the feminine police had printed their triumphant ode to conservative public opinion and bourgeois female surveillance activities in San Juan newspapers, flyers were distributed in Ponce's central plaza announcing a public meeting to protest "the persecution that prostitutes are experiencing in Puerto Rico." Government officials had effectively suspended the U.S. Constitution in their crackdown, the leaflet warned. "Such abuses cannot be tolerated."[37] The next night, a huge crowd numbering close to two thousand gathered at 8:00 P.M. in the plaza—a much bigger assembly than the usual turnout for public political debates. The atmosphere was charged with electricity. People from all social classes filled the plaza and stayed until nearly midnight, when the last speech was made.[38]

The two main speakers and organizers of the demonstration were Leopoldo Tormes Solís, the mulatto son of a black washerwoman and a small-scale Spanish merchant, and Rafael Martínez Nadal.[39] Both men were attorneys and staunch Republicanos. The two lambasted Kern's circular as abusive, inhumane, and antidemocratic. The antiprostitution campaign betrayed some of the most sacred principles of the U.S. Constitution, they cried, and the attorney general had consciously endorsed the punishment of women on the basis of unproven accusations. The crowd wildly applauded both Tormes and Martínez Nadal as they linked the campaign's violation of workingwomen's legal rights with the state's repression of strikes throughout the island and invoked the principles of individual liberties, habeas corpus, and innocence until proof of guilt. All these were crucial democratic rights that had become available to all Puerto Ricans only recently. They could not be abandoned now. The prostitutes' cause touched all citizens.

Even party loyalties, usually quite fierce in Puerto Rican political culture, could not be maintained while scores of Republicano judges, prosecutors, and police zealously carried out Kern's directives. Santiago Vivaldi, the Ponce district attorney and a fellow Republicano, came under especially vehement attack—he had betrayed the democratic principles to which he had sworn allegiance upon entering the legal profession, Tormes and Martínez Nada insisted.

Vivaldi leaped to the tribunal and delivered an impassioned rebuttal to his two party "coreligionists." Not all the arrested Ponce women had been convicted, he proclaimed—those who had deserved release had been pardoned by him personally. But all convicted women, he assured the crowd, were indeed prostitutes. The threat to national security and U.S. defense of worldwide democracy posed by these women was grave indeed—Puerto Rico had to have the courage to take radical action against them. Members of the crowd applauded enthusiastically.[40]

Evidently, the residents of Ponce were of two minds in their analysis of the connections between democracy and prostitution. Prostitutes could represent either the quintessential symbol of democracy's fragile nature, imperiled by state power run amok, or a threat to democracy's rule. *El Águila*'s waffling positions on prostitution and the state arrests was emblematic of this ambivalence. Alonso Gual clearly condemned police harassment of workingwomen, called for respectful treatment of all women by men, and warned that too zealous a campaign could violate citizens' constitutional rights. But ultimately he succumbed to the power of colonial saber rattling and supported the new state policy. Support of the U.S. armed forces and protection of their health was paramount, he insisted. Consequently, "it is acceptable to proceed (always in a humane manner) against women of the bad life."[41]

But the earlier cross-class consensus in favor of excluding disorderly plebeian women from the community of "decent" Ponce citizens had been shattered. *El Águila*'s support of the campaign was carefully qualified in ways unimaginable twenty years before. And key sectors of the populace, perhaps most notably dissident members of the prostatehood Republicano Party, recognized and were willing to oppose vociferously the repression inherent in the state's regulation of workingwomen's sexuality. Throughout the impassioned debates of 1918, however, no one publicly questioned the broader legitimacy of U.S. rule. Rather, for the opposition, abusive officials were driving the antiprostitution sweeps and had to be stopped to fulfill the utopian promise of justice and equality.

The protests escalated in the days following Ponce's mass meeting. Another Ponce lawyer wrote several times to the San Juan reformist Unión newspaper, *La Correspondencia,* to applaud Tormes and Martínez Nadal. "Where moral freedom does not exist, political freedom cannot exist," he asserted. Kern's policy of replacing officials who dared question the new policy was a direct threat to the right to dissent that Puerto Ricans had struggled long and hard to obtain. Other Ponce lawyers affirmed their opposition to the antiprostitution campaign in press communiqués.[42]

Thus, the refusal by individual workingwomen to submit to the state's repression and labeling of them as disreputable started the protests in Puerto Rico. Their insistence on the right to be treated as respectable citizens was taken up by male attorneys and journalists from Ponce—several of whom were of African descent. These intellectuals proved key in the development of an islandwide public discourse that challenged the colonial state's formidably organized crackdown against working-class women. Opposing the depiction of prostitutes as a diseased threat to national security and virility, they insisted that the repression against allegedly promiscuous women was a threat to the individual liberties of all Puerto Ricans.

The Socialist press also strengthened the chorus of protest. In keeping with their long-standing analysis of prostitutes as sisters of the working class, they called for solidarity with the targeted women, "virgins and martyrs of men and of society, eternal slaves of men's malignant passions." Prostitution was produced by poverty and wealthy men's sexual predation; its existence was an indictment of class exploitation, not the women themselves. Criminalizing the sale of sex, Socialists wrote, did not address the economic disparities at its root. The present state campaign was particularly ominous. Its systematic persecution of prostitutes violated basic Constitutional freedoms, targeted solely the poor, and made the dominant definitions of respectability even more rigid and oppressive. The state sweeps had created a "dictatorship of morality," where the law had become "the lash of an inhuman regime."[43]

Progressive, reform-minded Unionista also joined the drive to oppose the state's crackdown. In so doing, they openly defied the leadership of their party. Taking up the protests of individual arrested women and the criticisms broached in the Ponce mass meeting, they converted *La Correspondencia* into the island's central forum for the expression of dissenting views on the official prostitution policy. Throughout the months of August and September 1918, *La Correspondencia* gave front-page coverage to denunciations of the campaign and its authors' blatant disregard for individual civil rights. After being convicted on the basis of dubious evidence, many women were subsequently denied the right to appeal. Repression and denial of basic rights was no way to carry out social reform, especially when the women selling sex were not to blame for their position. "These women who are victims of misfortune, cannot find a propitious place of employment. . . . [They are] innocents, having committed no crime other than defending their own lives and those of their children who, dying of hunger, beg for a crust of bread and a tattered coat."[44] At stake was nothing less than the legitimacy of the entire judicial system and, implicitly, the state itself. The enforcement of Kern's draconian circular had to stop.[45] The force of Afro-Puerto Rican and other working peoples' voices had changed the landscape of sexual politics since Canta Claro penned his venomous columns; such an analysis would have been unthinkable twenty years before.[46]

Working people all over the island applauded *La Correspondencia*'s "valiant stance" against Kern's crackdown. Telegrams flooded in from workers—many of whom were male members of the FLT—in Ponce, Yauco, Cabo Rojo, Mayagüez, Aguas Buenas, Manatí, Cayey, Utuado, Arecibo, Bayamón, San Lorenzo, Humacao, Santurce, and San Juan. "One thousand workers of the Bayamón collective congratulate you for energetic campaign in favor of the people's rights. Stay at the pinnacle of protest. 'Democracia' and 'Tiempo' [the main San Juan–based Unión and Republicano newspapers, respectively] horribly servile. Do not stain reputation."[47] Santiago Iglesias, the president of the Socialist Party, wrote, "Congratulations on your virile campaign, defense of the people's rights." Five hundred Socialist tobacco rollers in San Lorenzo urged *La Correspondencia* to stand up to *La Democracia*'s and *El Tiempo*'s insults. A tobacco rollers local from Utuado commended the newspaper's editors for their position on the antiprostitution action, "all praise to socialism!" And three workers from Yauco encouraged the newspaper: "[Your] attitude saves nation from cowardly stigma for its silence before arbitrary orders and incorrect procedures. . . . The country is with you. Keep on swinging; there's ample reason to do so."[48]

Radical working men and women's growing social and political mobilizations and their inclusive discourse on prostitution were now bearing fruit. While the colonial state sought to save Puerto Rican men from the pernicious influences of "promiscuous" women, the discourses congealing in protest of the campaign insisted that manly men protect defenseless women from an abusive state. For the more radical sectors of the Puerto Rican working and professional classes, alleged prostitutes were no longer the darkened scourge of the community, as they had been in the days of Canta Claro and municipal regulation in Ponce. The new socialist and anarchist discourses of the early twentieth century had transformed prostitutes into the race-neutral, quintessential symbol of working-class exploitation. In addition, Afro-Puerto Rican popular sensibilities, now publicly articulated in the press, rejected the sharp racialized dichotomy between "respectable" and "disreputable" women that underlay the dominant discourse on feminine sexuality. The 1918 repression was also carried out amid accelerated female proletarianization and labor militancy. Workingwomen were constantly battling against police and employers for a living wage, decent working conditions, and physical integrity. Women of the laboring classes clearly could no longer be ignored or easily denigrated as they had been in the 1890s. By 1918, they had become undeniable allies in the fight for justice.

In this context, the women targeted by the antiprostitution campaign took on even broader meanings to their male allies. The crackdown itself constituted a profound betrayal of the democratic promise that had cemented U.S. colonial legitimacy for two decades among laboring Puerto Ricans of all races. The women came to represent hard-won civil liberties, cornerstones of that precious "democracy." Thus the attacks against them constituted an assault against all working people and ultimately against the nation as a whole. To the protesting working-class men, their defense was a simultaneous assertion of class solidarity, national dignity, and honorable virility.[49] To those of African descent, it may have been a question of racial loyalty as well.

Yet this oppositional male discourse sought to confirm male power (albeit in a more benevolent form) while it elevated the defense of threatened, deracialized, working-class womanhood to a national cause. Instead of vice-ridden whores, the targeted women were "helpless beings," "unfortunate victims," who desperately needed the protection of honorable, manly men. The idea of women banding together as a group and standing up for themselves seemed unspeakable to sympathetic men, even (perhaps especially) in this era of intense militancy by workingwomen. Men, they implicitly asserted, were the true political agents.

Other silences remained in the male discourses. Mass arrests, not the forced internal examinations, were protested. Apparently, women's civil rights included only the right to a fair hearing, not the right to control access to their bodies. Rarely was men's role in the transmission of venereal disease or the perpetuation of prostitution itself discussed.[50] Likewise, male protesters of the state policy largely failed to criticize the sexual double standard that allowed men multiple partners while demanding monogamy of women.

But men were not the only Puerto Ricans to challenge the antiprostitution campaign. Women's voices were more muted, but they were present. And they spoke in terms different from those of male counterparts. Women who openly opposed the campaign did not usually ask for male protection but rather defied police, prosecutors, and judges on their own, both individually or collectively. They also firmly denounced men's role in the perpetuation of prostitution and the insidious divisions that men reinforced between "respectable" and "disreputable" women.

As the scope of arrests broadened throughout the island, targeted women stepped up their protests to the press and the police. Carmen Selles and Mayra Rosario, both objects of attempted arrest, went to sympathetic newspapers with their stories and threatened to file charges against the police. Francisca Gotay of Ponce stormed down to the local police precinct in a rage after being accused of running a brothel. She defended her honor in typical street fashion, hurling curses at the police from the street and demanding that they come out to answer her challenge in person. When a Ponce policeman tried to arrest Salvadora Iglesias late one night, she called on her friends. They surrounded the officer and threatened him so severely that he finally fled in fright.[51]

Women accused of prostitution also defended themselves vigorously in court. The legal exonerations won by Leonor Crespo, Susana Torres, and Honoria Anaya in the early days of the campaign were only the beginning of a flood of litigation by targeted women throughout the island. In the space of four months, eighty-one appeals of convictions to District Court were filed from Ponce alone. Hundreds of convicted women and their families filed petitions for pardons as well, although the governor denied almost all of them.[52] Leopoldo Tormes, who had organized the mass meeting in Ponce, and his sister Herminia Tormes, also an attorney, represented scores of women. They pushed for speedy hearings, obtained numerous acquittals, filed appeals, and petitioned for pardons on behalf of those clients who ultimately were convicted.[53] Accused women's persistent legal challenges and individual protests ensured that the state's violation of civil liberties remained in the public spotlight; they thus played an important role in sustaining the opposition.

Working-class women also acted collectively in support of their persecuted sisters. The women tobacco workers in the San Juan "La Marina" factory, famous for their militant strikes and showdowns with police, sent word of their solidarity through *La Correspondencia.* Soon afterward, the Socialist women of Santurce held a demonstration to protest the antiprostitution campaign's trampling of workingwomen's constitutional rights. Their call to the streets included a condemnation of all men's sexual predation against women. "For some time our personality has been abandoned to the egotism of men, who in their insatiable sexual thirst toss us into the gulley and later, in the name of morality, unleash a new wave of persecutions against defenseless beings."[54]

Several months into the prostitution controversy, an anonymous author who claimed to be a working-class woman and signed her name as "Flor Oculta" (Hidden flower), wrote a piece in *El Águila* denouncing men's complicity in the sexual degradation of women. She pointed out that in all the public debate over prostitution and how to end it, this key issue had consistently been ignored. Men divided women into social/moral "categories, according to how [we] serve your interests." Those women shunted off into the mistress position were inevitably abandoned to a life of single motherhood, poverty, and shame and were often forced to turn to prostitution to survive. "If you [men] wish to regenerate these unhappy creatures, regenerate yourselves. Do not pretend that you can destroy in one rough collective blow what you have built for such a long time individually." The anonymous author ended her commentary with a famous poem by the eighteenth-century Mexican nun Sor Juana Inés de la Cruz denouncing men's subordination of women; it closed with the pointed lines: "¿O cual es más de culpar / aunque cualquier mal haga, / La que peca por la paga / o el que paga por pecar?"[55]

"Flor Oculta" left no doubt that men of all classes were personally responsible for women's sexual and economic sufferings—blaming a faceless capitalist system was as insufficient as blaming the women themselves. Within a few days, *El Águila* had received numerous positive responses to the piece. Clearly, some Ponce women shared her sentiments.[56] Neither manly workingmen nor hostile, "respectable" matrons could claim that they spoke for all women.

Effects of the Protests

As opposition to the antiprostitution campaign erupted around the island, supporters of the crackdown rallied to its defense. In the pages of *La Democracia,* Unión Party leaders took their renegade members to task for betraying the "cause of moralization." Puerto Rico's judicial system was perfectly trustworthy, they intoned; *La Correspondencia* and other protesters were sowing unfounded suspicion among the populace by their vociferous criticism of the state's policy. *La Democracia*'s editors began publishing reports of all the acquittals of women charged with prostitution in an attempt to recapture public faith in the judicial system. Howard Kern called press conferences and made speeches to conservative groups in which he reiterated repeatedly that the women's legal rights had not been violated. Municipal officials, prosecutors, and leaders of the Republicano and Unión Parties stepped up their calls to wartime loyalty and for protection of the troops' health. Supporters of the antiprostitution policy even leveled accusations of treason and pro-German sympathies against the opposition. Leopoldo Tormes, in particular, was singled out as dangerously insistent on the accused women's legal rights. The attorney general warned that Tormes' energetic representation of the targeted women posed a threat to the smooth workings of the war machine. Ultimately, advocates of the state's policy warned, an irreconcilable conflict lay between the enforcement of virtue and the preservation of individual rights. Whether focusing on the morality of male soldiers or the protection of "ladies," for them, "virtue" unquestionably deserved the upper hand.[57]

But the protests did not provoke only a hardening in the state's position. The public opinion of some sectors began to shift. Before the Ponce mass meeting, a columnist at *La Correspondencia* applauded the attorney general's attempt to enforce monogamy among women. But the same columnist turned against the campaign once protests began to explode. So many women were in jail, he noted, that the antiprostitution campaign resembled a second military draft. Men were beginning to fear that they could be arrested for their sexual adventures. Ultimately, there "is no defense for this policy," he concluded.[58] Even *La Democracia,* which consistently defended Kern and his campaign, was forced to admit that some "fallen" women were not to blame for their situation.[59]

Slight legal gains appeared as well. After a month of vociferous protests and unrelenting appeals of convictions, a federal judge pronounced that the Federal Court, rather than local officials, would handle all charges of prostitution. Women would be prosecuted only if they violated the "moral zone" around the Las Casas training camp; mass arrests across the island were to cease. Federal prosecutors were instructed to investigate carefully the evidence presented for each case before pressing charges. Men were proclaimed to have "identical responsibility" with women for sexual transgressions and the transmission of venereal diseases.

The opposition celebrated the decision as a triumph of the people against despotism.[60] But *El Águila* reports demonstrate that arrests of women in Ponce continued unabated; the victory seems to have been in theory alone. Only the great earthquake that rocked Puerto Rico in October 1918 stemmed the zest of the police for sexual surveillance.

Transforming Repression into Reform

A key aspect of the campaign supporters' attempt at legitimization in the face of public protest was their emphasis on rehabilitating and medically treating the arrested women. By 1918, a cure for some venereal diseases had been discovered; although the treatment was still quite toxic and provoked numerous side effects, it was effective. In addition, in the United States, the establishment of reformatories for convicted prostitutes was a common concern of the women staffing state agencies. Finally, Protestant evangelists in Puerto Rico emphasized the need for moral rehabilitation of "fallen women."[61] State officials in Puerto Rico, then, did not have far to look in their search for an answer to charges of indiscriminate repression against workingwomen.

Soon after the islandwide crackdown began, the attorney general announced that the Arecibo and Ponce district jails, now reserved exclusively for wayward women, would be converted into hospitals for the treatment of the inmates' venereal diseases. The mayor of Arecibo applauded the move, which held out the hope of rehabilitation to both the incarcerated women and society at large. All parties could trust that the women had been "submitted to the salvation of Science and Justice's joint action." The campaign was now presented as necessary for the *women's* own good, not only for the protection of public morals and the troops.[62]

In Ponce, the local press applauded the transformation of the prison into a "sanatorium for horizontals" staffed by a medical doctor, a physician's assistant, and three nurses. After a guided tour and lecture by the prison director, writers for *El Águila* reported that the institution was characterized by "cleanliness and tidiness throughout"; good, plentiful food; clean uniforms; and healthy work. Newspapers in Ponce and San Juan assured their readers that "the primary goal of the Government in confining [the women] is to cure them—not to treat them as prisoners. As soon as they are cured, they will be set free." Treatment, however, could be as lengthy as the police and doctors jointly deemed necessary; hundreds of women remained in the district prisons long after the war's end and the termination of the state campaign.[63]

Involuntary treatments were also a cornerstone of the new "curing facilities." The supervising Ponce personnel triumphantly pronounced in early 1919 that the women inmates had received substantially more mercury, salvarsan, and diarsenol (all extremely toxic treatments) in six months than they would have received in two years outside the jail's wall. "The physician in private practice is confronted with the fact that he cannot make a patient continue treatment persistently. We have been able to push the treatments to the utmost, and we get better results than in private practice."[64]

The coerced cures were an ever present reminder that despite the constant talk of hospitalization, medicine, and caring attention, these institutions were first and foremost prisons. As in the 1890s, their primary function was to isolate the incarcerated women from the rest of society. The dingy cells, iron window bars, barbed wire, and locked doors of municipal jails remained intact. All visitors were prohibited, except when accompanied by armed guards.[65]

The imprisoned women were quite clear about the true nature of their predicament, and they did not take kindly to it. In late August, the Ponce prison director prohibited inmates' friends and family from bringing them their customary cooked food, fruit, and cigarettes. More than three hundred women rioted in response, "shouting at the top of their lungs and insulting the Red Cross, the Attorney General, and other officials." Most refused to take their drug and mercury treatments. Only by throwing the most vociferous into solitary confinement were the women finally "reduced to obedience." Some time later, thirty-eight female prisoners set fires in the jail, receiving extended sentences for their troubles.[66]

Full social and moral rehabilitation of these women was necessary, supporters of the campaign insisted. Otherwise, they would return to their old ways, regardless of whether they had been cured of venereal diseases. Unlike the 1890s, many public commentators recognized that the roots of prostitution were economic, at least in part. Consequently, economic self-sufficiency was key to any attempt at rehabilitation. Interestingly enough, no mention was made in the press or government accounts of attempts to bind women into monogamous relationships, such as had occurred in the previous prostitution panic. The battle to reinscribe working-class women into the patriarchal family seems to have been lost; any large-scale efforts to do so were clearly doomed to failure. Instead, the incarcerated women should be taught skills that would allow them to earn their livings once released. Sewing, laundering, and literacy were the most commonly cited. The mayor of Ponce announced that the women prisoners "will dedicate themselves to labor appropriate to their sex, thus perhaps restoring these unfortunates to an honest life—part of a complete regeneration. They can be useful to the family and to society: it is never too late to change their ways."[67]

This emphasis on rehabilitation was a striking diversion from past practices; no such discourse or practice had existed during the 1890s. The proposed training programs, however, would have done little to end the incarcerated women's poverty. The vast majority of the women probably already had most of the skills in question; washing, ironing, and sewing were survival requirements for all women of the laboring classes. Indeed, rather than providing the imprisoned women with new income-earning options, the jails' rehabilitation efforts were primarily concerned with molding women into "disciplined," docile laborers. They could then be reinserted into the extremely narrow and ill-paid female labor market that had pushed some of them into the sale of sex to begin with. The salvageable women had to "cleanse themselves outwardly and inwardly" as they learned repentance and docility. They could do so successfully only through the efforts of reformers, who would strive for "the material well-being and moral conquest of these unfortunates."[68]

Middle- and upper-class women were the perfect candidates for this type of reform work. After the passage of the Prohibition referendum in Puerto Rico, in which they played a key role, the potential power of their activism could not be ignored. Since the outbreak of the war, large numbers of professional and wealthy Puerto Rican women had mobilized into war support organizations sponsored by the U.S. government, such as the Red Cross and the Council of National Defense.[69] In the eyes of conservative male elites and colonial officials, activities such as these, as well as the "ladies'" intervention into working-class family life, were vastly preferable to their increasing demands for female suffrage.

The state's campaign to reshape the values and behavior of incarcerated workingwomen combined both strands of "safe" female organizing. Thus bourgeois women, many of them prominent suffragists/feminists, were eagerly encouraged to collaborate in state reform as well as in surveillance of sexually suspect laboring women. In Ponce, the city's "ladies" were called on to carry out the "beautiful task of educational regeneration. . . . Now you are presented with an opportunity to undertake the most sublime of merciful works: lift up the fallen woman, bringing to her soul the treasures of rejuvenating pity that are overabundant in you. . . . Let your slogan be 'redeem the captives of vice!' "[70] This reform work would lend a crucial legitimizing element of humanitarianism to the mass jailings.

Interestingly enough, all the newspapers reviewed, other than the Socialists' *Unión Obrera* (which did not mention the issue), concurred in their endorsement of this middle- and upper-class female reform work. Alonso Gual's Afro-Puerto Rican Republicano publication *El Águila,* the dissident Unionista *La Correspondencia,* and the Unión Party leadership's *La Democracia* all enthusiastically supported the bourgeois women's moralizing mission, despite their bitter disagreements about the antiprostitution campaign itself. Consensus on the legal rights of sexually suspect, working-class women may have been impossible, but bourgeois women's moral superiority and responsibility for taming unruly women went unquestioned by most mainstream opinions.

Alonso Gual incorporated a subtle but quite pointed spin to his encouragement of reform work by Ponce's society ladies. Democracy and modernity required that they break out of their elitist isolation from "disreputable" women. "Ladies of Ponce: You must adapt to life in the present age: 'the world of the future will be a world of free democracies, of tolerance.' " Like his warnings to the Puerto Rican landed elite regarding the urgent need for redistribution of wealth and his rejection of racial hierarchies, the Afro-Puerto Rican Gual needled the wealthy, white women of Ponce, even as he echoed dominant sentiments about their ability to moralize less fortunate women.[71]

Thus by 1918, prodded by the force of female activism, many men were beginning to envision a new social role for women of the middle and upper classes. Bourgeois women's influence on society would not be exercised solely through moralizing their own families, as the nineteenth-century Liberals had hoped, but also through institution building and moral reform work. In addition to being the mothers of future male citizens, bourgeois women were to become the honorable mothers of disreputable women. No longer should they be carefully isolated from sexually dangerous women. In the process, they would both mold women of the laboring classes into a properly submissive femininity and remain safely segregated from the male spheres of formal government and the economy.

While policing and reshaping working-class women, the decidedly nonsexual matrons and "misses" of the "respectable" classes were to replace militant women workers and the dangerous "bawd" as Puerto Rico's public female presence. The reform activities of the ladies were celebrated by Unionista newspapers; for the most part, women's labor activism received smothering silence.[72] On the rare occasions when militant workingwomen's presence was acknowledged, they were painted as threatening and out of control, much like prostitutes.[73] Policemen facing women strikers on the picket line made this analogy much more directly, thrusting their genitals at the women, calling them sluts, and shouting that they should be incarcerated at the "women's jails." When the discursive exclusion of militant workingwomen failed, they were brutally forced out of public space—numerous strikes were met by beatings and imprisonment.[74]

Many bourgeois women activists took up the challenge to rehabilitate the jailed "prostitutes," now carrying their earlier institution-building and fundraising energies into personal contact with "the dangerous elements." For a few brief months, moral reform of sexually wayward women became the primary work of both illustrious ladies and forward-looking female professionals. By September 1918, "ladies" were organizing support committees in every city where women were detained. Respectable matrons raised money for the new venereal disease clinics; drummed up material donations of fabric, thread, and sewing machines; and taught work skills to the incarcerated women. Throughout the island, temperance societies and the "feminine police" were in the forefront of the movement.[75] In Ponce, daughters and wives of conservative landowners joined forces with social purity and temperance activists as well as outspoken feminists to visit the Ponce district jail on a weekly basis. They conversed with the inmates, exhorted them to change their immoral ways, taught them to read and write, and instructed them in sewing and embroidery.[76]

Bourgeois women were not simply tools of powerful men, however. Throughout the island, they had their own reasons for joining the campaign to contain prostitution and reform its practitioners. Like temperance organizing, their new activities provided middle-class women with a way to influence public discussions of morality. They helped open new societal expectations of women's role in the public arena. Finally, they facilitated bourgeois women's entry into the broader world of formal politics, despite many elite men's fear of such moves. Prosuffrage feminists played a leading role in organizing visits to imprisoned alleged prostitutes and offering them "moral uplift."[77]

Unfortunately, the sources of describing these moral reform activities are quite sketchy. Most consist of announcements of meetings, membership lists, or a few quick descriptions of jail visits by male journalists. No personal memoirs of the participants from this period have been preserved in public archives, as far as I know. My attempts to track down surviving family members of the women involved were all dead ends as well.

There are hints, however, that the women reformers may have viewed their ultimate goals somewhat differently than did the men around them. Puerto Rican female reformers never referred to the need for maintaining soldiers' health.[78] Rather, their meeting publicity and the few comments they published about their volunteer work in the prisons focused on transforming and aiding the incarcerated women. Overall, female reformers seem to have generated a more woman-centered vision than that articulated by male journalists and state officials. The Ponce reformers emphasized the woman-to-woman connection, although hierarchical and from a morally superior position. They spoke of forgiveness, mercy, "preaching virtue" "just as a mother would talk to her child" to the inmates, among whom "misery has sunk deep roots and vices have developed, extending like an oily stain over the sea. . . . All women called by love are invited to go [to the jail], along with the Committee or by themselves."[79] A detective of the "feminine police" in Arecibo insisted: "*Ours is a labor by women for women*. . . . All of our efforts should be focused on making the Arecibo jail . . . into a hospital, *into a home more than a jail*."[80]

It is also possible that Ponce reformers developed a program more progressive than those in Arecibo, Mayagüez, and San Juan. Ponce alone, out of the major cities in Puerto Rico, did not organize a squad of feminine police. In addition, the Ponce group focused on job creation and intensive literacy training, as well as instillment of labor discipline and moral reform. This may well reflect the influence of Herminia Tormes and Olivia Paoli, two quite remarkable and unorthodox "bourgeois" feminists.

Herminia Tormes headed the effort to reform women prisoners during World War I in Ponce. Although lighter skinned than her brother Leopoldo, Tormes too was proud of her African heritage, according to surviving family members. She was the first woman attorney in Puerto Rico. After representing many women targeted in the antiprostitution campaign, Tormes also became the first woman licensed to practice in the U.S. Circuit Court of Appeals in Boston, serving from 1926 to 1941 as the municipal judge of the town of Juana Díaz. After the war's end, she founded a school for prostitutes and, along with the Socialist organizer Moisés Echevarría, lobbied for the construction of a vocational school for women. Her niece remembers her as an outspoken, self-confident women, who always held her own in political and legal arguments with men and who had been no stranger to poverty as a child.[81]

Olivia Paoli, although much older and from a very different social background, worked alongside Herminia Tormes in her efforts to establish a school for women inmates in the Ponce jail during the war. The daughter of a once wealthy hacendado, Paoli married Mario Braschi, a radical Liberal journalist who was persecuted by the Spaniards during the 1880s for his political beliefs. When he died at an early age, leaving her with nine children, Paoli and her family were plunged into abject poverty. In the early days of the U.S. occupation, Paoli was forced temporarily to place several of her sons in public asylums because she could not feed them. She eked out a living for herself and her children as a teacher and census taker, eventually becoming a journalist, renowned in the 1930s for criticizing the roots of poverty in Puerto Rico and the inhuman conditions of its prisons and reformatories. A member of the progressive Liga Social Sufragista, which consistently pressed for universal female suffrage in alliance with working-class feminists, Paoli also joined the Socialist Party soon after it formed in 1915.[82]

These two women undoubtedly had a more radical outlook on prostitution and the state's wartime campaign than did many other female reformers. Both had known suffering firsthand, and were probably painfully aware of how fine a racial and class line existed between "women of the street" and "the angels of the home." Indeed, through her legal representation of targeted women, Herminia Tormes positioned herself among the opposition to the state's antiprostitution crusade. Her press releases also intimate as much, and they carefully avoid racially saturated moral language and refer to the imprisoned women as "inmates" (*recluidas*), rather than as "prostitutes," as they were commonly called in other articles.[83] Tragically, we have no direct written sources from either Paoli or Tormes, and the living relatives I was able to interview have no recollection of their work with the alleged prostitutes.

We can piece together, however, that unlike some other Ponce "ladies," Tormes did not spend much time spouting moral platitudes to the women inmates. Rather, with Paoli's assistance, she organized public school teachers to volunteer in the prison teaching the women to read and write—essential skills in wrenching oneself out of poverty, as she knew from personal experience. By the end of October 1918, Tormes had convinced Puerto Rico's commissioner of education to appoint a full-time teacher for the incarcerated women. She also attempted to establish special industries to offer the women prisoners work upon their release. After the war ended, Tormes pushed the Ponce division of the Council of National Defense to work on a proposal for economic development projects for Puerto Rico as a whole. She apparently understood that only systemic economic change would bring an end to the conditions that produced female poverty and prostitution.[84]

Even these most radical of the middle-class feminists, however, never openly denounced in print the state crackdown on workingwomen. Rather, they attempted to humanize the repression and retrain the jailed women for a more successful entrance into the formal labor market on their release. Neither did they overtly critique the sexual double standard during the wartime campaign. (Of course, it is possible that Tormes or Paoli may have penned the "Flor Oculta" letter, but we have nothing to indicate this.) This stands in great contrast to the United States, where from the nineteenth century on, middle-class feminists used critiques of prostitution to protest their own sufferings from male infidelity and sexual predation.[85] It also contrasts with the encoded discussions of predatory male sexuality in the writings of early Puerto Rican feminists, particularly the fiction of Ana Roqué de Duprey. Once again, respectability requirements during a public prostitution panic may have silenced more open radical critiques from middle- and upper-class women, whatever their racial identities.

Our understanding of the moral reform aspect of the antiprostitution campaign and responses to it is severely limited by the paucity of sources. But the jailhouse encounters of bourgeois and working-class women in Ponce were seemingly *not* the fruition of Luisa Capetillo's dream of cross-class female solidarity. Far from bringing women of all classes together in liberatory struggle, freely learning from and supporting one another, the wartime moral reform work appears to have reconfirmed hierarchies among women. Only Herminia Tormes and Olivia Paoli may have tried to create a more egalitarian relationship with the incarcerated women. Without the discovery of more detailed sources, though, we cannot ascertain whether this potential was ever reached.

Whatever their intentions, neither the female reformers nor the campaign's opponents had much time to develop their projects. On October 11, 1918, a great earthquake shook Puerto Rico. In Ponce, it destroyed countless homes and many public buildings, among them the cathedral in the central plaza and the graceful city theater. Thousands of people were wounded or left homeless, and tremors continued to be felt for months, sowing panic among the population. In addition, a severe influenza epidemic hit the island in November, putting unbearable strains on an already sorely inadequate public health system. More than three thousand fell ill in Ponce alone; medical doctors and the poor were the hardest hit. An atmosphere of dread pervaded Ponce during the last months of 1918. Even the end of the war in November could not eliminate the hollow ring from the feeble predictions of prosperity that newspapers printed periodically. Prophecies of imminent natural and political disasters began to appear among the popular classes, as did a series of religious miracles.[86]

Amid such chaos, the antiprostitution campaign seems to have ended as abruptly as it began. After mid-October, no arrests of suspicious women were reported in Ponce police logs or newspapers. The police had their hands full dealing with the deaths and dislocations of the earthquake. The nurses and doctors assigned to the prison's venereal disease "hospital" were sent to work with influenza victims. In November 1918, the funds available for prison expenses had been used up.[87] With the end of the war, the main rationale for arresting women suspected of "promiscuity" had disappeared. Most of those already imprisoned remained in jail until the summer of 1919, but no new arrests were made through the end of 1918.

By March 1919, the Ponce police seem to have returned to their old ways of dealing with prostitution. When neighbors complained of their noise or impropriety, the women were simply told to move. Arrests and prosecution, once again, dropped to an almost imperceptible level.[88] As Puerto Ricans found themselves caught up in the daily struggle to recover from the earthquake and influenza losses and as they no longer faced a massive arrest campaign, the protests against state repression also disappeared.

Thus, the close of the war, coupled with stunning natural and public health disasters, put an end to the fervor that had once again linked prostitution, respectability, and democracy in Puerto Rico's public debate. During the 1890s, these issues had been joined by the struggles over the terms of decency in Ponce. At that time, a misogynist, cross-class political consensus had been cemented by the antiprostitute sentiment. Twenty years later, however, much had changed. By the end of the second decade of U.S. rule in Puerto Rico, middle- and upper-class women, Afro-Puerto Ricans, and working-class women and men were vociferously articulating demands for political, social, and economic inclusion. As the United States pulled Puerto Rico into preparation for combat in World War I, colonial officials and their local allies tried desperately to reconsolidate a political consensus—this time in favor of U.S. rule. Panic about the German threat from abroad quickly translated into intensified internal repression of dissent and fears of "the enemy within."

As in the 1890s, official attention turned to working-class women defined as sexually wayward—the "natural" targets of stigmatization. Thousands of women were arrested across the island in the space of a few months. Police forces, judges, prosecutors, and other judicial officials quickly equated "prostitute" and "promiscuous"—a slippery, possibly racially loaded concept that was readily interpreted to mean any suspicion of extramarital sexual activity by working-class women.

But the consensus that emerged in 1890s Ponce around the necessity to exclude unruly, discursively darkened, plebeian women from the community of "decent" worthy citizens proved impossible to construct in 1918. Radical working-class women and men joined with dissident Republicanos and Unionistas—several of whom were of African descent—to denounce vehemently the state's antiprostitution crusade. Most of them refused to reproduce the racialized moral denigration of the targeted women that had been so prominent in the 1890s.

Two decades earlier, Canta Claro had insisted that prostitutes contaminated the "decent" working class. Their filth-ridden invasion had been accomplished by the Ponce elites' abrogation of the democratic process. Placing power in the hands of the people would effectively banish troublesome women from the working classes as well as from wealthy neighborhoods. During World War I, however, after two decades of sharpened class conflict, Canta Claro's arguments were turned on their heads. To hundreds of Puerto Rican women and men, the women accused of promiscuity represented the denial of legal rights and civil liberties to all impoverished, darker-skinned people. The defense, rather than the exclusion, of alleged prostitutes thus became a rallying cry of working people's class consciousness and Afro-Puerto Ricans' struggle for social equality. Their exoneration would herald the triumph of democracy and the establishment of a truly egalitarian society.

Not all the protesters articulated identical interests, however. While defending "wronged womanhood," Puerto Rican men simultaneously asserted their virility, their position as the true political leadership of the popular classes, and their exclusive right to judge working-class women's respectability. Women protesters, on the other hand, vigorously asserted their own political agency and denounced men's sexual abuse and categorization of women.

Throughout, the legitimacy of colonialism remained intact, despite U.S. officials' fears to the contrary. However loudly and persistently these groups may have challenged the state's indiscriminate crackdown against working women, none of them openly questioned the validity of colonial rule. Even the Socialists exempted U.S. rule from their sharp criticisms of capitalist exploitation. Indeed, the Unionista dissidents seemed to be warning that a continuation of the campaign would dangerously erode the populace's support for the United States. Their objections to the "arbitrary procedures" were meant to *preserve* colonial authority, not challenge it. Most protesters seemed to interpret the repressive crusade as a betrayal of U.S. democratic, egalitarian potential—not an indication that colonialism was incapable of instituting justice and equality in Puerto Rico.[89]

Middle-class and wealthy female reformers gave the arrests a human face through their "rehabilitation and moralization" work with the incarcerated women. During the 1890s, Puerto Rican bourgeois feminists had attempted to spread their message of moral transformation mainly through the power of the pen. Now, however, bourgeois female reformers physically took to the streets and jails to transform workingwomen in practice, not only discursively. They jockeyed with dissident men for the right to regulate and define working-class women's sexuality. In the process, they also asserted their right to occupy a place in public arenas and thus to transform Puerto Rican society.

Allegedly the embodiment of motherhood, morality, and "true woman-hood," most of the women reformers attempted to regenerate the dominant code of feminine respectability, now openly questioned by organized working people. Of the women touched by the antiprostitution campaign, these re-formers capitalized most effectively on the sexual controversy of World War I. Ultimately, the power of "respectability" won out again, even in a highly contested moment. Despite circumscribing them in a "woman's sphere of influence," the campaign confirmed their place in public and their impor-tance in shaping society. These same women would go on in the 1920s to sharpen their movement for suffrage and to establish the building blocks of the modern welfare state in Puerto Rico through their work as health care professionals, teachers, and social workers.

Once again, bourgeois feminists in Puerto Rico failed to protest state repression against sexually stigmatized workingwomen. This contrasts mark-edly with both Victorian England and the antebellum northern United States, where middle-class feminists built fragile alliances with working-class women in their battles against prostitution regulation. Perceptions of race may well have played a key role in creating this difference. Both British and U.S. feminists were able to identify more easily with prostitutes in these earlier periods because they perceived themselves as sharing a common racial/ ethnic identity. Ruth Rosen has suggested that feminist solidarity with pros-titutes began to wane once native-born women were replaced in the urban working classes by waves of immigrants in the late nineteenth century.[90] In Puerto Rico, particularly in the coastal regions where sugar and slavery had reigned during the nineteenth century and which reemerged as centers of social mobilization and economic activity under U.S. rule, plebeian women had long carried the taint of slavery and blackness in the eyes of the upper classes, regardless of their phenotypic characteristics. Cross-class alliances be-tween Puerto Rican women, therefore, were made particularly difficult; they would have required bridging a perceived racial, as well as a class, gap.

Class-race divisions among women may have been particularly acute when dealing with questions of sexuality, despite attempts by Socialists and Afro-Puerto Ricans to free moral definitions from racial connotations. In Puerto Rico, privileged women's individual and collective identities, whether in claiming the "whiteness" supposedly inherent in wealth and social status or in "blackening" the economically marginalized, were tightly intertwined with dominant definitions of honor and proper sexual behavior. For women of the professional and upper classes, challenging the division between "respectable" and "disreputable" womanhood probably would have meant questioning their own racial superiority as well.

Not surprisingly, most female reformers did not attempt to make common cause with the objects of their moralizing efforts. They expected incarcerated women to emulate them; identification on their part with these "unfortunates" was out of the question. Nor should it shock us that as the antiprostitution campaign was drawing to a close, Ana Roqué de Duprey, founder of the 1890s feminist publication *La Mujer* and now a prominent suffragist, insisted that only "honorable" women could be allowed in suffrage organizations.[91]

Certainly, Herminia Tormes fought on behalf of the accused women in court, attempting to better their material chances on release from prison by teaching them to read and write and actively seeking work for them. But Tormes herself, a mulatta born in poverty, seems to have been marginalized from the dominant bourgeois feminist circles. Angela Negrón Muñoz's 1930s survey of "great women" of Puerto Rico did not include an entry on Herminia Tormes, despite Tormes' prodigious achievements and the inclusion of many other women of her generation. Tormes' African heritage and her poverty-stricken social roots apparently rendered her "unprintable" to a mainstream feminist such as Negrón.[92] Tormes may be the exception that proves the rule: in Puerto Rico, it seems to have been easier to build cross-gender racial or class solidarity, no matter how fraught with tensions, than to bridge the class-race chasms dividing women from one another.

Conclusion

Throughout this book I have stressed the inseparability of political struggles and discourse—one cannot be understood without the other. Historically, people struggle over power, but they produce the meaning of their contests through discourses about legitimacy, justice, citizenship, and community.[1] In Puerto Rico, these discourses have often been produced through debates over racially coded moral values and sexual practices. In this book I have demonstrated that merging racial definitions with sexual norms and practices has often been an integral part of the formation of social movements, national identities, and state policies in Puerto Rico.

I have felt a special urgency about this project because in the Puerto Rican academy, sexuality has not usually been considered "political" or worthy of theoretical attention.[2] The intimate historical connections in Puerto Rico between racial identities and sexuality also remain largely ignored.[3] Such a position allows sexuality—and its frequent racial connotations—to remain relegated to the realm of "the natural," where its terms need not be subjected to serious scrutiny or struggle. As long as this state of affairs holds sway, any attempt to transform society will remain seriously hampered—not only because sexual options for women will be limited but also because "natural" sexual norms will continue to be invoked in the defense of repressive and unjust political positions and policies.

Creating a sexual threat—and thus a common enemy around which the community can bond in self-defense—is a particularly powerful way of constructing consensus in times of great social stress and change. In Puerto Rico during the late nineteenth and early twentieth centuries, the focus of such sexual panics was the prostitute—the dangerous, disreputable, and implicitly darkened workingwoman who had to be ripped out of the heart of the community. Both sexual cleansing campaigns emerged in response to organized challenges to the status quo. They were also based in fearful reaction to plebeian women's contestation of the social limits placed on them. During the 1890s, young women, many of African descent, migrated to the city of Ponce in record numbers, where they lived and loved outside the limits of the patriarchal family. By 1918, working-class women posed a different kind of threat: they were at the forefront of the labor mobilization sweeping the island.

Claiming moral respectability was the corollary to sexual demonization. Puerto Ricans who fashioned oppositional movements and discourses frequently used claims of special moral status to assert their superiority and consequent right to political and social leadership. The language of honor employed in such discourses invoked a variety of supposedly natural hierarchies. Groups such as the late-nineteenth-century Liberals sought to construct a coherent national identity by de-Africanizing the island's populace through moral reform. Many others, however, including the early labor activists and Afro-Puerto Rican Republicanos, deliberately rejected the nation as the primary referent for collective loyalty, instead seeking out other axes of identification. All these groups, however, built their projects at least partially on an attempt to reshape racialized moral norms.

Thus, the early bourgeois feminists claimed moral superiority over elite male Liberals and moral and racial superiority over plebeian women. Canta Claro, on the other hand, insisted that the locus of democracy rested in the respectable (male) poor. He defined his "imagined community" against the Liberals and even more vociferously in opposition to the alleged prostitutes of Ponce. But despite their conflicts with the Liberals, both Canta Claro and the early bourgeois feminists agreed with the elite male reformers on the necessity of excluding sexually and (at least for the feminists) racially threatening workingwomen from "decent" society. They were thus unable to break with the basic terms of the Liberal project. A conservative "respectability consensus" neutralized the radical potential of their class and gender critiques of Liberalism.

The U.S. invasion and subsequent emergence of the twentieth-century labor movement and Afro-Puerto Rican dissent fractured Liberal hegemony on the island, however. Working people were able to redraw radically the public lines of respectability. The women and men of the early Puerto Rican left proved that more inclusive popular sexual norms could be successfully politicized, that women's racial and moral status could be delinked, and that not all alliances built around sexuality necessarily supported the dominant social order. Working-class activists of both sexes challenged the racially loaded dominant distinctions between respectable and disreputable women. They insisted that women's alleged moral status was not determined by their racial identity and that it was artificially constructed by the various privileges or exploitation they experienced under capitalism. They also hailed the prostitute as sister and comrade, the quintessential representative of an oppressed, multiracial working class. Consequently, the mass arrests of alleged prostitutes during World War I provoked a radically different response than had Ponce's 1890s regulation campaign. Indeed, if the war had dragged on much longer, the colonial state might well have had trouble continuing to enforce its policy.

The new sexual enemies, according to male labor intellectuals, were external to the community: wealthy men, the descendants of Spanish slaveowners. Claiming the mantle of virile protectors of feminine virtue provided radical working-class men a platform from which to free themselves from the humiliating legacy of racial slavery, to challenge the hegemony of local male elites, and to assert control over plebeian women. They sought to construct a more inclusive social order than had their predecessors, but their project remained patriarchal, nonetheless.

In the end, the early labor movement activists retained solely the elements of the working-class discourse on sexuality that did not challenge workingmen's power over women. Because workingwomen were unable to establish themselves as authoritative voices, their analyses that denounced both capitalism and women's exploitation by *all* men were marginalized in the early left's internal hegemonization process. The sexual exploitation of women in prostitution provided a powerful trope through which to protest the ravages of capitalism and the poor's sufferings at the hands of the rich. But male leftists succeeded in deflecting attention away from their own complicity in women's subordination. Even radical notions of respectability excluded challenges to their totalizing legitimacy.

Enforcers of dominant sexual norms found that wielding the club of "decency" could be a very effective weapon in marginalizing socially or politically autonomous women. Despite this suffocating weight, however, women often attempted to assert their own unique voices and interests through sexual issues. From bourgeois and working-class feminists to women labor activists and divorce and *juicio verbal* petitioners, a wide spectrum of women seem to have recognized that sexual relations and concepts of honor held particular power in their lives. They insisted on enhanced reciprocity within heterosexual partnerships and an end to the sexual double standard, yearned for fulfillment of their sexual desires, and pointed out the complicity of even their closest male allies in women's subordination. For middle-class and elite women in particular, most of whom were protected to a certain extent by their status as white "respectable ladies," moral reform activism provided a way to enter the public sphere of political debate and action and to carve out a portion of that sphere as their own territory.

Race also haunted the politics of the period. It usually accompanied discussions of morality as it subtly wove its way through the discourses produced by Puerto Rico's political actors. Racial identities, however unstable, formed an integral part of nineteenth-century concepts of honor and social place. At crucial foundational points in Puerto Rican history, such as the early Liberal attempts to forge a national identity or the first years after the U.S. invasion, racial differences and hierarchies were directly addressed in public, either by elites seeking to morally reform a much too African populace or by Afro-Puerto Ricans simultaneously enraged at racial discrimination and hoping to gain acceptance into the new sociopolitical order.

Frequently, however, racial labels were conjured up indirectly in Puerto Rico by referring to other, racially loaded characteristics such as "disreputability," "respectability," and "honor." Thus, the self-proclaimed "respectable womanhood" of the early feminist movement was undeniably white, whereas the immoral, unruly women of Ponce's streets during the 1890s became symbolically black, whatever their phenotype or biological ancestry. The avoidance of direct racial naming did not diminish the power of such discourses' racial reverberations. It may have even extended their reach, allowing racial connotations to inhabit seemingly unrelated imagery and actions and rendering their force almost impossible to challenge frontally.

Finally, while engaged in crucial alliance building, Puerto Ricans sometimes pointedly rejected the use of racialized language. This strategic silencing did not signal the end of the significance of race to Puerto Rican politics, however. Rather, as Lillian Guerra and Peter Wade perceptively point out, such denial of racial differences *within* a community often simply shifts the focus of racial undesirability to those outside its bounds. Conscious internal erasure of racial difference can actually powerfully affirm racial hierarchies more generally.[4] In Ponce during the 1890s, public discussion of racial differences between men ceased, as elite Liberals and urban workingmen strove to build a race-neutral political fraternity. Ultimately, however, this new political configuration did not challenge the superiority of elite whiteness; it simply denied the importance of laboring men's racial identities. Neither did the alliance contest the denigration of Afro-Puerto Rican attributes; blackness was deflected from workingmen onto threatening plebeian women, now the repository for all that was dirty, defiled, and disgusting. A few years later, under a new colonial regime, early labor activists and Afro-Puerto Rican Republicano Party militants developed a different strategy for simultaneous racial labeling and silencing. They proudly claimed black or multiracial identities and denounced racism on the island, while carefully de-emphasizing the allegedly natural link between feminine racial and moral attributes. They pointedly refused to represent plebeian women in racial terms, thus bestowing potentially honorable status on them all—even prostitutes.

Despite the striking differences between these two strategies (they appear to be mirror images of each other), in both instances those who won "de-racialized" status were included only as subordinate members of the new community, subject to elite or male leadership. While both movements challenged some aspects of the dominant race/gender/class relationships, other aspects remained discouragingly resilient. Indeed, it seems that, at least in political relationships between men, the languages of race and class in Puerto Rico moved in and out of each other relatively fluidly, while women, whether incorporated or excluded, remained the clear "other" or polarity. Although always shaped by perceptions of race and class, gender seems to have continued to be a particularly powerful marker of difference for the male political actors in question, even as they and their female allies gave gendered power relations new meanings and devised new political projects around them.

Paying close attention to the role of gender and sexuality in shaping the ever shifting alliances built around race and class identities could well shed light on some unanswered questions about other historical periods or places. It might, for example, provide important clues to why, by the 1940s and 1950s in Puerto Rico, a political project that silenced racial difference in favor of cross-class cooperation once again reigned supreme—and did so for several decades. Such a development seems surprising, given the stubborn refusal of the island's popular classes to accept attempts to deflect attention away from elite racism and economic exploitation or from state officials' abuses of power during the first two decades of U.S. rule. Certainly, the populist economic and social reforms carried out during the 1940s and 1950s were key in winning widespread support, but we do not yet know how these sweeping changes were gendered or affected gender relations on the island. Our understanding of gender, sexuality, and popular culture is even sketchier. Lillian Guerra argues that men of the rural popular classes in many parts of the island constructed their communal identity around a fear of women's sexuality and an urgent desire to control it, as well as a generalized rejection of blackness. In addition, Arcadio Díaz Quiñones points out that Tomás Blanco, a preeminent intellectual of the period, attempted to target women as the most insidious practitioners of racism on the island. Blanco thus utilized a time-honored tradition in his attempt to soften the racial debates of his time—demonizing women as the threat to collective harmony. How might these two impulses, popular and elite, along with other, perhaps more inclusive ones, have converged to help produce a new, more enduring version of the racially silenced Puerto Rican "gran familia"?[5]

Analysis of gender and sexual relations may also help explain the power of racial democracy myths in countries such as Cuba. Clearly, Cuba's thirty years of independence struggles helped forge a potent, though contradictory sense of racially neutral, multiracial nationalism among men, as Ada Ferrer and Aline Helg masterfully point out. But does this provide the whole story, particularly considering the periodic violence, often large-scale and state-sponsored, that Cubans of African descent have faced over the last 150 years and their well-recognized historic difficulties in gaining political rights, socioeconomic parity, and respect for their cultural practices?[6] Have the racial conflicts among men been ameliorated somewhat in the nation-building process by the selective exclusion of women from community or movement membership, by the ceding of key patriarchal rights to plebeian men, or by women's own role in the creation of gender relations and sexual norms?

Vera Kutzinski began to explore some of these questions in her groundbreaking work on the cultural construction of mulattas—the mixed-race women who have for at least a century served as a primary signifier of Cuban national identity. Kutzinski argues that the mulatta "celebrates racial diversity while at the same time disavowing [exploitative] social realities," simultaneously expressing and erasing conflicts and anxieties about the new social orders created first by the rise of the sugar plantation in the nineteenth century and later, during the twentieth century, by U.S. domination. According to Kutzinski, the figure of the mulatta has been key in the creation of masculine national unity, but only as an idealized object, never as an autonomous agent, able to act on her own behalf. By the 1930s, focusing on the mulatta and her multiracial, allegedly always available sexuality allowed Cuban men of all races to avoid painful political questions through cultural synthesis. The mulatta, and representations of her, became the "site where men of European and African ancestry rhetorically reconcile their differences and, in the process, give birth to the paternalistic political fiction of a national multiculture in the face of a social system that resisted any real structural pluralism."[7]

As has occured at particular junctures in Puerto Rican history, it appears that Cuban men have constructed various versions of a racially harmonious fraternity, built at least in part through the use of women's racialized and sexualized bodies. The Cuban mulatta may have been celebrated, whereas the Puerto Rican prostitute was demonized, but at points they seem to have served analogous discursive purposes for men's conversations with one another.

It is here, however, that this study of Puerto Rico can hopefully provide ways to deepen analyses such as Kutzinski's, which seek to explore the nexus between race, sexuality, and politics. Prostitution in Puerto Rico, like the mulatta in Cuba, certainly evoked a particular set of dominant associations; alleged prostitutes were readily darkened, demonized, and rejected. But prostitution meant different things to different people in different historical contexts; prostitutes also could be fellow sufferers of exploitation, sisters in the struggle to survive, opportunities to prove the morally rehabilitative powers of "respectable ladies," or the supreme expression of wronged womanhood and democracy violated. Their defense could become the rallying cry of women and men uniting to challenge abuses of power. Finally, the targeted women themselves were active historical agents. In their responses to the campaigns, they shaped state strategies, devised their own concepts of citizenship, and fueled explosive protests of colonial policy. Culture, whether political or literary, is built on argument, even in times of consensus, and the seemingly powerless constantly affect these debates through their actions, values, and interests. Thus, the meanings surrounding the mulatta in Cuba will always have been multiple, even when one largely eclipsed the others. Also, Cuban women, whether plebeian or elite, of African descent or not, undoubtedly developed their own understandings of the mulatta's meanings; these have also become part of Cuba's national culture.

Much of the literature on sexuality and race, like Kutzinski's work, emphasizes the power that physically linked discourses lend to political projects which seek to contain, exclude, and exploit. Certainly, this tendency appeared frequently in turn-of-the-century Puerto Rico. But we must also look to the moments and movements that offer hopeful, however partial, alternatives. Working-class men and women forged powerful, though ambiguous, solidarities in their families and communities, within the early labor movement, and during the protests against the World War I antiprostitution campaign. Luisa Capetillo and Herminia Tormes dreamed of defeating injustice through cross-class, interracial connections among women. The creators of such alliances and visions never totally redrew the discursive map. They had to retain sufficient amounts of previously existing meanings, imagery, and social practices to remain rooted in popular culture and thus build a following. Indeed, those individuals like Capetillo and Tormes who sought to stretch the bounds of their social milieus too far failed to attract massive support for their projects. Despite these limits, though, this book demonstrates that organizers, intellectuals, and community members did make choices about which elements of popular culture to emphasize. Neither prostitution nor slavery, for example, had a single, unitary connotation—they could be either the root of a diseased, sickly collectivity or the symbol of a wronged people, worthy of protection and capable of dignified struggle. Sadly, most of the more inclusive, liberatory visions articulated in turn-of-the-century Puerto Rico were eventually marginalized or quelled or did not have time to develop into full-blown political projects. But this does not prevent us from learning from their visionary dreams as well as their shortcomings. Only when we listen to both will we be equipped to make our own choices in building the future.

Abbreviations and Acronyms

Ac.	Acontecimientos
Al.	Alcalde
AGPR	Archivo General de Puerto Rico
AHDSJ	Archivo Histórico Diocesano de San Juan
AMP	Archivo Municipal de Ponce
Ar.	Archivo
AS	Asuntos Sacramentales
Ay.	Ayuntamiento
Aud.	Audiencia
Ben.	Beneficencia
BIA	Records of the Bureau of Insular and Territorial Affairs
Cár.	Cárcel
Cen.	Censo
CIH	Centro de Investigaciones Históricas
Civ.	Civiles
Con.	Conciliaciones
Corr.	Correspondencia
CPR	Colección Puertorriqueña
Crim.	Criminales
Den.	Denuncias
Disp.	Dispensas
Div.	Divorcios
Exp. Civ.	Expedientes Civiles
FGE	Fondo de Gobernadores Espanoles
Fort.	Fortaleza
GA	Government Agencies
GCF	General Correspondence Files
GF	General File
Gob.	Gobierno
GRDJ	General Records of the Department of Justice
Hab.	Habitantes
Inf.	Informes
Infr.	Infracciones
J. de S.	Junta de Sanidad

Jud.	Fondo Judicial
Juic.	Juicios
Just.	Justicia
L.C.	Libro Copiador
LDN	Libro de Novedades
Leg.	Legajo
Legit.	Legitimación
List.	Listado
NP	Novedades de la Policía
Of.	Oficios
O.P.	Ordenes de la Policía
Pol.	Policía
PN	Protocolos Notariales
PPR	Policía de Puerto Rico
Pr.	Provisor
Pros.	Prostitución
RG	Record Group
Regl.	Reglamento
Rel.	Relaciones
Sec.	Secretaría
Sent.	Sentencias
S.P.	Seguridad Pública
Tr.	Tratado
UPR	Universidad de Puerto Rico
USNA	National Archives, Washington, D.C.
Ver.	Verbales

Notes

All translations are by the author.

Introduction

1   I have largely limited myself to analyzing the workings of heterosexuality. This is due in part to the paucity of archival sources available on same-sex sexual relations. It is also due to the confines of time and space that I faced. All studies have their limits; this one I regretfully accept.

2   A consensus seems to be emerging that given Puerto Rico's continued colonial subjection and its vibrant diaspora in the United States, culture, not the nation-state, is a particularly important locus of Puerto Ricans' national/collective identity. See, for example, Angel G. Quintero Rivera, *¡Salsa, sabor, y control! Sociología de la música "tropical"* (Mexico City: Siglo Veintiuno Editores, 1998) and Ruth Glasser, *My Music Is My Flag: Puerto Rican Musicians and Their New York Communities, 1917–1940* (Berkeley: University of California Press, 1994).

   One of the boldest rejections to date of the nationalism-colonialism dichotomy can be found in the collection edited by Frances Negrón-Muntaner and Ramón Grosfoguel, *Puerto Rican Jam: Essays on Culture and Politics* (Minneapolis: University of Minnesota Press, 1997), particularly their introduction with Chloe S. Georas, "Beyond Nationalist and Colonialist Discourses: The *Jaiba* Politics of the Puerto Rican Ethno-Nation," pp. 1–36. See also the journals *Bordes* and *El Centro*. For some important precursors, see José Luis González, *El país de cuatro pisos y otros ensayos,* 6th ed. (Río Piedras: Ediciones Huracán, 1987); Angel G. Quintero Rivera, *Patricios y plebeyos: Burgueses, hacendados, artesanos y obreros: Las relaciones de clase en el Puerto Rico de cambio de siglo* (Río Piedras: Ediciones Huracán, 1988); Juan Flores, *Divided Borders: Essays on Puerto Rican Identity* (Houston: Arte Público, 1993); Arcadio Díaz Quiñones, *La memoria rota* (Río Piedras: Ediciones Huracán, 1993).

3   Michel Foucault, *The History of Sexuality,* vol. 1, *An Introduction,* trans. Robert Hurley (New York: Random House, 1978); Lynn Hunt, *The Family Romance of the French Revolution* (Berkeley: University of California Press, 1992); Judith Walkowitz, *City of Dreadful Delight: Narratives of Sexual Danger in Late-Victorian London* (Chicago: University of Chicago Press, 1992); Ann Laura Stoler, *Race and the Education of Desire: Foucault's "History of Sexuality" and the Colonial Order of Things* (Durham: Duke University Press, 1995).

4   Some notable exceptions include Stuart Hall, whose corpus of relevant work is too extensive to cite here. For a sampling, see David Morley and Kuan-Hsing Chen, eds., *Stuart Hall: Critical Dialogues in Cultural Studies* (London: Routledge, 1996); Paul Gilroy, *The Black Atlantic: Modernity and Double Consciousness* (Cambridge: Harvard University Press, 1993); Florencia Mallon, *Peasant and Nation: The Making of Postcolonial Mexico and Peru* (Berkeley: University of California Press, 1994); and Frederick Cooper, "The Dialectics of Decolonization: Nationalism and Labor Movements in Postwar French Africa," in *Tensions of Empire: Colonial Cultures in a Bourgeois World,* ed. Cooper and Ann Laura Stoler (Berkeley: University of California Press, 1997), 406–35.

5   Anna Clark, *The Struggle for the Breeches: Gender and the Making of the British Working Class* (Berkeley: University of California Press, 1995); Lawrence Grossberg, ed., "On Postmodernism and Articulation: An Interview with Stuart Hall," in Morley and Chen, *Stuart Hall,* 143–44; Joan W. Scott, "Experience," in *Feminists Theorize the Political,* ed. Joan W. Scott and Judith Butler (New York: Routledge, 1992), 34.

6   Anne McClintock, *Imperial Leather: Race, Gender, and Sexuality in the Colonial Contest* (New York: Routledge, 1995), 5; Kathleen M. Brown, *Good Wives, Nasty Wenches, and Anxious Patriarchs: Gender, Race, and Power in Colonial Virginia* (Chapel Hill: University of North Carolina Press, 1996), 4.

7   Joan W. Scott, "On Language, Gender, and Working Class History," in *Gender and the Politics of History* (New York: Columbia University Press, 1988), 59.

8   Clark, *Struggle for the Breeches,* 7.

9   Mallon, *Peasant and Nation,* 5–6.

10 Miriam Jiménez Román discusses the alternating hostility and deafening silence that met Isabelo Zenón Cruz's *Narciso descubre su trasero: El negro en la cultura puertorriqueña* (1975) in "Un hombre negro del pueblo: José Celso Barbosa and the Puerto Rican 'Race' for Whiteness," *Centro* 8, nos. 1–2 (1996): 23–25. For some of the new scholarship on race in Puerto Rico, see CEREP, *La tercera raíz: Presencia africana en Puerto Rico* (San Juan: Instituto de Cultura Puertorriqueña, 1992); Angel G. Quintero Rivera, "The Somatology of Manners: Class, Race, and Gender in the History of Dance Etiquette in the Hispanic Caribbean," in *Ethnicity in the Caribbean,* ed. Gert Oostindie (London: Macmillan, 1996), 152–81; the articles in *Centro* 8, nos. 1–2 (1996); Luís Martínez-Fernández, *Torn between Empires: Economy, Society, and Patterns of Political Thought in the Hispanic Caribbean, 1840–1878* (Athens: University of Georgia Press, 1994); Jay Kinsbrunner, *Not of Pure Blood: The Free People of Color and Racial Prejudice in Nineteenth-Century Puerto Rico* (Durham: Duke University Press, 1996); and Lillian Guerra, *Popular Expression and National Identity in Puerto Rico: The*

Struggle for Self, Community, and Nation (Gainesville: University of Florida Press, 1998).

11 Stoler, *Race and the Education of Desire,* 45.

12 Peter Wade notes this pattern for Colombia and Latin America as a whole. See his masterful study of race, regionalism, and national identity *Blackness and Race Mixture: The Dynamics of Racial Identity in Colombia* (Baltimore: Johns Hopkins University Press, 1993). See also Guerra, *Popular Expression,* 212–64.

13 Mrinalini Sinha, "Reading *Mother India:* Empire, Nation, and the Female Voice." *Journal of Women's History* 6, no. 2 (summer 1994): 15. See also George L. Mosse, *Nationalism and Sexuality: Middle-Class Morality and Sexual Norms in Modern Europe* (Madison: University of Wisconsin Press, 1985); Edward Said, *Orientalism* (New York: Vintage, 1978), 6, 207; Leila Ahmed, *Women and Gender in Islam: Historical Roots of a Modern Debate* (New Haven: Yale University Press, 1992), 128–68; Partha Chatterjee, "The Nationalist Resolution of the Women's Question," in *Recasting Women: Essays in Indian Colonial History,* ed. Kumkum Sangari and Sudesh Vaid (New Brunswick: Rutgers University Press, 1990), 233–53; Lata Mani, "Contentious Traditions: The Debate on Sati in Colonial India," in Sangari and Vaid, *Recasting Women,* 88–126; Doris Sommer, *Foundational Fictions: The National Romances of Latin America* (Berkeley: University of California Press, 1991); and the essays in Andrew Parker et al., eds., *Nationalisms and Sexualities* (New York: Routledge, 1992).

14 Ann Laura Stoler and Frederick Cooper, "Tensions of Empire: Colonial Control and Visions of Rule," *American Ethnologist* 16 (November 1989): 614. See also Ann Laura Stoler, "Making Empire Respectable: The Politics of Race and Sexual Morality in Twentieth-Century Colonial Cultures," *American Ethnologist* 16 (November 1989): 634–60, and Stoler, "Carnal Knowledge and Imperial Power: Gender, Race, and Morality in Colonial Asia," in *Gender at the Crossroads: Towards an Anthropology of Power,* ed. Micaela di Leonardo (Berkeley: University of California Press, 1989).

15 Ann Laura Stoler, "Perceptions of Protest: Defining the Dangerous in Colonial Sumatra," *American Ethnologist* 12 (November 1985): 642–58; Stoler, "Rethinking Colonial Categories: European Communities and the Boundaries of Rule," *Comparative Studies in Society and History* 31 (November 1989): 134–61; Stoler, "Sexual Affronts and Racial Frontiers: European Identities and the Cultural Politics of Exclusion in Colonial Southeast Asia," *Comparative Studies in Society and History* 34, no. 3 (July 1992): 514–51; Laura Engelstein, *The Keys to Happiness: Sex and the Search for Modernity in Fin-de-Siècle Russia* (Ithaca: Cornell University Press, 1992); Isabel V. Hull, *Sexuality, State, and Civil Society in Germany, 1700–1815* (Ithaca: Cornell University Press, 1996); Sonya O. Rose,

"Sex, Citizenship, and the Nation in World War II Britain," *American Historical Review* 103, no. 4 (October 1998): 1147–76.

16   For an exploration of these issues in Puerto Rico during different historical periods, see Francisco A. Scarano, "The Jíbaro Masquerade and the Subaltern Politics of Creole Identity Formation in Puerto Rico, 1745–1823," *American Historical Review* 101, no. 5 (December 1996): 1398–1431; Arcadio Díaz Quiñones, "Tomás Blanco: Racismo, historia, esclavitud," introduction to *El prejuicio racial en Puerto Rico,* by Tomás Blanco, 3d ed. (Río Piedras: Ediciones Huracán, 1985), 13–91.

17   Antonio Gramsci, *Selections from the Prison Notebooks,* ed. and trans. Quintin Hoare and Geoffrey Nowell Smith (New York: International Publishers, 1971); Ernesto Laclau and Chantal Mouffe, *Hegemony and Socialist Strategy* (London: Verso, 1985); Raymond Williams, *Marxism and Literature* (Oxford: Oxford University Press, 1977).

18   Michel Foucault and Mary Douglas were among the first to deconstruct systematically assumptions about the naturalness and immutability of the human body. Foucault, *History of Sexuality,* and Mary Douglas, *Purity and Danger: An Analysis of Concepts of Pollution and Taboo* (London: Routledge, 1966). For a more recent treatment of such questions, see Emily Martin, *The Woman in the Body: A Cultural Analysis of Reproduction* (Boston: Beacon, 1987). Judith Butler has theorized gender difference as determined by performance rather than by biological distinctions. See her *Gender Trouble: Feminism and the Subversion of Gender Identity* (New York: Routledge, 1989).

19   Scott, *Gender and the Politics of History,* 46–50; Elaine M. Combs-Schilling, "Etching Patriarchal Rule: Ritual Dye, Erotic Potency, and the Moroccan Monarchy," *Journal of the History of Sexuality* 1, no. 4 (April 1991): 658–81.

20   Benedict Anderson's *Imagined Communities: Reflections on the Origin and Spread of Nationalism* (London: Verso, 1983) elaborated an analysis of nations as fictional but surprisingly enduring constructions. His insights (which did not include analyses of gender or sexuality) have spawned a vast literature on nationalism and its construction, which is too extensive to cite here.

21   Parker et al., introduction to *Nationalisms and Sexualities,* 5.

22   The quotes come from Steven Feierman, *Peasant Intellectuals: Anthropology and History in Tanzania* (Madison: University of Wisconsin Press, 1990), 4. Intellectuals who had access to print will, unfortunately, be privileged in this study. Many more popular intellectuals may well have played powerful roles in orally articulating the discourses and conflicts analyzed in the following pages. Without the preservation of their arguments and actions in written documents, however, their historical presence has been lost.

23   Ibid., p. 3.

24 Fernando Picó, *Libertad y servidumbre en el Puerto Rico del siglo XIX* (Río Piedras: Editorial Huracán, 1979); Laird Bergad, *Coffee and the Growth of Agrarian Capitalism in Nineteenth-Century Puerto Rico* (Princeton: Princeton University Press, 1983); Guerra, *Popular Expression*, 19–21, 227–37.

25 Francisco A. Scarano, *Sugar and Slavery in Puerto Rico: The Plantation Economy of Ponce, 1800–1850* (Madison: University of Wisconsin Press, 1984), esp. 7–8, 136–38. See also Pedro L. San Miguel, *El mundo que creó el azúcar: Las haciendas en Vega Baja, 1800–1873* (Río Piedras: Ediciones Huracán, 1989); Teresita Martínez-Vergne, *Capitalism in Colonial Puerto Rico: Central San Vicente in the Late Nineteenth Century* (Gainesville: University Press of Florida, 1992); and Andrés Ramos Mattei, *La hacienda azucarera: Su crecimiento y crisis en Puerto Rico (siglo XIX)* (Río Piedras: CEREP, 1981).

26 Quintero Riveva, *Patricios y plebeyos*, 37–78.

27 "Villa de Ponce. Ano de 1861. Resumen del Censo de almas de dicha villa verificados en el mes de Enero del espresado ano." AMP, Ay., Sec., Ar., Hab.

1 Respectable Ponce: Deciphering the Codes of Power, 1855–1898

1 This and all other quotes from the Astacio case are in "Sobre rapto de Teresa Astacio," 1894, AGPR, Jud., Ponce, Crim., box 38.

In nineteenth-century Puerto Rico, the term "pardo" had multiple nuances. Technically, it referred to an individual who was of three-quarters or more European heritage. It could also be used to refer to any light-skinned and/or straight-haired person of African descent. In addition, it was frequently used by "whites" to refer "politely" to people of African descent in general, while still affirming these individuals' nonwhiteness. The inscription of a person's birth in the parish "pardo" register indelibly marked him (and his descendants) as "black."

2 There is a growing literature on honor's role in the construction of power hierarchies in Latin America. Most of it focuses on the colonial period. See Sarah C. Chambers, "The Many Shades of the White City: Urban Culture and Society in Arequipa, Peru, 1780–1854" (Ph.D. diss., University of Wisconsin, Madison, 1992); Verena Stolcke, *Marriage, Class and Colour in Nineteenth-Century Cuba: A Study of Racial Attitudes and Sexual Values in a Slave Society*, 2d ed. (Ann Arbor: University of Michigan Press, 1989); Ramón A. Gutiérrez, *When Jesus Came, the Corn Mothers Went Away: Marriage, Sexuality and Power in New Mexico, 1500–1846* (Stanford: Stanford University Press, 1991); Patricia Seed, *To Love, Honor, and Obey in Colonial Mexico: Conflicts over Marriage Choice, 1574–1821* (Stanford: Stanford University Press, 1988); Susan M. Socolow, "Acceptable Partners: Marriage Choice in Colonial Argentina, 1778–1810," in *Sexuality and Marriage in Colonial Latin America*, ed. Asunción Lavrin (Lincoln: University of Nebraska Press, 1989), 209–251; Sue Ann Caulfield, *In*

Defense of Honor: Sexual Morality, Modernity, and Nation in Early-Twentieth-Century Brazil (Durham: Duke University Press, 1999); Martha de Abreu Esteves, *Meninas perdidas: Os populares e o cotidiano do amor no Rio de Janeiro de Belle Epoque* (Rio de Janeiro: Editora Paz e Terra, 1989); and Ana María Alonso, *Thread of Blood: Colonialism, Revolution, and Gender on Mexico's Northern Frontier* (Tucson: University of Arizona Press, 1995).

3   Steve J. Stern, *The Secret History of Gender: Women, Men, and Power in Late Colonial Mexico* (Chapel Hill: University of North Carolina Press, 1995), 11–21.

4   Michel Foucault pioneered the reconceptualization of power as operating from a multiplicity of discursive regimes rather than residing primarily in one group or set of social relations. Although he does not directly address questions of honor or respectability, Foucault's work has provided one of the inspirations for my thinking. In my view, however, Foucault tends to overemphasize the convergences of discourses and thus implicitly produces a picture of unremitting dominance. The following works by Foucault have been the most helpful for me: *Discipline and Punish: The Birth of the Prison,* trans. Alan Sheridan (New York: Pantheon, 1978); *The History of Sexuality;* and the interviews in *Power/Knowledge: Selected Interviews and Other Writings, 1972–1977,* ed. Colin Gordon (New York: Pantheon, 1980). Nancy Fraser provides an excellent overview and critique of Foucault's theory of power in *Unruly Practices: Power, Discourse and Gender in Contemporary Social Theory* (Minneapolis: University of Minnesota Press, 1989), 17–75.

5   Scarano, *Sugar and Slavery,* 3–34; Francisco A. Scarano, "The Jíbaro Masquerade and the Subaltern Politics of Creole Identity Formation in Puerto Rico, 1745–1823," *American Historical Review* 101, no. 5 (December 1996): 1398–1431; Jorge Ibarra, "Cultura e identidad nacional en el caribe hispánico: El caso puertorriqueño y el cubano," in *La nación soñada: Cuba, Puerto Rico y Filipinas ante el 98,* ed. Consuelo Navanjo, Miguel Puig-Samper, and Luis Miguel García Mora (Madrid: Doce Calles, 1996), 85–95.

6   Puerto Rican witnesses supporting women's claims in seduction and rape cases routinely stated that the women were "reputed to be pure"; this was accepted as evidence of the women's virginity. Ann Twinam shows that some elite white women in colonial Latin America had premarital sex and even bore illegitimate children while maintaining their reputations as honorable virgins. See her "Honor, Sexuality, and Illegitimacy in Colonial Spanish America," in *Sexuality and Marriage in Colonial Latin America,* ed. Asunción Lavrin (Lincoln: University of Nebraska Press, 1989), 118–55.

7   "Injurias a instancia de Da. Cecilia Miranda," Sent. 147, "Tomo de la Audiencia de lo criminal de Ponce, Minutas de Sentencias del Año 1890," AGPR, Jud., Ponce, Crim., box 6.

8 "Legitimación de D. Juan Serrallés," Jan. 11, 1867, AHDSJ, box J-223. For examples of unstable racial identities during the nineteenth century in urban San Juan, see Kinsbrunner, *Not of Pure Blood,* 96–97.

9 For a few examples of elites' disparaging remarks about such practices and their labeling of them as dangerously "black," see "Música del país," *La Democracia,* May 5, 1893, 2; "La bruja," *La Democracia,* June 7, 1893, 2; Salvador Brau, "La herencia devota," in *Almanaque de damas* (San Juan: Tipografía González Font, 1886); and Salvador Brau, *Hojas caídas* (San Juan: Tipografía La Democracia, 1909), 325.

10 These tenets emerge clearly from the testimony of witnesses in the hundreds of slander, seduction, and rape cases that survived from the nineteenth century. Accusations of sexual promiscuity or infidelity were the most common insults slung at women in attempts to dishonor them. The dominant honor code's requirements for women are also laid out Puerto Rico's colonial legislation. See *Código Penal para las islas de Cuba y Puerto Rico* (Madrid: Editorial Góngora, 1886), título 9, capítulos 1, 2, 5.

11 See, for example, "1853, Libro de Juicios de conciliación correspondiente á la 2a Teniencia del Alcalde de Ponce," no. 1, Oct. 7, 1853, AMP, Ay., Sec., Jud., Juic., Con.; "Sobre rapto de Francisca Vega," 1887, AGPR, Jud., Ponce, Crim., box 27; "D. Jose Colón demandando á D. José Vicente Ortiz," Sept. 17, 1860, "Villa de Ponce, Ano de 1860. Juicios Verbales celebrados en el Corregimiento en dicho año," no. 798, AMP, Ay., Sec., Jud., Juic., Ver.

12 *Código Penal,* título 9, capítulo 5; Don Enrique Vargas al Muy Iltre Sor. Gobernador de esta Diócesis, 1898, AHDSJ, Just., Corr., Pr., box J-236.

13 Gutiérrez (*When Jesus Came,* 208–36) and Stolcke (*Marriage,* 119–41) provide the most comprehensive analyses available of these aspects of the honor system in colonial New Mexico and Cuba, respectively.

14 Doña Nieves's mother actually petitioned the governor of Puerto Rico to discipline her wayward daughter. The surviving documents do not include the governor's final decision in the case. Doña Nieves Gaston contra Doña Cecilia Pordié Echeverne, Nov. 27, 1850, AGPR, FGE, box 534. See also Don Pedro Geli y Ros y Doña Brígida Collazo y Muñoz sobre reconocimiento de sus hijos naturales, 1902, AGPR, Jud., Ponce, Exp. Civ., box 14.

15 *Código Penal,* título 9, capítulo 1, 384; the penalties for female adultery are delineated on 382–85. The quotations are from p. 384. For cases of "respectable" white married women's extramarital affairs, see "D. Salvador Arena demandando a su esposa Da. Pilar Coll," 1849, AHDSJ, Just., AS, Div., box J-217; "Divorcio entre los esposos D. Vicente de Sárraga y Rengel y Da. Felisa Hernández Urbon," AHDSJ, Just., AS, Div., box J-216; "Sobre divorcio de D. Matías Deya con su legítima esposa Da. Petrona del Toro," 1862, AHDSJ, Just., AS, Div.,

box J-215; "Demanda de divorcio de D. José de la Rosa Rodríguez contra su esposa Da. Teresa Ortiz y Castillo," 1898, AHDSJ, Just., AS, Div.; "Sobre Envenenamiento," 1863–64, AGPR, Ponce, Crim., box 1.

16 See, for example, "Juan Laboy demandando al Comisario de Machuelo Arriba D. José María Alvarez," Sept. 10, 1852, "Juicios verbales del Corregimiento, Ponce. 1852," AMP, Ay., Sec., Jud., Juic., Ver.; "Manuel Rosado demandando á D. Francisco Fano," Jan. 10, 1856, AMP, Ay., Sec., Jud., Juic., Ver.; "Antonio Ríos demandando á D. Jaime Clavell," Aug. 22, 1844, AMP, Ay., Sec., Jud., Juic., Con.

17 "Da. Petronila de la Cruz, estado viuda demandando á D. Narciso Canet," "Cuaderno que contiene los juicios verbales celebrados los dos años espresados. Años de 1846 y 1847," AMP, Ay., Sec., Jud., Juic., Ver., and No. 33, Jan. 17, 1850, "Años de 1848 hasta el 52 inclusives. Copiador de oficios que se dirigen á los Senores Jueces Letrados y demás Autoridades de la Isla, y á particulares," AMP, Ay., Sec., Ar., L.C., Of.

18 "Un negro guapo; un negro muy jaquetón y atrevido." See "D. Ventura Toces demandando á Escolástico Negrón," Nov. 17, 1852, "Juicios verbales del Corregimiento. Ponce. 1852," AMP, Ay., Sec., Jud., Juic., Ver.

19 Needless to say, this requirement did not apply in cases of slaveowners' dealings with enslaved people. Ponce's nineteenth-century judicial documents are replete with cases brought by slaves against prominent Ponceños who had promised to allow them to buy their freedom but refused to sign the letters of manumission once the slaves had saved the agreed-on amounts. For a few examples, see "El Lcdo. D. Luis Antonio Becerra en su calidad de Síndico provisor de la misma . . . representando á la sierva Gabriela de la propiedad de Da. Asunción Brilé viuda de Fortier," July 24, 1852, "Juicios verbales del Corregimiento. Ponce. 1852," AMP, Ay., Sec., Jud., Juic., Ver.; "El Síndico D. Jesús María Toro en representación del siervo Hipólito de la dotación de la hacienda Catalina demandando a D. Miguel Moler dueño de aquella," Oct. 4, 1855, "Villa de Ponce. Año 1855. Juicios verbales celebrados en el Corregimiento en dicho año," AMP, Ay., Sec., Jud., Juic., Ver.

20 See, for example, Juan Bautista Rivera to El Gobernador de Puerto Rico, Nov. 11, 1862, AGPR, FGE, box 145.

21 "José Colón demandando á Teodoro Ruiz," Oct. 9, 1860, "Villa de Ponce, Año de 1860. Juic. verbales celebrados en el Corregimiento en dicho año," AMP, Ay., Sec., Jud., Juic., Ver. See Stern, *Secret History of Gender,* 151–88, for an insightful analysis of plebeian Mexican men's violence toward each other.

22 See, for example, "D. Antonio Maldonado demandando á D. Nelson Boisjoli," Jan. 10, 1852, AMP, Ay., Sec., Jud., Juic., Ver.

23 "Por delito de allanamiento de morada y lesiones contra Juan González Delgado," Sent. 206, *Audiencia de lo criminal de Ponce: Sentencias dictadas en el 30*

trimestre de 1895, AGPR, Jud., Crim., Ponce, box 44. Some examples of other such cases are "Lesiones graves conta Antonio Castaing," Sent. 96, and "Lesiones," Sent. 85, Causa 642, both in *Tomo de la audiencia de lo criminal de Ponce: Minutas de sentencias del año 1890,* AGPR, Jud., Crim., Ponce, box 6.

24   For some examples, see "Reconocimiento de hijos naturales," Mar. 18, 1865, p. 114, AGPR, PN, Ponce, Notary D. Joaquín Mayoral, 1865, box 2209; "Por rapto contra Juan Aniceto Vega," Sent. 415, *Audiencia de lo Criminal de Ponce. Minutas de sentencias dictadas por la Sala de Justicia de esta Audiencia en octubre, noviembre, y diciembre, 1891,* AGPR, Ponce, Jud., Crim., box 37; and "Eulalia Martínez demandando á María del Rosario Rodríguez y á una hija de ésta Felícita Rosado," Nov. 8, 1860, "Villa de Ponce, Año de 1860. Juicios Verbales celebrados en el Corregimiento en dicho año," AMP, Ay., Sec., Jud., Juic., Ver. See also Guerra, *Popular Expression,* 143–49, 179–81, 193–94.

25   "Muerte de envenenamiento de Doña Rosa Besant," 1877, AGPR, Jud., Crim., Ponce, box 7.

26   Yvonne Laborde, interview, March 14, 1992.

27   "Muerte de María Sánchez," Causa 1065, 1896, AGPR, Ponce, Jud., Crim., box 48.

28   "D. José María Avendaño demandando á Da. Gumersinda Salmás," June 22, 1860, and "Doña Rosa Méndez demandando à D. Enrique Duvver," Aug. 20, 1860, both in "Villa de Ponce, Año de 1860. Juicios Verbales celebrados en el Corregimiento en dicho año," no. 798, AMP, Ay., Sec., Jud., Juic., Ver.; "Copiador de oficios dirigidos á las autoridades locales y particulares," 1873, no. 133, AMP, Ay., Ar., L.C., Of.

29   Sent. 86, *Tomo de la Audiencia de lo Criminal de Ponce: Minutas de sentencias del año 1890,* AGPR, Ponce, Jud., Crim., box 6.

30   "Por rapto, contra D. Felix Fernández y Pacheco," Sent. 154, *Audiencia de lo Criminal de Ponce: Sentencias dictadas el segundo trimestre, 1891,* AGPR, Ponce, Jud., Crim., box 66.

31   Pamela Scully discusses a similar phenomenon in "Rape, Race, and Colonial Culture: The Sexual Politics of Identity in the Nineteenth-Century Cape Colony, South Africa," *American Historical Review* 100, no. 2 (April 1995): 335–59.

32   "El pueblo de Puerto Rico v. Clotilde Rivera," May 18, 1918, AGPR, Jud., Ponce, Crim., box 92. See also "Sobre violación de Juana Teodora Pérez y Torres," 1901, AGPR, Ponce, Jud., Crim., box 102; "Sobre violación de Salomé González," 1887, AGPR, Ponce, Jud., Crim., box 31; and "Trato sobre la libertad de la esclava Agripina de D. Pablo Niuri," Oct. 7, 1865, AMP, Ay., Sec., Jud., Juic.

33   "Muerte de envenenamiento de Doña Rosa Besant," 1877, AGPR, Ponce, Jud., Crim., box 7. Isidora Vives, the enslaved mistress of Don Salvador Vives, a prominent Ponce landowner and politician, was given her freedom for her "good services." In addition, Vives willed her three thousand pesos, to be paid at

the rate of fifteen pesos per month, but Vives's legal wife prevented Isidora from receiving the money. Guillermo Baralt, *La Buena Vista, 1833–1904: Estancia de frutos menores, fábrica de harinas y hacienda cafetalera* (San Juan: Fideicomiso de Conservación de Puerto Rico, 1988), 64, 66. See also "Por violación versus Guillermo V. Cintrón," July 5, 1923, AGPR, Ponce, Jud., Crim., box 103; and "D. Loreto Dantín demandando á Rafael Penalver," Sept. 20, 1852, AMP, Ay., Sec., Jud., Juic., Ver.

34   "1842. Conciliaciones," no. 244, and "Juicios de conciliación celebrados en la Alcaldía 2a de Ponce," Dec. 2, 1843, Años 1844 y 1845, both in AMP, Ay., Sec., Jud., Juic., Con.; "Doña Rosa Méndez demandando á D. Enrique Duvver," Aug. 20, 1860, in "Villa de Ponce, Año de 1860. Juicios verbales celebrados en el Corregimiento en dicho año," no. 798, AMP, Ay., Sec., Jud., Juic., Ver.; "Por D. Gumersindo Rivas a nombre de D. Vicente Gazol sobre reconocimiento de hijo," AHDSJ, Legit., box J-223.

35   D. José María Ortiz, plaintiff, Oct. 5, 1853, "1853. Libro de Juicios de conciliación correspondiente á la 1a y 2a Tenencia de Alcalde de Ponce," no. 1, AMP, Ay., Sec., Jud., Juic., Con.

36   Eighty-one percent of court cases brought by white mistresses resulted in a financial settlement close or equal to what the woman requested. I found only ten women of African descent who filed financial claims in court against their white former lovers between 1840 and 1870; none of them demanded marriage or financial compensation for the woman's sullied honor.

37   For a few examples, see Da. Ana Escalona v. D. Sebastian Llompart (untitled court case), 1893, AHDSJ, Just., AS, Div., box J-216; Da. Catalina Vizcarrondo v. D. Epifanio Vizcarrondo (untitled court case), AHDSJ, Just., AS, Div., box J-216; "Discernimiento de Da. Salustiana Capó," 1877, AHDSJ, Just., AS, Div., box J-215; Da. Isabel Casanova v. D. Anastacio Martínez (untitled court case), 1890, AHDSJ, Just., AS, Div., box J-216.

38   During the nineteenth century, married women were able to garner some state assistance in tracking down wayward husbands and demanding child support from them. For examples, see untitled memorandum to the Alcalde de Yauco, June 17, 1872, in "Copiador de Oficios dirigidos a las Autoridades locales y particulares," 1872, no. 129, AMP, Ay., Sec., Ar., L.C., Of.; memorandum to the Alcalde Municipal Delegado en Caguas, June 8, 1876, "Copiador de oficios dirigidos á las Autoridades locales y particulares, año de 1875 y 76 y 1877," no. 139, AMP, Ay., Sec., Ar., L.C., Of.

39   Magistrates' denial of honor to plebeian women in such cases had a material motivation—granting validity to the claims of mistresses against other "respectable" men would have opened the door to a similar use of their own sexual adventures.

40 Eric R. Wolf, "San José: Subcultures of a 'Traditional' Coffee Municipality," in *The People of Puerto Rico: A Study in Social Anthropology,* ed. Julian H. Steward (1956; reprint, Urbana: University of Illinois, 1972), 171–264, and Sidney W. Mintz, "Cañamelar: The Subculture of a Rural Sugar Plantation Proletariat," in Steward, *People of Puerto Rico,* 314–418.

41 See the various "Relaciones de los que fueron sorprendidos en juegos prohibidos," 1850–1856, AGPR, FGE, box 529; "La morena liberta María de la Cruz Mercado, demandando a Nolverto [*sic*] del Toro," "Juicios verbales del ano 1844 y 1845," AMP, Ay., Sec., Jud., Juic., Ver.; "D. Ulpiano González demandando á D. Isais Ruiz," Oct. 15, 1857, no. 229, "Cuaderno de juicios verbales por el Corregimiento. 1857," AMP, Ay., Sec., Jud., Juic., Ver.; D. "Pedro José Torres en representación de su esclavo Felix, demandando á Hilario Rivas," Sept. 12, 1859, "Juicios Verbales, Corregimiento. 1859," AMP, Ay., Sec., Jud., Juic., Ver.; "Contra Ramón Rodríguez (a) el Indio y Simón Santos sobre tentativa de violación el 10 y lesiones el 20," 1886, AGPR, Ponce, Jud., Crim., box 9.

42 "Isla de Puerto Rico: Villa de Ponce. La Cantera and Sabanetas. Padrón nominal del número de almas de dicho barrio, 1860," AMP, Ay., Sec., Ar., Hab., box 1860–1860. For later-nineteenth-century descriptions of interracial relationships, see Henry K. Carroll, *Report on the Island of Puerto Rico* (Washington, D.C.: Governmental Printing Office, 1899), 690–712.

43 In 1860, better than one-third of the "white" *comerciantes* of the rural barrio of Sabanetas were married to Afro-Puerto Rican women. "Isla de Puerto Rico: Villa de Ponce. Sabanetas. Padrón nominal del número de almas de dicho barrio, 1860," AMP, Ay., Sec., Ar., Hab., box 1860–1860. See also "Manuel Rosado demandando á D. Francisco Fano," Jan. 10, 1856, "Juicios Verbales. Tenencias Alcalde," 1856, no. 221, AMP, Ay., Sec., Jud., Juic., Ver.; "D. José María Avendaño demandando á Da. Gumersinda Salmás," June 22, 1860, and "Da. Concepción Figueroa en representación de su hija Da. María Merchona Gallard demandando á Francisco de Rivera," June 25, 1860, both in "Villa de Ponce, Año de 1860. Juicios Verbales celebrados en el Corregimiento en dicho año," no. 798, AMP, Ay., Sec., Jud., Juic., Ver.; no. 25, Nov. 27, 1860, "1853 al 1864. Copiador de informes," AMP, Ay., Sec., Ar., L.C., Inf.

44 There were ten such families in the plebeian barrio of La Cantera alone. See "Isla de Puerto Rico: Villa de Ponce. La Cantera. Padrón nominal del número de almas de dicho barrio, 1860," AMP, Ay., Sec., Ar., Hab., box 1860–1860. For further examples, see "Al Juez," Feb. 16, 1857, and Feb. 13, 1857, "1857 al 60 incs. Copiador de oficios al Juez Letrado del Distrito," no. 805, AMP, Ay., Sec., Ar., L.C., Of.

45 The very existence of such cases shows that many people of African descent did not accept the marginal Dons' claim to superiority. For a few examples, see

"D. Narciso López contra María Florina, liberta," Jan. 31, 1843, "Juicios verbales celebrados en la Alcaldía 2a," AMP, Ay., Sec., Jud., Juic., Ver.; "D. Camilo Simonpietri demandando á Andrea Maze," Dec. 20, 1845, "Juicios verbales del año 1844 y 1845," AMP, Ay., Sec., Jud., Juic., Ver., "Madama Bartolo demandando á la morena Rosa," May 5, 1852, "Juicios verbales del Corregimiento. Ponce, 1852," AMP, Ay., Sec., Jud., Juic., Ver. Susan Socolow notes a similar pattern in colonial Buenos Aires, where elites viewed all plebeians as a dishonorable mass, while Spanish-born artisans considered themselves racially purer than others of their class ("Acceptable Partners," 234).

46   "Doña María González en unión de su hija Doña Julia Guevara demandando á Don Gumersindo y Da. Dolores Rivas," Oct. 30, 1852, "Juicios verbales del Corregimiento: Ponce, 1852," AMP, Ay., Sec., Jud., Juic., Ver. The popular saying, "y tu abuela, dónde está?" [and your grandmother, where is she?] refers to the African antecedents that so many Puerto Ricans still strive to hide.

47   Quintero Rivera, "Somatology of Manners," 175–78.

48   "José Dergniz, vecino de Guayama, demandando á D. Fernando Monica," Sept. 5, 1855, "Villa de Ponce. Año 1855. Juicios verbales celebrados en el Corregimiento en dicho año," AMP, Ay., Sec., Jud., Juic., Ver. Pamela Scully discusses analogous divisions between "blacks" and "coloureds" in mid-nineteenth-century Cape colony, South Africa ("Rape, Race, and Colonial Culture").

49   No. 229, Aug. 3, 1857, "Cuaderno de juicios verbales por el Corregimiento, 1857," AMP, Ay., Sec., Jud., Juic., Ver.

50   No. 798, Dec. 14, 1860, "Villa de Ponce, Año de 1860. Juicios Verbales celebrados en el Corregimiento en dicho año," AMP, Ay., Sec., Jud., Juic., Ver. See also Rosario Rentas v. Alejandro Torres (untitled court case), 1874, AHDSJ, box J-217.

51   "D. Pedro González demandando á María Nicolasa Moreno i María Andrea Vega," Nov. 20, 1856, "Juicios Verbales. Tenencias Alcalde. 1856," AMP, Ay., Sec., Jud., Juic., Ver.

52   "Juan Laboy demandando al Comisario de Machuelo Arriba D. José María Alvarez," Sept. 10, 1852, "Juicios verbales del Corregimiento. Ponce. 1852," AMP, Ay., Sec., Jud., Juic., Ver.

53   See "Por rapto de Ercilia Reyes," Sept. 10, 1896, AGPR, Ponce, Jud., Crim., box 19, for plebeian youths' wonderfully rich description of their methods of flirtation, courtship, and preparation of "marital space" before running off together.

54   *Código Penal,* título 13, capítulo 1, artículos 261–62.

55   Of the surviving rapto cases from the nineteenth century ($N = 211$), 50 percent included no mention of how long the parents had waited to file their complaint. Forty-six percent of all parents went to court within a week of the rapto; the remaining 4 percent filed after waiting several months or longer.

56 "Por rapto de Inés Serna Lugo," June 14, 1896, AGPR, Ponce, Jud., Crim., box 19.

57 Stolcke, *Marriage,* 100–141; Gutiérrez, *When Jesus Came,* 215–26. See also Seed, *To Love, Honor, and Obey.*

58 The one exception was Santos Vargas, the initial lover of Teresa Astacio, whose story opened this chapter. He, however, was not only facing a jail sentence but had been deserted for another man as well.

59 Gutiérrez, *When Jesus Came,* 221.

60 "Sobre rapto de Guadalupe Rodríguez," May 27, 1888, AGPR, Ponce, Jud., Crim., box 8.

61 "Por rapto de Ercilia Reyes," Sept. 10, 1896, AGPR, Ponce, Jud., Crim., box 19.

62 "Sobre violación de Juana Teodora Pérez y Torres," 1901, AGPR, Ponce, Jud., Crim., box 102.

63 "Isla de Puerto Rico: Villa de Ponce. La Cantera. Padrón nominal del número de almas de dicho barrio, 1860," AMP, Ay., Sec., Ar., Hab., box 1860–1860. Eric Wolf's and Sidney Mintz's classic studies of rural Puerto Rico in the 1940s seem to confirm the now time-worn argument that worries about controlling access to women's reproductive capacities, based in desires to pass on property to clearly definable heirs, form the underlying motivations for men's interest in regulating women's sexuality. Wolf and Mintz found an overriding concern among the landowning "white" coffee peasantry for maintaining young women's virginity and practicing lifelong marriage, while the women of the multiracial sugar proletariat tended to practice serial monogamy (Wolf, "San José"; Mintz, "Cañamelar").

The 1860 census reflects analogous patterns even within the municipality of Ponce. The largely highland barrio of Machuelo Arriba, where a smallholding peasantry continued to survive, showed a marriage rate hovering around 50 percent for both free Afro-Puerto Ricans and whites. In the sugar barrio of Sabanetas, however, only one-third of free people of African descent were married, compared with 43 percent of all whites.

64 "Sobre rapto de Francisca Vega," 1887, AGPR, Ponce, Jud., Crim., box 27.

65 Women former slaves were the only exception to this pattern; 59 percent were married. The reasons for this discrepancy are not clear. It may reflect a greater concern for respectability among those women who had suffered the humiliation of slavery. It also may indicate that women were freeing themselves from slavery through sexual alliances with men who paid for their freedom and subsequently married them. "Censo del Depto. 5" [undated—filed with and recorded by the same scribe as the censuses between 1841 and 1847], AGPR, FGE, box 15.

66 "Isla de Puerto Rico: Villa de Ponce. La Cantera."

67 "Sobre hurto de seis pesos a Lorenza Moró," 1892, AGPR, Ponce, Jud., Crim., box 90. For further examples of this sort, see the rapto cases for 1890 in AGPR, Ponce,

Jud., Crim., box 6; the witnesses living in concubinage include a sweetmaker, mule drivers, and vegetable stand owners.

68　See, for example, no. 25, Oct. 13, 1866, "Corregimiento de Ponce, año de 1866: Juicios sobre faltas ó injurias leves celebrados desde setiembre [*sic*] hasta Diciembre del referido año," AMP, Ay., Sec., Jud., Juic., Untitled, [Juan Bautista Rivera to the governor of Puerto Rico], Nov. 11, 1862, AGPR, FGE, box 145.

69　Mintz noted in 1948 that for the sugar workers in the coastal plains near Ponce, adult life was married life but that "marriage" more often than not meant consensual relationships that dissolved and re-formed with different people several times over the course of an individual's life. Seventy percent of all couples in the community Mintz studied were living in consensual union ("Cañamelar," 375–80). Henry Carroll, a late-nineteenth-century North American observer of Puerto Rico, also commented on the high incidence of consensual unions among working people in the coastal areas.

　　For specific nineteenth-century examples, see "Bonifacia Ortiz demandando á Pedro Eustaquio Figueroa y á José Charlotín," Oct. 6, 1862, "Ponce, Año de 1862. Juicios vervales [*sic*] ante el 20 Teniente," AMP, Ay., Sec., Jud., Juic., Ver.; No. 798, Dec. 14, 1860, "Villa de Ponce, Año de 1860. Juicios Verbales celebrados en el Corregimiento en dicho año," AMP, Ay., Sec., Jud., Juic., Ver.; "Consejo de familia de la menor Juana María Moñí," Jan. 26, 1897, AGPR, Ponce, Jud., Crim., box 100; "Por delito de violación a Juana Montalvo," 1892, AGPR, Ponce, Jud., Crim., box 42.

70　"Contra Juana Garay Hernández sobre Hurto de dinero y ropa a Olivorio Garay," Causa 1711, 1894, AGPR, Ponce, Jud., Crim., box 2.

71　For examples, see "Por delito de violación a Juana Montalvo," Sent. 372, Causa 238, rollo 359, 1892, AGPR, Ponce, Jud., Crim., box 42; and "El Pueblo de Puerto Rico contra Juan Sánchez y Mercedes González por adulterio," Dec. 25, 1903, AGPR, Ponce, Jud., Crim., box 76. See also "Consejo de la familia de la menor Juana María Moñí," Jan. 26, 1897, AGPR, Ponce, Jud., Crim., box 100, and Sent. 419, *Tomo de sentencias de la Audiencia de lo Criminal de Ponce, Cuarto trimestre, Año de 1891,* AGPR, Ponce, Jud., Crim., box 5.

72　Sidney Mintz's anthropological research from the 1940s supports my contention that the flexibility of consensual union partnerships was an important consideration for those who entered into them ("Cañamelar," 378). For Alejandrina's testimony, see "Causa Criminal sobre rapto contra Don Miguel Santiago," 1893, AGPR, Ponce, Jud., Crim., box 14.

73　$N = 83$ for Afro-Puerto Rican women; $N = 23$ for "white" women.

74　Again, Mintz's research from the 1940s supports my conclusion. He found that most parents who wanted their daughters to marry were concerned primarily with financial well-being, not with marriage per se ("Cañamelar," 377).

75 "D. Jose Colón demandando á D. José Vicente Ortiz," Sept. 17, 1860," Villa de Ponce, Año de 1860. Juicios Verbales celebrados en el Corregimiento en dicho año," no. 798, AMP, Ay., Sec., Jud., Juic., Ver.; "Bonifacia Ortiz demandando á Pedro Eustaquio Figueroa y á José Charlotín," Oct. 6, 1862, "Ponce, Año de 1862. Juicios vervales [*sic*] ante el 20 Teniente," no. 860, AMP, Ay., Sec., Jud., Juic., Ver.; "José Lindore Laporte en representación de su esposa Victoria Conde demandando á Isabel Roche," Nov. 4, 1860, "Ponce, Año de 1861. Juicios vervales [*sic*] ante el 20 Teniente," no. 873, AMP, Ay., Sec., Jud., Juic., Ver.

76 For examples of women's conflicts with their partners' mistresses, see "Doña Rosa Méndez demandando á D. Enrique Duvver," Aug. 20, 1860, "Villa de Ponce, Año de 1860. Juicios Verbales celebrados en el Corregimiento en dicho año," no. 798, AMP, Ay., Sec., Jud., Juic., Ver.; "Eulalia Martínez demandando á María del Rosario Rodríguez y á una hija de ésta Felícita Rosado," Nov. 8, 1860, "Villa de Ponce, Año de 1860. Juicios Verbales celebrados en el Corregimiento en dicho año," no. 798, AMP, Ay., Sec., Jud., Juic., Ver.; and Sent. 138, causa 30, rollo 35, "Tomo de Sentencias del segundo trimestre, 1891," AGPR, Ponce, Jud., Crim., box 66. Kathleen Brown provides an illuminating discussion of the uses of gossip in colonial Virginia in *Good Wives,* 100–104, 145–49, 306–13.

77 See, for example, "El pueblo de Puerto Rico vs. Eladio Maldonado," Feb. 14, 1907, AGPR, Ponce, Jud., Crim., box 92; "Contra Manuel Patos sobre rapto de Lorenza Torres Rivera," Jan. 22, 1900, AGPR, Ponce, Jud., Crim., box 105.

78 For a few examples, see Minuta 88, Oct. 28, 1889, *Audiencia de Ponce, Sección segunda, minutas de sentencias, 1889,* AGPR, Ponce, Jud., Crim., box 66; Sent. 71, contra Juan Miguel Ortiz Padilla, *Audiencia de lo Criminal de Ponce. Sentencias dictadas en el primer trimestre de 1892,* AGPR, Ponce, Jud., Crim., box 26; Juan Bautista Rivera to the Governor of Puerto Rico, Nov. 11, 1862, AGPR, FGE, box 145; "Contra Juana Garay Hernández sobre Hurto de dinero y ropa a Olivorio Garay," Causa 1711, 1894, AGPR, Ponce, Jud., Crim., box 2.

79 "Cayetano Cambreleng con su hija menor Belén en representación de ella demandando á José Jaime Napoleoni," Aug. 22, 1857, "Cuaderno de juicios verbales por el Corregimiento. 1857," AMP, Ay., Sec., Jud., Juic., Ver.

80 Manuela was eventually acquitted of her husband's adultery charges. See "El pueblo de Puerto Rico contra Manuela Guiets y Juan Nieves por adulterio," Aug. 23, 1903, AGPR, Ponce, Jud., Crim., box 76.

81 "Por delito de violación a Juana Montalvo," Sent. 372, causa 238, rollo 359, 1892, AGPR, Ponce, Jud., Crim., box 42.

82 Sent. 287, 1892, AGPR, Ponce, Jud., Crim., box 3.

83 Stern, *Secret History of Gender,* 45–150. Heidi Tinsman provides an extremely insightful analysis of the shifting historical bases for domestic violence in late-twentieth-century rural Chile; see "Household Patrones: Wife-Beating and Sex-

ual Control in Rural Chile, 1964–1988," in *The Gendered Worlds of Latin American Women Workers: From Household and Factory to the Union Hall and Ballot Box*, ed. John D. French and Daniel James (Durham: Duke University Press, 1997), 264–96. See also Alonso, *Thread of Blood*, 217–32.

84   "Homicidio contra Julio Clausell," Sent. 419, causa 88, 1891, AGPR, Ponce, Jud., Crim., box 5; "Nicolasa Figueroa demandando á su esposo D. Francisco Fernández," Oct. 7, 1857, "Cuaderno de juicios verbales por el Corregimiento. 1857," no. 229, AMP, Ay., Sec., Jud., Juic., Ver. See *Tomo de la Audiencia de lo Criminal de Ponce. Minutas de Sentencias del Año 1890*, AGPR, Ponce, Jud., Crim., box 6, for many similar cases, as well as "Bacilia Mercado demandando á Juan de la Rosa Chavarría," Feb. 10, 1853, "Juicios verbales del Corregimiento. Ponce, 1852," AMP, Ay., Sec., Jud., Juic., Ver.; "Da. Marcelina Rodríguez demandando á su esposo D. Joaquín Casal," Oct. 24, 1859, "Juicios Verbales, Corregimiento. 1859," AMP, Ay., Sec., Jud., Juic., Ver.; "Francisca Ortiz demandando á su esposo D. Vicente Moré," Sept. 22, 1860, "Juana García Moreno demandando á su marido José Roini," Jan. 25, 1860, no. 798, and "María Felipa Ruiz demandando á su marido Gregorio Martínez," July 13, 1860, no. 798, all three in "Villa de Ponce, Año de 1860. Juicios Verbales celebrados en el Corregimiento en dicho año," AMP, Ay., Sec., Jud., Juic., Ver.

85   See "Noticias," *La Democracia*, May 8, 1893, July 3, 1893, Mar. 21, 1894, May 29, 1894.

86   "Sobre lesiones a Carlos Perault, contra Juan Lugo Negrón," 1895, AGPR, Ponce, Jud., Crim., box 67; "Sobre lesiones a Miguel Fernández," 1888, AGPR, Ponce, Jud., Crim., box 28.

87   For examples, see "Por el delito de lesiones contra Gregorio Rosado Cortés," Sent. 10, *Audiencia de lo Criminal de Ponce: Sentencias dictadas en el primer trimestre de 1891*, AGPR, Ponce, Jud., Crim., box 25; "Sobre lesiones a Miguel Fernández," 1880, AGPR, Ponce, Jud., Crim., box 28; "Por delito de lesiones contra Regino Figueroa Díaz y Juan José Figueroa," 1897, AGPR, Ponce, Jud., Crim., box 90.

88   "Sobre violación de María Margarita Marcucci," 1885, AGPR, Ponce, Jud., Crim., box 27.

89   "Sobre rapto de Daniela Colón y Collazo," 1897, AGPR, Ponce, Jud., Crim., box 21.

2   Motherhood, Marriage, and Morality: Male Liberals and Bourgeois Feminists, 1873–1898

1   See Luis Antonio Figueroa, "Facing Freedom: The Transition from Slavery to Free Labor in Guayama, Puerto Rico, 1860–1898" (Ph.D. diss., University of Wisconsin, Madison, 1991), and Ileana María Rodríguez-Silva, "Freedmen and

Freedwomen: Processes of Social Reconfiguration in Post-Emancipation Puerto Rico (1873–1876)" (Master's thesis, University of Wisconsin, Madison, 1997), for discussions of former slaves' struggles with planters and the state over the terms of freedom. Rodríguez-Silva also perceptively analyses the fragmentation of consensus between local elites and Spanish colonial authorities after 1850 on pages 44–84.

2   During the nineteenth century, the linking of middle- and upper-class women's education, enlightened motherhood, and the formation of good citizens was common among Liberals throughout Latin America. In Mexico, this theory of "respectable" women's "social utility" emerged as early as the colonial Bourbon reforms in the late eighteenth century and was periodically touted by Liberals throughout the following 120 years. In Cuba, the discourse arose during the twin struggles for independence and the abolition of slavery, beginning in 1868, and reached its culmination in José Martí's fiery abolitionist and nationalist arguments of the 1880s and 1890s. In Brazil, women were the first to take up the call for female education; men appear to have been much more conservative on this and most other questions of women's emancipation than in other major Latin American nations. The issue did not develop into a central component of nineteenth-century Brazilian elite male discourse, although a few statesmen did argue that educated mothers would be beneficial to national progress. Women's education became much more central to official Brazilian reform projects in the twentieth century, between the two world wars. For Mexico, see Silva Marina Arrom, *The Women of Mexico City, 1790–1857* (Stanford: Stanford University Press, 1985), 15–32; Anna Macías, *Against All Odds: The Feminist Movement in Mexico to 1940* (Westport, Conn.: Greenwood, 1982), 6–9, 17; and Carmen Ramos Escandón, "Señoritas porfirianas: Mujer e ideología en el México progresista, 1880–1910," in *Presencia y transparencia: La mujer en la historia de México,* ed. Carmen Ramos Escandón (México: El Colegio de México, 1987), 143–61. For Cuba, see K. Lynn Stoner, *From the House to the Streets: The Cuban Woman's Movement for Legal Reform, 1898–1940* (Durham: Duke University Press, 1991), 17–32; for Brazil, see June E. Hahner, *Emancipating the Female Sex: The Struggle for Women's Rights in Brazil, 1850–1940* (Durham: Duke University Press, 1990), 26–36, 47–53, and Susan K. Besse, *Restructuring Patriarchy: The Modernization of Gender Inequality in Brazil, 1914–1940* (Chapel Hill: University of North Carolina Press, 1996), 110–28.

3   Asunción Lavrin notes concerns about women's sexuality among a few male and female Southern Cone reformers of the 1890s. These focused mainly on venereal disease and public health, however. See *Women, Feminism, and Social Change in Argentina, Chile, and Uruguay, 1890–1940* (Lincoln: University of Nebraska Press, 1995), 126–29.

4 Notable exceptions to this racial characterization of the Liberal Autonomists were José Celso Barbosa, a black physician, and Ramón Baldorioty de Castro, a mulatto journalist.

Autonomism was not a monolithic ideology or political program. Two main tendencies emerged in Puerto Rico during this period: the Cuban Party's platform and the Canadian model. The Cubans called for the Caribbean colonies to have more say in decisions relating to local administrative and economic questions such as infrastructure, education, budgetary priorities, and tariffs. The Canadian model went further, demanding much broader political autonomy, along with the economic and administrative decentralization advocated by the Cubans. Ponce Liberals tended to sympathize with the Cuban Party's version. See Francisco A. Scarano, *Puerto Rico: Cinco siglos de historia* (San Juan: McGraw-Hill, 1993), 517–18.

5 See Quintero Rivera, *Patricios y plebeyos: Burgueses, hacendados, artesanos y obreros: Las relaciones de clase en el Puerto Rico de cambio de siglo* (Río Piedras: Ediciones Huracán, 1988), 23–98, for a fascinating discussion of Ponce as the alternate capital of Puerto Rico. More than a dozen Liberal newspapers and magazines were published in Ponce during this period. Many of them were eventually repressed by the Spanish authorities.

6 "Ponce y su término Municipal: Observaciones Generales," letter from Mayor of Ponce to Governor of Puerto Rico, Mar. 20, 1887, AGPR, FGE, box 535.

7 For accounts of the *componte*, as the repression was called, in Ponce, see Eduardo Neumann, *Verdadera y auténtica historia de la ciudad de Ponce, desde sus primitivos tiempos hasta la época contemporanea* (1911; San Juan: Instituto de Cultura Puertorriqueña, 1987), 229–41.

8 As Ileana Rodríguez-Silva has pointed out, this discourse of social harmony served the Liberals' political interests. Puerto Rico experienced a good deal of social conflict during the nineteenth century, although much of it centered on individual, less frontal challenges to authority. See "Freedmen," 21–32. For some examples of collective popular rebellions on the island, see Guillermo Baralt, *Esclavos rebeldes: Conspiraciones y sublevaciones de esclavos en Puerto Rico (1795–1873)* (Río Piedras: Ediciones Huracán, 1982), and Olga Jiménez de Wagenheim, *El grito de Lares: Sus causas y sus hombres* (Río Piedras: Ediciones Huracán, 1985).

9 Salvador Brau, "Las clases jornaleras de Puerto Rico: Su estado actual, causas que lo sostienen y medios de propender al adelanto moral y material de dichas clases" (1882), reprinted in *Ensayos: Disquisiciones sociológicas* (Río Piedras: Editorial Edil, 1972), 14. See also Brau, "Rafael Cordero" (1891), in *Ensayos*, 158, and Francisco del Valle Atiles, *El campesino puertorriqueño: Sus condiciones físicas,*

intelectuales y morales, causas que las determinan y medios para mejorarlas (San Juan: Tipografía de J. González Font, 1887), 13, 75.

10 Del Valle, *El campesino,* 147.

11 Luís Muñoz Rivera, "22 de marzo," *La Democracia,* Mar. 22, 1892; del Valle, *El campesino,* 132–34, 145–51; Ada Ferrer, "To Make a Free Nation: Race and the Struggle for Independence in Cuba, 1868–1898" (Ph.D. diss., University of Michigan, Ann Arbor, 1995), 34–37; "Carta de Isaura," *La Azucena,* December 20, 1875, 25; "La mujer en sociedad," *La Azucena,* November 30, 1875, 7. Salvador Brau was one of the few Liberals who understood that the poor had their own moral codes and were not simply submerged in sexual chaos. Nonetheless, Brau still agreed with his contemporaries that the rural poor's African elements and the "vices" of concubinage and gambling were great obstacles to developing Puerto Rico's productive potential. He thus concurred with the Liberals' linking of racial reconstitution, labor discipline, and moral reform. See his 1883 essay on popular culture "La danza puertorriqueña," in *Ensayos,* 75–91; his 1886 essay "La campesina," in *Ensayos,* 111–22; his novella *¿Pecadora?* (1890; reprint, Río Piedras: Editorial Edil, 1975); his 1882 blueprint for social reform "Las clases jornaleras," 29–38; and "La herencia devota," in *Almanaque de damas* (San Juan: Tipografía González Font, 1886).

12 Ann Laura Stoler, *Race and the Education of Desire: Foucault's "History of Sexuality" and the Colonial Order of Things* (Durham: Duke University Press, 1995), 6, 10.

13 Angel G. Quintero Rivera argues that the danza was Puerto Rico's first national music, reaching across class and race lines; see *Patricios y plebeyos,* pp. 46–78. He has also developed a compelling analysis of Puerto Rican bourgeois identity and the danza in "The Somatology of Manners: Class, Race, and Gender in the History of Dance Etiquette in the Hispanic Caribbean," in *Ethnicity in the Caribbean,* ed. Gert Oostindie (London: Macmillan Education, 1996), 152–81.

14 Luis Muñoz Rivera, "Por patria semper," *La Democracia,* September 1, 1892; Brau, "La danza," p. 90; Mariano Abril, "Música del país," *La Democracia,* May 5, 1893, p. 2. Manuel González García provides an illuminating counterpoint to this discourse of degenerate mulatta sexual infection in his novel *El escándalo: Novela naturalista* (San Juan: Tipografía de Arturo Córdova, 1894), in which the magnetically attractive son of a mulatta and a wealthy Spaniard passes as white and enters high society. There, he robs money, seduces respectable women, and threatens the local social order. The young man was "a fount of immorality among his friends, who he perverted within a matter of days" (26).

15 Brau, "La danza," 91. Most eminent Liberals refused to acknowledge such close cultural, social, and potentially even biological association with Afro-Puerto

Ricans, however. Luís Muñoz Rivera was fond of insisting that Spain was "our race, our blood, our origin" and persistently differentiated between the elite Puerto Rican "sons of Spain" and Puerto Rico's ignorant, racially ambiguous "people" ("El separatismo," *La Democracia,* Aug. 10, 1890; "En la atalaya," *La Democracia,* Mar. 17, 1892; "El centenario," *La Democracia,* Oct. 1, 1892).

Mariano Abril also lashed out in rage at Eva Canel's dramatic production *La mulata,* in which an allegedly Spanish attorney publicly claimed his mulatta mother and renounced his wealthy Spanish merchant father. Abril called the play "a joke, without one original thought or trace of ingenuity. Filled with empty phrases" and proof that women were useless as playwrights. Clearly the story line was far from "empty," judging from Abril's virulent reaction ("Perfil del día," *La Democracia,* Apr. 3, 1895).

16 Brau, "La danza," 88–91; Luis Muñoz Rivera, "Ni hechos ni palabras," *La Democracia,* Mar. 17, 1892; Mariano Abril, "Música del país," *La Democracia,* May 5, 1893, p. 2. Puerto Rican Liberal Autonomists were not alone in expressing such concerns. Ann L. Stoler notes that throughout French, British, and Dutch colonies, "discourses on self-mastery were productive of racial distinctions, of clarified notions of 'whiteness' and what it truly meant to be European." These discourses sprang from the colonial elites' fear of popular transgressions (*Education of Desire,* 8 [quotation], 102–23).

17 Quintero Rivera, *Patricios y plebeyos,* 46–78, 193–229. Familial imagery, meanings, and methods of asserting power over others have often been used to assert political legitimacy. For colonial Mexico, see Stern, *Secret History of Gender,* 189–213. For Latin American independence struggles, see Mary Lowenthal Felsteiner, "Family Metaphors: The Language of an Independence Revolution," *Comparative Studies in Society and History* 25, no. 1 (January 1983): 154–80. For early modern Europe, see Lynn Hunt, *The Family Romance of the French Revolution* (Berkeley: University of California Press, 1992).

18 Note how, twenty years after abolition, Muñoz Rivera deftly appropriated the suffering of enslaved Africans for elite white men. See Muñoz Rivera, "22 de marzo." Other examples can be found in "Efemérides," *La Democracia,* Mar. 22, 1893; "El insulto," *La Democracia,* Jan. 3, 1893; "Lo que manda el decoro," *La Democracia,* Jan. 5, 1893; and "Paralelos," *La Democracia,* June 28, 1893.

19 "Ser periodista; *dirigir las masas; / engendrar las corrientes populares; /* luchar por las ideas luminosas / y por las causas grandes." See Luís Muñoz Rivera, "XXXIV," in *Retamas* (1891), reprinted in *Obras Completas,* ed. Eugenio Fernández Méndez (San Juan: Instituto de Cultura Puertorriqueña, 1960), 53; emphasis mine. In a similar vein, see Muñoz Rivera's other pieces: "¿Escalón? ¿Para Qué?" *La Democracia,* May 5, 1894; "Ni hechos ni palabras"; and "Al país, la verdad," *La Democracia,* Apr. 24, 1896.

20 Manuel Zeno Gandía, *La charca* (1894; San Juan: Instituto de Cultura Puerto-rriqueña, 1987), 17. See also Manuel González García, *La primera cría* (San Juan: Tipografía del Boletín Mercantil, 1892), 28.

21 Brau, *¿Pecadora?* 189; emphasis mine. For another particularly graphic example of the invocation of a cross-class brotherhood of workers, see "Balada: Trabajar es orar," *La Azucena,* Dec. 10, 1870, 19. See also Salvador Brau, *¿Pecadora?* 198–200; Brau, "Las clases jornaleras," 47–59; Brau, "Rafael Cordero," 147–59; and Zeno Gandía, *La charca,* 6–11, 16–17, 23–25, 34, 44.

22 See, for example, Brau, *¿Pecadora?* and Zeno Gandía, *La charca,* 17.

23 Del Valle, *El campesino,* 12–13 (quotation), 73–75; Gabriel Ferrer, *La mujer en Puerto Rico: Sus necesidades presentes y los medios más fáciles y adecuados para mejorar su porvenir* (Puerto Rico: Imprente de "El Agente," 1881), 19–21, 34–37.

24 Thomas E. Skidmore, *Black into White: Race and Nationality in Brazilian Thought* (1974; Durham: Duke University Press, 1993); Winthrop Wright, *Café con leche: Race, Class, and National Image in Venezuela* (Austin: University of Texas Press, 1990); Nancy Leys Stepan, *"The Hour of Eugenics": Race, Gender, and Nation in Latin America* (Ithaca: Cornell University Press, 1991); Aline Helg, "Race in Argentina and Cuba, 1880–1930: Theory, Policies, and Popular Reaction," in *The Idea of Race in Latin America, 1870–1940,* ed. Richard Graham (Austin: University of Texas Press, 1990), 37–69.

25 See, for example, del Valle, *El campesino,* 133. For analogous European cases of Liberal reformers' nation-building zest for moral and familial reform, see Isabel V. Hull, *Sexuality, State, and Civil Society in Germany, 1700–1815* (Ithaca: Cornell University Press, 1996), and Laura Engelstein, *The Keys to Happiness: Sex and the Search for Modernity in Fin-de-Siècle Russia* (Ithaca: Cornell University Press, 1992).

26 Brau, "Las clases jornaleras," 32 (quotations); del Valle, *El campesino,* 134, 136, 156; Quintín Negrón Sanjurjo, "La escuela rural," *La Democracia,* May 14, 1895; G. Ferrer, *La mujer,* 19–22, 34–36.

27 Del Valle, *El campesino,* 12–13, 73; Ferrer, *La mujer,* 19–25, 35; "Parricidio," *La Democracia,* May 18, 1893, pp. 1–2.

28 Brau, "La campesina," 116. See also del Valle, *El campesino,* 136, and G. Ferrer, *La mujer,* 34–35.

29 G. Ferrer, *La mujer,* 20, 34–36; del Valle, *El campesino,* 135–36; González García, *La primera cría,* 29–32. Salvador Brau, as usual, had a more sympathetic analysis of rural men's "oversexed" behavior, although he did not question this general characterization of their sexual practices. Brau insisted that poverty and in-justice wracked men's bodies and incited their passions. His solution was to propose the democratization of benevolent patriarchal rights. If paid a decent wage and provided with chaste, loving wives who exercised moral influence

while properly submitting to them, jornaleros would soon flower into productive, humble, appropriately moral, and, implicitly, less African workers. See Brau, *¿Pecadora?* esp. 198, and "Las clases jornaleras."

30 Salvador Brau and Manuel Zeno Gandía, not surprisingly, were the only exceptions I encountered. Brau passionately denounced the rape of poor women by hacendados in *¿Pecadora?* He too, however, turned a blind eye to the possible perpetration of such abuses by Liberals themselves. The wise Doctor Bueno (Dr. Good), who in the novella represents the progressive character of liberalism, would never have contemplated sex outside marriage, much less with an unwilling *peona*. In *La charca*, Zeno Gandía created a similar dichotomy between Galante, the evil, dissolute landowner, and Juan del Salto, the wise, paternal Liberal hacendado.

31 During the late nineteenth and early twentieth centuries, colonial officials in Southeast Asia developed similar strategies. They sought to create a recognizable, uniform European identity among colonists by encouraging the immigration of European women and the formation of "pure," bourgeois white families. Again, harnessing the socialization capacities of "respectable" women was key to creating a coherent, dependable collectivity (Ann Laura Stoler, "Making Empire Respectable: The Politics of Race and Sexual Morality in Twentieth-Century Cultures," *American Ethnologist* 16 (November 1989): 634–60. See María de Fátima Barceló Miller, *La lucha por el sufragio femenino en Puerto Rico, 1896–1935* (Río Piedras: Ediciones Huracán, 1997), 39–52, for an initial foray into the Liberals' linkage of women's education and Puerto Rico's modernization.

32 María Fernanda Baptista Bicalho argues that in late-nineteenth-century Brazil, similar discussions of the need to develop responsible white mothers were in part an attempt to reclaim the active mothering of white children from enslaved and recently freed black women (conversation with the author, June 11, 1993).

33 The newspapers published by Liberal men for bourgeois women include *La Azucena,* edited by Alejandro Tapia Rivera during the 1870s in Ponce and San Juan; *Las Hijas de Eva* (1880); *El Ramillete,* edited by José de Diego from Aguadilla (1887), Humacao (1897), and San Juan; and *El Almanaque de las Damas,* edited by Manuel Fernández Juncos in 1886. Gabriel Ferrer's essay *La mujer en Puerto Rico* won a national contest in 1881 for the best analysis of "the woman question." It was published in book and pamphlet form and distributed widely throughout the island.

Calls for women's education emerged through the colonized world during this period. In Egypt and India, such movements were in full swing by the 1890s. See Leila Ahmed, *Women and Gender in Islam: Historical Roots of a Modern Debate* (New Haven: Yale University Press, 1992), 138–43, and Partha Chatterjee, "The Nationalist Resolution of the Women's Question," in *Recast-*

ing Women: Essays in Indian Colonial History, ed. Kumkum Sangari and Sudesh Vaid (New Brunswick: Rutgers University Press, 1990), 245–52.

34   See, for example, "Carta de Julia," *La Azucena,* Dec. 10, 1870, p. 17; "Solución a la charada," ibid., p. 22; "Conversación con mis lectoras," ibid., Aug. 15, 1874, p. 1; Manuel Fernández Juncos, "Prólogo" to *La mujer,* by G. Ferrer, xii, xiv; and G. Ferrer, *La mujer,* 12–16. Mexican Liberals seem to have aired similar complaints about elite women. See Ramos Escandón, "Señoritas," 151, and Macías, *Against All Odds,* 8.

35   Fernández Juncos, "Prólogo," xv.

36   Ibid. This was the Liberals' version of making bourgeois women the compañera rather than the hembra of their men. See "Carta de Isaura," *La Azucena,* Nov. 20, 1870, 1–3; Alejandro Tapia Rivera, "El aprecio a la mujer es barómetro de civilización," *La Azucena,* Nov. 30, 1870, p. 10; G. Ferrer, *La mujer,* 5–6, 38–39; Fernández Juncos, "Prólogo."

37   "Se deja / Picar de cualquier abeja." See "La flor del café," *Guirnalda de Puerto Rico,* Mar. 30, 1856, p. 3. Similar sentiments were expressed frequently in later publications. See, for example, "¡El matrimonio en baja!" *La Democracia,* Sept. 21, 1891, p. 3, and "¿Qué haré?" *La Democracia,* June 6, 1894, p. 3.

38   G. Ferrer, *La mujer,* 17–19; "Adúltera," *La Democracia,* May 2, 1893, p. 3.

39   The quote is from Tapia, "El aprecio a la mujer," p. 10.

40   Alejandro Tapia, "La mujer en sociedad," *La Azucena,* Nov. 30, 1875, p. 7. See also Brau, "La danza," 88–89, and his "La herencia devota," *Almanaque de damas* (San Juan: Tipografía González Font, 1886).

41   Alejandro Tapia, "La mujer en sociedad," p. 7; G. Ferrer, *La mujer,* 53.

42   G. Ferrer, *La mujer,* 53. Note that Ferrer's insistence on the submissive union of elite women to their husbands is only one step removed from plebeian men's assertions of their right to discipline their lovers physically. Both male discourses warned against the unruliness of *altanera* (haughty, uppity) women.

43   *La Democracia*'s humor section, "Recortes," was also filled with jokes and popular sayings, such as, "A woman will dominate, when she is not dominated," which laid bare the conflict between men and women within the bourgeois family. See, for example, the issues for Oct. 22, 1891; Oct. 24, 1891; Nov. 5, 1891; June 22, 1892; and Feb. 11, 1892. See also "Adúltera," 3.

44   Note Rodríguez's play with the gender of the onerous term "frivolous," which so permeated contemporary Liberal discussions of bourgeois women. Lola Rodríguez Tió, "La influencia de la mujer en la civilización," reprinted in Lola Rodríguez de Tió, *Obras completas,* 4 vols. (San Juan: Instituto de Cultura Puertorriqueña, 1971), 4:83.

45   For character sketches of nineteenth-century Puerto Rican feminists who were closely involved in the Liberal Party and its causes, see Angela Negrón Muñoz,

Las mujeres de Puerto Rico: Desde el período de colonización hasta el primer tercio del siglo XX (San Juan: Imprenta de Venezuela, 1935), 49, 67, 83, 90, 99, 104, 119, 121, 123, 127, 133, 137. Feminism and Liberalism had a close relationship elsewhere in Latin America. In Mexico, many feminists were passionate adherents of the Partido Liberal Mexicana, which resisted the regime of Porfirio Díaz in the early twentieth century. In Cuba, nineteenth-century elite women's political activism centered in the nationalist struggle. Women's support organizations were key in Cuba's Ten Years' War of 1868–78, and during the 1890s, women formed their own Revolutionary Clubs on the island and throughout the Cuban diaspora in the United States. See Shirlene Soto, *The Emergence of the Modern Mexican Woman: Her Participation in Revolution and Struggle for Equality, 1910–1940* (Denver: Arden, 1990), 19–26, and Stoner, *House to the Streets,* 17–32.

46   The vast majority of the authors published in *La Mujer* were from the coastal sugar centers of Ponce, Mayagüez, and Arecibo. But poetry and letters were received from towns in the center of the island as well ("Noticias," *La Mujer,* July 29, 1894, p. 3; "Estafeta de Ponce," *La Democracia,* Jan. 16, 1895, p. 3).

47   See, for example, the short stories by Ana Roqué in *Sara la obrera y otros cuentos* (Ponce: Imprenta Manuel López, 1895) and her novel *Luz y sombra* (Ponce: Tipografía de Q. N. Sanjurjo, 1903). The latter was written in 1894 and not published for almost a decade ("Advertencia," ibid). Carmela Eulate Sanjurjo, another prolific and rather conservative feminist of the period, wrote the novel *La muñeca* (1895; reprint, Río Piedras: Editorial de la Universidad de Puerto Rico, 1987).

48   Other Latin American feminist movements also encompassed a wide range of political positions. K. Lynn Stoner has examined the various, often conflictual strains of elite, "first-wave" Cuban feminism in *House to the Streets.* During the nineteenth century, however, most Latin American feminists seem to have focused on demanding equal education for women, with a lesser emphasis on reforming national civil codes to protect women's right to their property and custody of their children after marriage. Although it did not inspire widespread attention until the twentieth century in Latin America, suffrage appeared as a feminist demand in the 1880s in Mexico and Brazil; the Cuban abolitionist Ana Betancourt first called for the female vote in 1869. Until further research is done on the history of feminism in Latin America and the Caribbean, we cannot know whether the issues of morality and sexuality raised in this chapter were also important to nineteenth-century feminists throughout the region. For a broad overview of feminists' political and social demands in the Southern Cone, where sexuality was briefly politicized in the 1890s, see Lavrin, *Women, Feminism, and Social Change.*

49   In India, nineteenth-century women also took up and redirected debates that had originally been male-defined. Like the early Puerto Rican feminists, they recognized that the family and sexuality were central to women's subordination; their critiques frequently focused on the oppression of women within marriage. See Uma Chakravarti, "Whatever Happened to the Vedic *Dasi?* Orientalism, Nationalism, and a Script for the Past," in *Recasting Women: Essays in Indian Colonial History,* ed. Kumkum Sangari and Sudesh Vaid (New Brunswick: Rutgers University Press, 1990), 66–76, and Vir Bharat Talwar, "Feminist Consciousness in Women's Journals in Hindi, 1910–1920," in *Recasting Women,* ed. Sangari and Vaid, 213–25.

50   Journalism and fiction writing were also crucial tools for early feminists in other parts of Latin America. Brazilian feminists were among the first to publish their own periodicals; they began to do so in 1852. Feminist newspapers proliferated throughout the continent in the 1880s. Hahner, *Emancipating the Female Sex,* 26–36, 72–73; Soto, *Emergence,* 19–29; Ramos Escandón, "Señoritas," 151; Francine Masiello, *Between Civilization and Barbarism: Women, Nation, and Literary Culture in Modern Argentina* (Lincoln: University of Nebraska Press, 1992). See also Ericka Kim Verba, "The *Círculo de Lectura de Señoras* and the *Club de Señoras* of Santiago, Chile: Middle- and Upper-Class Feminist Conversations (1915–1920)," *Journal of Women's History* 7, no. 3 (fall 1995): 6–33.

51   Of all the male Liberals writing about "the woman question," only Gabriel Ferrer mentioned this topic, but he did not develop it as a central theme (*La mujer,* 17).

52   Ana Roqué, "¿Deberá ser limitada la instrucción de la mujer? (II)," *La Mujer,* Mar. 28, 1894, p. 1; J. N. Bouilly, "El obrador filial," *La Mujer,* Feb. 2, 1894, p. 3; Ibid., May 10, 1894; "La mujer puertorriqueña," *La Mujer,* Mar. 28, 1894, p. 2.

53   Lillian Torres-Braschi, *Olivia: Vida de Olivia Paoli, Viuda de Braschi (1855–1942)* (Barcelona: I. G. Manuel Pareja, n.d.), 7, 17–18; Negrón Muñoz, *Las mujeres,* 91, 110, 114, 119, 127.

54   Carmela Eulate, "La mujer," *La Mujer,* Feb. 2, 1894, p. 2; Ana Roqué, "Nuestro Programa," *La Mujer,* Feb. 2, 1894, p. 1; "La instrucción de la mujer," *La Mujer,* Apr. 4, 1894, p. 2; "La mujer en el Congreso Hispano-Portugúes, Americano de Madrid (II)," *La Mujer,* June 10, 1894, p. 1.

55   See, for example, Ana Roqué, "¿Deberá ser limitada la educación de la mujer? (IV)," *La Mujer,* Apr. 24, 1894, p. 1. Compare her analysis with that of Rosendo Cordero of the town of Juana Díaz; Cordero implied that women's main problems were their immorality and their inability to distinguish right from wrong— not their economic vulnerability ("La instrucción de la mujer"). Both Cordero and Roqué agreed, however, that the panacea for women was education.

56   Ana Roqué, "Nuestro programa," *La Mujer,* Feb. 2, 1894, p. 1. See also Eulate, "La mujer," 2; "La instrucción de la mujer," *La Mujer,* Apr. 4, 1894, p. 2; and "La mujer en el Congreso Hispano-Portugúes," 1. The sole exception to the feminists' proposal for class-specific feminine education was the attempt by the editorial board of *La Mujer* to finance the preparation of several low-income women at Puerto Rico's Normal School for teachers (Roqué, "Nuestro programa"). See Soto, *Emergence,* 16, for a brief description of early Mexican feminist attempts at cross-class educational work.

57   Eulate, "La mujer."

58   Ana Roqué, "Sara la obrera," in *Sara la obrera,* 14; "Candelaria," *La Mujer,* September 10, 1894, p. 2; Ana Roqué, "El ramo de jacintos," in *Sara la obrera,* 59–66; Ana Roqué, "Andina," in *Sara la obrera,* 34; Roqué, *Luz y sombra,* 1–8, 38–40, 50–51, 73–74.

59   Eulate, "La mujer."

60   Ibid.; Roqué, "Nuestro programa." See also Lola Baldoni, "A la mujer," *La Mujer,* Mar. 8, 1894, pp. 1–2; Carmela Eulate, "Influencia de la mujer," *La Mujer,* Apr. 24, 1894, pp. 1–2. Compare the feminist insistence on innate feminine moral superiority with the article by Rosendo Cordero in which he claims that education would above all help women distinguish right from wrong ("La instrucción de la mujer," 2).

61   "Muerte de envenamiento de Doña Rosa Besant," 1877, box 7, and Causa 1065, "Muerte de María Sánchez," 1896, both in AGPR, Ponce, Jud., Crim., box 48.

62   Yvonne Laborde, interview by author, Ponce, Mar. 13, 1992; Elsa Guillermina Salich Laborde, interview by author, Ponce, Mar. 6, 1992.

63   Roqué, "La serenata de los ángeles," in *Sara la obrera,* 69–72.

64   Puerto Rican feminists were not alone in their concerns. Early Mexican feminists denounced the double standard as well; they proclaimed that a single sexual standard for men and women was a "constant longing of feminists" (Macías, *Against All Odds,* 14; Ramos Escandón, "Señoritas," 153). European women also vigorously opposed the practice of concubinage by colonist men in Southeast Asia during the late nineteenth century, on the grounds that it condoned the sexual double standard within European colonial communities (Stoler, "Making Empire Respectable," 641). For the Puerto Rican feminist line, see, for example, Roqué, "¿Deberá ser limitada . . . ? (IV)"; Roqué, *Luz y sombra,* 8; and Eulate, "La mujer."

65   Roqué, "Sara la obrera," 21; Ana Roqué, "Los gorros," in *Sara la obrera,* 76; and Roqué, *Luz y sombra,* 70–71.

66   Roqué, "La serenata de los ángeles," 69. See also Eulate's discussion of Cleopatra in "Influencia de la mujer," 1–2. Similar competitions with plebeian women for their husband's financial resources, attentions, and loyalty may well have under-

lain the uncompromising resistance many early-twentieth-century elite Cuban feminists mounted to legislation that would have equalized illegitimate and legitimate children's rights. See Stoner, *House to the Streets*, 49, 62–77, 160–65. Nell Irvin Painter explores the sexual competition between enslaved and slave-owning women in the U.S. antebellum South in "Three Southern Women and Freud: A Non-Exceptionalist Approach to Race, Class, and Gender in the Slave South," in *Feminists Revision History*, ed. Ann-Louise Shapiro (New Brunswick: Rutgers University Press, 1994), 195–216.

67 It was not uncommon for women to die in childbirth during the nineteenth century. Large numbers of these types of cases appear in the archives of the Catholic Church, as a result of widowers petitioning to marry their deceased wife's younger sisters. See the scores of proceedings in AHDSJ, Just., Disp., box J-96. The advertisements for quack cures of syphilis and gonorrhea which littered Puerto Rican newspapers of the period are ample testimony to the widespread presence of these diseases. Weekly and sometimes daily ads appeared in every newspaper I reviewed.

68 Roqué, *Luz y sombra*, 26–27. See also Baldoni, "A la mujer"; Roqué, "La serenata de los ángeles"; Roqué, "El ramo de jacintos."

69 Roqué, *Luz y sombra*, 71.

70 Ibid., 50–51.

71 Ibid., 26–27, 17, 70–73.

72 Ibid.

73 Ibid., 42–46; Roqué, "Sara la obrera," 21; Roqué, "Los gorros," 81–82.

74 Perhaps the best example of this implication is to be found in "La serenata de los ángeles." See also "¿Deberá ser limitada . . . ? (II)."

75 "Pongámonos en lo cierto," *La Mujer*, June 10, 1894, p. 2; Roqué, "Nuestro programa." Lest readers accuse me of expecting too much from these early feminists, I remind them of the more inclusive (although still paternalistic) stance taken by many bourgeois feminists in Victorian England. There, women such as Josephine Butler publicly defended prostitutes from police harassment and invasive medical examinations. I suspect that the lack of a deep-rooted tradition of radical, class-based politics in nineteenth-century Puerto Rico and the profound racial divisions that haunted the island's social relations were key factors in preventing such attempts at cross-class gender solidarity from emerging among early Puerto Rican feminists. See Judith Walkowitz, *Prostitution and Victorian Society: Women, Class, and the State* (Cambridge: Cambridge University Press, 1980), and Walkowitz, *City of Dreadful Delight: Narratives of Sexual Danger in Late-Victorian London* (Chicago: University of Chicago Press, 1992), 84–93, 133–34, 159–60. Antoinette Burton argues that the hierarchical paternalistic attitudes of Butler and the Ladies National Association toward alleged

prostitutes intensified once they turned their attention to India. The British feminists saw "their" empire, and their role within it, as the ultimate instrument of benevolent reform for Indian women. Burton, *Burdens of History: British Feminists, Indian Women, and Imperial Culture, 1865–1915* (Chapel Hill: University of North Carolina Press, 1994), 127–69.

76   Roqué, "Nuestro programa," 1.

77   Roqué, "Sara la obrera," 12–13; Roqué, "El ramo de jacintos," 59–66.

78   Roqué, "Sara la obrera," 13; Roqué, "Andina," 30–31; Roqué, "La virgen del mar," in *Sara la obrera,* 54. This substitution of an idealized native Indian element for the African in Puerto Rico's plebeian ethnic mix is typical of Puerto Rican racism. The indigenous inhabitants of Puerto Rico were effectively eliminated within a few generations after the conquest. Thus, unlike the peoples of Africa, whose cultures and phenotypes were (and still are) a powerful presence on the island, "Indians" were safe for Puerto Rican elites to claim as a part of the national heritage. See also Roqué, "La Hada del Sorata," in *Sara la obrera,* 41–47, whose main character is a blond-haired, blue-eyed "Andean" girl.

79   See, for example, Roqué, "¿Deberá ser limitada . . . ? (II)."

80   "Por los fueros de la verdad," *La Mujer,* May 25, 1894, p. 2. See also "Pongámonos en lo cierto."

81   Middle-class Indian women reformers also intervened in the nationalist discourse to position themselves as the sole legitimate interpreters of women's experience. See Mrinalini Sinha's articles "Reading *Mother India*" and "Gender in the Critiques of Colonialism and Nationalism: Locating the "Indian Woman," in *Feminists Revision History,* ed. Ann-Louise Shapiro, 246–75.

82   Celia, "La mujer puertorriqueña," *La Mujer,* March 28, 1894, p. 2.

83   Eulate, "Influencia de la mujer," 2.

3   Decent Men and Unruly Women: Prostitution in Ponce, 1890–1900

1   Salvador Brau, "Rafael Cordero," reprinted in *Ensayos: Disquisiciones sociológicas* (Río Piedras: Editorial Edil, 1972), 147–59.

2   "Contra Isabel Salguero por ejercer el tráfico de higiene," Dec. 31, 1896, AMP, Ay., Sec., Ben., Den., Pros.

3   Ponce's prostitution regulations were part of a movement that swept Puerto Rico during the last decade of the nineteenth century. San Juan, Mayagüez, Guayama, Coamo, and Caguas also attempted to institute distinct prostitution zones and medical surveillance during this period. It is not yet clear whether the broader political and social ramifications of these campaigns mirrored those of Ponce. José Flores Ramos, "Virgins, Whores, and Martyrs: Prostitution in the Colony, 1898–1919," in *Puerto Rican Women's History: New Perspectives,* ed.

Felix V. Matos Rodríguez and Linda C. Delgado (Armonk, N.Y.: M. E. Sharpe, 1998), 83–104; Fernando Picó, *1898: La guerra despúes de la guerra* (Río Piedras: Ediciones Huracán, 1987), 178; Luís Figueroa, conversation with the author, April 4, 1990; "Noticias Generales," *La Democracia,* Dec. 5, 1898, p. 3; Margarita Flores, conversation with the author, February 10, 1991.

4 Sonya O. Rose has identified an analogous occurrence in Britain during World War II, when anxieties about working-class women's alleged sexual relationships with non-European men demarcated the national community of "decent" citizens ("Sex, Citizenship, and the Nation," *American Historical Review* 103, no. 4 (October 1998): 1147–76.

5 Judith Walkowitz develops a brilliant analysis of such complex uses and effects of prostitution discourses in urban England in *City of Dreadful Delight: Narratives of Sexual Danger in Late-Victorian London* (Chicago: University of Chicago Press, 1992). Unlike their British counterparts, Puerto Rican feminists did not intervene in the public debates over prostitution until the twentieth century.

6 Mariano Negrón Portillo claims that the progressive national vision advanced in the 1890s in *La Democracia* was quite egalitarian. Negrón asserts that the Liberals became conservative in their positions on workers, race, and women's role in the family only in the twentieth century, when they lost political hegemony under U.S. colonial rule (*El autonomismo puertorriqueño: Su transformación ideológica (1895–1915)* (Río Piedras: Ediciones Huracán, 1981). I agree that most of the nineteenth-century Liberals were quite enlightened for their day. But I locate the roots of Liberal twentieth-century conservatism in the hierarchical paternalism that permeated the nineteenth-century views of even the party's most progressive members. Consequently, I do not see such a radical break between pre- and post-U.S. occupation male elite Liberal politics. Nineteenth-century prostitution policy in Ponce is a good example of the repression against "undesirables" employed by Liberals before their turn toward overtly conservative traditionalism. Yet Liberal positions were not unchanging; the racialized gender boundaries of who they considered worthy of inclusion or exclusion in their imagined communities did shift over time.

7 Astrid Cubano Iguina, *El hilo en el laberinto: Claves de la lucha política en Puerto Rico (Siglo XIX)* (Río Piedras: Ediciones Huracán, 1990), 88–103; Francisco A. Scarano, *Puerto Rico: Cinco siglos de historia* (San Juan: McGraw-Hill, 1993), 460–70; Ileana María Rodríguez-Silva, "Freedmen and Freedwomen: Processes of Social Reconfiguration in Post-Emancipation Puerto Rico (1873–1876)" (Master's thesis, University of Wisconsin, Madison, 1997), 89–93. See also Andrés Ramos Mattei, *La sociedad del azúcar en Puerto Rico: 1870–1910* (Río Piedras: Universidad de Puerto Rico, 1988), for a discussion of Ponce's changing social and economic relations during the late nineteenth century.

8   "Villa de Ponce, Año 1871, Censo general de habitantes," AMP, Ay., Sec., Ar.,
     Cen., Hab.; Eduardo Neumann, *Verdadera y auténtica historia de la ciudad de
     Ponce, desde sus primitivos tiempos hasta la época contemporanea* (1911; San Juan:
     Instituto de Cultura Puertorriqueña, 1987); Rodríguez-Silva, *Freedmen*, 103–12,
     161–62; "Ciudad de Ponce. Año 1897, Censo general de habitantes," AMP, Ay.,
     Sec., Ar., Cen., Hab.

9   "Ponce y su término municipal: Observaciones generales," March 20, 1887,
     folios 2–4, AGPR, FGE, box 535, entry 290. The "Noticias" section of *La Demo-
     cracia* had notices of this sort almost daily throughout the 1890s. An example of
     the frequent antibeggar diatribes is Luis Muñoz Rivera, "El país de los pro-
     yectos," *La Democracia*, May 12, 1893. For plebeians' confrontations with the
     Spanish Guardia Civil, see "Por disparo de arma de fuego y lesiones, contra
     Ramón Rey Jusino," Sent. 191, Causa 113, rollo 173, AGPR, Ponce, Crim., box 48,
     and "Por lesiones contra Venancio Medina y Morán," Sent. 161, Causa 568,
     Tomo de Sentencias del 1892, abril–mayo, AGPR, Ponce, Crim., box 35; "La estafeta
     de Ponce," *La Democracia*, Mar. 22, 1895; Mariano Abril, "La bruja," *La Demo-
     cracia*, June 7, 1893, p. 2. For illuminating elite journalistic descriptions of Afro-
     Puerto Ricans, see "Asesinato de Cotorruelo," *La Democracia*, May 1, 1893, p. 2;
     "Parricidio," *La Democracia*, May 18, 1893; and "La mujer hermosa," *La Demo-
     cracia*, Apr. 30, 1892, p. 2.

10 Actas del Ayuntamiento, Feb. 16, 1894; "Asilo para pobres," *La Democracia*,
     June 14, 1893, p. 2; "Noticias," *La Democracia*, May 22, 1894, p. 3; Actas del
     Ayuntamiento, Oct. 4, 1897, entry 8. Indeed, the latter half of the nineteenth
     century was the age of "curing and isolation" in Puerto Rico. A veritable explo-
     sion of such institutions followed the 1846 construction of the Casa de Bene-
     ficencia in San Juan. Teresita Martínez-Vergne argues that the initial push
     to build these institutions was a Liberal-inspired political project ("The Lib-
     eral Concept of Charity: *Beneficencia* Applied to Puerto Rico, 1821–1868," in
     *The Middle Period in Latin America: Values and Attitudes in the Seventeenth–
     Nineteenth Centuries*, ed. Mark D. Szuchman [Boulder: Lynne Rienner, 1989],
     167–84). Félix V. Matos Rodríguez explores the role of elite women in the
     founding of such charitable institutions. See *Women and Urban Change in San
     Juan, Puerto Rico, 1820–1868* (Gainesville: University of Florida Press, 1999),
     101–24. See also Fernando Picó, *El día menos pensado: Historia de los presidarios
     en Puerto Rico (1793–1993)* (Río Piedras: Ediciones Huracán, 1994).

11 Rodríguez argues that libertas in particular moved to the city of Ponce from the
     countryside, where they sought an alternative to plantation life in urban domes-
     tic service (*Freedmen*, 103–12, 161–62; see also "Ciudad de Ponce. Año 1897,
     Censo General de Habitantes," AMP, Ay., Sec., Ar., Hab., Cen.; and José de

Olivares, *Our Islands and Their People as Seen with Camera and Pencil* [St. Louis: N. D. Thompson, 1899], 303–4).

12   See, for example, "Por lesiones contra Carlos Martínez (a) Chulín, Juana Rosaly y Robles, y Eustaquia Navarro y Velásquez (a) Guachinanga," Sent. 190, "*Audiencia de lo Criminal de Ponce. Sentencias dictadas el Segundo Trimestre, 1891*," AGPR, Ponce, Crim., box 66. See also the "Noticias" section in *La Democracia* during the 1890s. "Sobre lesiones a Justina González," July 24, 1895, AGPR, Ponce, Crim., box 33; "Sobre hurto de seis pesos a Lorenza Moró," 1892, AGPR, Ponce, Crim., box 90. For rich testimony about poor urban women's social lives and nocturnal physical mobility, see "Por rapto de Ercilia Reyes," 1896, AGPR, Ponce, Crim., box 19; "Sobre rapto de Ramona Caraballo," 1902, AGPR, Ponce, Crim., box 100; and "Ciudad de Ponce. Año 1897. Censo de habitantes," AMP, Ay., Sec., Ar., Hab., Cen. Today, elderly residents of Ponce's black, working-class neighborhood of San Antón tell stories passed on to them by their parents of how young Afro-Puerto Ricans would walk for miles to attend one of these dances: "It was one of the only times they felt free, those bombas. They'd dance until the rising sun sent them home!" Interviews with Doña Librada Roque and Doña Josefina Cabrera, Ponce, April 14, 1992.

13   See, for example, "Oficial. Al pueblo," *La Democracia,* Oct. 31, 1891; "Carta al Sr. Alcalde de Ponce," *La Democracia,* June 5, 1893, p. 3.

14   "Sección local," *El obrero,* Nov. 19, 1889, p. 3.

15   See, for example, "Estafeta de Ponce," *La Democracia,* Jan. 16, 1895, p. 3; "Por los fueros de la verdad," *La Mujer,* May 25, 1894, p. 2; "Pongámonos en lo cierto," *La Mujer,* June 10, 1894.

16   See "La mujer y la guerra," *La Democracia,* Mar. 8, 1898, p. 2; "Sólo por mujeres," *La Democracia,* Mar. 10, 1898, p. 2; "Noticias Generales," *La Democracia,* Nov. 24, 1898, p. 3.

17   See, for example, "Marimachos," *La Democracia,* Feb. 19, 1898; "Curiosa costumbre," *La Democracia,* Mar. 10, 1898, p. 2; and "El feminismo triunfa," *La Democracia,* May 27, 1898.

18   Luís Muñoz Rivera, "El dedo en la llaga," *La Democracia,* June 5, 1893.

19   Unfortunately, the 1897 Ponce census omitted all reference to racial identities— a telling indication of the general political move toward silencing public discussion of race. Therefore, I could not definitively ascertain whether the percentage of artisans of African descent in the city increased between the abolition of slavery in 1873 and the 1890s. In 1875, however, 65 percent of Ponce's urban artisans who appeared in the surviving census records were categorized as mulatto or black, even though the two barrios whose records are available were known for having a relatively large number of white residents. By the mid-

1890s, a generation later, it is quite conceivable that an even larger percentage were of African ancestry.

20   "El obrero puertorriqueño: Sus antecedentes," *El obrero,* Nov. 19, 1880. See also Ramón Romero Rosa, *Musarañas: Opúsculo sobre ciertas preocupaciones y costumbres que son un estorbo a los trabajadores puertorriqueños para le compenetración de los revindicadores ideales del obrerismo universal* (San Juan: Tipografía de El Carnaval, 1904), 12–16. Artisans' newspapers published in Ponce included *El Artesano* (1874), *Heraldo del Trabajo* (1878–80), *El Obrero* (1889–90), and *Revista Obrera* (1893). The Círculo Ponceño de Artesanos and the Sociedad Protectora de la Inteligencia del Obrero nourished worker culture and education in Ponce during the late nineteenth century. Mutual societies, such as the Taller Benéfico de Artesanos, and cooperatives were founded by Ponce tobacco workers, shoemakers, and masons in the 1890s. Angel G. Quintero Rivera, *Patricios y plebeyos: Burgueses, hacendados, artesanos y obreros: Las relaciones de clase en el Puerto Rico de cambio de siglo* (Río Piedras: Ediciones Huracán, 1988), 71; Gervasio L. García and Angel G. Quintero Rivera, *Desafío y solidaridad: Breve historia del movimiento obrero puertorriqueño* (Río Piedras: Ediciones Huracán, 1982), 18–23; Angel G. Quintero Rivera, "The Somatology of Manners: Class, Race, and Gender in the History of Dance Etiquette in the Hispanic Caribbean," in *Ethnicity in the Caribbean,* ed. Gert Oostindie (London: Macmillan, 1996), 152–81.

21   Luis Muñoz Rivera, "El uno de mayo," *La Democracia,* May 1, 1893; "Augurios tristes," *La Democracia,* Jan. 26, 1895. See also "A la revista," *La Democracia,* Apr. 10, 1894, p. 2; "Crónica," *La Democracia,* Apr. 11, 1894, p. 2; "Cuestión social," *La Democracia,* May 14, 1894, p. 2; "Angelitos!" *La Democracia,* Apr. 10, 1894, p. 2; "Filosofía anarquista," *La Democracia,* Apr. 11, 1894, p. 2; and "Zona neutral," *La Bomba,* Mar. 24, 1895.

22   Brau, "Rafael Cordero"; Luis Muñoz Rivera, "Las clases obreras," *La Democracia,* Apr. 6, 1894, p. 2. Brau reassured his readers that Rafael Cordero never openly challenged racial hierarchies, instead encouraging his students to cross racial barriers solely through individual relationships. Thus, Cordero had helped maintain social rankings even as he fostered cross-class, interracial intimacy ("Rafael Cordero," 156–59). See Quintero Rivera, *Patricios y plebeyos,* 54–80, for an insightful analysis of the "stratified integration" of Afro-Puerto Rican workingmen into Ponce's proto-national culture.

23   Luis Muñoz Rivera, "¿Escalón? ¿Para qué?" *La Democracia,* May 5, 1894. See also Muñoz Rivera, "Obreros en el ayuntamiento," *La Democracia,* Dec. 3, 1898, p. 2; J. N. Bouilly, "El obrador filial," *La Mujer,* Feb. 2, 1894, p. 3; "Pongámonos en lo cierto," 2. Ada Ferrer analyzes a similar process of deracialized political alliance building between Cuban men of differing racial backgrounds during the struggles for independence from Spain, particularly during times of height-

ened black political activism, in "To Make a Free Nation: Race and the Struggle for Independence in Cuba, 1868–1898" (Ph.D. diss., University of Michigan, Ann Arbor, 1995).

24 For examples of artisan support of Liberal candidates and agendas, see "Los obreros hablan," *La Democracia*, May 18, 1894, p. 2, and "Villa de Vega," *La Democracia*, June 5, 1894, p. 3.

25 These discursive strategies during the 1890s in Ponce provided a historical precedent to those noted by Arcadio Díaz Quiñones for prominent Puerto Rican elite intellectuals and by Lillian Guerra for working people during the 1930s and 1940s. Both twentieth-century groups attempted to downplay racial differences among members of their own community and simultaneously confirmed the ideal of whiteness more generally. Those outside the circle of membership were the "real" blacks, both threatening and inferior. Thus, racial hierarchies were legitimated, even while being "discursively collapsed" or "homogenized" within the community in question. The Ponce campaign to regulate prostitution vividly illuminates how powerful a role gender and sexuality can play in determining who is designated as racially undesirable and "other" (Díaz Quiñones, "Tomás Blanco: Racismo, historia, esclavitud," introduction to *El prejuicio racial en Puerto Rico*, by Tomás Blanco, 3d ed. [Río Piedras: Ediciones Huracán, 1985], 13–91; Guerra, *Popular Expression and National Identity in Puerto Rico: The Struggle for Self, Community, and Nation* [Gainesville: University of Florida Press, 1998], 212–42).

26 Lynn Hunt, *The Family Romance of the French Revolution* (Berkeley: University of California Press, 1992), 11; Ann Laura Stoler, *Race and the Education of Desire: Foucault's "History of Sexuality" and the Colonial Order of Things* (Durham: Duke University Press, 1995), 7. Gail Hershatter demonstrates how anxieties about political crises, nationalism, and growing female autonomy were expressed in Shanghai debates about prostitution, in *Dangerous Pleasures: Prostitution and Modernity in Twentieth-Century Shanghai* (Berkeley: University of California Press, 1997), 139–69.

27 See Francisco del Valle Atiles, *El campesino puertorriqueño: Sus condiciones físicas, intelectuales, y morales, causas que las determinan y medios para mejorarlas* (San Juan: Tipografía de J. González Font, 1887), 12–13, 20–25, 59–61, 72–75; del Valle Atiles, "Eugenesis: La base más firme de nuestro progreso," in *Conferencias dominicales dadas en la Biblioteca Insular de Puerto Rico* (San Juan: Bureau of Supplies, Printing, and Transportation, 1913), 9–22; and del Valle Atiles, *Un estudio de 168 casos de prostitución: Contribución al examen del problema del comercio carnal en Puerto Rico* (San Juan: Tipografía "El Compás," 1919). Ann Stoler notes that eugenics discourses lent legitimacy to colonial officials' anxieties about European "degeneracy" in colonized Southeast Asia ("Making Em-

pire Respectable: The Politics of Race and Sexual Morality in Twentieth-Century Colonial Cultures," *American Ethnologist* 16 (November 1989): 644.

28 Interview with José Ramón Rivera, an Arecibo "druggist and property owner," in Henry K. Carroll, *Report on the Island of Porto Rico* (Washington, D.C.: Government Printing Office, 1899), 733. See also Francisco del Valle Atiles, *El campesino,* 132–39; *La Salud,* no. 2, Sept. 23, 1883, p. 21; "Lavaderos de la Capital," *La Salud,* no. 3, Sept. 30, 1883, p. 42; Ramón Gandía Córdova, *Estado Actual de Ponce: Sus necesidades y medios para satisfacerlas* (Ponce: Tipografía "La Democracia," 1899). See also AMP, Ay., Sec., Ben., Inf., J. de S., Mar. 3 and Mar. 18, 1899. Socialist physicians in Argentina argued that capitalism created the oppressive conditions that ruined workers' health. See Hector Recalde, "Prostitutas reglamentadas: Buenos Aires, 1875–1934," *Todo Es Historia* 24, no. 285 (March 1991): 72–94, and Donna J. Guy, *Sex and Danger in Buenos Aires: Prostitution, Family, and Nation in Argentina* (Lincoln: University of Nebraska Press, 1991).

29 Stoler, *Race and the Education of Desire,* 34–35. For discussions of hygiene movements in other parts of the Americas, see Sueann Caulfield, "The Birth of Mangue: Race, Nation, and the Politics of Prostitution in Rio de Janeiro, 1850–1942," in *Sex and Sexuality in Latin America,* ed. Donna J. Guy and Daniel Balderston (New York: New York University Press, 1997), 85–100; Guy, *Sex and Danger;* Donna J. Guy, " 'White Slavery,' Citizenship, and Nationality in Argentina," in *Nationalisms and Sexualities,* ed. Andrew Parker et al. (New York: Routledge, 1992), 201–17; Recalde, "Prostitutas reglamentadas"; Mary Nash, ed., *Mujer, familia y trabajo en España, 1875–1936* (Barcelona: Anthropos, Editorial del hombre, 1983), 37–40; Nancy Leys Stepan, *"The Hour of Eugenics": Race, Gender, and Nation in Latin America* (Ithaca: Cornell University Press, 1991); Allan M. Brandt, *No Magic Bullet: A Social History of Venereal Disease in the United States since 1880,* 2d ed. (New York: Oxford University Press, 1987).

30 A syphilis clinic on the Calle Comercio in Ponce was also advertised during 1898 in *La Democracia.*

31 *Reglamento de higiene de la prostitución de Ponce. Aprobado por el Excmo. Sr. Gobernador General de la Provincia en 19 de junio de 1894* (Ponce: Imprenta de M. López, 1895), articles 1, 31, and 36 (hereinafter *Reglamento,* 1894). Eight speculums were purchased by the city of Ponce to equip doctors making the hygiene rounds. "Expediente apuntando las cuentas trimestrales rendidas por la Junta Auxiliar de Higiene Pública de Ponce," Oct. 6, 1894, AGPR, FGE, box 536.

32 *Ciudad de Ponce: Reglamento de higiene de la prostitución,* August 12, 1898, article 24, held in CPR (hereinafter *Reglamento,* 1898).

33 "Capítulo Último," in *Reglamento,* 1894, articles 8–9, 14–18, 22–25, 34, 37; "Relación de las Guardias Municipales y donde prestan servicios," AMP, Ay., Sec., S.P., List., Pol.

34 "Por hurto contra Anabel Meléndez," 1890, AGPR, Ponce, Crim., box 24.

35 "Relación de las mujeres de vida licenciosa que existen en la actualidad en esta Ciudad," July 7, 1893, AMP, Ay., Sec., Ben., Tr.

36 The only exceptions were two pairs of sisters, one from Guayama and the other from Cayey. "Relación de las mugeres de vida hairada [*sic*] que viven en las calles de la Salud y Aurora lugar denominada Vista Alegre," Apr. 9, 1892, AMP, Ay., Sec., Ben., Rel.; "Relación de las mujeres de vida licenciosa que existen en la actualidad en esta Ciudad," July 7, 1893, AMP, Ay., Sec., Ben., Tr.

37 This small-scale and relatively informal structure seems to have survived the regulation campaign of the 1890s, despite municipal officials' hopes to the contrary. "El Pueblo de Puerto Rico contra José Cabrera por infracción del artículo 288 del Código Penal," July 21, 1904, AGPR, Ponce, Jud., Crim., box 54; "El Pueblo de Puerto Rico contra Vicenta Fernández y Lorenzo Moreno por infracción del artículo 288 del Código Penal," July 21, 1904, AGPR, Ponce, Jud., Crim., box 54; "El Pueblo de Puerto Rico contra Angel Gautier (a) Angelita por infracción del artículo 288 del Código Penal," July 21, 1904, AGPR, Ponce, Jud., Crim., box 54; "Quejas de vecinos sobre mujeres escandalosas," 1916, AGPR, Ponce, Crim., box 91.

   Jill Harsin describes the regulated brothels established in Paris during the nineteenth century in *Policing Prostitution in Nineteenth-Century Paris* (Princeton: Princeton University Press, 1985), 280–321. For Buenos Aires, see Donna J. Guy, *Sex and Danger,* 22, 47, and Recalde, "Prostitutas Reglamentadas," 77; for Guatemala City, see David McCreery " 'This Life of Misery and Shame': Female Prostitution in Guatemala City, 1880–1920," *Journal of Latin American Studies* 18, no. 2: 333–53, 337–38. Beth Bailey and David Farber describe prostitution at an industrial level of intensity in Honolulu, Hawaii, during World War II in "Hotel Street: Prostitution and the Politics of War," *Radical History Review* 52 (winter 1992): 54–78.

38 "Relación de las casas de pupilas, citas, y meretrices que deben abonar sus cuotas del mes de octubre 1894," AMP, Ay., Sec., Ben., Tr.; "Relación de las mugeres," April 9, 1892; "Relación de las mujeres de vida licenciosa que existen en la actualidad en esta Ciudad," July 7, 1893, AMP, Ay., Sec., Ben., Tr.

39 "Legajo que comprende los partes diarios del puesto de orden público y demás comprobantes que con aquellos se relacionan," Jan. 1884, AMP, Ay., Sec., Jud., Den.; "Libro Diario, 1896. Anotaciones de hechos acontecidos diariamente," AMP, Ay., Sec., Jud., Den. (hereinafter "Libro Diario"); and "Relaciones de las denuncias dadas por la Policía Municipal desde el día 13 de enero hasta el 30 de abril de 1895," AMP, Ay., Sec., Jud., Den.

40 "Proyecto de Cárcel del partido judicial de Ponce: Modificaciones, 1898," p. 2, AMP, Ay., Sec., O.P., Pro., Cár.; "Incoado por orden del último Sr. Alcalde Vice

Presidente de la Junta Auxiliar de Cárceles en averiguación de ciertos hechos ocurridos en el Departamento de las Mujeres," 1888, AMP, Ay., Sec., Jud., Inv.; and Manuel N. Domenech, Arquitecto Municipal, "Memoria," Feb. 1, 1898, AMP, Ay., Sec., Jud., Inf.

41   Historians of prostitution have noted similar trends elsewhere in Europe and the Americas. The stigmatization and repression of regulatory campaigns seems to have consistently created an identity and full-time occupation of "prostitute" for many women who previously exchanged sex for cash as only one of a variety of income-generating strategies. For examples, see Guy, *Sex and Danger;* McCreery, " 'This Life of Misery and Shame,' " 333–53; Judith Walkowitz, *Prostitution and Victorian Society: Women, Class, and the State* (Cambridge: Cambridge University Press, 1980); Harsin, *Policing Prostitution;* and Laurie Bernstein, *Sonia's Daughters: Prostitutes and their Regulation in Imperial Russia* (Berkeley: University of California Press, 1995).

42   Cases of refusal to register can be found in the Archivo Municipal de Ponce, in the Beneficencia, Judicial, or Seguridad Pública sections of the Ayuntamiento, Secretaría division. Some examples of fine nonpayment are "Relación de las casas de pupilas, citas, y meretrices," and "Cuerpo de Policía Municipal de la Ciudad de Ponce, Relación que se cita," Oct. 17, 1894, AMP, Ay., Sec., S.P., Rel., List. Counterfeit passbooks are denounced in *Reglamento,* 1894, article 6. For denunciations against registered women, see "Relaciones de las denuncias dadas por la Policía Municipal desde el día 13 de enero hasta el 30 del abril de 1895," AMP, Ay., Sec., Jud., List., Den. (hereinafter "Relaciones de las denuncias"), Jan. 28, 1895, Carmen Mayoral; Ibid., Mar. 23, 1895, Eugenia Fornier; "Contra Dominga Velásquez," June 1896, AMP, Ay., Sec., Ben., Den., Pros., box 1894–1897. Doctors' complaints are in *Reglamento,* 1898, article 31.

43   "Libro Diario," July 14, 1896; "Sobre oficio del Doctor Rendón interesando se disponga la completa incomunicación del Asilo de Higiene," Nov. 21, 1899, AMP, Ay., Sec., Ben., Tr., box 1893–1917. For the widespread reliance on isolation rather than effective therapeutic treatment of infectious diseases, see Actas de la Junta local de Sanidad, Nov. 20, 1887, and Nov. 21, 1890, AMP, Ay., Sec., Ben., J. de S.

44   "Libro Diario," July 14, 1896. See also *Reglamento,* 1898, article 31; "Relaciones de las denuncias," Feb. 1895, Felipa Rodríguez and María Torni; "Libro Diario," Aug. 20, 1895; "Estafeta de Ponce," *La Democracia,* Feb. 1, 1895, p. 3; and "Noticias Generales," *La Democracia,* Dec. 10, 1898, p. 3.

45   For some examples of such unruly-prostitute equations, see "Estafeta de Ponce," *La Democracia,* Apr. 2, 1895, p. 3, Apr. 15, 1895, p. 3, Apr. 16, 1895, p. 3, and Apr. 17, 1895, p. 3. Only 29.4 percent of the total population of Ponce was literate in 1897; the illiteracy rates of the popular classes must have been even

higher (Neumann, *Verdadera y auténtica historia,* 86). Walkowitz extensively analyzes the media's role in the creation of moral panics in *City of Dreadful Delight,* 84–134.

46 See, for example, the denunciation of "Magdalena" to the police by "respectable families" living on the poverty-stricken Aurora Street, the center of one of the new prostitution zones. Magdalena allowed different men into her house at various times. No such complaint ever arose from poor families before 1894. "Contra Magdalena Usera por Egercer el tráfico de higiene," July 1897, AMP, Ay., Sec., Ben., Den., Pros., box 1897–1899. See also "Metralla," *La Bomba,* Feb. 23, 1895, p. 3; "Bombas y Bombos," *La Bomba,* Mar. 13, 1895, p. 3; "Metralla," *La Bomba,* Mar. 16, 1895, p. 3; *La Bomba,* Apr. 7, 1895, p. 3; "La estafeta de Ponce," *La Democracia,* Jan. 8, 1895, p. 3, Jan. 16, 1895, p. 3, and Feb. 23, 1895, p. 3.

47 "Cartera de Ponce," *La Democracia,* June 19, 1895, p. 3. For additional examples, see *La Democracia,* Mar. 26, 1894, p. 3; "Noticias," *La Democracia,* Apr. 11, 1894, p. 3; and "Cartera de Ponce," *La Democracia,* June 14, 1895, p. 3.

48 See, for example, *La Democracia,* June 5, 1895, p. 3, June 18, 1895, p. 3, June 2, 1895, p. 3, Apr. 29, 1895, p. 3, and June 19, 1895, p. 3; "Libro Diario," Sept. 21, 1896; and "Contra Adelina Cueva por dedicarse al tráfico de higiene sin estar inscrita," Oct. 1896, AMP, Ay., Sec., Ben., Den., Pros., box 1894–1897. For some examples of bomba dancers' harassment by police, see "Estafeta de Ponce," *La Democracia,* Apr. 29, 1895, and June 2, 1895.

49 "Estafeta de Ponce," *La Democracia,* Apr. 29, 1895, p. 3; "Libro Diario," Feb. 7, 1895, AMP, Ay., Sec., Jud., List., Den.

50 "La estafeta de Ponce," *La Democracia,* June 28, 1898, p. 3.

51 "Relaciones de las denuncias," Feb. 12, 1895; "Contra Gervasia Rodríguez y Monserrate Nazario por ejercer el tráfico de higiene sin autorización," Dec. 1896, AMP, Ay., Sec., Ben., Den., Pros., box 1894–1897; "Contra Isabel Salguero por ejercer el tráfico de higiene," ibid., Dec. 30, 1896.

52 *Reglamento,* 1898; "Relación de las meretrices que han sido dadas de baja por órden del Senor Alcalde. . . ," July 31, 1899, AMP, Ay., Sec., Ben.; "Dando de baja á la meretriz Ezequiela Saldaño," Jan. 10, 1899, AMP, Ay., Sec., Ben., Tr., box 1893–1917.

53 "Contra las individuas Eugenia Bautista y Josefa Torres, por ejercer el tráfico de higiene sin estar inscrita para ello," Dec. 1898, AMP, Ay., Sec., Ben., Den., Pros., box 1897–1899; "Contra María Vega por Infracción Regl. Higiene," Dec. 7, 1898, AMP, Ay., Sec., Ben., Den., Pros., box 1897–1899.

54 "Sobre amenazas y hurto contra no hay procesado," 1899, AGPR, Ponce, Crim., box 14; "Por lesiones a Clemencia Colón contra Jesús Pérez Martín y Juan de la Cruz Santiago, causa 770, Dec. 14, 1897, AGPR, Ponce, Crim., box 46, folio 25; Juan José Baldrich, conversation with author, May 16, 1991. The oral accounts

from Cayey of artisans not only accepting prostitutes but actually marrying them may reflect the more radically inclusive sexual politics that developed among anarchist cigar makers there in the early twentieth century. I will explore this movement in subsequent chapters of this book. In England also, Walkowitz notes that some urban laborers were willing to acknowledge their lovers' prostitution history in court (*Prostitution in Victorian Society*, 182–83).

55   "Contra María Vega por Infracción Regl. Higiene," Dec. 7, 1898, AMP, Ay., Sec., Ben., Den., Pros., box 1897–1899; "Astrea," *La Patria*, Apr. 21, 1899, p. 2.

56   See, for example, Aug. 3, 1857, no. 229, "Cuaderno de juicios verbales por el Corregimiento. 1857," AMP, Ay., Sec., Jud., Juic., Ver.; "Cayetano Cambreleng con su hija menor Belén en representación de ella demandando á José Jaime Napoleoni," Aug. 22, 1857, "Cuaderno de juicios verbales por el Corregimiento," AMP, Ay., Sec., Jud., Juic., Ver.

57   "At present," a resident of the section wrote, [Vista Alegre] "has one registered live-in brothel, one house for sexual trysts, six houses owned by a wealthy man who fixes them up to rent them to prostitutes, and seven houses rented by prostitutes and owned by different people." See "Victoria de las mesalinas," *La Democracia*, Dec. 2, 1898, p. 3. See also "Libro Diario," Sept. 1896, Dominga Velásquez; "Olvidada diez y nueve años," *La Democracia*, Nov. 28, 1898, p. 3; and *La Bomba*, Feb. 7, 1895, pp. 2–3.

58   Stuart Hall points out that the creation of identities and meanings is always a two-sided process. To be successful, they must provoke or spring from popular choice and agency, not simply be "summoned" or imposed from without. See his "Introduction: Who Needs Identity?" in *Questions of Cultural Identity*, ed. Stuart Hall and Paul de Gay (London: Sage, 1996), 12.

59   "Contra Ramón Torres por proteger la prostitución," Nov. 1896, AMP, Ay., Sec., Ben., Den., Pros., box 1894–1897; "Contra María Vega por Infracción Regl. Higiene."

60   García and Quintero Rivera, *Desafío y solidaridad*, 30–34. See Picó, *1898*, 81–143, for a detailed description of the actions of the *partidas sediciosas* in the highlands and the sugar fields of Ponce. See Mariano Negrón Portillo, *Las turbas republicanas, 1900–1904* (Río Piedras: Ediciones Huracán, 1990), for a detailed discussion of the violence between plebeian Republican and Liberal sympathizers in the early years of U.S. rule. The conflicts in Ponce are covered on pages 158–66.

61   Unfortunately, *La Nueva Era* and its counterparts in the local press have not been preserved in accessible archives. The exchanges between Mayoral and various local newspapers are traceable only in the Canta Claro column responses. However, the few issues of the Ponce Republican paper *La Patria* that

have survived from this period refer to Canta Claro's campaign as a familiar part of Ponce political culture. See "Astrea," *La Patria*, Apr. 2, 1899, p. 2. See also "Me salió al encuentro," *La Democracia*, Nov. 16, 1898, p. 3; "Justicia para el pobre, hermano," *La Democracia*, Dec. 27, 1898, p. 3; "Remitido: Primer apuro de Canta Claro," *La Democracia*, Nov. 18, 1898, p. 3; "Segundo Apuro de Canta Claro," *La Democracia*, Nov. 21, 1898, p. 3; "Sobre instancia de Don Ramón Mayoral para que se destinen á otro sitio las meretrices que viven en 'Vista Alegre' por no poderse sufrir los escándalos que proporcionan al vecindario," Sept. 4, 1898, AMP, Ay., Sec., Ben., Tr., box 1893–1918; "Por virtud de escrito del vecino D. Ramón Mayoral Barnés al Señor Presidente del concejo de Secretarios de esta Isla, quejándose del Reglamento de Higiene de la prostitución de la misma," Jan. 21, 1899–Mar. 17, 1899, ibid.; "Sobre escrito de D. Ramón Mayoral pidiendo la traslación á otro sitio de las prostitutas de Vista Alegre," Jan. 30, 1899, ibid.

62 "Actuales Gestiones de la Alcaldía de Ponce," *La Democracia*, Dec. 6, 1898, p. 2; "Citaciones," Nov. 1898, AMP, uncatalogued at the time of my research; Alcalde de Ponce to Hon. Sr. Presidente, in "Por virtud de escrito del vecino D. Ramón Mayoral Barnés al Señor Presidente del concejo de Secretarios de esta Isla."

63 Other indications of the growing popular independence from Liberal political positions surfaced in *La Democracia* during the same months. In early November, artisans held a public meeting in Ponce to elect their own representative to Washington, D.C. A week later, several workers expressed anger at the paper for its antiworker attitudes since winning control of the municipal government some months before. See *La Democracia*, Nov. 2, 1898, p. 3, and "Una hoja," *La Democracia*, Nov. 9, 1898, p. 2.

64 Gervasio García and Angel G. Quintero Rivera trace the development of artisanal culture in Ponce and San Juan. They acknowledge that nineteenth-century Puerto Rican urban artisans carefully distinguished between themselves and unskilled (male) workers, fearing competition from cheap labor and production of low-quality products. Proletarianization, especially in the tobacco sector, they argue, erased these distinctions and laid the material basis for a radically inclusive working-class culture. As Marcia Rivera pointed out in "El feminismo obrero en la lucha de clases (1900–1920)," *Claridad-En Rojo*, Mar. 1981, pp. 13–19, García and Quintero Rivera are silent on the gendered nature of nineteenth-century male artisans' self-definition, although they briefly discuss the feminism of twentieth-century male socialists and anarchists. García and Quintero Rivera, *Desafío y solidaridad*, 67–86; Quintero Rivera, *Patricios y plebeyos*, 82–98, 106–25, 252–74; Quintero Rivera, "Socialista y tabaquero; La proletarización de los artesanos," *Sin Nombre* 8, no. 4 (March 1978): 100–137.

65   "Por virtud de escrito del vecino D. Ramón Mayoral Barnés al Señor Presidente del concejo de Secretarios de esta Isla." "Estalló la bomba," *La Democracia,* Nov. 10, 1898, p. 3; "Castigada por un error," *La Democracia,* Nov. 8, 1898, p. 3.

66   "Un alcalde satisfecho," *La Democracia,* Nov. 30, 1898, p. 3. See also "A los que no les va, ni les viene," *La Democracia,* Dec. 7, 1898, p. 3.

67   Appeals for justice to the U.S. high command in Puerto Rico and the U.S. president in Washington, D.C., by working people were common in the first years following the 1898 invasion, even in the face of sometimes quite brutal abuses of Puerto Ricans by U.S. troops. See, for example, "El fuego lento," *El Cañón,* Dec. 2, 1898, p. 2.

68   "Por virtud de escrito del vecino D. Ramón Mayoral Barnés al Señor Presidente del concejo de Secretarios de esta Isla." See also "Sobre instancia de Don Ramón Mayoral para que se destinen á otro sitio las meretrices que viven en 'Vista Alegre,' " and Canta Claro, "Estalló la bomba," *La Democracia,* Nov. 10, 1898, p. 3.

69   "Confirmación de la arbitrariedad," *La Democracia,* Dec. 14, 1898, p. 3. Mayoral's phrase "zone of stone" refers to the wealthy center of the city, where residents could afford large homes built of stone ("La honradez vencida por la prostitución," *La Democracia,* Dec. 29, 1898, p. 3).

70   "Por virtud de escrito del vecino D. Ramón Mayoral Barnés al Señor Presidente del concejo de Secretarios de esta Isla." See also his columns in *La Democracia.*

71   Note that to Mayoral, an urban worker, rural areas were empty of decency, just as his community had been for the urban elites. "Tercer apuro de Canta Claro," *La Democracia,* Nov. 22, 1898, p. 3. See also, "La residencia de las hetairas," *La Democracia,* Nov. 25, 1898, p. 3; "Me salió al encuentro," *La Democracia,* Nov. 16, 1898, p. 3; and "Levantó ampolla el cáustico," *La Democracia,* Dec. 24, 1898, p. 3.

72   "Sección local," *El Obrero,* Nov. 19, 1889, p. 3. See also *La Bomba,* Feb. 7, 1895, 2–3; "Metralla," *La Bomba,* Feb. 23, 1895, p. 3; "Bombas y bombos," *La Bomba,* Mar. 13, 1895; "Metralla," *La Bomba,* Mar. 16, 1895; "Bombas y bombos," *La Bomba,* Mar. 28, 1895, p. 3; *La Bomba,* Apr. 7, 1895, p. 3; "Sobre escrito de D. Ramón Mayoral pidiendo la traslación á otro sitio de las prostitutas de Vista Alegre," Jan. 30, 1899; "Remitido: Primer apuro de Canta Claro," *La Democracia,* Nov. 18, 1898, p. 3.

73   See chapter 9 of Florencia Mallon, *Peasant and Nation: The Making of Postcolonial Mexico and Peru* (Berkeley: University of California Press, 1994), for an extended discussion of local intellectuals' role in surveillance and control of popular discourses. See also Steven Feierman, *Peasant Intellectuals: Anthropology and History in Tanzania* (Madison: University of Wisconsin Press, 1990).

4   Marriage and Divorce in the Formation of the New Colonial Order, 1898–1910

1   The 1910 International Feminist Congress in Buenos Aires made divorce one of its principal demands. At that time, only Uruguay, of all the Latin American nations attending, had legalized divorce for religious marriages. Mexican women were still debating divorce's merits and dangers in 1925. Even Cuban women, whose feminist movement was one of the most effective of the early twentieth century, did not gain the right to divorce until 1917. Several Latin American countries, including Chile, allegedly one of the region's most "modern" nations, have still not fully legalized divorce today. Francesca Miller, *Latin American Women and the Search for Social Justice* (Hanover, N.H.: University Press of New England, 1991), 74–75, 92; K. Lynn Stoner, "On Men Reforming the Rights of Men: The Abrogation of the Cuban Adultery Law, 1930," *Cuban Studies* 21 (1991): 83–99.

2   For extended discussions of the assaults on wealthy landowners and their property that punctuated the months following the U.S. invasion of Puerto Rico, see Fernando Picó, *1898: La guerra despúes de la guerra* (Río Piedras: Ediciones Huracán, 1987); Kelvin A. Santiago-Valles, *"Subject People" and Colonial Discourses: Economic Transformation and Social Disorder in Puerto Rico, 1898–1947* (Albany: State University of New York Press, 1994), 77–99; and Blanca Silvestrini de Pacheco, *Violencia y criminalidad en Puerto Rico, 1898–1973: Apuntes para un estudio de historia social* (Río Piedras: Editorial Universitaria, 1980), 13–51.

3   For the U.S. labor movement's fight for the eight-hour day, see David Roediger, *Our Own Time: A History of American Labor and the Working Day* (London: Verso, 1989). The struggles over divorce in the United States are delineated in Glenda Riley, *Divorce: An American Tradition* (New York: Oxford University Press, 1991), and William L. O'Neill, *Divorce in the Progressive Era* (New Haven: Yale University Press, 1967; reprint, New York: New Viewpoints, 1973). Divorce advocates during the Progressive Era (1890–1920) included social scientists, liberal clergy, and feminists. Nineteenth-century feminists, however, led the drives to legitimize and defend divorce in the United States.

4   Alice L. Conklin, "Colonialism and Human Rights, a Contradiction in Terms? The Case of France and West Africa, 1895–1914," *American Historical Review* 103, no. 2 (April 1998): 422. See also Louis A. Pérez Jr. "Incurring a Debt of Gratitude: 1898 and the Moral Sources of United States Hegemony in Cuba," *American Historical Review* 104, no. 2 (April 1999): 356–99.

5   "Divorcio entre los esposos Don Domingo Dertrés y Doña Emilia Ríos," 1853, AHDSJ, Just., AS, Div., 1819–1886, box J-215; "Sobre divorcio de D. Matías Deya con su legítima esposa Da. Petrona del Toro," 1862, ibid.; Untitled [D. Salvador

Arena versus Da. Pilar Coll], 1849, AHDSJ, AS, Div., 1842–1926, box J-217. Silvia Marina Arrom discusses ecclesiastical divorce in nineteenth-century Mexico in *The Women of Mexico City, 1790–1857* (Stanford: Stanford University Press, 1985), 206–85.

6   "Discernimiento de divorcio," Da. Salustiana Capó de Durucú, 1877, AHDSJ, Just., AS, Div., 1819–1886, box J-215.

7   Ibid.; "Demanda de divorcio por mal trato de obra y de palabra e injurias graves promovida por Da. Julia Romañat de Bozzo contra su esposo D. Luis Bozzo y García," 1898, AHDSJ, Just., AS, Div., 1888–1963, box J-216.

8   Silvia Arrom found a similar distribution of cases in her study of early-nineteenth-century ecclesiastical divorce in Mexico. The vast majority of petitioners were women; 99 percent of them alleged abuse and cruelty, whereas only one-third also charged lack of financial support or adultery (*Women of Mexico City,* 229). In her study of divorce in colonial Brazil, María Beatriz Nizza da Silva also found that women brought the great bulk of divorce suits. She argues, however, that male physical abuse and adultery were deemed unbearable only by women when a husband had completely abandoned his wife and the material and social base of a married woman's livelihood had disappeared ("Divorce in Colonial Brazil: The Case of Sao Paulo," in *Sexuality and Marriage in Colonial Latin America,* ed. Asunción Lavrin [Lincoln: University of Nebraska Press, 1989], 311–40).

9   Untitled [Juana Soler versus Victor Marquez], 1894, AHDSJ, Just., AS, Div., box J-217.

10 See, for example, "Causa de divorcio entre los esposos D. Sebastian Viñas y Da. Santos Lavrieu," 1872, AHDSJ, Just., AS, Div., 1819–1886, box J-215; Untitled [Da. María Eduarda Calderón versus D. Narciso Eduviges Gámbaro], 1897, AHDSJ, Just., AS, Div., 1842–1926, box J-217; No. 389, "Declarativo—Divorcio: Don José de la Rosa y Rodríguez con Da. Teresa Ortiz y Castillo sobre divorcio," 1901, AGPR, Jud., Ponce, Exp. Civ., box 6; and "Doña Natividad Maldonado de Marcano sobre Depósito para establecer divorcio," 1901, AGPR, Jud., Ponce, Civ., box 5. Ponce's civil judicial cases at the Archivo General de Puerto Rico were in uncatalogued boxes. I numbered them as I reviewed them; all box numberings cited are obtained from this informal process.

11 "Incidente—En la causa de divorcio entre Juan Portalín Díaz y Micaela Díaz, sobre el depósito de ésta," 1863, AHDSJ, Just., AS, Div., 1819–1886, Caja J-215.

12 Ibid.

13 Francisco A. Scarano discusses the class composition and early agendas of the two major parties in *Puerto Rico: Cinco siglos de historia* (San Juan: McGraw-Hill, 1993), 556–58, 575–76. Edgardo Meléndez analyzes the early Republican

Party's positions in *Puerto Rico's Statehood Movement* (New York: Greenwood, 1988), 33–55.

14 Historians of this period discuss the high hopes held by Puerto Ricans of almost all classes for U.S. rule. See Mariano Negrón Portillo, *El autonomismo puertorriqueño: Su transformación ideológica (1895–1914)* (Río Piedras: Ediciones Huracán, 1981), 36–51; Negrón Portillo, "Puerto Rico: Surviving Colonialism and Nationalism," in *Puerto Rican Jam: Essays on Culture and Politics,* edited by Frances Negrón-Muntaner and Ramón Grosfoguel (Minneapolis: University of Minnesota Press, 1997), 39–56; Picó, *1898,* 73–79; and Angel G. Quintero Rivera, *Patricios y plebeyos: Burgueses, hacendados, artesanos y obreros. Las relaciones de clase en el Puerto Rico de cambio de siglo* (Río Piedras: Ediciones Huracán, 1988), 99–116. Lillian Guerra points out that great resentment of Spain's regime, particularly memories of slavery and the libreta, formed the basis for much of the U.S. support (*Popular Expression and National Identity in Puerto Rico: The Struggle for Self, Community, and Nation* (Gainesville: University of Florida Press, 1998), 203–9.

For a few examples of Afro-Puerto Rican enthusiasm for U.S. rule, see Negrón-Portillo, "Surviving Colonialism and Nationalism," 41, 43; "La Censura," *La Patria,* Apr. 10, 1899, p. 3; "Al País," *El águila de Puerto Rico,* Jan. 9, 1902, p. 1; "Los esclavos," ibid., Mar. 8, 1902, p. 2; and "Serviles?" ibid., June 19, 1902, p. 2.

The Federales worried about support from Afro-Puerto Ricans for the U.S. presence in Puerto Rico and hostility toward local elite rule. See Mariano Abril, "Crónica," *La Democracia,* June 16, 1898, p. 2.

15 "Sobre estado sanitario de la Ciudad de Ponce," Apr. 1–4, 1899, AMP, Ay., Sec., Ben., Inf., J. de S.

16 Scarano, *Puerto Rico,* 604–10.

17 General Order no. 54, May 2, 1899, Military Department of Puerto Rico, *General Orders and Circulars, October 1898–May 1900,* AGPR. For other "benevolent reforms" by decree, see ibid., nos. 33 and 193. Edward J. Berbusse provides a chronology of the various military governors and their decrees in *The United States in Puerto Rico, 1898–1900* (Chapel Hill: University of North Carolina Press, 1966), 88–106. See also Governor Hunt's speech asserting the "intensely American" "right to organize to secure better wages by peaceable measures." Reprinted in *El águila de Puerto Rico,* Jan. 16, 1902, p. 4.

18 Order no. 145, Sept. 21, 1899, *General Orders and Circulars.*

19 Stuart B. Schwartz, "The Hurricane of San Ciriaco: Disaster, Politics, and Society in Puerto Rico, 1899–1901," *Hispanic American Historical Review* 72, no. 3 (August 1992): 303–34; Trumbull White, *Our New Possessions . . . a Graphic*

Account, Descriptive and Historical, of the Tropic Islands of the Sea Which Have Fallen under Our Sway, Their Cities, People and Commerce, Natural Resources and the Opportunities They Offer to Americans (Book 2—Puerto Rico) (Boston: J. Q. Adams, 1898), 342–46; General George W. Davis to Editor, *El Combate,* June 7, 1899, AGPR, Fortaleza, box 24; Order no. 35, Mar. 20, 1899, and Order no. 193, Nov. 28, 1899, both in *General Orders and Circulars,* Berbusse, *United States,* 88–91.

Gervasio García and Angel Quintero Rivera have pointed out that Puerto Rican workers were not blind to the contradiction between the often repressive colonial policies of the United States and its reputation as the standard bearer of democracy and equality. They frequently tried (unsuccessfully) to resolve this contradiction by appealing directly to the federal government in Washington and demanding that it correct the "mistakes" its agents were committing in Puerto Rico (García and Quintero Rivera, *Desafío y solidaridad,* 88–91; Quintero Rivera, *Patricios y plebeyos,* 106–27).

20 The prohibition of Puerto Rican self-governance codified in the Foraker Act did not garner complete consensus in the U.S. Congress. A number of U.S. legislators vehemently opposed the Foraker Act. Some argued that its denial of direct elected representation made a mockery of U.S. democracy. Others insisted that the United States should not become an imperialist nation, which it would become by holding Puerto Rico as a colony. In the end, however, these more progressive views did not prevail (Berbusse, *United States in Puerto Rico,* 149–65).

For detailed discussions of the Foraker Act and its implications for Puerto Rico, see Lyman J. Gould, *La ley Foraker: Raíces de la política colonial de los Estados Unidos* (Río Piedras: Editorial Universitaria, 1969), and María Dolores Luque de Sánchez, *La ocupación norteamericana y la ley Foraker (la opinión pública puertorriqueña) 1898–1904* (Río Piedras: Editorial de la Universidad de Puerto Rico, 1980). Scarano provides a succinct overview of the Foraker Act in *Puerto Rico,* 572–75.

21 See Eileen J. Findlay, "Love in the Tropics: Marriage, Divorce, and the Construction of Benevolent Colonialism in Puerto Rico, 1898–1910," in *Close Encounters of Empire: Writing the Cultural History of U.S.–Latin American Relations,* ed. Gilbert M. Joseph, Catherine C. LeGrand, and Ricardo D. Salvatore (Durham: Duke University Press, 1998), 139–72, for a detailed analysis of the representational uses of Puerto Rico by U.S. imperialists.

22 See the testimony of various U.S. officials to the Senate in "Industrial and Other Conditions . . . Senate Hearings," pp. 88, 191–92, entry 5, GCF, BIA, RG 350, USNA. See also the speech of Connecticut Representative Ebenezer J. Hill, recorded in the *Appendix to the Congressional Record, April 11, 1900,* 177; comments and questions of various representatives in *Committee Reports, Hearings,*

and Acts of Congress . . . Fifty-Ninth Congress, 144–48; Henry K. Carroll, *Report on the Island of Porto Rico* (Washington, D.C.: Government Printing Office, 1899), 35, 663, 691–712; de Olivares, *Our Islands,* 287; and Rowe, *The United States and Porto Rico,* 110–14.

23 Governor Davis' report, cited in a speech by U.S. Representative Ebenezer J. Hill, from Connecticut, in *Appendix to the Congressional Record,* Apr. 11, 1900, p. 177. See also de Olivares, *Our Islands,* 330–31; and Schwartz, "Hurricane of San Ciriaco," 321–23.

24 The term is Ann Stoler's, although she does not discuss the United States extensively (*Race and the Education of Desire: Foucault's "History of Sexuality" and the Colonial Order of Things* [Durham: Duke University Press, 1995], 15).

25 For overviews of the Progressive Era and its activists, see Arthur S. Link and Richard L. McCormick, *Progressivism* (Arlington Heights, Ill.: Harlan Davidson, 1983), and Daniel T. Rodgers, "In Search of Progressivism," *Reviews in American History* 10, no. 4 (December 1982): 113–32.

26 Order no. 50, Apr. 22, 1899, *General Orders;* emphasis mine.

27 *Report of Brigadier General George W. Davis, U.S.V., on Civil Affairs of Puerto Rico, 1899* (Washington, D.C.: Government Printing Office), app. C, 701. See also Carroll, *Report,* 693–757, 762–63, 795–96; Rowe, *United States and Porto Rico,* 110–14; de Olivares, *Our Islands,* 287; *First Annual Report of Charles H. Allen, Governor of Puerto Rico, Covering the Period from May 1, 1900, to May 1, 1901* (Washington, D.C.: Government Printing Office, 1901), 34–35; U.S. Attorney General to the President, June 23, 1902, "letters sent Feb. 25, 1902–Aug. 31, 1906," 1:456–58, BIA, 1902–1906, GRDJ, RG 60, USNA; *Report of Brigadier-General George W. Davis,* app. C, 686.

28 William H. Hunt, *Third Annual Report of the Governor of Porto Rico, covering the Period from July 1, 1902, to June 30, 1903* (Washington, D.C.: Government Printing Office, 1903), 54.

29 Ibid.; *Fourth Annual Report of the Governor of Porto Rico, covering the Period from July 1, 1903–June 30, 1904* (Washington, D.C.: Government Printing Office, 1904), 30.

30 *Report of Brigadier-General George W. Davis,* app. C, 687; Carroll, *Report,* 35, 663, 691–712; de Olivares, *Our Islands,* 331.

31 Rowe, *United States,* 113, 164–65; Carroll, *Report,* 691–93; *Report of Brigadier-General George W. Davis,* app. C, 687. At the turn of the century, divorce was a contentious issue on the mainland. Despite this lack of political consensus at home, U.S. officials apparently unanimously advocated its usefulness, appropriating the arguments of North American feminists and social scientists. For discussions of the debates that raged in the United States between 1880 and 1920 about the appropriateness of divorce, see Riley, *Divorce,* 11–131, and O'Neill,

Divorce in the Progressive Era. During the 1890s, numerous states placed restrictions on divorce, although none outlawed it altogether.

32   *Report of Brigadier-General George W. Davis,* app. C, p. 686; Perfecta Montalvo to Brigadier General George W. Davis, June 10, 1899, AGPR, Fort., box 24; Expediente 4441, June 30, 1899, AGPR, Fort., box 25; "Civil Marriage, Divorce, Ecclesiastical Laws Governing Same: To War Secretary," Feb. 7, 1900, Expediente 7253, AGPR, Fort., box 37; and Rowe, *United States,* 164.

33   Berbusse provides a brief discussion of anticlericalism among Liberals. Salvador Brau, José de Diego, Mariano Abril, and Luis Muñoz Rivera, some of the "founding fathers" of Puerto Rican Liberal Autonomism, were all Masons and enthusiastic advocates of the separation of church and state (Berbusse, *United States in Puerto Rico,* 72, 198–200).

34   O'Neill demonstrates that this type of reasoning was also common among defenders of divorce in the United States during this period. Ultimately, divorce advocates insisted in the Progressive Era, happiness was a right of married couples; once companionship and love broke down, divorce was a perfectly moral response (*Divorce in the Progressive Era,* 230–66).

35   "Demanda de divorcio—Doña Elisa Giménez y Ramírez contra D. José Colón y Carrasquillo por malos tratamientos de obra," 1901, AGPR, Ponce, Exp. Civ., box 7. See also "Demanda de divorcio, Don Ramón y Vega contra Doña María Medina y Padilla," 1902, AGPR, Ponce, Exp. Civ., box 15. Puerto Rican elites were not alone in their linkage of family reform and the institution of a new political order. Stoner points out that Cuban male politicians associated the criminalization of wife killing with the establishment of a "bourgeois, republican order" ("On Men Reforming the Rights of Men"). See also Susan Besse, "Crimes of Passion: The Campaign against Wife-Killing in Brazil, 1910–1940," *Journal of Social History* 22, no. 4 (summer 1989): 653–66. In the early days of the American Revolution, divorce petitions linked revolutionary republican principles such as "life, liberty, and the pursuit of happiness" and "freedom from tyranny and misrule" to the right to dissolve unworkable marriages (Riley, *Divorce,* 30–33).

36   See, for example, "Report on the Civil and Criminal Laws of Puerto Rico," Apr. 12, 1899, Expediente 8062, AGPR, Fort., box 43; "Report on Marriage and Divorce," June 28, 1899, Expediente 4854, AGPR, Fort., box 25.

37   I found no evidence of protests against legalization of divorce from the Catholic Church during this period. This surprising silence is attributable to a number of factors. First, the U.S. restructuring of church-state relations dealt a devastating blow to the Catholic Church. The Spanish state's direct subsidies had provided the vast bulk of the church's income; these funds evaporated after the U.S. invasion. In addition, U.S. officials and anticlerical Puerto Rican municipal

officers asserted control over church property on the island. The resultant legal battles were not resolved until 1906, when the U.S. Supreme Court found in the church's favor. Until then, however, the simple day-to-day economic survival of parish priests and the physical and juridical integrity of the church seem to have absorbed most of the hierarchy's attention. They were also kept busy defending the right of women's religious orders to staff hospitals; U.S. officials launched a campaign to purge the nuns in 1901. See Berbusse, *United States in Puerto Rico*, 139–41, 191–210; *Committee Reports, Hearings, and Acts of Congress Corresponding Thereto: Sixtieth Congress, 1907–1909*, 347–51, Legislative Division, Y.4, In7 6, C73, USNA.

The Catholic hierarchy did not, however, completely ignore questions of marriage and divorce. They protested moves to legalize civil marriage and to allow ministers of other faiths to celebrate weddings. Marriage, ultimately, seems to have been more important than divorce in the hierarchy's political strategies: if the Catholic Church could maintain control over the terms of marriage, divorce would not be nearly as great a threat to its power.

38 *Revised Statutes and Codes of Porto Rico Containing All Laws Passed at the First and Second Sessions of the Legislative Assembly in Effect after July 1, 1902, including the Political Code, the Penal Code, the Code of Criminal Procedure, the Civil Code* (San Juan: Boletín Mercantil Press, 1902), title 4, chap. 3.

39 Ibid., title 9, chap. 1. Proposed modifications in patria potestad provoked impassioned protests from Federales such as Julian Blanco, who argued that democratizing authority within the family would produce "the most deplorable and dissolute anarchy." See "El nuevo código civil: VI," *La Democracia*, Jan. 27, 1902, p. 1. See also "El nuevo código civil: VII," *La Democracia*, Jan. 29, 1902, p. 1. Clearly such protests had an effect; mothers' wishes were unequivocally subordinated to those of fathers in the final draft of the Civil Code.

40 Only one in twenty of all women petitioners came from wealthy, landowning backgrounds. Another one in ten were from the middle-class and professional sectors. Two-fifths were married to artisans or day laborers, and the social standing of one-third was unidentified. Male petitioners ranged broadly. One in ten were of elite status and one in four from the professional middling sectors. One of every six male plaintiffs were artisans and day laborers. Almost one-half of all male plaintiffs were not identified by class.

41 This is reflected not only in the rapidity of the courts' processing of cases but also in the increasingly formulaic nature of the language used to draw up divorce petitions. After 1906, very little witness testimony and no lengthy judicial reasoning were included in the transcripts of the cases. This contrasted sharply with the detail of charges, testimony, and sentences that characterized the early files, when the terms of divorce were still being negotiated.

42   The intervening years' divorce percentages of total civil cases filed in Ponce are as follows: 1902–4 percent (N = 302); 1903–4.3 percent (N = 300); 1904–2.7 percent (N = 226); 1905–no record of cases filed; 1906–15.2 percent (N = 250); 1907–14.3 percent (N = 263); 1908–14 percent (N = 223); 1909–12.4 percent (N = 201); 1910–16 percent (N = 233); 1911–22 percent (N = 253).

43   See, for example, "María Otero (único apellido) contra José Gregorio Torres sobre divorcio," 1902, AGPR, Jud., Ponce, Exp. Civ., box 15; "Doña Carmen Lucca y Sánchez contra Don Miguel Napoleoni Thillet sobre divorcio," 1904, ibid., box 40; "María Angustias Anguita y Ribarte contra Ercilio de la Cruz y Rivera: Sobre divorcio," 1902, ibid., box 12.

44   "Doña Plácida La O Rios contra Don Ramón Alvarado sobre divorcio," 1903, ibid., box 18.

45   "María Angustias Anguita y Ribarte contra Ercilio de la Cruz y Rivera: Sobre divorcio," 1902, ibid., box 12; "Juana López Lugo v. Ramón Mas Orca: Divorcio," 1904, ibid., box 42; "Antonia Rendón v. Francisco Maldonado: Divorcio," 1906, ibid., box 42.

46   "Ramón Ortiz Zayas vs. María Rita Ortiz née López," 1910, ibid., box 36. See also "Doña Marta Estrella Rodríguez y Mateu contra Don Eugenio Montalvo y González. Sobre divorcio," 1903, ibid., box 22, and "Dóña Mercedes Velez contra Don Luis Castro Arciatore sobre divorcio," 1903, ibid., box 24.

47   "José Martínez vs. Mercedes Almodóvar: Acción divorcio," 1910, ibid., box 38.

48   "Demanda de divorcio: Doña Elisa Giménez y Ramírez contra Don José Colón y Carrasquillo por malos tratamientos de obra," 1901, ibid., box 7.

49   "Carlota Prieto y Cruz versus Juan José Príncipe y Medrano: Acción de divorcio," 1909, ibid., box 28. See also "Doña Petronila Quiles contra Don Francisco Perez Fabio. Sobre divorcio," 1903, ibid., box 21, and "Don Carlos Cercado y Zayas contra Doña Micaela Castello y Feliciano sobre divorcio," 1903, ibid., box 27.

50   "Felicidad conyugal," *La Democracia,* Jan. 4, 1902, p. 3.

51   "Doña Petronila Quiles contra Don Francisco Perez Fabio. Sobre divorcio"; "Doña Andrea Corsina Martínez y Torres contra Don Juan Antonio Olivencia sobre divorcio," 1903, ibid., box 27; "Elisa Ferrer Piñiero vs. José López Súarez, divorcio," 1906, ibid., box 43.

52   "Don Juan Martínez y Torres contra Doña Juana Evangelista Rodríguez sobre divorcio," 1903, ibid., box 23. See also "Don Luis Basante y Lespier contra Doña Rafaela Nuñez y Fernández, sobre divorcio," 1903, ibid., box 20, and "Francisco Muñiz Senque versus Isabel Torres y Medina, acción divorcio," 1909, ibid., box 28.

53   See, for example, "María Otero (único apellido) contra José Gregorio Torres sobre divorcio" (quotation); "Demanda de divorcio: Doña Elisa Giménez y

Ramírez contra Don José Colón y Carrasquillo por malos tratamientos de obra," 1901, AGPR, Jud., Ponce, Exp. Civ., box 7; "Doña Bernardina del Valle y Rojas contra Don Domingo Aurelio Cruz Rivera sobre divorcio," 1903, ibid., box 19.

54 "Doña Petronila Quiles contra Don Francisco Perez Fabio, sobre divorcio"; "Doña Andrea Corsina Martínez y Torres contra Don Juan Antonio Olivencia sobre divorcio," 1903, AGPR, Jud., Ponce, Exp. Civ., box 27; "Elisa Ferrer Piñiero vs. José López Súarez, divorcio," 1906, ibid., box 43.

55 "Ezequiela Rosa del Busto vs. Simón Pierluisi y Crau: Divorcio," 1904, ibid., box 39.

56 "Doña Mercedes Velez contra Don Luis Castro Arciatore sobre divorcio," 1903, ibid., box 24. See also "Doña María de la Paz Franceschi y Antongiorgi contra su esposo, Don Antonio Sánchez y Cintrón, sobre divorcio," 1903, ibid., box 18.

57 "El pueblo de Puerto Rico vs. Edmundo Steinacher: Adulterio, 1905," ibid., box 46.

58 "María F. Irizary Quiñones contra Ramón del Toro Seda sobre divorcio," 1910, ibid., box 47; "Doña Nicolasa Torres y Ledesma contra Don Bartolomé Deffendini y Mattey, sobre divorcio," 1902, ibid., box 16; "Doña Mart Estrell Rodríguez y Mateu contra Don Eugenio Montalvo y González," 1903, ibid., box 22.

59 "Doña Carmen Lucca y Sánchez contra Don Miguel Napoleoni Tillet sobre divorcio," 1904, ibid., box 40.

60 See "El Pueblo de Puerto Rico vs. Edmundo Steinacher: Adulterio," 1905, ibid., box 46; "María Angustias Anguita y Ribarte contra Ercilio de la Cruz y Rivera: Sobre divorcio," 1902, ibid., box 12; and "Doña Carmen Lucca y Sánchez contra Don Miguel Napoleoni Tillet sobre divorcio," 1904, ibid., box 40.

61 This may have influenced women in their framing of divorce petitions. María Irizarry, for example, first requested a divorce based on her husband's public affair with his mistress. She later amended her complaint, however, to eliminate all references to her husband's adultery. Instead, she provided lengthy descriptions of his physical abuse, as well as his refusal to support her financially or to live with her. María's petition for divorce was approved only three months after filing the amended complaint ("María F. Irizary [*sic*] Quiñones contra Ramón del Toro Seda sobre divorcio," 1910, ibid., box 7).

62 See, for example, "María F. Irizary [*sic*] Quiñones contra Ramón del Toro Seda sobre divorcio," 1906, ibid., box 47.

63 Foucault most clearly delineated his analysis of the modern forms of power in *Discipline and Punish: The Birth of the Prison,* trans. Alan Sheridan (New York: Pantheon, 1978); *The History of Sexuality,* vol. 1, *An Introduction,* trans. Robert Hurley (New York: Random House, 1978); and *Power/Knowledge: Selected Interviews and Other Writings, 1972–1977,* ed. Colin Gordon (New York: Pantheon, 1980).

64   Foucault, *History of Sexuality,* 103; *Discipline and Punish,* 180.

65   Mary Louise Pratt, borrowing from the Cuban intellectual Fernando Ortiz, calls such processes "transculturation." She notes that "while subjugated peoples cannot control what emanates from the dominant culture, they do determine to varying extents what they absorb into their own, and what they use it for." See her *Imperial Eyes: Travel Writing and Transculturation* (New York: Routledge, 1992), 6.

66   Leila Ahmed, *Women and Gender in Islam: Historical Roots of a Modern Debate* (New Haven: Yale University Press, 1992), 145–64.

67   Interviews with Doña Hipólita Gonzalez, Ponce, Apr. 1, 1994; Doña Ramona García, Ponce, Mar. 20, 1994; and Doña Carmen Rodríguez, May 24, 1994.

68   Guerra, *Popular Expression,* 179–81.

69   The limits of the new colonial paternalist judicial system emerge even more clearly when compared with the court system set up jointly by the Chilean state and the Braden copper mine in the early twentieth century. These judges also enforced women's restriction to the home, motherhood, and financial dependence on men but in turn disciplined violent or financially inconsistent husbands. See Thomas Miller Klubock, "Morality and Good Habits: The Construction of Gender and Class in the Chilean Copper Mines, 1904–1951," in *The Gendered Worlds of Latin American Women Workers,* ed. John French and Daniel James (Durham: Duke University Press, 1997), 232–63.

5   Slavery, Sexuality, and the Early Labor Movement, 1900–1917

1   Joan W. Scott, *Gender and the Politics of History* (New York: Columbia University Press, 1988), 49.

2   For some analogous examples elsewhere, see the essays in Sonia Kruks, Rayna Rapp, and Marilyn B. Young, eds., *Promissory Notes: Women in the Transition to Socialism* (New York: Monthly Review, 1989); Dora Barrancos, *Anarquismo, educación y costumbres en la Argentina de principios del siglo* (Buenos Aires: Editorial Contrapunto, 1990); Deborah Levenson-Estrada, "The Loneliness of Working-Class Feminism: Women in the 'Male World' of Labor Unions, Guatemala City, 1970s," in *The Gendered Worlds of Latin American Women Workers: From Household and Factory to the Union Hall and Ballot Box* (Durham: Duke University Press, 1997), 208–31.

3   During the last decades of the nineteenth century, coffee had usurped sugar as Puerto Rico's primary export. After the U.S. occupation, however, the coffee industry began to crumble. Unlike sugar and tobacco, coffee did not enjoy tariff protection from "foreign" (non-U.S.) competition in U.S. markets. This, combined with the loss of its preferential access to traditional Cuban and Spanish

markets, spelled the coffee industry's downfall. Francisco Scarano, *Puerto Rico: Cinco siglos de historia* (San Juan: McGraw-Hill, 1993), 592–93.

4   Scarano, *Puerto Rico*, 584–90; Gervasio L. García and Angel G. Quintero Rivera, *Desafío y solidaridad: Breve historia del movimiento obrero puertorriqueño* (Río Piedras: Ediciones Huracán, 1982), 67–81.

5   Scarano, *Puerto Rico*, 590–92; Angel G. Quintero Rivera, "Socialista y tabaquero: La proletarización de los artesanos," *Sin nombre* 8, no. 4 (March 1978): 12; Amilcar Tirado Avilés, "Notas sobre el desarrollo de la industria del tabaco en Puerto Rico y su impacto en la mujer puertorriqueña, 1898–1920," *Centro* 2, no. 7 (winter 1989–90): 18–23. Juan José Baldrich provides an account of the brief but intense struggle of smallholding highland tobacco growers against U.S. monopoly capital's control over tobacco prices in the 1930s in *Sembraron la nosiembra: Los cosecheros de tabaco puertorriqueño frente a las corporaciones tabacaleras, 1920–1934* (Río Piedras: Ediciones Huracán, 1988).

6   Yamila Azize Vargas, *La mujer en la lucha* (Río Piedras: Editorial Cultural, 1985), 40–60; Marcia Rivera, "Incorporación de las mujeres al mercado de trabajo en el desarrollo del capitalismo (esbozo para un análisis)," in *La mujer en la sociedad puertorriqueña*, ed. Edna Acosta Belén (Río Piedras: Ediciones Huracán, 1980), 41–65. For complaints about the low wages of urban women workers, see "Notas de Ponce," *Unión Obrera*, Sept. 11, 1911, p. 3, and "La mujer obrera en Puerto Rico," *Justicia*, Feb. 6, 1915, p. 1. Needlework did not take off as a significant industry in Puerto Rico until the 1920s. By 1930, however, it had become one of the principal economic activities of the island, employing at least forty thousand women. See María del Carmen Baerga, "Exclusion and Resistance: Household, Gender, and Work in the Needlework Industry in Puerto Rico, 1914–1940" (Ph.D. diss., State University of New York, Binghamton, 1996); Scarano, *Puerto Rico*, 593–95; Juan José Baldrich, "Gender and the Decomposition of the Cigar-Making Craft in Puerto Rico, 1899–1934," in *Puerto Rican Women's History*, ed. Felix V. Matos Rodríguez and Linda C. Delgado (Armonk, N.Y.: M. E. Sharpe, 1998), 105–25.

7   See García and Quintero Rivera, *Desafío y solidaridad*, 34–81, for an overview of this period. Mariano Negrón Portilla discusses the violence between workers loyal to the Republicano Party and FLT members in *Las turbas republicanas, 1900–1904* (Río Piedras: Ediciones Huracán, 1990). Rubén Dávila Santiago describes the short-lived attempt of a small group of workers to establish "moralizing circles" as an alternative to both the FLT and the Republicano-affiliated Federación Regional in 1907 (*El derribo de las murallas: Orígenes intelectuales del socialismo en Puerto Rico* [Río Piedras: Editorial Cultural, 1988], 137–45).

8   Angel G. Quintero Rivera, *Patricios y plebeyos: Burgueses, hacendados, artesanos y*

obreros. Las relaciones de clase en el Puerto Rico de cambio de siglo (Río Piedras: Ediciones Huracán, 1988), 109.

9   Santiago Iglesias, often hailed as the father of Puerto Rican socialism, was the leader of the "reformist" group (Dávila Santiago, *El derribo,* 58–60, 88, 141–45). For critiques of Iglesias by Ramón Romero Rosa and Andrés Rodríguez Vera, see Rafael Bernabé, *Respuestas al colonialismo en la política puertorriqueña, 1899–1929* (Río Piedras: Ediciones Huracán, 1996), 92–98.

10   Dávila Santiago, *El derribo,* 201.

11   Julio Ramos provides a compelling portrait of the radical tobacco workers' culture that stretched throughout the Spanish-speaking Caribbean and its diaspora in Florida and New York City. He points out that owners of the tobacco factories fought hard to end the practice of worker readers; employers' attempts to eliminate these positions were even the focus of several strikes. See *Amor y anarquía: Los escritos de Luisa Capetillo* (Río Piedras: Ediciones Huracán, 1992), 19–27. See also Patricia Cooper, *Once a Cigarmaker: Men, Women, and Work Culture in American Cigar Factories, 1900–1919* (Urbana: University of Illinois Press, 1987).

12   During the twentieth century, Quintero Rivera has pointed out that the economic and political reorganization of the island by the United States destroyed Ponce's role as Puerto Rico's "alternate capital." The bulk of the island's port activity was redirected from Ponce to San Juan. The state's economic role was increased drastically, and its administrative offices were centralized in San Juan. Municipal autonomy was dramatically curtailed as well, furthering the rapid move toward political and economic centralization. Ponce's previous position as the island's center of economic activity collapsed (*Patricios y plebeyos,* 82–92). In addition, Liberal power was strongest in Ponce, cemented by the antiprostitute "decency" consensus of the 1890s. Consequently, it may have been more difficult for the popular classes there to challenge directly the Liberals' "seignorial project" than in San Juan, where the Liberals had never gained the same hegemonic force. Finally, Afro-Puerto Rican, twentieth-century political activity in Ponce seems to have been rooted in the Republicano Party. This may have discouraged people of African descent in Ponce from placing their political loyalties as definitively with the Socialists as they apparently did in other towns.

13   "Noticias," *Unión Obrera,* Sept. 25, 1906; "Labor Organization in Ponce," *Porto Rico Workingman's Journal,* Mar. 1905, 40; *Unión Obrera,* Mar. 4, 1907, p. 4, and Mar. 7, 1907, p. 2; "El 10 de mayo de Ponce," *Unión Obrera* (Edición de San Juan), May 9, 1903, p. 1; *Unión Obrera,* Apr. 21, 1907; *Unión Obrera,* May 7, 1907.

14   Rubén Dávila Santiago, *Teatro obrero en Puerto Rico (1900–1920) Antología* (Río

Piedras: Editorial Edil, 1985), 12, 89; Julio Ramos also characterizes the early
radical worker culture in Puerto Rico as extremely heterogenous and felicitously
"undisciplined" (*Amor y anarquía,* 27).

15 "El ideal del siglo XX," *Voz Humana,* Sept. 2, 1906; p. 1.

16 See Anna Clark, *The Struggle for the Breeches: Gender and the Making of the
British Working Class* (Berkeley: University of California Press, 1995), for a
brilliant analysis of the gendered, open-ended making of the English working
classes through a rhetoric of domesticity. Lynn Hunt develops an analogous
argument about the power of family metaphors in French revolutionary politics
in *The Family Romance of the French Revolution* (Berkeley: University of California Press, 1992).

17 See, for example, Ramón Romero Rosa [R. del Romeral], *Musarañas: Opúsculo
sobre ciertas preocupaciones y costumbres que son un estorbo á los trabajadores
puertorriqueños para la compenetración de los revindicadores ideales del obrerismo
universal* (San Juan: Tipografía de El Carnaval, 1904); Juan Vilar, *Páginas libres*
(San Juan: Compañía Editorial Antillana, 1915); "Moralidad," *Porto Rico Workingman's Journal,* 1905, p. 13; "Noticias," *Unión Obrera,* Nov. 19, 1906; and
"Cualidades morales que debe tener el obrero organizador," *Justicia,* Nov. 29,
1914, p. 3. For a discussion of various groups' use of modernity discourses in the
Puerto Rican temperance campaign, see Mayra Rosario Urrutia, "Reconstruyendo la nación: La idea del progreso en el discurso anti-alcohol, 1898–1917)," in
La nación soñada: Cuba, Puerto Rico y Filipinas ante el 98, ed. Consuelo Naranjo,
Miguel Puig-Samper, and Luis Miguel García Mora (Madrid: Doce Calles,
1996), 585–94.

18 Romero Rosa, *Musarañas,* 28–29. Eugenio Sánchez, Jesús Colón, and Sotero
Figueroa are some of the better-known Afro-Puerto Rican leftists. Six FLT workers attacked by Republicano gangs in Mayagüez in 1902 were black. Hoja suelta,
1902, CPR, Colección obrero. The U.S. informant Henry K. Carroll observed
that nine of the eleven FLT island leaders were "colored men" (*Report,* 51). Most
of the rank-and-file members of Cayey's local Socialist Party were of African
descent (Juan José Baldrich, conversation with author, March 25, 1991).

19 " 'La Democracia' miente," *El Combate Obrero,* Dec. 3, 1910, p. 2; "Gompers en
su puesto," *El Combate Obrero,* Dec. 9, 1910, p. 2. Black insurgents in Cuba's
Guerra Chiquita (1879–80) also lambasted liberals for their racism (Ada Ferrer,
"To Make a Free Nation: Race and Struggle for Independence in Cuba, 1868–
1898" (Ph.D. diss., University of Michigan, Ann Arbor, 1995), 156.

20 Romero Rosa, *Musarañas,* 12–14, 24, 29–30; Eduardo Conde, "Cuestión de
razas," *Unión Obrera,* June 14, 1903, p. 1; Eugenio Sánchez, "Programa de la
federación, *Federación Libre,* Feb. 9, 1902, p. 1.

21   *Procedimientos del Sexto Congreso Obrero de la Federación Libre de Trabajo de Puerto Rico (1910),* 122, 126–27, CPR; Romero Rosa, *Musarañas,* 12–14, 24, 29–30; Conde, "Cuestión de razas," 1; Sánchez, "Programa de la federación," 1.

22   See, for example, La Unión Obrera Central de Ponce, "¡22 de marzo de 1873!" *Unión Obrera,* Mar. 21, 1907, p. 2. This interplay of race and class discourses broadens Ann Stoler's analysis of how "the working of race through the language of class" can provide ways of talking about "at once overlapping and interchangeable" identities. Stoler focuses solely on the European bourgeoisie. Clearly, however, working-class people have also devised ways of simultaneously raising and silencing these questions (*Race and the Education of Desire,* 11, 100, 123–30).

      Rebecca J. Scott asserts that for many Afro-Cuban men during this period, class and racial identities were also inseparable. The right to organize around their work, to be a "race of color," and to be full citizens formed part of a whole, complex identity ("'The Lower Class of Whites' and 'The Negro Element': Race, Social Identity, and Politics in Central Cuba, 1899–1909," in *La nación soñada,* ed. Naranjo, Puig-Samper, and García Mora, 179–91.

23   For examples, see El Negrito, "A mis hermanos de raza," *La Defensa,* Sept. 9, 1900; "Los esclavos," *El Águila,* Mar. 8, 1902, p. 2; "¿Serviles?" *El Águila,* June 19, 1902, p. 2; "Entre los albañiles," ibid.; "¡¡Solo es esclavo quien merece serlo!!" hoja suelta, n.d., CPR, Colección obrera; "No hay tal servidumbre," *El Águila,* June 25, 1902, p. 2; "Discurso pronunciado por el Señor Pedro Carlos Timothee," *El Águila,* Mar. 6, 1902, p. 1; and "Entre los albañiles," *El Águila,* June 19, 1902, p. 2. For a rare criticism of racism *within* the Republicano Party, see Luís Felipe Dessus, "El cinismo de ayer," *La Justicia* (Ponce), May 3, 1901. Lillian Guerra notes that the Puerto Rican elite began to elaborate a highly idealized, emphatically white *jíbaro* (highland peasant) as the national symbol during the early twentieth century (*Popular Expression and National Identity in Puerto Rico: The Struggle for Self, Community, and Nation* (Gainesville, University of Florida, 1998), 79–90. The race of this new representation may well have been constructed in response to Afro-Puerto Ricans' more aggressive political assertion of their racial identity and interests during the early years after the U.S. occupation.

24   Sánchez, "Programa de la federación, p. 1. See also, Romero Rosa, *Musarañas,* 12–14, 24, 29–30, and Conde, "Cuestión de razas," 1.

25   "Los esclavos," 2; El Negrito, "A mis hermanos de raza"; "Los esclavos," 2; "¿Serviles?" 2; "Entre los albañiles"; "¡¡Solo es esclavo quien merece serlo!!" Miriam Jiménez-Román argues that José Celso Barbosa, the celebrated black founder and leader of the Republicano Party, was never able to escape this contradiction. While he helped open discussion on race in Puerto Rican politics, denouncing racism on the island, asserting the importance of blackness to

Puerto Ricans' individual and collective identities, and refusing "honorary white" status himself, Barbosa was unable to break with the hope of being integrated into both the "great Puerto Rican family" and the colonial metropolis. Thus, he limited himself to denouncing individual racists, without addressing structural or institutional racism. See "Un hombre (negro) del pueblo: José Celso Barbosa and the Puerto Rican 'Race' toward Whiteness," *Centro* 8, nos. 1–2 (1996): 8–29.

For some fascinating parallels between Afro-Cuban and Afro-Puerto Rican strategies of silencing and articulating racial questions, see Vera M. Kutzinski, *Sugar's Secrets: Race and the Erotics of Cuban Nationalism* (Charlottesville: University of Virginia Press, 1993), 81–100.

26 Tirado, "Notas," 23. For illuminating discussions of women's labor in the Puerto Rican textile industry of the early twentieth century, see Lydia Milagros González García, *Una puntada en el tiempo: La industria de la aguja en Puerto Rico (1900–1929)* (Río Piedras: CEREP, 1990); María del Carmen Baerga, "Exclusion and Resistance"; and Baerga, ed., *Género y trabajo: La industria de la aguja en Puerto Rico y el Caribe hispánico* (Río Piedras: Editorial de la Universidad de Puerto Rico, 1993).

27 "El 10 de mayo de Ponce"; "Movimiento obrero," *Unión Obrera* (Edición de San Juan), May 9, 1903, p. 2; "Noticias," *Unión Obrera*, Sept. 25, 1906, p. 3; "Noticias," *Unión Obrera*, Mar. 4, 1907, p. 4; *Unión Obrera*, Mar. 7, 1907, p. 2; and *Unión Obrera*, Apr. 21, 1907, Dec. 18, 1904, Nov. 20, 1918, Oct. 14, 1919, and May 7, 1907.

28 Quintero Rivera, "Socialista y tabaquero," 117, and *Patricios y plebeyos*, 267–74. Yamila Azize heartily concurs, insisting that from the very beginning, most male tobacco workers had a "progressive attitude toward women" owing to their "high cultural level" (*La mujer en la lucha*, 50–94, 118–31). For other celebratory accounts of the gender inclusiveness of the island's early labor movement, see Tirado, "Notas," 23–29, and García and Quintero Rivera, *Desafío y solidaridad*, 75–78. Julio Ramos was the first to take exception to this heroic, feminist, male left narrative in his insightful essay on Luisa Capetillo (*Amor*, 11–58).

29 Barceló Miller, *La lucha por el sufragio*, 66–69; Baerga, "Exclusion and Resistance."

30 Levenson-Estrada, "Loneliness," 221–27; Clark, *Struggle for the Breeches*, 59–62, 126–28, 158–96.

31 Juan José Baldrich has begun to outline a similar argument in "Gender and Decomposition." He notes that Puerto Rican male cigar rollers encouraged the organization of women in the cigar industry but stubbornly opposed their admittance into the core of the craft—cigar rolling itself.

32 "Las calumnias oficiales," *Luz y vida*, Aug. 30, 1909, p. 5.

33   "Noticias," *El Combate,* Dec. 3, 1910, p. 3. See also Edmundo Dantes [José Limón de Arce], *Rendención* (San Juan: Tipografía "El Alba," 1906), reproduced in Dávila, *Teatro obrero,* 143, 183–202; Juan S. Marcano, "Páginas Rojas," 1919, excerpted in Angel G. Quintero Rivera, *Lucha obrera en Puerto Rico* (Río Piedras: CEREP, 1972), 67; Santiago Valle y Velez, *Magdalena* (Mayagüez: Imprenta "Gloria," 1908), 27, 68; Alejandro Sux, "Surge mujer!" *Unión Obrera,* Sept. 7, 1911, p. 3.

34   "Noticias," *El Combate,* Dec. 3, 1910, p. 3.

35   Meredith Tax discusses the American Federation of Labor's undercutting of the Women's Trade Union League in *The Rising of the Women* (New York: Monthly Review, 1980), 102–9, 115–23. For Britain, see Clark, *Struggle for the Breeches.* For the Chilean mining working class, see Klubock, "Morality and Good Habits: The Construction of Gender and Class in the Chilean Copper Mines, 1904–1951," in *The Gendered Worlds of Latin American Women Workers: From Household and Factory to Union Hall and Ballot Box,* ed. John French and Daniel James (Durham: Duke University Press, 1998), 232–63.

36   "Dignificación de la mujer," *Unión Obrera,* Aug. 21, 1906, p. 3. See also "Nuestra enseñanza," *Unión Obrera,* Jan. 11, 1910, p. 2; Marcano, "Páginas Rojas," 66, 67; and Dantes, *Redención,* 171.

37   Jesús M. Balsac, "Primero de Mayo," and Paca Escabí de Peña, "Nuestra misión," both in *Páginas del obrero* (Mayagüez: Imprenta la Protesta, 1904); Vilar, *Páginas libres,* 77; Valle y Velez, *Magdalena,* 57; Angel María Dieppa, *El porvenir de la sociedad humana* (San Juan: Tipografía "El eco," 1915), 30; Romero Rosa, *Musarañas,* 43.

38   J. Elias Levis, "La huelga," *El Tipógrafo,* Apr. 16, 1911, 2. See also the female characters in Magdaleno González's plays. In "Los crímenes sociales," Guita, a young, working-class girl, persistently explains to her brother the nature of class exploitation and the need to develop strategic, collective forms of resistance. Juanita, the daughter of the local capitalist, sympathizes with the workers, defends hungry children from the police and wealthy bullies, and by the end of the drama cries out that she embraces the workers' cause. Magdaleno González, "Los crímenes sociales," in *Arte y rebeldía* (Caguas, 1920), reprinted in Dávila, *Teatro obrero,* 319–20, 322–23, 327–29, 334.

39   For some examples, see Juan de M. Velez, "Ocho años despúes," *Unión Obrera,* Apr. 2, 1905; Juan Vilar, "Así está la sociedad," *Unión Obrera,* Oct. 13, 1911, p. 3; Magdaleno González, "Pelucín el limpiabotas a la obra del sistema capitalista," in *Arte y rebeldía,* reprinted in Dávila, *Teatro obrero,* 341–54.

40   Dávila cites at least six plays and novels in which such rapes play a central role (*Teatro obrero,* 94). See also "A las uniones . . . ," May 22, 1902 [unattributed flyer, CPR]; "¡¡No importa!!" *Unión Obrera,* Nov. 21, 1906; "La hija del crímen,"

Luz y vida, Sept. 30, 1909, 9–10; "The Tyranny of the House of Delegates of Porto Rico," 1913, reprinted in Quintero Rivera, *Lucha obrera,* 50–51.

41 "La ramera," *El comunista,* Dec. 18, 1920, p. 3. See also Dieppa, *El porvenir,* 29–31; "10 de mayo: '¿Civilizados?'" *Unión Obrera,* May 1, 1907; "20 Congreso obrero de Puerto Rico: Labor que tiene que ejecutar," *Unión Obrera* (Edición de San Juan), July 19, 1903, p. 1; "¿Quienes somos?" *El comunista,* July 10, 1920, p. 1; Dieppa, *El porvenir,* 29, 31; and Juan Vilar, "La Ramera," in *Páginas libres,* 74–75.

42 Elizabeth Quay Hutchinson argues that the early Chilean left's discourse on prostitution expressed male workers' distress about their *own* economic vulnerability and lack of control over women's sexuality, not concern about prostitutes themselves ("'El fruto envenenado del arbol capitalista': Women Workers and the Prostitution of Labor in Urban Chile, 1896–1925," *Journal of Women's History* 9, no. 4 [winter 1998]: 131–51). This may have been partially the case in Puerto Rico as well, but the massive working-class rejection of the U.S. colonial state's jailing and harassment of alleged prostitutes during World War I demonstrates that laboring Puerto Ricans' new public discourses on sexuality could actually translate into significant shifts in political practices.

43 "Lazo de amor libre," *Unión Obrera,* Mar. 30, 1907, p. 1; Dávila Santiago, *El derribo,* 182–84; Luís Figueroa, conversation with author, February 25, 1989; Juan José Baldrich, conversation with author, April 4, 1991; Norma Valle Ferrer, *Luisa Capetillo: Historia de una mujer proscrita* (Río Piedras: Editorial Cultural, 1990), 81.

44 Venancio Cruz, *Hacia el porvenir* (San Juan: Tipografía República Española, n.d.), 49, 99–105; Julio Camba, "Matrimonios," *El comunista,* Oct. 30, 1920, 2–3; Dieppa, *El porvenir,* 30, 41, 47, 50–55; Dávila Santiago, *El derribo,* 182; Valle y Velez, *Magdalena,* 57–58; Juan José López, *Voces libertarias* (San Juan: Tipografía La Bomba, n.d.), 9; "Matrimonios y divorcio," *Unión Obrera,* Mar. 7, 1907, p. 1, and Mar. 8, 1907, p. 1.

45 Of all the free-lover anarchists, Luisa Capetillo was the most explicit in her references to Puerto Rican popular sexual norms (*Mi opinión,* vii, 28–29, 78; Capetillo, "La influencia de las ideas modernas," and "En el campo, amor libre," both in *Influencias de las ideas modernas: Notas y apuntes, escenas de la vida* (San Juan: Tipografía Negrón Flores, 1916), 42–43 and 181–85, respectively.

46 "Censura dolorosa," *El criterio libre,* May 7, 1900, p. 2.

47 "Federación Libre: Acta de la asamblea celebrada la noche del día del 6 de julio de 1900," CPR, Colección obrera.

48 *Procedimientos del Sexto Congreso Obrero de la Federación Libre de Trabajadores de Puerto Rico, celebrado del 18 al 24 de marzo de 1910, en la ciudad de Juncos* (San Juan: Tipografía de M. Burillo, 1910), 102–3.

49   "Adelanto y desmoralización," *Federación Obrera,* Feb. 4, 1899, p. 3. See also "Don Simón: ¿Va usté mirando?" *Federación Obrera,* Jan. 21, 1899; "¡Siempre socialista!" ibid.; "Triqui-Traque," ibid.

50   Federación Libre de los Trabajadores de Puerto Rico, *Actuaciones de la Segunda y Tercera Asambleas Regulares de Tabaqueros de Puerto Rico* (San Juan: Tipografía Murillo, 1914), 48. The quotation from Baldrich is in his "Gender and the Decomposition of the Cigar-Making Craft, 118.

51   *Unión Obrera,* Nov. 10, 1915, cited in Azize, *La mujer,* 70; "La independencia de la mujer del siglo XX," *Justicia,* June 26, 1915.

52   20 congreso obrero de Puerto Rico: Labor que tiene que ejecutar," *Unión Obrera* (Edición de San Juan), July 19, 1903, p. 1; R. del Romeral [Ramón Romero Rosa], "En serio y en broma," *Unión Obrera* (Edición de San Juan), June 14, 1903; Dantes, *Redención,* 141; "¡¡No importa!!" 2; Torres de Solon, "La hija del crímen," *Luz y vida,* Sept. 30, 1909, 9–10; "Ironía de patricios," *Unión Obrera,* Jan. 25, 1910, p. 1; Juan Vilar, *Páginas libres,* 74–75; "¿Quienes somos?" *El comunista,* July 10, 1920.

53   Ramón Romero Rosa was the one exception. He did discuss male artisans' sexual objectification of women in their nineteenth-century casinos and social events. But his treatment of this "contradiction" within the working class implied that he saw it as a practice rooted in a prepolitical, unenlightened age, now quickly passing from the stage of history (*Musarañas,* 11–12).

54   Dantes, *Redención,* 164–75.

55   "El infierno del gobierno invisible en Puerto Rico," *Justicia,* July 28, 1924, 6.

56   Dieppa, *El porvenir;* R. del Romeral [Ramón Romero Rosa] *Unión Obrera* (Edición de San Juan), Mar. 1, 1903, p. 1; Marcano, *Páginas Rojas,* 66.

57   Again, the exception was Ramón Romero Rosa, who wrote enthusiastically that "Puerto Rico will become great, with its women's work in workshops and factories, which will moralize our society. . . . We have to put an end to what was said until very recently—that women were only good for household chores" ([R. del Romeral], "En serio y en broma," *Unión Obrera* (Edición de San Juan), May 17, 1903, p. 2).

58   Dieppa, *El porvenir,* 47.

59   Cruz, *Hacia el porvenir,* 40. See also Dieppa, *El porvenir,* 47.

60   [Untitled], *Luz y vida,* Sept. 15, 1909, p. 6.

61   "Casos y cosas," *Luz y vida,* Dec. 30, 1909, p. 6; emphasis mine.

62   Valle y Velez, *Magdalena,* 57. See also Dieppa, *El porvenir,* 47.

63   Dieppa, *El porvenir,* 47.

64   Vilar, *Páginas libres,* 36; Dieppa, *El porvenir,* 47.

65   "¡Surge, mujer!" *Unión Obrera,* Sept. 7, 1911, p. 3; emphasis mine. See also

Alfonso Torres, "El amor y el ideal," *Luz y vida,* Aug. 30, 1909, p. 4, and Marcano, *Páginas Rojas,* 67.

66 Romero Rosa, *Musarañas,* 11.

67 Amilcar Tirado asserts that atheism, the necessity of class struggle, and the importance of worker education were all absorbed by women through their exposure to radical male tobacco culture. By implication, then, women were simply receptors of male ideas, not intellectuals and historical actors in their own right. Tirado reduces even Luisa Capetillo, who clearly acknowledged her intellectual and political debts to other women, to an example of a woman radicalized solely by her contact with the male-led and male-conceptualized labor movement. In his article Tirado quotes only one woman, who recounted in properly feminine form, "Basilio taught me how to understand our problems, and when he died, he left me with a different consciousness ("Notas," 26). Angel Quintero Rivera, Gervasio García, and Rubén Dávila Santiago paint equivalent pictures of the early Puerto Rican left. Quintero (*Lucha obrera*) and Dávila (*Teatro obrero*) should be given credit, though, for beginning to make Capetillo's work available to the general public; they included excerpts from her plays in their collections of workers' writings. Quintero also encouraged some of the first feminist historians, such as Yamila Azize, in their research.

68 Azize, *La mujer,* 50, 93–95; Valle Ferrer, *Luisa Capetillo,* 67; *Unión Obrera,* Nov. 10, 1915, cited in Azize, *La mujer,* 70.

69 Capetillo, *Mi opinión,* preface. Information on Capetillo's mother and father are in Valle Ferrer, *Luisa Capetillo,* 40–46.

70 Valle Ferrer, *Luisa Capetillo,* 54–57.

71 Capetillo, *Influencias,* prologue.

72 Capetillo, "La mujer en la época primitiva," in *Mi opinión,* 148.

73 Luisa Capetillo, *Ensayos libertarios* (Arecibo: Imprenta Unión Obrera, 1907). The essays contained in this collection were written between 1904 and 1907. Prostitution was also the only sexual issue deemed to be "political" by Argentinian male anarchists in the early twentieth century. Maxine Molyneux, "No God, No Boss, No Husband: Anarchist Feminism in Nineteenth-Century Argentina," *Latin American Perspectives* 13, no. 1 (winter 1986): 136–37. Julio Ramos notes the shift in Capetillo's thinking to include nonproduction issues; he contends that Capetillo was the first proletarian woman to infuse the woman question with "specificity and autonomy" (*Amor,* 51–53).

74 Capetillo, "Influencias de las ideas modernas," 50. See also Luisa Capetillo, "Recuerdo á la Federación Libre," in *Mi opinión,* 182.

75 Capetillo, "La mujer en la época primitiva," 150. See also Luisa Capetillo, "Notas, apuntes, pensamientos, conceptos, definiciones, sentencias y reflex-

iones filosófícas, naturistas, psicológicas, moralistas," in *Influencias,* 53, 56, 92–93; Capetillo, "Influencias de las ideas modernas," 41; Capetillo, *Mi opinión,* 15–16.

76   Capetillo, "La corrupción de los ricos y la de los pobres, ó como se prostituye una rica y una pobre," in *Influencias,* 179; Capetillo, *Mi opinión,* 6–10, 16–19, 26–29, 30–32, 74–78; Luisa Capetillo, "Notas," in *Influencias,* 53; Capetillo, *Influencias,* 76, 93.

77   Capetillo, *Mi opinión,* 7–9, 16–17, 51, 74–78 (quotation from 28); Capetillo, "Influencias de las ideas modernas," 41, 49, 91–93.

78   Capetillo, *Mi opinión,* 9, 17–18.

79   Capetillo, *Mi opinión,* 17. See also *Mi opinión,* 9–13, 17–19, 27–28; "Las influencias de las ideas modernas," 49, 93; and "Notas," 56.

80   Cite from Magdalena Vernet, "El amor libre," reprinted in Capetillo, *Mi opinión,* 38–55 (quotation is on 44). See also Capetillo, *Mi opinión,* 70–74; "Notas," 66; and *Influencias,* 93.

81   Some limits remained firm, however. Women's sensuality could only be heterosexual. To Capetillo, masturbation and sexual relationships between women were reprehensible. Both were products of parents' obsessive attempts to regulate their daughter's sexual interactions with boyfriends (*Mi opinión,* 29, 34). Thus, the "laws of nature" that Capetillo mustered in defense of women's sexual autonomy and pleasure could also be turned against any sexual expression that challenged the boundaries of heterosexuality. Better to acknowledge women's sexual capacities and defy the dominant honor code than to allow even more dangerous sexual practices.

82   Capetillo, *Mi opinión,* 16–17, 34–35.

83   More than twenty years after the publication of the nineteenth-century newspaper *La Mujer,* Ana Roqué de Duprey continued to insist on the exclusion of "disreputable" women—with all this term's race and class connotations intact—from the feminist community. "All suffragists should always behave in a well-educated manner, never using indecorous or unseemly words. Only honorable women should be admitted to suffragist groups, as a way of ensuring the morality of the social order" ("Mandamientos del sufragismo," *Album puertorriqueño,* 12).

84   Capetillo, "La corrupción," in *Influencias,* 167–80; Capetillo, *Mi opinión,* 8, 18, 23–25, 28–29, 34–35, 135–37.

85   Capetillo, "Influencias de las ideas modernas," 6–50.

86   Capetillo, *Mi opinión,* xi; Capetillo, "Influencias de las ideas modernas," 41; Capetillo, "Notas," 56. For analogous examples of the isolation of women challenging male dominance within their social movements, see Levenson-Estrada, "Loneliness," 220–28; Susan K. Besse, *Restructuring Patriarchy: The Modernization of Gender Inequality in Brazil, 1914–1940* (Chapel Hill: Univer-

sity of North Carolina Press, 1996), 164–98; and Paulette Pierce, "Boudoir Politics and the Birthing of the Nation: Sex, Marriage, and Structural Deflection in the National Black Independent Party," in *Women Out of Place: The Gender of Agency and the Race of Nationality,* ed. Brackette F. Williams (New York: Routledge, 1996), 216–44.

87 Capetillo, *Mi opinión,* 183; Capetillo, "Cartas interesantes de un ácrata de Panamá," in *Influencias,* 150–51. Historians' interviews during the 1970s and 1980s with Capetillo's male contemporaries confirm her complaints. See Valle Ferrer, *Luisa Capetillo,* 77–78, 80, 100–101, and Quintero Rivera, *Luchas obreras,* 34.

88 See Dávila Santiago, *El derribo,* 181–216, for a discussion of this repression and its role in the consolidation of the reformist leadership's power within the Puerto Rican left.

89 Ibid., 192–203.

90 Historians of Argentinan working-class feminism have noted a similar pattern. With the emergence of socialism as the dominant force within the left, anarchist critiques of the family, male dominance, and authoritarian power more generally were all dropped. Molyneux, "No God," 139–41; María del Carmen Feijoo, "Las trabajadoras porteñas a comienzos del siglo," in *Mundo urbano y cultura popular: Estudios de historia social argentina,* ed. Diego Armus (Buenos Aires: Editorial Sudamérica, 1990), 305–9.

6 Saving Democracy: Debating Prostitution during World War I

1 Gervasio L. García and Angel G. Quintero Rivera, *Desafío y solidaridad: Breve historia del movimiento obrero puertorriqueño* (Río Piedras: Ediciones Huracán, 1982), 93–95; Francisco Scarano, *Puerto Rico: Cinco siglos de historia* (San Juan: McGraw-Hill, 1993), 590, 610–16. For an example of seamstresses' letters, see "Obreras, bordadoras, caladoras, y costureras, relatan a *El Águila* su triste situación," *El Águila,* Oct. 10, 1918, p. 5; for petitions, see AGPR, Fort., between January 1917 and January 1920; "Problema inquietante," *El Águila,* Nov. 6, 1918, p. 2; *El Águila,* Dec. 28, 1918, p. 8.

2 "Cuestión palpitante: Defensa del hogar," *Unión Obrera,* Aug. 10, 1918, p. 1; *El Águila,* Aug. 22, 1918, p. 1; "A través de la isla: Ponce," *La Correspondencia,* Aug. 9, 1918. Lillian Guerra argues that, although they rarely openly challenged colonial hegemony, by about 1915, the popular classes felt much more ambivalent about U.S. rule than during the first years after the 1898 invasion (*Popular Expression and National Identity in Puerto Rico: The Struggle for Self, Community, and Nation* (Gainesville: University of Florida Press, 1998), 186–211.

3 Pedro Vásquez Ríos, "La mujer obrera en Ponce," *Unión Obrera,* Aug. 13, 1918, p. 3.

4   "Peticiones recibidas en la Cámara de Representantes," *La Democracia,* Nov. 30, 1918, p. 10.

5   "Vean que son mujeres," *El Águila,* Aug. 22, 1918, p. 1. For examples of other women's strikes, see "La mujer obrera en Ponce," 3; "Escogedoras de café en huelga," *El Águila,* Nov. 8, 1918, p. 8; "Huelga de despalilladoras," *El Águila,* Dec. 2, 1918, p. 1; "Importante Debate," *El Águila,* May 28, 1919, pp. 5–6; "Solucionada en varios talleres," *El Águila,* June 19, 1919, p. 1; "Huelga de despalilladoras," *La Democracia,* Aug. 30, 1918, p. 4.

6   Mayra Rosario Urrutia, "Hacia un mundo abstemio: La prohibición del alcohol en Puerto Rico" (Ph.D. diss., Universidad de Puerto Rico, Río Piedras, 1993). Early Puerto Rican bourgeois suffragist organizations and publications called for the vote for literate women only. After the United States failed to extend the suffrage to Puerto Rican women in 1920, feminists on the island made a short-lived, cross-class coalition to advocate unrestricted female electoral rights. By 1924, this cross-class unity had splintered, however, with the more conservative bourgeois feminists again advocating the vote only for literate women. The Liga Social Sufragista, a group of progressive bourgeois suffragists, continued to press for universal suffrage alongside working-class women activists. Literate women finally won the vote in 1929; in 1936, suffrage was extended to all Puerto Rican women. María de Fátima Barceló Miller, *La lucha por el sufragio femenino en Puerto Rico, 1896–1935* (Río Piedras: Ediciones Huracán, 1997); Yamila Azize Vargas, *La mujer en la lucha* (Río Piedras: Editorial Cultural, 1985), 93–146.

7   "El abandono de la niñez y la delincuencia infantil," *El Águila,* July 19, 1918, p. 2.

8   The individuals to whom I refer as Afro-Puerto Rican either publicly claimed this identity in the press or were identified as such by surviving family members.

During the first two decades of U.S. rule, the Republicano Party was a quite diverse grouping, Before the death of its Afro-Puerto Rican leader, José Celso Barbosa, and the party's 1924 alliance with the Unionistas, urban artisans and Afro-Puerto Ricans figured heavily among its activists. From 1919 until Barbosa's death in 1921, Republicanos even made local alliances with the Socialists; these informal coalitions briefly took power in municipal governments in Ponce, Arecibo, and Fajardo. But sugar hacendados and wealthier *colonos* were also joining the professionals and smaller merchants who had historically formed the bulk of the Republican leadership. These more conservative sectors eventually pulled the party away from its dialogue with the Socialists and into a national alliance with the Unión Party. See Rafael Bernabé, *Respuestas al colonialismo en la política puertorriqueña, 1899–1929* (Río Piedras: Ediciones Huracán, 1996); Edgardo Meléndez, *Puerto Rico's Statehood Movement* (New York: Greenwood, 1988); Angel G. Quintero Rivera, *Conflictos de clase y política en Puerto Rico,* 5th ed. (Río Piedras: Ediciones Huracán, 1986), 38–40, 53, 76–105;

and Angel G. Quintero Rivera, *Patricios y plebeyos: Burgueses, hacendados, artesanos y obreros. Las relaciones de clase en el Puerto Rico de cambio de siglo* (Río Piedras: Ediciones Huracán, 1988), 129–89.

9 "Sucesos y comentos," *El Águila,* Sept. 27, 1918, p. 1; "La realidad se impone," *El Águila,* May 3, 1919, p. 2; "El partido republicano y la raza de color en Porto Rico," *El Águila,* June 10, 1919; ibid., June 11, 1919; ibid., June 12, 1919; "Confiemos," *El Águila,* Apr. 11, 1919, p. 2; "Pasado, presente, porvenir," *El Águila,* June 26, 1919, p. 2; "Realidades del ambiente: El 375," *El Águila,* Sept. 30, 1918, p. 7; "El regimiento 475, el Dr. Barbosa, y los Sres. Godreau," *El Águila,* Oct. 5, 1918, p. 1; "Fiesta en honor del Regimiento 375: Discurso del Señor J.A. Becerril," *El Águila,* Nov. 6, 1918, p. 3.

10 "Asilos para niños desamparados," *El Águila,* Apr. 4, 1918, p. 2. See also "El abandono de la niñez y la delincuencia infantil," *El Águila,* July 19, 1918, p. 2; "La riqueza como arma," *El Águila,* Apr. 16, 1919, p. 2; "De la riqueza irresponsable," *La Correspondencia,* Aug. 19, 1918, p. 5; "La canción del dolor," *Mujer,* June 23, 1923, p. 16; "No hubiera mendigos si el mundo social se humanizara," *Mujer,* June 23, 1923, p. 24; M. Meléndez Muñoz, "El trabajo y la vida de las obreras," *Puerto Rico Ilustrado,* Apr. 13, 1918, p. 34.

11 "Abusivo proceder de un policía," *El Águila,* May 23, 1918, p. 1; "La policía en Berlina: Un juez poco cauto," *El Águila,* May 22, 1918, p. 2; "Respeto y defensa a la mujer," *El Águila,* May 25, 1918, p. 2; "Redención de la mujer," *El Águila,* Aug. 20, 1918, p. 2; "Un grupo de mujeres de buena voluntad," *El Águila,* Sept. 15, 1918, p. 4; "Que las dejen en el gimnasio," *El Águila,* Oct. 25, 1918, p. 8.

12 Ruth Rosen, *The Lost Sisterhood: Prostitution in America, 1900–1918* (Baltimore: Johns Hopkins University Press, 1982); Barbara Meil Hobson, *Uneasy Virtue: The Politics of Prostitution and the American Reform Tradition* (New York: Basic, 1987); Mary E. Odem, *Delinquent Daughters: Protecting and Policing Adolescent Female Sexuality in the United States, 1885–1920* (Chapel Hill: University of North Carolina Press, 1995).

13 Rosen, *Lost Sisterhood,* 19–33; Hobson, *Uneasy Virtue,* 157–59; Odem, *Delinquent Daughters.*

14 Allan M. Brandt, *No Magic Bullet: A Social History of Venereal Disease in the U.S. since 1800,* 2d ed. (New York: Oxford University Press 1987), 87. See also Brandt, *No Magic Bullet,* 60–77, 84–94; Hobson, *Uneasy Virtue,* 167, 175–80; Rosen, *Lost Sisterhood,* 33–37; Nancy K. Bristow, *Making Men Moral: Social Engineering during the Great War* (New York: New York University Press, 1996); Odem, *Delinquent Daughters;* "Man Power Bill," May 22, 1918, AGPR, Fort., box 730, GF 2220.

15 Argentina experienced its own "white slavery" scare during this period; it was intensely anti-Semitic. See Donna J. Guy, *Sex and Danger in Buenos Aires:*

Prostitution, Family, and Nation in Argentina (Lincoln: University of Nebraska Press, 1991), and Guy, " 'White Slavery,' Citizenship, and Nationality in Argentina" in *Nationalisms and Sexualities,* ed. Andrew Parker et al. (New York: Routledge, 1992), 201–17.

16   AGPR, Fort., box 721, GF 1742; AGPR, Fort., box 729, GF 1910; AGPR, Fort., box 727, GF 1901, Apr. 9, 1918; "La Bandera Roja," *El Águila,* Nov. 29, 1918, p. 4; "Casi un decreto implantando la ley marcial," *El Águila,* Nov. 29, 1918, p. 1; "Subject: Censorship of Foreign Mails in Porto Rico," Feb. 17, 1918, Report no. 50, AGPR, Fort., box 724, GF 2010; AGPR, Fort., 1918, box 720, GF 1798; AGPR, Fort., 1918, box 722, GF 1850; "Juicio por violar la ley de espionaje," *El Águila,* July 19, 1918, p. 1; "Arrestado por la ley de espionaje," *La Correspondencia,* Aug. 9, 1918, p. 2; AGPR, PPR, NP, Ponce, LDN no. 11, Mar. 31, 1918–May 16, 1918, Apr. 8, 1918, pp. 41, 42, and Apr. 19, 1918, p. 86; "Quejas de unas madres," *La Correspondencia,* Aug. 26, 1918, p. 8; "Ponce a la altura de su deber," *El Águila,* June 6, 1918, p. 1; "Manifiesto: Cuerpo de Vigilancia de la American Defense Society, Capítulo de Ponce," *El Águila,* June 6, 1918, p. 1.

17   Howard L. Kern, *Special Report of the Attorney General of Porto Rico to the Governor of Porto Rico concerning the Suppression of Vice and Prostitution in Connection with the Mobilization of the National Army at Camp Las Casas* (San Juan: Bureau of Supplies, Printing, and Transportation, 1919), 3–5; George Shanton to the Governor of Porto Rico, June 21, 1918, AGPR, Fort., box 732, GF 2460; "El próximo paso," *La Democracia,* Nov. 4, 1918, p. 1; Conference of State and Provincial Boards of Health of North America to Governor of Puerto Rico, May 11, 1918, AGPR, Fort., box 730, GF 2026.

18   Tomás Bryan, "La campaña de la prostitución," *La Democracia,* Aug. 29, 1918, p. 7. See also "Información general," *La Democracia,* Sept. 5, 1918, p. 2, and Luís Samalea Iglesias, "El momento actual," *La Democracia,* Sept. 5, 1918, p. 4.

19   Department of Justice of Porto Rico, *Laws of Porto Rico in Regard to Prostitution, Adultery, Sale of Intoxicating Liquors, etc.* (San Juan: Bureau of Supplies, Printing, and Transportation, 1918), 3–5; "Declaraciones que ha hecho el Attorney General Mr. Kern sobre un problema social," *La Democracia,* Aug. 13, 1918, p. 1.

20   Department of Justice of Porto Rico, *Laws of Porto Rico,* 4–5; emphasis mine.

21   Howard Kern to Angel Acosta Quintero, August 10, 1918, in Kern, *Special Report,* 23; G. Shanton, Chief Insular Police, to Gov. Yager, June 8, 1918, AGPR, Fort., box 732, GF 2017/1.

22   Kern, *Special Report,* 6; "Por el campamento las Casas," *La Democracia,* Aug. 12, 1918, p. 4; Sept. 3, 1918, p. 4; "La carcel de mujeres," *La Correspondencia,* Aug. 9, 1918, p. 1.

23   See the Libros de Novedades, Policía de Puerto Rico, Ponce, in AGPR, between 1916 and 1918 for these patterns.

24 See, for example, Vol. June 9, 1916–Sept. 12, 1916, p. 130, July 21, 1916; ibid., 103–4, July 11, 1916; ibid., p. 93, July 7, 1916; Vol. Dec. 27, 1915–June 9, 1916, p. 136, Apr. 4, 1916; ibid., p. 272, May 27, 1916; ibid., p. 49, Feb. 1, 1916; ibid., p. 60, Feb. 16, 1916; ibid., p. 7, Dec. 30, 1915, all in AGPR, PPR, NP, Ponce, LDN.

25 Vol. Dec. 27, 1915–June 9, 1916, p. 263, May 26, 1916, p. 263, AGPR, PPR, NP, Ponce, LDN; Vol. II, p. 97, Mar. 8, 1918, AGPR, PPR, NP, Ponce, LDN; "Quejas de vecinos sobre mujeres escandalosas," June 16, 1916, AGPR, Crim., Ponce, box 91.

26 "Más de cien mujeres en la cárcel," *El Águila*, Aug. 15, 1918, p. 1; "Ponce," *La Correspondencia*, Aug. 17, 1918, p. 4; "Notas de Ponce," *La Democracia*, Aug. 20, 1918, p. 7; "Desde Aguadilla," *La Democracia*, Aug. 26, 1918, p. 6; "Desde Ponce," *La Democracia*, Sept. 6, 1918, p. 1; "Notas de Ponce," *La Democracia*, Sept. 14, 1918, p. 4.

27 "La cárcel de mujeres," *La Correspondencia*, Aug. 9, 1918, p. 1; Kern, *Special Report*, 8–10.

28 "Las de 5 millas," *Unión Obrera*, Sept. 12, 1918, p. 2; "Misconduct of Civilian towards Convoy," AGPR, Fort., box 740, GF 2145.

29 Vol. 17, pp. 51–53, Sept. 28 and 29, 1918, AGPR, PPR, NP, Ponce, LDN; "A través de la isla: Ponce," *La Correspondencia*, Aug. 3, 1918, p. 4; Vol. 17, p. 3, Sept. 22, 1918, AGPR, PPR, NP, Ponce, LDN; "Por la moral," *El Águila*, Sept. 22, 1918, p. 8; "La cruzada contra las horizontales," *El Águila*, Aug. 20, 1918, p. 6; "Importantes servicios," *El Águila*, Oct. 18, 1918, p. 8.

30 Vol. 17, p. 10, Sept. 22, 1918, AGPR, PPR, NP, Ponce, LDN; Vol. 17, p. 22, Sept. 24, 1918, AGPR, PPR, NP, Ponce, LDN; Vol. 17, p. 23, Sept. 25, 1918, AGPR, PPR, NP, Ponce, LDN; Vol. 17, pp. 52–53, Sept. 28, 1918, AGPR, PPR, NP, Ponce, LDN; "¿Metió la pata otro policía?" *La Correspondencia*, Aug. 20, 1918, p. 1; "Siguen los abusos," *La Correspondencia*, Sept. 23, 1918, p. 2. For crackdown strategies in Manatí, which Kern considered a particularly badly vice-ridden city, see "Manatí por dentro," *La Correspondencia*, Aug. 14, 1918, p. 3.

31 "Información general," *La Democracia*, Aug. 22, 1918, p. 2; "Policía femenina en Mayagüez," *La Correspondencia*, Aug. 26, 1918, p. 8; "Entrega de credenciales," *La Correspondencia*, Aug. 28, 1918, p. 5; "Policía femenina," *La Correspondencia*, Sept. 21, 1918, p. 8.

32 Tomás Bryan, "La campaña a la prostitución," *La Democracia*, Sept. 30, 1918, p. 7.

33 "Varias notas," *Unión Obrera*, Aug. 14, 1918, p. 3; "Queja y felicitación de una madre," *El Águila*, Sept. 10, 1918, p. 6.

34 "A las damas de Puerto Rico," *La Correspondencia*, Aug. 14, 1918, p. 3, and *La Democracia*, Aug. 14, 1918, p. 6. See also "Felicitando al Attorney General," *La Correspondencia*, Aug. 26, 1918, p. 2.

35 Judges from Camuy, San Sebastián, Mayagüez, Aguadilla, Vieques, and Arecibo

expressed their support of the policy. Kern, *Special Report,* exhibits 33–62, pp. 56–71; Eugenio Fernández García, ed., *El libro de Puerto Rico* (San Juan: El Libro Azul Publishing, 1923), 137; "Lo que opina el fiscal Campillo," *La Correspondencia,* Sept. 21, 1918, p. 1; "Con su permiso," *La Correspondencia,* Sept. 7, 1918, p. 1; Manuel Ledesma to Gov. Yager, Sept. 18, 1918, AGPR, Fort., box 735, GF 2020/1.

36   "El peligro de las sospechas," *El Águila,* Aug. 19, 1918, p. 1; "Grave acusación contra una Srta.," *El Águila,* May 21, 1918, p. 1; "El peligro de las sospechas," *El Águila,* Aug. 19, 1918, p. 1; Tomás Bryan, "La campaña de la prostitución," *La Democracia,* Aug. 29, 1918, p. 7; "Abusivo proceder de un policía," *El Águila,* May 23, 1918, p. 1; "Susana Torres era pura," *La Correspondencia,* Aug. 19, 1918, p. 1.

37   "Mitín esta noche," *El Águila,* Aug. 20, 1918, p. 1.

38   "Importante acto público," *La Democracia,* Aug. 24, 1918, p. 2.

39   Leopoldo Tormes was acutely conscious of his African heritage; he frequently told his children stories of their foremothers' struggles under slavery (Doña Gladys Tormes, conversation with author, July 30, 1990).

I have not been able to ascertain how Martínez Nadal identified himself racially. But Edgardo Meléndez notes that he was the principal opponent of the Republicans' 1924 alliance with the Unión Party; Martínez Nadal passionately disagreed with more conservative Republicanos' insistence on making common cause with the Unionistas to defeat the Socialists. He accused the pact's advocates of selling Puerto Rico to the United States and the rich (Meléndez, *Puerto Rico's Statehood Movement* [New York: Greenwood, 1988], 51).

40   "El mitín de anoche," *El Águila,* Aug. 21, 1918, p. 1; "De la isla: Ponce," *La Correspondencia,* Aug. 24, 1918, p. 4; "Importante acto público," *La Democracia,* Aug. 24, 1918, p. 3. Leopoldo Tormes is a good example of the ideological complexity of the Republicano Party before its 1924 alliance with the Unionistas. An avid supporter of statehood as the only viable path to "regional integrity," Tormes also seems to have maintained a consistently critical stance vis-à-vis government repression against working people. A few months after the anti-prostitution campaign ended, Tormes appeared in the spotlight again, this time representing the Socialist Sandalio Alonso who had been thrown in jail for leading a demonstration of striking seamstresses to the plaza in Ponce ("Contra Sandalio E. Alonso," *El Águila,* June 27, 1919, p. 1). As noted earlier, such grassroots-level cooperation between Republicanos and Socialists was not uncommon, particularly during the immediate postwar years. See Meléndez, *Statehood Movement,* 40–50.

41   "El peligro de las sospechas," *El Águila,* Aug. 19, 1918, p. 1; "Redención de la mujer," *El Águila,* Aug. 20, 1918, p. 2.

42 "Una carta sabrosa," *La Correspondencia,* Aug. 29, 1918, p. 1; "Sin sobre," *La Correspondencia,* Sept. 10, 1918, p. 1; "Falsos rumores," *El Águila,* Sept. 14, 1918, p. 1.

43 "Del Ambiente," *Unión Obrera,* Aug. 24, 1918, p. 2; "Varias notas," *Unión Obrera,* Aug. 14, 1918, p. 3; "La prostitución y el estado," *Unión Obrera,* Aug. 27, 1918, p. 1; "¿Donde vamos a parar," *Unión Obrera,* Sept. 9, 1918, p. 2; "Las de 5 millas," *Unión Obrera,* Sept. 12, 1918, p. 2; Manuel F. Rojas, "Continuamos nuestra réplica," *Unión Obrera,* Sept. 24, 1918, p. 1.

44 José P. Marchán, "Voz de alarma ante un attorney," *La Correspondencia,* Aug. 23, 1918, p. 3. See also "Se ha querido extraviar la opinion," *La Correspondencia,* Sept. 5, 1918, p. 1; "Como se acumulan pruebas contra las acusadas," *La Correspondencia,* Aug. 26, 1918, p. 1; "Misericordiosamente. . . ," *La Correspondencia,* Aug. 21, 1918, p. 1.

45 "¡¡Basta Ya!! El Attorney General está violando las leyes del País," *La Correspondencia,* Aug. 20, 1918, p. 1. José Flores Ramos explores the protests of the pro-independence Unionista dissident Luis Dalta in "Virgins, Whores, and Martyrs: Prostitution in the Colony, 1898–1919," in *Puerto Rican Women's History: New Perspectives,* ed. Félix V. Matos Rodríguez and Linda C. Delgado (Armonk, N.Y.: M. E. Sharpe, 1998), 95–97.

46 These dissident Unionistas did not completely abandon their elitist Liberal heritage, however. Despite the fact that Afro-Puerto Rican Republicanos had organized autonomous protests of the state's antiprostitution campaign in Ponce and that the socialist FLT had for decades developed its own counter-hegemonic discourse on prostitution, the editors of *La Correspondencia* crowed that *they* were the sole legitimate representative of the people, the voice of the masses who until now had been "a bunch of humiliated, ignorant clods, insulted by their exploiters" ("Con esa gente. . . ," *La Correspondencia,* Aug. 24, 1918, p. 1).

47 "El pueblo con nosotros," *La Correspondencia,* Aug. 21, 1918, p. 1.

48 "El pueblo está con nosotros," *La Correspondencia,* Aug. 23, 1918, p. 1; "Carta que nos fortalece: El país honrado con nosotros," *La Correspondencia,* Aug. 23, 1918, p. 1; "El pueblo con nosotros," *La Correspondencia,* Aug. 24, 1918, p. 1; " 'Esa gente' con nosotros," *La Correspondencia,* Aug. 26, 1918, p. 1; "El pueblo con nosotros," *La Correspondencia,* Aug. 27, 1918, p. 1.

49 Male Socialists asserted their "true manhood" in opposition to the evilly feminine, immoral nature of wealthy Unionistas. When the Unionista leadership ransacked the Socialist Party offices in San Juan and had several leaders arrested without a warrant, a Socialist commentator lashed out: "What more could they do besides panic, once the rotting pool of their prostituted consciences had been discovered? They violated the Law, degraded the Constitution, prostituted pub-

lic trust. . . . The purity of our ideals are your envy; the manliness of our attacks, your nightmares. Fickle, lewd women that you are. Men of effeminate judgement. You are not the reality of woman, but the wicked degradation of both sexes" ("Silvanard" [pseud.], "Canallezca conspiración. . . ?" *Unión Obrera,* Aug. 29, 1918, p. 3).

50   The one exception was a passing comment by Alonso Gual in *El Águila* that unscrupulous men infected women with venereal diseases ("Redención de la mujer," *El Águila,* Aug. 20, 1918, p. 2).

51   "¿Donde vamos a parar?" *Unión Obrera,* Sept. 9, 1918, p. 2; "Abusos de la persecución, *La Correspondencia,* Sept. 11, 1918, p. 1; vol. 17, Oct. 7, 1918, pp. 108–9, AGPR, PPR, NP, Ponce, LDN; Nov. 11, 1918–Jan. 20, 1918, Dec. 15, 1918, p. 160, AGPR, PPR, NP, Ponce, LDN.

52   "Susana Torres era pura," *La Correspondencia,* Aug. 19, 1918, p. 1; "Los tribunales de Puerto Rico no inspiran confianza a los acusados," *La Correspondencia,* Aug. 19, 1918, p. 1; "No todas son sentenciadas," *El Águila,* Aug. 22, 1918, p. 1. For examples of women's petitions to the governor for pardons, see "Solicitud de indulto," *El Águila,* Nov. 6, 1918, p. 3; "No perdona," *La Correspondencia,* Sept. 20, 1918, p. 2; "Indultos denegados," *La Correspondencia,* Aug. 23, 1918, p. 2; "Sobre indultos," *La Democracia,* Sept. 10, 1918, p. 4; and "Solicitud denegada," *La Democracia,* Nov. 9, 1918, p. 2.

53   See "Habeas Corpus," *El Águila,* Aug. 16, 1918, p. 8; "En la corte federal," *La Correspondencia,* Sept. 18, 1918, p. 2; and "Infractoras al art. 287," *La Correspondencia,* Sept. 5, 1918, p. 8.

54   "Convocatoria a todas las damas que pertenecen a la sección de Santurce," *Unión Obrera,* Aug. 31, 1918, p. 1; "El pueblo con nosotros," *La Correspondencia,* Aug. 29, 1918, p. 1.

55   "Which is guiltier / whatever evil they may have committed / She who sins for pay / or he who pays for the sin?" "Vale más precaver que tener que remediar," *El Águila,* Oct. 9, 1918, pp. 3, 6.

56   "Felicitación para 'Flor Oculta,'" *El Águila,* Oct. 11, 1918, p. 1.

57   See, for example, "Por el prestigio de nuestros tribunales de justicia," *La Democracia,* Aug. 20, 1918, p. 4; "¡Y basta!" *La Democracia,* Aug. 21, 1918, p. 4; "La integridad de nuestros cortes," Aug. 24, 1918, p. 4; "Información general," *La Democracia,* Sept. 5, 1918, p. 2; "Declaraciones que ha hecho el Attorney General Mr. Kern sobre un problema social," *La Democracia,* Aug. 13, 1918, p. 1; "The Meeting of the Rotary Club Tuesday," in Kern, *Special Report,* 57; Luís Samalea Iglesias, "Acción Social," *La Democracia,* Aug. 23, 1918, p. 4; "Desde Aguadilla," *La Democracia,* Aug. 26, 1918, p. 6; "Lo que opina el fiscal Campillo," *La Democracia,* Sept. 21, 1918, p. 1; Manuel Ledesma to Gov. of Puerto Rico, Sept. 18, 1918, AGPR, Fort., box 735, GF 2020/1; Howard Kern to Santiago Vivaldi

Pacheco, Aug. 23, 1918, in Kern, *Special Report,* 25; "Redención de la mujer," *El Águila,* Aug. 20, 1918, p. 2; and "La campaña a la prostitución," *La Democracia,* Aug. 31, 1918, p. 6.

58 "Croniquilla," *La Correspondencia,* Aug. 10, 1918, p. 2. See also "Croniquilla," *La Correspondencia,* Aug. 13, 1918, p. 2, Aug. 21, 1918, p. 2, Aug. 22, 1918, p. 2, and Aug. 23, 1918, p. 2.

59 "Información general," *La Democracia,* Sept. 5, 1918, p. 2.

60 "A 10 millas de distancia," *La Correspondencia,* Sept. 6, 1918, p. 1. See also José de Julian Acosta to Howard L. Kern, Sept. 2, 1918, in Kern, *Special Report,* 69.

61 Flores, "Virgins, Whores, and Martyrs," 94.

62 "Cárcel de mujeres," *La Correspondencia,* Aug. 7, 1918, p. 5; "En Arecibo," *La Democracia,* Aug. 28, 1918, p. 4; Manuel Ledesma to Governor of Puerto Rico, Sept. 18, 1918, AGPR, Fort., box 735, GF 2020/1; "En Arecibo," *La Democracia,* Aug. 28, 1918, p. 4.

63 "Información general," *La Democracia,* Aug. 21, 1918, p. 2; "Transformado en sanatorio," *El Águila,* Aug. 19, 1918, p. 1; "Sobre la reclusión de ciertas mujeres," *El Águila,* Aug. 19, 1918, p. 2; "Los que cumplen condeno," *El Águila,* May 16, 1919, p. 8; "Para la cárcel de Arecibo," *El Águila,* Apr. 4, 1919, p. 1. As the district jails in Mayagüez and San Juan were dedicated to the imprisonment of alleged prostitutes, they too were equipped with hospital annexes ("Una sala especial," *La Democracia,* Aug. 26, 1918, p. 2; "Nuevo hospital para mujeres," *La Democracia,* Sept. 9, 1918, p. 5).

64 Quotation from "Medical Reports of the District Jail at Ponce" in Kern, *Special Report,* p. 35. See also AGPR, Fort., box 738, GF 2103, Aug. 28, 1918, and Sept. 17, 1918.

65 "Transformado en sanatorio," *El Águila,* Aug. 19, 1918, p. 1.

66 "Movimiento carcelario," *El Águila,* June 14, 1919, p. 8; "El suceso de ayer," *El Águila,* Aug. 27, 1918, p. 1.

67 L. Yordan Dávila, "Salus Populi, Suprema Lex," *El Águila,* Aug. 17, 1918, p. 5; "Redención de la mujer," *El Águila,* Aug. 20, 1918, p. 2; "Uno de los aspectos del vicio," *El Águila,* Aug. 22, 1918, p. 2; "Una cárcel para mujeres," *La Correspondencia,* Aug. 15, 1918, p. 1; "Un grupo de mujeres de buena voluntad visita la cárcel de Ponce," *El Águila,* Sept. 15, 1918, p. 4; "Con hechos y con palabras," *El Águila,* Sept. 11, 1915, p. 4.

68 "Un grupo de mujeres de buena voluntad visita la cárcel de Ponce," 4.

69 The Council of National Defense was founded in April 1917 in the United States to mobilize middle-class women in support of the war. A few months later, most of the prominent women of Ponce had signed on as members of Puerto Rico's chapter, as had women leaders of local groups such as the Club de Damas, the Liga Femínea de Temperancia, the Anti-Tuberculosis League, the Beggars and

Orphans' Asylums, and a variety of churches. The women rolled bandages, sold war bonds, and provided assistance to the families of soldiers. "Constitution of the Porto Rico Division of the Woman's Committee of the Council of National Defense" [n.d.], AGPR, Fort., box 730, GF 2008; "La salvación de los niños," *La Correspondencia,* Aug. 16, 1918, p. 3; "Cruz Roja Americana, Rama de Ponce," *El Águila,* Apr. 3, 1918, p. 5; "Defensa Nacional de Mujeres," *El Águila,* Apr. 4, 1918, p. 1; "Obra de verdadera patriotismo: Cómo actúa la mujer puertorriqueña," *El Águila,* Apr. 5, 1918, p. 8; Kern, *Special Report,* 41–44.

70   "Redención de la mujer." See also "Un grupo de mujeres de buena voluntad visita la cárcel de Ponce," 4.

71   "Un grupo de mujeres de buena voluntad visita la carcel de Ponce."

72   For a few examples, see "Comité Central de Bienestar Social," *La Democracia,* Oct. 8, 1918, p. 7; "La salvación de los niños," *La Correspondencia,* Aug. 16, 1918, p. 3; "Altruista asociación," *La Correspondencia,* Sept. 28, 1918, p. 5.

73   See, for example, "Colisión entre huelguistas y policía," *La Democracia,* Aug. 30, 1918, p. 4. The reporter for *La Democracia* claimed that striking women attacked the police, whereupon the officers were "forced" to use their nightsticks in self-defense, leaving twenty-nine women wounded. Contrast this version to that of *Unión Obrera,* Aug. 5, 1918, p. 2, and Aug. 12, 1918, p. 1. Ironically, the suffragists themselves were portrayed several years later as prostitutes and lesbians. Gladys M. Jiménez-Muñoz, "Literacy, Class, and Sexuality in the Debate on Women's Suffrage in Puerto Rico during the 1920s," in *Puerto Rican Women's History,* ed. Matos Rodríguez and Delgado, 161–63.

74   "¿Policías o rufianes?" *Unión Obrera,* Sept. 13, 1918, pp. 1, 2; "Vean que son mujeres," *El Águila,* Aug. 22, 1918, p. 1; "Obreros de Juncos," *Unión Obrera,* Oct. 10, 1918, p. 1.

75   "Acción social," *La Democracia,* Sept. 13, 1918, p. 2; "Comité Central de Bienestar Social," *La Democracia,* Oct. 8, 1918, p. 7; "Altruista asociación," 5.

76   Virginia B. Haughwout to Howard L. Kern, Oct. 4, 1918, in Kern, *Special Report,* 55–56; "Comité de Bienestar Social," *El Águila,* Sept. 27, 1918, p. 6; "A las Sras. de Ponce que forman parte de la 'Defensa Nacional,'" *El Águila,* Oct. 14, 1918, p. 6; "Ecos de la ciudad," *El Águila,* Oct. 18, 1918, p. 8.

77   Both Judith Walkowitz and Gail Hershatter discuss similar uses of prostitution rehabilitation work and discourses by women activists. See Walkowitz, *Prostitution and Victorian Society: Women, Class, and the State* (Cambridge: Cambridge University Press, 1980), and *City of Dreadful Delight: Narratives of Sexual Danger in Late-Victorian London* (Chicago: University of Chicago Press, 1992), 88–103, 132–34; Hershatter, *Dangerous Pleasures: Prostitution and Modernity in Twentieth-Century Shanghai* (Berkeley: University of California Press, 1997), 245–66.

78 The North American women active in the movement, however, stressed the troop venereal disease issue quite strenuously. See "Acción social," 2.

79 "A las Sras. de Ponce que forman parte de la 'Defensa Nacional,' " 6 (quotations); Haughwout to Kern, 55–56.

80 "A las damas de Puerto Rico," *La Correspondencia,* Aug. 14, 1918, p. 3; emphasis mine.

81 Newspaper clippings "Licenciada Herminia Tormes García"; José P. Alcala, "Semblanza de la Juez Herminia Tormes García"; and "Homenaje postumo a la Lcda. Herminia Tormes," all undated, in AMP, Archivo Vertical, "Tormes García, Herminia"; conversations with Doña Gladys Tormes, June 15, 16, and 17, 1990.

82 Communications between Olivia Paoli de Braschi and Board of Charities, Dec. 24, 1900–Feb. 25, 1901, AGPR, Fort., box 87, GF 1116; Lillian Torres-Braschi, *Olivia: Vida de Olivia Paoli, viuda de Braschi (1855–1942)* (Barcelona: I. G. Manuel Pareja, n.d.), 17–18, 129–30; Angela Negrón Muñoz, *Las mujeres de Puerto Rico: Desde el período de colonización hasta el primer tercio del siglo XX* (San Juan: Imprenta de Venezuela, 1935), 102–4.

83 See, for example, "A las maestras de Ponce," *El Águila,* Oct. 11, 1918, p. 3.

84 Ibid.; "Se necesita una profesora," *El Águila,* Oct. 31, 1918, p. 1; "Invitación de la Defensa Nacional, Rama de Ponce," *El Águila,* Dec. 21, 1918, p. 8; "La defensa nacional en Ponce," *Album Puertorriqueño,* Jan. 1, 25, 1919, p. 16.

85 Brandt, *No Magic Bullet,* 86–87; Rosen, *Lost Sisterhood,* 1–13, 51–68; Hobson, *Uneasy Virtue,* 151–52; Lori Ginzberg, *Women and the Work of Benevolence: Morality, Politics, and Class in the Nineteenth-Century U.S.* (New Haven: Yale University Press, 1990).

86 "Más detalles del terremoto en Ponce," *El Águila,* Oct. 14, 1918, p. 1; "Con satánicos propósitos," *El Águila,* Nov. 22, 1918, p. 8; "Faltan médicos," *El Águila,* Nov. 23, 1918, p. 1; "Ponce en estado epidémico," *El Águila,* Nov. 23, 1918, p. 1; "Terrible situación en Guayama," *El Águila,* Nov. 25, 1918, p. 1; "Por la salud del pueblo," *El Águila,* Nov. 26, 1918.

87 "Expediente sobre acuerdo adoptado para que se retorne al Hospital Correspondiente las 3 nurses que prestan servicio en el Hospital de Mujeres (antes Cárcel del Distrito)," no. 53, Nov. 1918, AMP, Ay., Gob., a.m., Ac., Ben.; Kern, *Special Report,* 49–54; Message of the Governor of Porto Rico to the Ninth Legislature, Feb. 10, 1919, GF 1500/9, AGPR, Fort.

88 Vol. Mar. 19, 1919–May 18, 1919, p. 12, Mar. 20, 1919, AGPR, PPR, NP, Ponce, LDN; ibid., p. 15, Mar. 21, 1919; ibid., p. 61, Mar. 29, 1919; ibid., vol. 21, p. 96, June 8, 1919; ibid., vol. Mar. 23, 1920–Apr. 25, 1920, p. 46, Mar. 31, 1920.

89 The central role played by Leopoldo Tormes and other Republicanos in creating and maintaining the opposition raises important questions about the consciousness of prostatehood Puerto Ricans. The protests of Gual, Tormes, and Mar-

tínez Nadal seem to confirm Edgardo Meléndez's arguments that Republicanos during this early period were not unquestioning supporters of the U.S. colonial project. Rather, they envisioned statehood as a means for Puerto Ricans to gain control over their own economic and political destiny; once a state, the island would become a "Republic within a Republic." Meléndez asserts that Barbosa and other like-minded Republicans rejected the colonial status codified by the Jones Act as the institutionalization of subservience to foreign domination (*Statehood Movement,* 33–48).

90 Rosen, *Lost Sisterhood,* 62–66.

91 "Mandamientos del sufragismo," *Album Puertorriqueño,* Feb. 10, 1919, pp. 11–12.

92 Angela Negrón Muñoz, *Las mujeres.*

Conclusion

1 Florencia Mallon, *Peasant and Nation: The Making of Postcolonial Mexico and Peru* (Berkeley: University of California Press, 1994), 312.

2 One of the few exceptions to this general rule is the U.S. policy of mass sterilization in Puerto Rico, which clearly linked colonial control of the island to control over women's reproductive capacities. The campaign began in the 1940s, continued for decades, and by the 1970s had left 35 percent of women of childbearing age sterile. See Annette B. Ramírez de Arellano and Conrad Seipp, *Colonialism, Catholicism, and Contraception: A History of Birth Control in Puerto Rico* (Chapel Hill: University of North Carolina Press, 1983), and Margarita Ostolaza Bey, *Política sexual en Puerto Rico* (Río Piedras: Ediciones Huracán, 1989), 74–97.

  See also the initial explorations of the literary and contemporary connections between sexuality and exceedingly malleable Puerto Rican "national" identities in Frances Negrón-Muntaner and Ramón Grosfoguel, eds., *Puerto Rican Jam: Essays on Culture and Politics* (Minneapolis: University of Minnesota Press, 1997); Yolanda Martínez-San Miguel, "Deconstructing Puerto Ricanness through Sexuality: Female Counternarratives on Puerto Rican Identity (1894– 1934)," 127–39; and Manuel Guzmán, " 'Pa'la Escuelita con Mucho Cuida'o y por la Orillita': A Journey through the Contested Terrains of the Nation and Sexual Orientation," 209–28.

3 Angel G. Quintero Rivera has made an initial insightful foray into this question with "The Somatology of Manners: Class, Race, and Gender in the History of Dance Etiquette in the Hispanic Caribbean," in *Ethnicity in the Caribbean,* ed. Gert Oostindie (London: Macmillan, 1996), 152–81.

4 Lillian Guerra, *Popular Expression and National Identity in Puerto Rico: The Struggle for Self, Community, and Nation* (Gainesville: University of Florida,

1998), 212–42; Peter Wade, *Blackness and Race Mixture: The Dynamics of Racial Identity in Colombia* (Baltimore: Johns Hopkins University Press, 1993), 18–19.

5 Lillian Guerra, *Popular Expression;* Arcadio Díaz Quiñones, "Tomás Blanco: Racismo, historia, esclavitude," introduction to *El prejuicio racial en Puerto Rico,* by Tomás Blanco, 3d ed. (Río Piedras: Ediciones Huracán, 1985), 13–73.

6 Ada Ferrer, "To Make a Free Nation: Race and the Struggle for Independence in Cuba, 1868–1898" (Ph.D. diss., University of Michigan, Ann Arbor, 1995); Aline Helg, *Our Rightful Share: The Afro-Cuban Struggle for Equality, 1886–1912* (Chapel Hill: University of North Carolina Press, 1995).

7 Vera M. Kutzinski, *Sugar's Secrets: Race and the Erotics of Cuban Nationalism* (Charlottesville: University of Virginia Press, 1993), 12–13.

Selected Bibliography

Published Primary Sources

Brau, Salvador. "La campesina," 1886. Reprinted in Brau, *Ensayos: Disquisiciones sociológicas*. Río Piedras: Editorial Edil, 1972.

———. "Las clases jornaleras de Puerto Rico: Su estado actual, causas que lo sostienen y medios de propender al adelanto moral y material de dichas clases," 1882. Reprinted in Brau, *Ensayos: Disquisiciones sociológicas*. Río Piedras: Editorial Edil, 1972.

———. "La danza puertorriqueña," 1883. Reprinted in Brau, *Ensayos: Disquisiciones sociológicas*. Río Piedras: Editorial Edil, 1972.

———. "La herencia devota." In *Almanaque de damas*. San Juan: Tipografía González Font, 1886.

———. *Hojas Caídas*. San Juan: Tipografía La Democracia, 1909.

———. *¿Pecadora?* 1890. Reprint, Río Piedras: Editorial Edil, 1975.

———. "Rafael Cordero," 1891. Reprinted in Brau, *Ensayos: Disquisiciones sociológicas*. Río Piedras: Editorial Edil, 1972.

Browne, G. Waldo. *The New America and the Far East: A Picturesque and Historic Description of These Lands and Peoples*. Boston: Marshall Jones, 1901.

Capetillo, Luisa. *Ensayos libertarios*. Arecibo: Imprenta Unión Obrera, 1907.

———. *La humanidad en el futuro*. San Juan: Tipografía Real Hermanos, 1910.

———. *Influencias de las ideas modernas: Notas y apuntes, escenas de la vida*. San Juan: Tipografía Negron Flores, 1916.

———. *Mi opinión sobre las libertades, derechos, y deberes de la mujer, como compañera, madre, y ser independiente*. San Juan: Times Publishing, 1911.

Carroll, Henry K. *Report on the Island of Porto Rico*. Washington, D.C.: Governmental Printing Office, 1899.

Cruz, Venancio. *Hacia el porvenir*. San Juan: Tipografía República Española, n.d.

Dantes, Edmundo [Jose Limón de Arce]. *Redención*. San Juan: Tipografía "El Alba," 1906.

De Olivares, José. *Our Islands and Their People as Seen with Camera and Pencil*. St. Louis: N. D. Thompson, 1899.

Dieppa, Angel María. *El porvenir de la sociedad humana*. San Juan: Tipografía "El eco," 1915.

Del Valle Atiles, Francisco. *El campesino puertorriqueño: Sus condiciones físicas, intelectuales, y morales, causas que las determinan y medios para mejorarlas.* San Juan: Tipografía de J. González Font, 1887.

Eulate Sanjurjo, Carmela. *La muñeca.* 1895. Reprint, Río Piedras: Editorial de la Universidad de Puerto Rico, 1987.

Fernández García, Eugenio. *El libro de Puerto Rico.* San Juan: El Libro Azul Publishing, 1923.

Ferrer, Gabriel. *La mujer en Puerto Rico: Sus necesidades presentes y los medios más fáciles y adecuados para mejorar su porvenir.* Puerto Rico: Imprente de "El Agente," 1881.

Gandia Cordova, Ramon. *Estado actual de Ponce: Sus necesidades y medios para satisfacerlas.* Ponce: Tipografía "La Democracia," 1899.

González García, Manuel. *El escándalo: Novela naturalista.* San Juan: Tipografía de Arturo Córdova, 1894.

———. *La primera cría.* San Juan: Tipografía del Boletin Mercantil, 1892.

Kern, Howard. *Special Report of the Attorney General of Porto Rico to the Governor of Porto Rico concerning the Suppression of Vice and Prostitution in Connection with the Mobilization of the National Army at Camp Las Casas.* San Juan: Bureau of Supplies, Printing, and Transportation, 1919.

López, Juan José. *Voces libertarias.* San Juan: Tipografía La Bomba, n.d.

Morris, Charles. *Our Island Empire: A Hand-Book of Cuba, Porto Rico, Hawaii, and the Philippine Islands.* Philadelphia: J. B. Lippincott, 1899.

Muñoz Rivera, Luis. *Retamas.* 1891. Reprinted in *Obras completas,* edited by Eugenio Fernández Méndez. San Juan: Instituto de Cultura Puertorriqueña, 1960.

Negrón Muñoz, Angela. *Las mujeres de Puerto Rico: Desde el período de colonización hasta el primer tercio del siglo XX.* San Juan: Imprenta de Venezuela, 1935.

Neumann, Eduardo. *Verdadera y auténtica historia de la ciudad de Ponce, desde sus primitivos tiempos hasta la época contemporanea.* 1911. Reprint, San Juan: Instituto de Cultura Puertorriqueña, 1987.

Romero Rosas, Ramón. *Musarañas: Opúsculo sobre ciertas preocupaciones y costumbres que son un estorbo a los trabajadores puertorriqueños para la compenetración de los revindicadores ideales del obrerismo universal.* San Juan: Tipografía de El Carnaval, 1904.

Roqué de Duprey, Ana. *Luz y sombra.* Ponce: Tipografía de Q. N. Sanjurjo, 1903.

———. *Sara la obrera y otros cuentos.* Ponce/ Imprenta Manuel López, 1895.

Rowe, L. S. *The United States and Porto Rico.* New York: Longmans, Green, 1904.

Torres-Braschi, Lillian. *Olivia: Vida de Olivia Paoli, viuda de Braschi (1855–1942).* Barcelona: I. G. Manuel Pareja, n.d.

Valle y Velez, Santiago. *Magdalena.* Mayagüez: Imprenta "Gloria," 1908.

Vilar, Juan. *Páginas libres.* San Juan: Conpañía Editorial Antillana, 1914.

White, Trumbull. *Our New Possessions . . . a Graphic Account, Descriptive and Historical, of the Tropic Islands of the Sea Which Have Fallen under Our Sway, Their Cities, People and Commerce, Natural Resources and the Opportunities They Offer to Americans (Book 2, Puerto Rico).* Boston: J. Q. Adams, 1898.

Zeno Gandía, Manuel. *La charca.* 1894. Reprint, San Juan: Instituto de Cultura Puertorriqueña, 1987.

Principal Newspapers Cited

El Águila de Puerto Rico (Ponce, 1902–20)

Album puertorriqueño (1918–19)

La Azucena (Ponce, 1870–75)

La Bomba (Ponce, 1895)

El Cañon (Ponce, 1898)

Canta Claro (Ponce, 1899)

El Combate Obrero (Arecibo, 1910)

El Comunista (Bayamón, 1920)

La Correspondencia (San Juan, 1917–20)

El Criterio Libre (San Juan, 1900)

La Democracia (Ponce and San Juan, 1891–99, 1902–20)

Ensayo Obrero (San Juan, 1893)

Federación Obrera (1899)

La Justicia (San Juan, 1914–24)

Luz y vida (1909)

La Mujer (Humacao, 1894)

Mujer (San Juan, 1923)

El Obrero (Ponce, 1889)

La Patria (Ponce, 1899)

Porto Rico Workingmen's Journal (1905)

El Porvenir Social (San Juan, 1899)

Puerto Rico Ilustrado (1915–20)

Revista Obrera (Ponce, 1893)

La Salud (Puerto Rico [probably San Juan], 1883)

El Tiempo (San Juan, 1917–20)

El Tipógrafo (San Juan, 1911)

Unión Obrera (Mayagüez, Ponce, and San Juan, 1905–20)

Yo Acuso (Cataño, 1918)

Archives and Depositories

The primary sources consulted for this book were found in a number of archives and libraries in the United States and Puerto Rico. Principal among them were the Archivo General de Puerto Rico (AGPR) in Puerta de Tierra; the Archivo Histórico Diocesano de San Juan (AHDSJ) in San Juan; the Colección Puertorriqueña (CPR) at the main library of the Universidad de Puerto Rico, Río Piedras (UPR); and the Archivo Municipal de Ponce (AMP) in the city of Ponce. I also consulted a number of sources at the Centro de Investigaciones Históricas (CIH), located at the History Department, UPR. The holdings of the United States National Archives (USNA) in Washington, D.C., were also invaluable to me.

Secondary Sources

Ahmed, Leila. *Women and Gender in Islam: Historical Roots of a Modern Debate.* New Haven: Yale University Press, 1992.

Alonso, Ana María. "Progress as Disorder and Dishonor: Discourses of Serrano Resistance." *Critique of Anthropology* 8, no. 1 (1990): 13–33.

——. *Thread of Blood: Colonialism, Revolution, and Gender on Mexico's Northern Frontier* (Tucson: University of Arizona Press, 1995).

Anderson, Benedict. *Imagined Communities: Reflections on the Origin and Spread of Nationalism.* London: Verso, 1983.

Arrom, Silvia Marina. *The Women of Mexico City, 1790–1857.* Stanford: Stanford University Press, 1985.

Azize Vargas, Yamila. *La mujer en la lucha.* Río Piedras: Editorial Cultural, 1985.

——, ed. *La mujer en Puerto Rico: Ensayos de investigación.* Río Piedras: Ediciones Huracán, 1987.

Baerga, María del Carmen. "La articulación del trabajo asalariado y no asalariado: Hacia una reevaluación de la contribución femenina a la sociedad puertorriqueña (el caso de la industria de la aguja)." In *La mujer en Puerto Rico: Ensayos de investigación,* edited by Yamila Azize Vargas, 89–113. Río Piedras: Ediciones Huracán, 1987.

——. "Exclusion and Resistance: Household, Gender, and Work in the Needlework Industry in Puerto Rico, 1914–1940." Ph.D. diss., State University of New York, Binghamton, 1996.

——. "Women's Labor and the Domestic Unit: Industrial Homework in Puerto Rico during the 1930s." *Centro* 2, no. 7 (winter 1989–90): 32–39.

——, ed. *Género y trabajo: La industria de la aguja en Puerto Rico y el caribe hispánico.* Río Piedras: Editorial de la Universidad de Puerto Rico, 1993.

Bailey, Beth, and David Farber. "Hotel Street: Prostitution and the Politics of War." *Radical History Review* 52 (winter 1992): 54–78.

Balderston, Daniel, and Donna J. Guy, eds. *Sex and Sexuality in Latin America.* New York: New York University Press, 1997.

Baldrich, Juan José. "Gender and the Decomposition of the Cigar-Making Craft in Puerto Rico, 1899–1934." In *Puerto Rican Women's History: New Perspectives,* edited by Felix V. Matos Rodríguez and Linda C. Delgado, 105–25. Armonk, N.Y.: M. E. Sharpe, 1998.

——. *Sembraron la no-siembra: Los cosecheros de tabaco puertorriqueños frente a las corporaciones tabacaleras (1920–1934).* Río Piedras: Ediciones Huracán, 1988.

Banerjee, Sumanta. "Marginalization of Women's Popular Culture in Nineteenth-Century Bengal." In *Recasting Women: Essays in Indian Colonial History,* edited by Kumkum Sangari and Sudesh Vaid, 127–79. New Brunswick: Rutgers University Press, 1990.

Baralt, Guillermo. *La Buena Vista, 1833–1904: Estancia de frutos menores, fábrica de harinas y hacienda cafetalera.* San Juan: Fideicomiso de Conservación de Puerto Rico, 1988.

——. *Esclavos rebeldes: Conspiraciones y sublevaciones de esclavos en Puerto Rico (1795–1873).* Río Piedras: Ediciones Huracán, 1982.

Barceló Miller, María de Fátima. "Halfhearted Solidarity: Women Workers and the Women's Suffrage Movement in Puerto Rico during the 1920s." In *Puerto Rican Women's History: New Perspectives,* edited by Felix V. Matos Rodríguez and Linda C. Delgado, 126–42. Armonk, N.Y.: M. E. Sharpe, 1998.

——. *La lucha por el sufragio femenino en Puerto Rico, 1896–1935.* Río Piedras: Ediciones Huracán, 1997.

——. "Las urnas sobrias: Sufragistas y temperancistas en la década de 1910." Paper presented at the Universidad del Sagrado Corazón, Santurce, Puerto Rico, March 8, 1989.

Barrancos, Dora. *Anarquismo, educación y costumbres en la Argentina de principios del siglo.* Buenos Aires: Editorial Contrapunto, 1990.

——. "Anarquismo y sexualidad." In *Mundo urbano y cultura popular: Estudios de historia social argentina,* edited by Diego Armus, 17–37. Buenos Aires: Editorial sudamericana, 1990.

Baud, Michiel. " 'Constitutionally White: The Forging of a National Identity in the Dominican Republic." In *Ethnicity in the Caribbean,* edited by Gert Oostindie, 121–51. London: Macmillan, 1996.

Bellucci, Mabel. "Anarquismo, sexualidad y emancipación femenina: Argentina alrededor del 1900." *Nueva Sociedad* 109 (September–October 1990): 141–47.

Berbusse, Edward J. *The United States in Puerto Rico, 1898–1900*. Chapel Hill: University of North Carolina Press, 1966.

Bergad, Laird. *Coffee and the Growth of Agrarian Capitalism in Nineteenth-Century Puerto Rico*. Princeton: Princeton University Press, 1983.

Bernabé, Rafael. *Respuestas al colonialismo en la política puertorriqueña, 1899–1929*. Río Piedras: Ediciones Huracán, 1996.

Besse, Susan K. "Crimes of Passion: The Campaign against Wife-Killing in Brazil, 1910–1940." *Journal of Social History* 22, no. 4 (summer 1989): 653–66.

———. *Restructuring Patriarchy: The Modernization of Gender Inequality in Brazil, 1914–1940*. Chapel Hill: University of North Carolina Press, 1996.

Borges, Dain Edward. *The Family in Bahia Brazil, 1870–1945*. Stanford: Stanford University Press, 1992.

———. "Puffy, Ugly, Slothful, and Inert: Degeneration in Brazilian Social Thought, 1880–1940." *Journal of Latin American Studies* 25, no. 2 (May 1993): 235–56.

Boyer, Richard. "Women, La Mala Vida, and the Politics of Marriage." In *Sexuality and Marriage in Colonial Latin America*, edited by Asunción Lavrin, 252–86. Lincoln: University of Nebraska Press, 1989.

Brandt, Allan M. *No Magic Bullet: A Social History of Venereal Disease in the U.S. since 1880*. 2d ed. New York: Oxford University Press, 1987.

Bristow, Nancy K. *Making Men Moral: Social Engineering during the Great War*. New York: New York University Press, 1996.

Brown, Kathleen M. *Good Wives, Nasty Wenches, and Anxious Patriarchs: Gender, Race, and Power in Colonial Virginia*. Chapel Hill: University of North Carolina Press, 1996.

Burton, Antoinette. *Burdens of History: British Feminists, Indian Women, and Imperial Culture, 1865–1915*. Chapel Hill: University of North Carolina Press, 1994.

———. "From Child Bride to 'Hindoo Lady': Rukhumabai and the Debate on Sexual Respectability in Imperial Britain." *American Historical Review* 103, no. 4 (October 1998): 1119–46.

Bush, Barbara. "White 'Ladies,' Coloured 'Favourites,' and Black 'Wenches': Some Considerations on Sex, Race, and Class Factors in Social Relations in White Creole Society in the British Caribbean." *Slavery and Abolition* 2, no. 3 (December 1981): 245–62.

Butler, Judith. *Gender Trouble: Feminism and the Subversion of Gender Identity*. New York: Routledge, 1989.

Butler, Judith, and Joan Scott, eds. *Feminists Theorize the Political*. New York: Routledge, 1992.

Caulfield, Sueann. "The Birth of Mangue: Race, Nation, and the Politics of Prostitution in Rio de Janeiro, 1850–1942." In *Sex and Sexuality in Latin America*, edited by Daniel Balderston and Donna J. Guy, 85–100. New York: New York University, 1997.

———. "Getting into Trouble: Dishonest Women, Modern Girls, and Women-Men in the Conceptual Language of *Vida Policial,* 1925–1927." *Signs* 19, no. 1 (Autumn 1993): 146–76.

———. *In Defense of Honor: Sexual Morality, Modernity, and Nation in Early-Twentieth-Century Brazil.* Durham: Duke University Press, 1999.

CEREP. *La tercera raíz: Presencia africana en Puerto Rico.* San Juan: Instituto de Cultura Puertorriqueña, 1992.

Chakravarti, Uma. "Whatever Happened to the Vedic *Dasi?* Orientalism, Nationalism, and a Script for the Past." In *Recasting Women: Essays in Indian Colonial History,* edited by Kumkum Sangari and Sudesh Vaid, 27–87. New Brunswick: Rutgers University Press, 1990.

Chambers, Sarah C. "The Many Shades of the White City: Urban Culture and Society in Arequipa, Peru, 1780–1854." Ph.D. diss., University of Wisconsin, Madison, 1992.

Chatterjee, Partha. "The Nationalist Resolution of the Women's Question." In *Recasting Women: Essays in Indian Colonial History,* edited by Kumkum Sangari and Sudesh Vaid, 233–53. New Brunswick: Rutgers University Press, 1990.

———. *Nationalist Thought and the Colonial World: A Derivative Discourse?* London: Zed, 1986.

Clark, Anna. *The Struggle for the Breeches: Gender and the Making of the British Working Class.* Berkeley: University of California Press, 1995.

———. "Whores and Gossips: Sexual Reputation in London, 1770–1825." In *Current Issues in Women's History,* edited by Anna Angerman et al., 231–48. London: Routledge, 1990.

Combs-Schilling, Elaine M. "Etching Patriarchal Rule: Ritual Dye, Erotic Potency, and the Moroccan Monarchy." *Journal of the History of Sexuality* 1, no. 4 (April 1991): 658–81.

Conklin, Alice L. "Colonialism and Human Rights, a Contradiction in Terms? The Case of France and West Africa, 1845–1914." *American Historical Review* 103, no. 2 (April 1998): 419–42.

Connelly, Mark Thomas. *The Response to Prostitution in the Progressive Era.* Chapel Hill: University of North Carolina Press, 1980.

Cooper, Frederick. "The Dialectics of Decolonization: Nationalism and Labor Movements in Postwar French Africa." In *Tensions of Empire: Colonial Cultures in a Bourgeois World,* edited by Cooper and Ann Laura Stoler, 406–35. Berkeley: University of California Press, 1997.

Cooper, Patricia. *Once a Cigarmaker: Men, Women, and Work Culture in American Cigar Factories, 1900–1919.* Urbana: University of Illinois Press, 1987.

Cruz Monclova, Lidio. *Baldorioty de Castro (Su Vida, Sus Ideas).* San Juan: Instituto de Cultura Puertorriqueña, 1973.

———. *Historia de Puerto Rico (siglo XIX) Tomo 3, Tercera Parte (1885–1898).* Río Piedras: Editorial Universitaria, 1964.

Cubano Iguina, Astrid. *El hilo en el laberinto: Claves de la lucha política en Puerto Rico (Siglo XIX).* Río Piedras: Ediciones Huracán, 1990.

Curet, Jose. "About Slavery and the Order of Things: Puerto Rico, 1845–1873." In *Between Slavery and Free Labor: The Spanish-Speaking Caribbean in the Nineteenth Century,* edited by Manuel Moreno Fraginals, Frank Moya Pons, and Stanley Engerman, 117–40. Baltimore: Johns Hopkins University Press, 1985.

———. *Los amos hablan.* Río Piedras: Editorial Cultural, 1986.

———. *De la esclavitud a la abolición.* Río Piedras: CEREP, 1979.

———. "From Slave to Liberto: A Study on Slavery and Its Abolition in Puerto Rico." Ph.D. diss., Columbia University, 1980.

Dávila Santiago, Rubén. *El derribo de las murallas: Orígenes intelectuales del socialismo de Puerto Rico.* Río Piedras: Editorial Cultural, 1988.

———. *Teatro Obrero en Puerto Rico (1900–1920) Antología.* Río Piedras: Editorial Edil, 1985.

Davis, Darién. "¿Criollo Mulato? Cultural Identity in Cuba, 1930–1960." In *Ethnicity, Race, and Nationality in the Caribbean,* edited by Juan Manuel Carrión, 69–95. San Juan: Institute of Caribbean Studies, 1997.

De la Fuente, Alejandro. "Negros y electores: Desigualdad y políticas raciales en Cuba, 1900–1930." In *La nación soñada: Cuba, Puerto Rico y Filipinas ante el 98,* edited by Consuelo Naranjo, Miguel Puig-Samper, and Luis Miguel García Mora, 163–77. Madrid: Doce Calles, 1996.

Díaz, Arlene. "'Necesidad hizo parir mulatas': Liberalismo, nacionalidad e ideas sobre las mujeres en la Cuba del siglo XIX." In *Género, familia y mentalidades en América Latina,* edited by Pilar Gonzalbo Aizpuru, 199–226. Río Piedras: Editorial de la Universidad de Puerto Rico, 1997.

Díaz Quiñones, Arcadio. "Tomás Blanco: Racismo, historia, esclavitud." Introduction to *El prejuicio racial en Puerto Rico,* by Tomás Blanco, 13–91. 3d ed. Río Piedras: Ediciones Huracán, 1985.

———. *La memoria rota.* Río Piedras: Ediciones Huracán, 1993.

Douglas, Mary. *Natural Symbols: Explorations in Cosmology.* New York: Pantheon, 1970.

———. *Purity and Danger: An Analysis of Concepts of Pollution and Taboo.* London: Routledge, 1966.

DuBois, Ellen Carol, and Linda Gordon. "Seeking Ecstasy on the Battlefield: Danger and Pleasure in Nineteenth-Century Feminist Thought." In *Pleasure and Dan-*

ger: Exploring Female Sexuality, edited by Carole S. Vance, 31–49. Boston: Routledge and Kegan Paul, 1984.

Engelstein, Laura. *The Keys to Happiness: Sex and the Search for Modernity in Fin-de-Siècle Russia.* Ithaca: Cornell University Press, 1992.

Esteves, Martha de Abreu. *Meninas perdidas: Os populares e o cotidiano do amor no Rio de Janeiro de Belle Epoque.* Rio de Janeiro: Editora Paz e Terra, 1989.

Farnsworth-Alvear, Ann. "Talking, Fighting, Flirting: Workers' Sociability in Medellín Textile Mills, 1935–1950." In *The Gendered Worlds of Latin American Women Workers: From Household and Factory to the Union Hall and Ballot Box,* edited by Daniel James and John French, 147–75. Durham: Duke University Press, 1997.

Feierman, Steven. *Peasant Intellectuals: Anthropology and History in Tanzania.* Madison: University of Wisconsin Press, 1990.

Feijoo, María del Carmen. "Las trabajadoras porteñas a comienzos del siglo." In *Mundo urbano y cultura popular: Estudios de historia social argentina,* edited by Diego Armus, 181–311. Buenos Aires: Editorial Sudamérica, 1990.

Felsteiner, Mary Lowenthal. "Family Metaphors: The Language of an Independence Revolution." *Comparative Studies in Society and History* 25, no. 1 (January 1983): 154–80.

Ferrer, Ada. "To Make a Free Nation: Race and the Struggle for Independence in Cuba, 1868–1898." Ph.D. diss., University of Michigan, Ann Arbor, 1995.

Figueroa, Luis Antonio. "Facing Freedom: The Transition from Slavery to Free Labor in Guayama, Puerto Rico, 1860–1898." Ph.D. diss., University of Wisconsin, Madison, 1991.

Findlay, Eileen J. "Decency and Democracy: The Politics of Prostitution in Ponce, Puerto Rico, 1890–1900." *Feminist Studies* 23, no. 3 (fall 1997): 471–501.

———. "Domination, Decency, and Desire: The Politics of Sexuality in Ponce, Puerto Rico, 1870–1920." Ph.D. diss., University of Wisconsin, Madison, 1995.

———. "Free Love and Domesticity: Sexuality and the Shaping of Working-Class Feminism in Puerto Rico, 1900–1917." In *Identity and Struggle at the Margins of the Nation-State: The Laboring Peoples of Central America and the Hispanic Caribbean,* edited by Aldo Lauria-Santiago and Aviva Chomsky, 229–59. Durham: Duke University Press, 1998.

———. "Love in the Tropics: Marriage, Divorce, and the Construction of Benevolent Colonialism in Puerto Rico, 1898–1910." In *Close Encounters of Empire: Writing the Cultural History of U.S.–Latin American Relations,* edited by Gilbert M. Joseph, Catherine C. LeGrand, and Ricardo D. Salvatore, 139–72. Durham: Duke University Press, 1998.

Flores, Juan. *Divided Borders: Essays on Puerto Rican Identity.* Houston: Arte Público, 1993.

Flores Ramos, José. "Virgins, Whores, and Martyrs: Prostitution in the Colony, 1898–1919." In *Puerto Rican Women's History: New Perspectives,* edited by Felix V. Matos Rodríguez and Linda C. Delgado, 83–104. Armonk, N.Y.: M. E. Sharpe, 1998.

Foucault, Michel. *Discipline and Punish: The Birth of the Prison.* Translated by Alan Sheridan. New York: Pantheon, 1978.

——. *The History of Sexuality.* Vol. 1, *An Introduction.* Translated by Robert Hurley. New York: Random House, 1978.

——. "Two Lectures." In *Power/Knowledge: Selected Interviews and Other Writings, 1972–1977,* edited by Colin Gordon, 78–109. New York: Pantheon, 1980.

Franco, Jean. *Plotting Women: Gender and Representation in Mexico.* New York: Columbia University Press, 1989.

Fraser, Nancy. *Unruly Practices: Power, Discourse, and Gender in Contemporary Social Theory.* Minneapolis: University of Minnesota Press, 1989.

French, William. "Prostitutes and Guardian Angels: Women, Work, and the Family in Porfirian Mexico." *Hispanic American Historical Review* 72, no. 4 (November 1992): 529–54.

García, Gervasio L. *Historia crítica, historia sin coartadas: Algunos problemas de la historia de Puerto Rico.* Río Piedras: Ediciones Huracán, 1989.

García, Gervasio L., and Angel G. Quintero Rivera. *Desafío y solidaridad: Breve historia del movimiento obrero puertorriqueño.* Río Piedras, Ediciones Huracán, 1982.

Gilfoyle, Tim. *City of Eros: New York City, Prostitution, and the Commercialization of Sex, 1790–1920.* New York: W. W. Norton, 1992.

Gilroy, Paul. *The Black Atlantic: Modernity and Double Consciousness.* Cambridge: Harvard University Press, 1993.

Ginzberg, Lori. *Women and the Work of Benevolence: Morality, Politics, and Class in the Nineteenth-Century U.S.* New Haven: Yale University Press, 1990.

Glasser, Ruth. *My Music Is My Flag: Puerto Rican Musicians and Their New York Communities, 1917–1940.* Berkeley: University of California Press, 1994.

González, José Luis. *El país de cuatro pisos y otros ensayos.* 6th ed. Río Piedras: Ediciones Huracán, 1987.

González García, Lydia Milagros. *Una puntada en el tiempo: La industria de la aguja en Puerto Rico (1900–1929).* Río Piedras: CEREP, 1990.

González García, Lydia Milagros, and Angel G. Quintero Rivera. *La otra cara de la historia: La historia de Puerto Rico desde su cara obrera.* Vol. 1, *1800–1925.* Río Piedras: CEREP, 1984.

Gordon, Linda. *Heroes of Their Own Lives: The Politics and History of Family Violence, Boston, 1880–1960.* New York: Viking, 1988.

Gould, Lyman J. *La ley Foraker: Raíces de la política colonial de los Estados Unidos.* Río Piedras: Editorial Universitaria, 1969.

Graham, Richard, ed. *The Idea of Race in Latin America, 1870–1940.* Austin: University of Texas Press, 1990.

Gramsci, Antonio. *Selections from the Prison Notebooks.* Edited and translated by Quintin Hoare and Geoffrey Nowel Smith. New York: International Publishers, 1971.

Griswold, Robert L. *Family and Divorce in California, 1850–1890: Victorian Illusions and Everyday Realities.* Albany: State University of New York Press, 1982.

Grosfoguel Ramón, Frances Negrón-Muntaner, and Chloe Georas. "Beyond Nationalist and Colonialist Discourses: The *Jaiba* Politics of the Puerto Rican Ethno-Nation." In *Puerto Rican Jam: Essays on Culture and Politics,* edited by Negrón-Muntaner and Grosfoguel, 1–36. Minneapolis: University of Minnesota Press, 1997.

Grossberg, Lawrence, ed. "On Postmodernism and Articulation: An Interview with Stuart Hall." In *Stuart Hall: Critical Dialogues in Cultural Studies,* edited by David Morley and Kuan-Hsing Chen, 131–50. London: Routledge, 1996.

Guerra, Lillian. *Popular Expression and National Identity in Puerto Rico: The Struggle for Self, Community, and Nation.* Gainesville: University of Florida Press, 1998.

Gullón Abao, Alberto José. "Un acercamiento a la prostitución cubana de fines del siglo XIX." In *La nación soñada: Cuba, Puerto Rico y Filipinas ante el 98,* edited by Consuelo Naranjo, Miguel Puig-Samper, and Luis Miguel García Mora, 447–507. Madrid: Doce Calles, 1996.

Gutiérrez, Ramón A. *When Jesus Came, the Corn Mothers Went Away: Marriage, Sexuality, and Power in New Mexico, 1500–1846.* Stanford: Stanford University Press, 1991.

Guy, Donna J. *Sex and Danger in Buenos Aires: Prostitution, Family, and Nation in Argentina.* Lincoln: University of Nebraska Press, 1991.

——. " 'White Slavery,' Citizenship, and Nationality in Argentina." In *Nationalisms and Sexualities,* edited by Andrew Parker, Mary Russo, Doris Sommer, and Patricia Yaeger, 201–17. New York: Routledge, 1992.

——. "White Slavery, Public Health, and the Socialist Position on Legalized Prostitution in Argentina, 1913–1936." *Latin American Research Review* 23, no. 3 (1988): 60–80.

Guzmán, Manuel. " 'Pa'la Escuelita con Mucho Cuida'o y por la Orillita': A Journey through the Contested Terrains of Nation and Sexual Orientation." In *Puerto Rican Jam: Essays on Culture and Politics,* edited by Frances Negrón-Muntaner and Grosfoguel, 209–28. Minneapolis: University of Minnesota Press, 1997.

Hahner, June E. *Emancipating the Female Sex: The Struggle for Women's Rights in Brazil, 1850–1940.* Durham: Duke University Press, 1990.

Hall, Stuart. "Introduction: Who Needs Identity?" In *Questions of Cultural Identity,* edited by Stuart Hall and Paul de Gay, 1–17. London: Sage, 1996.

Harsin, Jill. *Policing Prostitution in Nineteenth-Century Paris.* Princeton: Princeton University Press, 1985.

Helg, Aline. *Our Rightful Share: The Afro-Cuban Struggle for Equality, 1886–1912.* Chapel Hill: University of North Carolina Press, 1995.

——. "Race in Argentina and Cuba, 1880–1930: Theory, Policies, and Popular Reaction." In *The Idea of Race in Latin America, 1870–1940,* edited by Richard Graham, 37–69. Austin: University of Texas Press, 1990.

Hershatter, Gail. *Dangerous Pleasures: Prostitution and Modernity in Twentieth-Century Shanghai.* Berkeley: University of California Press, 1997.

Hewitt, Nancy A. " 'The Voice of Virile Labor': Labor Militancy, Community Solidarity, and Gender Identity among Tampa's Latin Workers, 1880–1921." In *Work Engendered: Toward a New History of American Labor,* edited by Ava Baron, 142–67. Ithaca: Cornell University Press, 1991.

Hine, Darlene Clark. "Rape and the Inner Lives of Black Women in the Middle West: Preliminary Thoughts on the Culture of Dissemblance." *Signs* 14, no. 4 (summer 1989): 912–20.

Hobson, Barbara Meil. *Uneasy Virtue: The Politics of Prostitution and the American Reform Tradition.* New York: Basic, 1987.

Hodes, Martha. "The Sexualization of Reconstruction Politics: White Women and Black Men in the South after the Civil War." In *American Sexual Politics: Sex, Gender, and Race since the Civil War,* edited by John C. Fout and Martha Shaw Tantillo, 59–74. Chicago: University of Chicago Press, 1993.

Hull, Isabel V. *Sexuality, State, and Civil Society in Germany, 1700–1815.* Ithaca: Cornell University Press, 1996.

Hunt, Lynn. *The Family Romance of the French Revolution.* Berkeley: University of California Press, 1992.

Hunt, Margaret. "Wife Beating, Domesticity, and Women's Independence in Eighteenth-Century London." *Gender and History* 4, no. 1 (spring 1992): 10–33.

Hutchinson, Elizabeth Quay. " 'El fruto envenenado del arbol capitalista': Women Workers and the Prostitution of Labor in Urban Chile, 1896–1925." *Journal of Women's History* 9, no. 4 (winter 1998): 131–51.

Ibarra, Jorge. "Cultura e identidad nacional en el caribe hispánico: El caso puertorriqueño y el cubano." In *La nación soñada: Cuba, Puerto Rico y Filipinas ante el 98,* edited by Consuelo Naranjo, Miguel Puig-Samper, and Luis Miguel García Mora, 85–95. Madrid: Doce Calles, 1996.

James, Daniel, and John French. *The Gendered Worlds of Latin American Women Workers: From Household and Factory to the Union Hall and Ballot Box.* Durham: Duke University Press, 1997.

James, Winston. "Afro-Puerto Rican Radicalism in the U.S.: Reflection on the Political Trajectories of Arturo Schomberg and Jesús Colón." *Centro* 8, nos. 1–2 (1996): 92–127.

Jiménez de Wagenheim, Olga. "La mujer en el Puerto Rico del siglo XIX." *Centro* 2, no. 7 (winter 1989–90): 10–17.

———. *El grito de Lares: Sus causas y sus hombres.* Río Piedras: Ediciones Haracán, 1985.

Jiménez-Muñoz, Gladys. "Literacy, Class, and Sexuality in the Debate on Women's Suffrage in Puerto Rico during the 1920s." In *Puerto Rican Women's History: New Perspectives,* edited by Felix V. Matos Rodríguez and Linda C. Delgado, 143–70. Armonk, N.Y.: M. E. Sharpe, 1998.

———. "A Storm Dressed in Skirts: Ambivalence in the Debates on Women's Suffrage in Puerto Rico, 1927–1929." Ph.D. diss., State University of New York at Binghamton, 1993.

Jiménez-Román, Miriam. "Un hombre (negro) del pueblo: José Celso Barbosa and the Puerto Rican 'Race' toward Whiteness." *Centro* 8, nos. 1–2 (1996): 8–29.

Kannabiran, Vasantha, and K. Latitha. " 'That Magic Time': Women in the Telengana People's Struggle." In *Recasting Women: Essays in Indian Colonial History,* edited by Kumkum Sangari and Sudesh Vaid, 180–203. New Brunswick: Rutgers University Press, 1990.

Kinsbrunner, Jay. *Not of Pure Blood: The Free People of Color and Racial Prejudice in Nineteenth-Century Puerto Rico.* Durham: Duke University Press, 1996.

Klubock, Thomas Miller. "Morality and Good Habits: The Construction of Gender and Class in the Chilean Copper Mines, 1904–1951." In *The Gendered Worlds of Latin American Women Workers: From Household and Factory to the Union Hall and Ballot Box,* edited by John French and Daniel James, 232–63. Durham: Duke University Press, 1997.

Kruks, Sonia, Rayna Rapp, and Marilyn B. Young, eds. *Promissory Notes: Women in the Transition to Socialism.* New York: Monthly Review, 1989.

Kutzinski, Vera M. *Sugar's Secrets: Race and the Erotics of Cuban Nationalism.* Charlottesville: University of Virginia Press, 1993.

Laclau, Ernesto. *Politics and Ideology in Marxist Theory.* London: Verso, 1979.

Laclau, Ernesto, and Chantal Mouffe. *Hegemony and Socialist Strategy.* London: Verso, 1985.

Lavrin, Asunción. *Women, Feminism, and Social Change in Argentina, Chile, and Uruguay, 1890–1940.* Lincoln: University of Nebraska Press, 1995.

———. "Women, Labor, and the Left: Argentina and Chile, 1890–1925." *Journal of Women's History* 1, no. 2 (fall 1989): 88–116.

———, ed. *Sexuality and Marriage in Colonial Latin America.* Lincoln: University of Nebraska Press, 1989.

Levenson-Estrada, Deborah. "The Loneliness of Working-Class Feminism: Women in the 'Male World' of Labor Unions, Guatemala City, 1970s." In *The Gendered Worlds of Latin American Women Workers: From Household and Factory to the Union Hall and Ballot Box,* edited by John French and Daniel James, 208–31. Durham: Duke University Press, 1997.

Link, Arthur S., and McCormick, Richard L. *Progressivism.* Arlington Heights, Ill.: Harlan Davidson, 1983.

Littlewood, Barbara, and Linda Mahood. "Prostitutes, Magdalenes, and Wayward Girls: Dangerous Sexualities of Working Class Women in Victorian Scotland." *Gender and History* 3, no. 2 (summer 1991): 160–75.

Luque de Sánchez, María Dolores. *La ocupación norteamericana y la ley Foraker (la opinión pública puertorriqueña) 1898–1904.* Río Piedras: Editorial de la Universidad de Puerto Rico, 1980.

Macías, Anna. *Against All Odds: The Feminist Movement in Mexico to 1940.* Westport, Conn.: Greenwood, 1982.

MacLean, Nancy. "The Leo Frank Case Reconsidered: Gender and Sexual Politics in the Making of Reactionary Populism." *Journal of American History* 78, no. 3 (December 1991): 917–48.

Mallon, Florencia. *Peasant and Nation: The Making of Postcolonial Mexico and Peru.* Berkeley: University of California Press, 1994.

Mari, Lata. "Contentious Traditions: The Debate on Sati in Colonial India." In *Recasting Women: Essays in Indian Colonial History,* edited by Kumkum Sangari and Sudesh Vaid, 88–126. New Brunswick: Rutgers University Press, 1990.

Martin, Emily. *The Woman in the Body: A Cultural Analysis of Reproduction.* Boston: Beacon, 1987.

Martínez-Fernández, Luis. *Torn between Empires: Economy, Society, and Patterns of Political Thought in the Hispanic Caribbean, 1840–1878.* Athens: University of Georgia Press, 1994.

Martínez-San Miguel, Yolanda. "Deconstructing Puerto Ricanness through Sexuality: Female Counternarratives on Puerto Rican Identity (1894–1934)." In *Puerto Rican Jam: Essays on Culture and Politics,* edited by Ramón Grosfoguel and Frances Negrón-Muntaner, 127–39. Minneapolis: University of Minnesota Press, 1997.

Martínez-Vergne, Teresita. *Capitalism in Colonial Puerto Rico: Central San Vicente in the Late Nineteenth Century.* Gainesville: University Press of Florida, 1992.

———. "The Liberal Concept of Charity: *Beneficencia* Applied to Puerto Rico, 1821–1868." In *The Middle Period in Latin America: Values and Attitudes in the Seventeenth–Nineteenth Centuries,* edited by Mark Szuchman, 167–84. Boulder: Lynne Rienner, 1989.

Masiello, Francine. *Between Civilization and Barbarism: Women, Nation, and Literary Culture in Modern Argentina.* Lincoln: University of Nebraska Press, 1992.

Matos Rodríguez, Félix V. "La mujer y el derecho en el siglo XIX en San Juan, Puerto Rico (1820–1862)." In *Género, familia y mentalidades en América Latina,* edited by Pilar Gonzalbo Aizpuru, 227–65. Río Piedras: Editorial de la Universidad de Puerto Rico, 1997.

——. *Women and Urban Change in San Juan, Puerto Rico, 1820–1868.* Gainesville: University of Florida Press, 1999.

Matos Rodríguez, Félix V., and Linda C. Delgado, eds. *Puerto Rican Women's History: New Perspectives.* Armonk, N.Y.: M. E. Sharpe, 1998.

Mayo Santana, Raúl, and Mariano Negrón Portilla. *La esclavitud urbana en San Juan.* Río Piedras: Ediciones Huracán, 1992.

McClelland, Keith. "Some Thoughts on Masculinity and the 'Representative Artisan' in Britain, 1850–1880." *Gender and History* 1, no. 2 (1989).

McClintock, Anne. *Imperial Leather: Race, Gender, and Sexuality in the Colonial Contest.* New York: Routledge, 1995.

McCreery, David. " 'This Life of Misery and Shame': Female Prostitution in Guatemala City, 1880–1920." *Journal of Latin American Studies* 18, no. 2 (Nov. 1986): 333–53.

Meléndez, Edgardo. *Puerto Rico's Statehood Movement.* New York: Greenwood, 1988.

Menéndez, Nina, "Garzonas and Feministas in Cuban Women's Writing of the 1920s: *La vida manda* by Ofelia Rodríguez Acosta." In *Sex and Sexuality in Latin America,* edited by Daniel Balderston and Donna J. Guy, 174–84. New York: New York University Press, 1997.

Miller, Francesca. *Latin American Women and the Search for Social Justice.* Hanover, N.H.: University Press of New England, 1991.

Mintz, Sidney W. "Cañamelar: The Subculture of a Rural Sugar Plantation Proletariat." In *The People of Puerto Rico: A Study in Social Anthropology,* edited by Julian H. Steward, 314–418. 1956. Reprint, Urbana: University of Illinois Press, 1972.

Molyneux, Maxine. "No God, No Boss, No Husband: Anarchist Feminism in Nineteenth-Century Argentina." *Latin American Perspectives* 13, no. 1 (winter 1986): 119–45.

Morley, David, and Kuan-Hsing Chen, eds. *Stuart Hall: Critical Dialogues in Cultural Studies.* London: Routledge, 1996.

Mosse, George L. *Nationalism and Sexuality: Middle-Class Morality and Sexual Norms in Modern Europe.* Madison: University of Wisconsin Press, 1985.

Naranjo Oveido, Consuelo. "En búsqueda de lo nacional: Migraciones y racismo en Cuba (1880–1910)." In *La nación soñada: Cuba, Puerto Rico y Filipinas ante el 98,* edited by Consuelo Naranjo, Miguel Puig-Samper, and Luis Miguel García Mora, 149–62. Madrid: Doce Calles, 1996.

Naranjo, Consuelo, Miguel Puig-Samper, and Luis Miguel García Mora, eds. *La nación soñada: Cuba, Puerto Rico y Filipinas ante el 98.* Madrid: Doce Calles, 1996.

Nash, Mary, ed. *Mujer, familia y trabajo en España, 1875–1936.* Barcelona: Anthropos, Editorial del hombre, 1983.

Negrón-Muntaner, Frances, and Ramón Grosfoguel, eds. *Puerto Rican Jam: Essays on Culture and Politics.* Minneapolis: University of Minnesota Press, 1997.

Negrón Portillo, Mariano. *El autonomismo puertorriqueño: Su transformación ideológica (1895–1914).* Río Piedras: Ediciones Huracán, 1981.

———. "Puerto Rico: Surviving Colonialism and Nationalism." In *Puerto Rican Jam: Essays on Culture and Politics,* edited by Frances Negrón-Muntaner and Ramón Grosfoguel, 39–56. Minneapolis: University of Minnesota Press, 1997.

———. *Las turbas republicanas, 1900–1904.* Río Piedras: Ediciones Huracán, 1990.

Nizza Da Silva, María Beatriz. "Divorce in Colonial Brazil: The Case of Sao Paulo." In *Sexuality and Marriage in Colonial Latin America,* edited by Asunción Lavrin, 311–40. Lincoln: University of Nebraska Press, 1989.

Odem, Mary E. *Delinquent Daughters: Protecting and Policing Adolescent Female Sexuality in the United States, 1885–1920.* Chapel Hill: University of North Carolina Press, 1995.

O'Neill, William L. *Divorce in the Progressive Era.* New Haven: Yale University Press, 1967; reprint, New York: New Viewpoints, 1973.

Ostolaza Bey, Margarita. *Política sexual en Puerto Rico.* Río Piedras: Ediciones Huracán, 1989.

Painter, Nell Irvin. "Three Southern Women and Freud: A Non-Exceptionalist Approach to Race, Class, and Gender in the Slave South." In *Feminists Revision History,* edited by Ann-Louise Shapiro, 195–216. New Brunswick: Rutgers University Press, 1994.

Parker, Andrew, Mary Russo, Doris Sommer, and Patricia Yaeger, eds. *Nationalisms and Sexualities.* New York: Routledge, 1992.

Pateman, Carole. *The Disorder of Women.* Stanford: Stanford University Press, 1989.

———. *The Sexual Contract.* Stanford: Stanford University Press, 1988.

Peiss, Kathy, and Christina Simmons, eds. *Passion and Power: Sexuality in History.* Philadelphia: Temple University Press, 1989.

Picó, Fernando. *Al filo del poder: Subalternos y dominantes en Puerto Rico, 1739–1910.* Río Piedras: Editorial de la Universidad de Puerto Rico, 1993.

———. *El día menos pensado: Historia de los presidarios en Puerto Rico (1793–1993).* Río Piedras: Ediciones Huracán, 1994.

———. *1898: La guerra despúes de la guerra.* Río Piedras: Ediciones Huracán, 1987.

———. *Libertad y servidumbre en el Puerto Rico del siglo XIX.* Río Piedras: Ediciones Huracán, 1979.

Pierce, Paulette. "Boudoir Politics and the Birthing of the Nation: Sex, Marriage, and

Structural Deflection in the National Black Independent Party." In *Women Out of Place: The Gender of Agency and the Race of Nationality,* edited by Brackette F. Williams, 216–44. New York: Routledge, 1996.

Poovey, Mary. *Uneven Developments: The Ideological Work of Gender in Mid-Victorian England.* Chicago: University of Chicago Press, 1988.

Pratt, Mary Louise. *Imperial Eyes: Travel Writing and Transculturation.* New York: Routledge, 1992.

Quintero Rivera, Angel G. *Conflictos de clase y política en Puerto Rico.* 5th ed. Río Piedras: Ediciones Huracán, 1986.

——. *Patricios y plebeyos: Burgueses, hacendados, artesanos y obreros. Las relaciones de clase en el Puerto Rico de cambio de siglo.* Río Piedras: Ediciones Huracán, 1988.

——. *¡Salsa, Sabor, y control! Sociología de la música "tropical."* Mexico City: Siglo Veintiuno Editores, 1998.

——. "Socialista y tabaquero: La proletarización de los artesanos." *Sin Nombre* 8, no. 4 (1978): 100–137.

——. "The Somatology of Manners: Class, Race, and Gender in the History of Dance Etiquette in the Hispanic Caribbean." In *Ethnicity in the Caribbean,* edited by Gert Oostindie, 152–81. London: Macmillan, 1996.

Ramírez de Arellano, Annette B., and Conrad Seipp. *Colonialism, Catholicism, and Contraception: A History of Birth Control in Puerto Rico.* Chapel Hill: University of North Carolina Press, 1983.

Ramos, Julio. *Amor y anarquía: Los escritos de Luisa Capetillo.* Río Piedras: Ediciones Huracán, 1992.

Ramos Escandón, Carmen. "Señoritas porfirianas: Mujer e ideología en el México progresista, 1880–1910." In *Presencia y transparencia: La mujer en la historia de México,* edited by Ramos Escandón, 143–61. México: El Colegio de México, 1987.

Ramos Mattei, Andrés. *La hacienda azucarera: Su crecimiento y crisis en Puerto Rico (siglo XIX).* San Juan: CEREP, 1981.

——. *La sociedad del azúcar en Puerto Rico: 1870–1910.* Río Piedras: Universidad de Puerto Rico, 1988.

Recalde, Hector. "Prostitutas reglamentadas: Buenos Aires, 1875–1934." *Todo Es Historia* 24, no. 285 (March 1991): 72–94.

Riley, Glenda. *Divorce: An American Tradition.* New York: Oxford University Press, 1991.

Rivera, Marcia. "Incorporación de las mujeres al mercado de trabajo en el desarrollo del capitalismo (esbozo para un análisis)." In *La mujer en la sociedad puertorriqueña,* edited by Edna Acosta Belén, 41–65. Río Piedras: Ediciones Huracán, 1980.

Rodgers, Daniel T. "In Search of Progressivism." *Reviews in American History* 10, no. 4 (December 1982): 113–32.

Rodríguez-Silva, Ileana María. "Freedmen and Freedwomen: Processes of Social Reconfiguration in Post-Emancipation Puerto Rico (1873–1876). Master's thesis, University of Wisconsin, Madison, 1997.

Rodríguez Villanueva, Carlos A. "Amor furtivo y comportamiento demográfico en el Puerto Rico del Siglo XVII: Relaciones pre- y extramaritales vistas a través del clero y la respuesta del pueblo." Paper presented at the Association of Caribbean Historians, Santo Domingo, March 1991.

———. "El control de la natalidad a través del siglo XIX y la Pastoral: Bayamón, Camuy y la familia en Guaynabo (Apuntes para una historia de los nacimientos)." Paper presented at the Third Conference of Church Historians, San Juan, September 1987.

Roediger, David. *Our Own Time: A History of American Labor and the Working Day.* London: Verso, 1989.

Roper, Lyndal. "Discipline and Respectability: Prostitution and the Reformation in Augsberg." *History Workshop,* no. 19 (1985): 3–28.

Rosario Urrutia, Mayra. "Convicciones Anti-Alcohol de mujeres prohibicionistas: '¡Sin pisa, sin ron, sin botella!' " Paper presented at the Universidad del Sagrado Corazón, Santurce, Puerto Rico, March 8, 1989.

———. "Hacia un mundo abstemio: La prohibición del alcohol en Puerto Rico. Ph.D. diss., Universidad de Puerto Rico, Río Piedras, 1993.

———. "La génesis de la conciencia anti-alcohólica bajo el dominio hispánico." *Op. Cit.: Boletín del Centro de Investigaciones Históricas* 8 (1994–95): 167–200.

———. "Reconstruyendo la nación: La idea del progreso en el discurso anti-alcohol, 1898–1917." In *La nación soñada: Cuba, Puerto Rico y Filipinas ante el 98,* edited by Consuelo Naranjo, Miguel Puig-Samper, and Luis Miguel García Mora, 585–94. Madrid: Doce Calles, 1996.

Rose, Sonya O. "Sex, Citizenship, and the Nation in World War II Britain." *American Historical Review* 103, no. 4 (October 1998): 1147–76.

Rosen, Ruth. *The Lost Sisterhood: Prostitution in America, 1900–1918.* Baltimore: Johns Hopkins University Press, 1982.

Ruggiero, Kristin. "Honor, Maternity, and the Disciplining of Women: Infanticide in Late-Nineteenth-Century Buenos Aires." *Hispanic American Historical Review* 72, no. 3 (August 1992): 353–73.

Ryan, Mary P. *Women in Public: Between Banners and Ballots, 1825–1880.* Baltimore: Johns Hopkins University Press, 1990.

Said, Edward. *Orientalism.* New York: Vintage, 1978.

San Miguel, Pedro L. *La isla imaginada: Historia, identidad, y utopía en La Española.* San Juan: Editorial Isla Negra; Santo Domingo: Ediciones Librería La Trinitaria, 1997.

——. *El mundo, que creó el azúcar: Las haciendas en Vega Baja, 1800–1873.* Río Piedras: Ediciones Huracán, 1989.

Santiago-Valles, Kelvin A. "'Forcing Them to Work and Punishing Whoever Resisted': Servile Labor and Penal Servitude under Colonialism in Nineteenth-Century Puerto Rico." In *The Birth of the Penitentiary in Latin America: Essays on Criminology, Prison Reform, and Social Control, 1830–1940,* edited by Carlos Aguirre and Ricardo D. Salvatore, 123–68. Austin: University of Texas Press, 1996.

——. *"Subject People" and Colonial Discourses: Economic Transformation and Social Disorder in Puerto Rico, 1898–1947.* Albany: State University of New York Press, 1994.

Scarano, Francisco A. *Inmigración y clases sociales en el Puerto Rico del siglo XIX.* Río Piedras: Ediciones Huracán, 1981.

——. "The Jíbaro Masquerade and the Subaltern Politics of Creole Identity Formation in Puerto Rico, 1745–1823." *American Historical Review* 101, no. 5 (December 1996): 1398–1431.

——. *Puerto Rico: Cinco siglos de historia.* San Juan: McGraw-Hill, 1993.

——. "Slavery and Free Labor in the Puerto Rican Sugar Economy, 1815–1873." In *Comparative Perspectives on Slavery in New World Plantation Societies,* edited by Vera Rubin and Arthur Tuden, 553–63. New York: New York Academy of Sciences, 1977.

——. *Sugar and Slavery in Puerto Rico: The Plantation Economy of Ponce, 1800–1850.* Madison: University of Wisconsin Press, 1984.

Schwartz, Stuart B. "The Hurricane of San Ciriaco: Disaster, Politics, and Society in Puerto Rico, 1899–1901." *Hispanic American Historical Review* 72, no. 3 (August 1992): 303–34.

Scott, Joan W. *Gender and the Politics of History.* New York: Columbia University Press, 1988.

——. "Experience." In *Feminists Theorize the Political,* edited by Judith Butler and Joan Wallach Scott, 22–40. New York: Routledge, 1992.

Scott, Rebecca J. "'The Lower Class of Whites' and 'The Negro Element': Race, Social Identity, and Politics in Central Cuba, 1899–1909." In *La nación soñada: Cuba, Puerto Rico y Filipinas ante el 98,* edited by Consuelo Naranjo, Miguel Puig-Samper, and Luis Miguel García Mora, 179–91. Madrid: Doce Calles, 1996.

——. *Slave Emancipation in Cuba: The Transition to Free Labor, 1860–1899.* Princeton: Princeton University Press, 1985.

Scully, Pamela. "Rape, Race, and Colonial Culture: The Sexual Politics of Identity in the Nineteenth-Century Cape Colony, South Africa." *American Historical Review* 100, no. 2 (April 1995): 335–59.

——. *To Love, Honor, and Obey in Colonial Mexico: Conflicts over Marriage Choice, 1574–1821*. Stanford: Stanford University Press, 1988.

Silvestrini de Pacheco, Blanca. *Los trabajadores puertorriqueños y el Partido Socialista (1932–1940)*. Río Piedras: Editorial Universitaria, 1978.

——. *Violencia y criminalidad en Puerto Rico, 1898–1973: Apuntes para un estudio de historia social.* Río Piedras: Editorial Universitaria, 1980.

——. "Women and Resistance: Herstory in Contemporary Caribbean History." Elsa Goveia Memorial Lecture, Department of History, University of the West Indies, Mona, 1989.

Sinha, Mrinalini. "Gender in the Critiques of Colonialism and Nationalism: Locating the 'Indian Woman.'" In *Feminists Revision History,* edited by Ann-Louise Shapiro, 246–75. New Brunswick: Rutgers University Press, 1994.

——. "Reading *Mother India:* Empire, Nation, and the Female Voice." *Journal of Women's History* 6, no. 2 (summer 1994): 6–44.

Skidmore, Thomas E. *Black into White: Race and Nationality in Brazilian Thought.* 1974. Reprint, Durham: Duke University Press, 1993.

Smith-Rosenberg, Carroll. *Disorderly Conduct: Visions of Gender in Victorian America.* New York: A. A. Knopf, 1985.

Socolow, Susan M. "Acceptable Partners: Marriage Choice in Colonial Argentina, 1778–1810." In *Sexuality and Marriage in Colonial Latin America,* edited by Asunción Lavrin, 209–51. Lincoln: University of Nebraska Press, 1989.

Sommer, Doris. *Foundational Fictions: The National Romances of Latin America.* Berkeley: University of California Press, 1991.

Soto, Shirlene. *The Emergence of the Modern Mexican Woman: Her Participation in Revolution and Struggle for Equality, 1910–1940.* Denver: Arden, 1990.

Stallybrass, Peter, and Allon White. *The Politics and Poetics of Transgression.* London: Methuen, 1986.

Stansell, Christine. *City of Women: Sex and Class in New York, 1789–1860.* Urbana: University of Illinois Press, 1987.

Stepan, Nancy Leys. *"The Hour of Eugenics": Race, Gender, and Nation in Latin America.* Ithaca: Cornell University Press, 1991.

Stern, Steve J. *The Secret History of Gender: Women, Men, and Power in Late Colonial Mexico.* Chapel Hill: University of North Carolina Press, 1995.

Stolcke, Verena. *Marriage, Class, and Colour in Nineteenth-Century Cuba: A Study of Racial Attitudes and Sexual Values in a Slave Society.* 2d ed. Ann Arbor: University of Michigan Press, 1989.

Stoler, Ann Laura. "Carnal Knowledge and Imperial Power: Gender, Race, and Morality in Colonial Asia." In *Gender at the Crossroads: Towards an Anthropology of Power,* edited by Micaela di Leonardo. Berkeley: University of California Press, 1989.

———. "Making Empire Respectable: The Politics of Race and Sexual Morality in Twentieth-Century Colonial Cultures." *American Ethnologist* 16 (November 1989): 634–60.

———. "Perceptions of Protest: Defining the Dangerous in Colonial Sumatra." *American Ethnologist* 12 (November 1985): 642–58.

———. *Race and the Education of Desire: Foucault's "History of Sexuality" and the Colonial Order of Things.* Durham: Duke University Press, 1995.

———. "Rethinking Colonial Categories: European Communities and the Boundaries of Rule." *Comparative Studies in Society and History* 31 (November 1989): 134–61.

———. "Sexual Affronts and Racial Frontiers: European Identities and the Cultural Politics of Exclusion in Colonial Southeast Asia." *Comparative Studies in Society and History* 34, no. 3 (July 1992): 514–51.

Stoler, Ann Laura, and Frederick Cooper. "Tensions of Empire: Colonial Control and Visions of Rule." *American Ethnologist* 16 (November 1989): 609–21.

———, eds. *Tensions of Empire: Colonial Cultures in a Bourgeois World.* Berkeley: University of California Press, 1997.

Stoner, K. Lynn. *From the House to the Streets: The Cuban Woman's Movement for Legal Reform, 1898–1940.* Durham: Duke University Press, 1991.

———. "On Men Reforming the Rights of Men: The Abrogation of the Cuban Adultery Law, 1930." *Cuban Studies* 21 (1991): 83–99.

Szuchman, Mark D. *Order, Family, and Community in Buenos Aires, 1810–1860.* Stanford: Stanford University Press, 1988.

———, ed. *The Middle Period in Latin America: Values and Attitudes in the Seventeenth–Nineteenth Centuries.* Boulder, Colo.: Lynne Rienner, 1989.

Talwar, Vir Bharat. "Feminist Consciousness in Women's Journals in Hindi, 1910–20." In *Recasting Women: Essays in Indian Colonial History,* edited by Kumkum Sangari and Sudesh Vaid, 204–32. New Brunswick: Rutgers University Press, 1990.

Tax, Meredith. *The Rising of the Women.* New York: Monthly Review, 1980.

Tinsman, Heidi. "Household Patrones: Wife-Beating and Sexual Control in Rural Chile, 1964–1988." In *The Gendered Worlds of Latin American Women Workers: From Household and Factory to the Union Hall and Ballot Box,* edited by John French and Daniel James, 264–96. Durham: Duke University Press, 1997.

Tirado Avilés, Amilcar. "Notas sobre el desarrollo de la industria del tabaco en Puerto Rico y su impacto en la mujer puertorriqueña, 1898–1920." *Centro* 2, no. 7 (winter 1989–90): 18–29.

Twinam, Ann. "Honor, Sexuality, and Illegitimacy in Colonial Spanish America." In *Sexuality and Marriage in Colonial Latin America,* edited by Asunción Lavrin, 118–55. Lincoln: University of Nebraska Press, 1989.

Valle Ferrer, Norma. *Luisa Capetillo: Historia de una mujer proscrita.* Río Piedras: Editorial Cultural, 1990.

Verba, Ericka Kim. "The *Círculo de Lectura de Señoras* and the *Club de Señoras* of Santiago, Chile: Middle- and Upper-Class Feminist Conversations (1915–1920)." *Journal of Women's History* 7, no. 3 (fall 1995): 6–33.

Wade, Peter. *Blackness and Race Mixture: The Dynamics of Racial Identity in Colombia.* Baltimore: Johns Hopkins University Press, 1993.

Walkowitz, Daniel. "The Making of a Feminine Professional Identity: Social Workers in the 1920s." *American Historical Review* 95, no. 4 (October 1990): 1051–75.

Walkowitz, Judith. *City of Dreadful Delight: Narratives of Sexual Danger in Late-Victorian London.* Chicago: University of Chicago Press, 1992.

——. *Prostitution and Victorian Society: Women, Class, and the State.* Cambridge: Cambridge University Press, 1980.

White, E. Frances. "Africa on My Mind: Gender, Counter-Discourse, and African-American Nationalism." *Journal of Women's History* 2, no. 1 (spring 1990): 73–97.

White, Luise. *The Comforts of Home: Prostitution in Colonial Nairobi.* Chicago: University of Chicago Press, 1990.

Williams, Raymond. *Marxism and Literature.* Oxford: Oxford University Press, 1977.

Wolf, Eric R. "San José: Subcultures of a 'Traditional' Coffee Municipality." In *The People of Puerto Rico: A Study in Social Anthropology,* edited by Julian H. Steward, 171–264. 1956. Reprint, Urbana: University of Illinois Press, 1972.

Wolfe, Joel. "Anarchist Ideology, Worker Practice: The 1917 General Strike and the Formation of Sao Paulo's Working Class." *Hispanic American Historical Review* 71, no. 4 (November 1991): 809–46.

——. *Working Women, Working Men: Sao Paulo and the Rise of Brazil's Industrial Working Class, 1900–1955.* Durham: Duke University Press, 1993.

Wright, Winthrop. *Café con leche: Race, Class, and National Image in Venezuela.* Austin: University of Texas Press, 1990.

Zimmerman, Eduardo A. "Racial Ideas and Social Reform: Argentina, 1890–1916." *Hispanic American Historical Review* 72, no. 1 (February 1992): 23–46.

Index

Eileen J. Suárez Findlay is Assistant Professor of History at American University.

Library of Congress Cataloging-in-Publication Data

Findlay, Eileen J. Suárez.

Imposing decency : the politics of sexuality and race in Puerto Rico, 1870–1920 / Eileen J. Suárez Findlay.

p.   cm. — (American encounters/global interactions)   Includes index.

ISBN 0-8223-2375-3 (cl. : alk. paper). —

ISBN 0-8223-2396-6 (pa. : alk. paper)

1. Prostitution—Government policy—Puerto Rico—History.

2. Puerto Rico—Moral conditions.   3. Puerto Rico—Race relations.

4. Puerto Rico—Social policy.   5. Puerto Rico—Colonization.

I. Title.   II. Series.

HQ164.A5F56 1999   306'.097295—dc21   99-25911   CIP